Fiber Optic Video Transmission

The Complete Guide

Fiber Optic Video Transmission

The Complete Guide

by David R. Goff
President & CTO
Force, Incorporated

Edited by
Kimberly Hansen

Assistant Editor
Michelle K. Stull

Focal Press

OXFORD AMSTERDAM BOSTON LONDON NEW YORK PARIS
SAN DIEGO SAN FRANCISCO SINGAPORE SYDNEY TOKYO

Focal Press is an imprint of Elsevier Science.

Library of Congress Cataloging-in-Publication Data

Goff, David R.

Fiber optic video transmission : the complete guide / by David R. Goff ; edited by Kimberly Hansen ; assistant editor Michelle K. Stull.

p. cm.

Include bibliographical references and index.

ISBN 0-240-80488-0 (pbk. : alk. paper)

1. Optical communications. 2. Fiber optics. I. Hansen, Kimberly S. II. Stull, Michelle K. III. Title.

TK5103.592.F52 G64 2002

621.382'75-dc21   2002040838

British Library Cataloging-in-Publication Data

A catalogue record for this book is available from the British Library.

The publisher offers discounts on bulk orders of this book.

For information, please contact:
Manager of Special Sales
Elsevier Science
200 Wheeler Road
Burlington, MA 01803
Tel: (781) 313-4700
Fax: (781) 313-4882

For information on all Focal Press publications available, contact our World Wide Web home page at: http://www.focalpress.com

10 9 8 7 6 5 4 3 2 1

Printed in the United States of America

Contents

Contents

Contents

Contents

Contents

Contents

Contents

Contents

Contents

Preface

About This Book

Fiber optic engineers just love to design transmission systems for digital data transport. With data rates ever increasing, today engineers seriously contemplate the leap of transmission rates from 10 Gb/s to 40 Gb/s. Three to five years down the road, they may push for 160 Gb/s. Data transmission better utilizes fiber's capabilities, simplifying transport, switching, and other forms of manipulation, doesn't it? Well, yes and no. Digitized video and audio signal transport has three important considerations.

First, good quality digitized video and audio signals can generate a lot of data per second — enough to swamp even relatively high speed data networks. Second, video and audio often require real time delivery. Real time means every second of the signal must contain both one full second of video and one full second of audio. Data files, often not time critical, can tolerate pauses and interruptions. On the other hand, video and audio transmission must deliver the information continuously, with little or no breaks. Third, video and audio will continue to use a variety of analog transmission formats for many years to come.

Despite the media's obsession with digital everything, the broadcast industry has entered the golden age of analog, sending more analog signals than ever before. While the role of analog will no doubt diminish as time goes on, it still fills a large niche by providing a simple, low-cost way to transport video and audio. So while we will address HDTV, MPEG, QAM and the other hot topics of the day, we will also provide a firm foundation for understanding AM and FM video and audio transmission.

Fiber optics and video are popular topics these days. Both are established technologies; video, in approximately its present form, has been around for more than 50 years and fiber optics for more than 30 years. Despite their longevity, both technologies have undergone stunning advances in recent years. The figure below shows the progress that has been made in fiber optic technology over the past two decades. In 1980, a typical fiber could carry about 45 Mb/s. Today, 22 years later, a single fiber can carry more than 3.5 terabits per second of data. Moore's law, which states that computer power will double every 18 months, has long been considered to be the pinnacle of technological achievement. The dashed line that represents Moore's Law has an arbitrary starting point so that growth rates can be compared. While the computational power of computers has increased an impressive 26,000 times over the 22-year period, fiber has increased over 110,000 times during the same period of time.

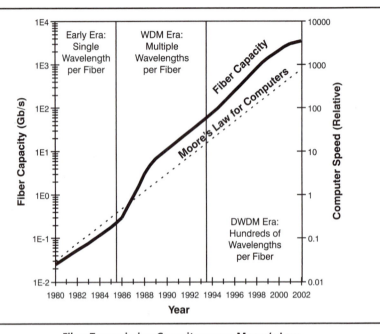

Fiber Transmission Capacity versus Moore's Law

Scope of This Book

Fiber Optic Video Transmission: The Complete Guide discusses at length for the first time under one cover, the intricacies involved with transporting video signals over optical fiber. This book evolved from educational material developed for my company's customers and also from my perception of a void of material in the marketplace. It attempts to present the information in a clear cut and straightforward manner, taking a very practical look at fiber optic and video technologies and their associated industries. Because of this approach, the text will not dwell on theoretical issues, that while valid and important, often only serve to confuse those trying to apply the science. *Fiber Optic Video Transmission: The Complete Guide* presents the essential concepts of fiber optics and video applications and gives the reader a good feeling of how the technologies really work rather than presenting endless pages of mind-numbing equations.

The book also includes brief discussions of the history of fiber optics and video industries, important in order to clarify why many things are done the way they are. By having some sense of history, what worked and what did not, it becomes easier to predict what the future will bring. Hopefully the reader will find all the answers sought within this book.

Having written that, it would be satisfying to say that this book contains the last word in fiber optics and video transmission. Unfortunately, the enormity of the scope required some fine-tuning. I made a key concession, choosing to focus primarily on NTSC video and its digital derivatives while providing basic overviews of other common formats. PAL and SECAM (and others) have equal value as television standards, and a number of concepts are common to all three. If you are reading this book on the couch in front of a TV using the PAL or SECAM video format, I apologize in advance for having to limit my focus.

Acknowledgments

The content of this book has benefitted from the input of a great many people to whom I am thankful. I would especially like to thank the editor, Kimberly Hansen Norris, whose skill as a writer, graphic designer and advanced desktop publisher helped make this book possible. Kimberly's ability to take hundreds of pages of technical descriptions and turn them into clear, concise prose is a major key to the usability and ultimate success of this book.

I also sincerely thank assistant editor, Michelle Stull, who quickly became a real asset to the writing team. For many hard hours, Michelle's talent and attention to detail went into creating and revising numerous illustrations, rewriting and polishing the text, and providing considerable skill as a proofreader.

Thanks also goes Mr. Bill Lindblom, one of the pioneers of fiber optic video transmission, for teaching me the intricacies of video over the years.

A special acknowledgment also goes to my loving wife Maria for her patience as I toiled over the manuscript. Her support has made this project possible.

I must also thank all of those who reviewed the manuscript and contributed significantly to make this a useful reference guide for the fiber optics and video industries and its present and future customers, including:

- Terry Forkner, SBC Ameritech
- Dr. Ira Jacobs, Virginia Tech Bradley Dept. of Electrical and Computer Engineering
- Edward T. Kopakowski, Olson Technology, Inc.
- C. William Lindblom, Force, Inc.
- Robert F. Martin, Force, Inc.
- John Megna, JDS Uniphase
- Joe Preschutti, Preschutti and Associates, Inc.

Finally, I wish to thank the companies that provided information and illustrations or photographs, including:

- Force, Inc.
- Hopecom, Inc.
- Optical Communication Products, Inc.
- PD-LD, Inc.
- Dr. Don Davis, Bandwidth9 Systems Division

Fiber optic video transmission continues to evolve, even as you read this book. The end result is far from clear at this point. However, it is clear that fiber optics and video transmission will be intimately inter-related for many years to come. Hopefully, this guide will serve as a road map to the basic concepts, as new and more complex techniques and schemes develop.

David R. Goff

President & CTO
Force, Incorporated
825 Park Street, Christiansburg, VA 24073
TEL: (540) 382-0462
E-mail: dgoff@forceinc.com

Fiber Optic Video Transmission

The Complete Guide

Chapter 1

The Intersection of Two Cornerstone Technologies

This book discusses the convergence of two of the great technology forces of the last few decades: video transmission and fiber optic transmission. Video, like data and audio, represents an essential element in any modern communication system. However, fundamental differences set video transmission apart from data and audio transmission. Video signals require huge amounts of transmission capacity, or bandwidth, as well as one or more associated audio channels, and the system must transmit a continuous, uninterrupted signal in order to achieve proper reception. This contrasts sharply with data, where pauses in data reception are often only minor annoyances.

In its earliest incarnation, video signals traveled through the air — wireless using today's jargon. Video signal transmission used analog techniques and each channel consumed about 6 MHz of bandwidth. Over decades, the TV industry and technology evolved until more than 80 channels could be transported using the VHF and UHF bands. Audio shared a similar history, evolving into wireless AM and FM transmission formats, each requiring 10 kHz to 100 kHz of bandwidth per signal.

In parallel with the development of TV and radio, the telephone industry quietly advanced techniques for digitizing voice signals and then converting their copper-wired infrastructure to a fiber-based infrastructure. The telecommunications industry offered optical fiber its first large-scale application. In this process, an analog-to-digital (A/D) converter sampled 4 kHz analog voice channels 8,000 times per second, using an 8-bit format, to become 64 kb/s data channels. This 8-bit sampling format reduced the voice signals to 256 distinct levels, which proved adequate to reconstruct speech with little loss of clarity.

Broadcast quality digital audio soon followed, but in this application, the analog-to-digital conversion generated considerably more data. The initial CD format required sampling the audio signal 44,100 times per second using 16-bit words. The 16-bit words digitized the analog audio into 65,536 distinct levels providing much higher signal fidelity and higher bandwidth (20 kHz) as well. A stereo analog signal converted to the standard CD digital format generates a data rate of 1.411 Mb/s, 22 times higher than that required for voice telephone. New high-quality audio standards, such as DVD-audio, increase the sampling rate to 96 kHz using 24-bit words. This brings the number of distinct digitized levels to 16.8 million, increases the audio bandwidth to 48 kHz (well beyond the range of human hearing), and increases the digital data rate for a stereo audio signal to 4.6 Mb/s!

From Analog to Digital

As the demand for video increased, researchers considered ways to convert it to a digital format. This conversion presented some thorny issues compared to voice and audio; video required far more bandwidth. A typical uncompressed digitized video signal uses a minimum data rate of 270 Mb/s. In this case, the video is sampled at an effective rate of 27 million times per second using 10-bit words, giving 1,024 distinct digitized levels. (Actually, the brightness, or luminance, is sampled 13.5 million times each second and two additional color components are each sampled 6.75 million times per second, totalling 27 million samples per second.) The 270 Mb/s data stream also embeds audio and control signals.

Next generation HDTV video signals increase the serial data rate for a single uncompressed channel to 1,485 Mb/s, the equivalent bandwidth of 23,203 digitized telephone voice signals. Fiber provides the means to transmit more than one terabit of data per second. That enables fiber to transmit over 1,000 uncompressed HDTV signals and hundreds of thousands of MPEG compressed video signals at 19.4 Mb/s each. A few such signals would swamp even a gigabit data transport link.

In the late 1980s, Nicholas Negroponte of MIT's Media Lab developed a theory on the future of media that became known as the "Negroponte Switch." This theory proposed that information once transmitted over the air — such as broadcast TV — would soon switch to wired architectures (fiber optic and copper). In contrast, wired services, chiefly voice telephony, would move to a predominantly wireless architecture, allowing for greater mobility. Despite numerous exceptions, communications and media have indeed made the "Negroponte Switch." Most viewers receive today's television signals over wired architectures (cable TV), and a few minutes spent in any public place attests to the growing dominance of the cell phone in voice communications. Only the advance of fiber optic technology can support the "Negroponte Switch" because only fiber can provide the huge bandwidth needed.

Today, video transmission and fiber optic technology are intertwined and interdependent. Each technology supports and benefits from the other. Fiber provides the bandwidth needed to transport a multitude of video signals, which at the same time increases the demand for fiber. Today there exist literally dozens of ways to transport video over fiber. And despite the battle cries of the digitizers, the industry still uses amplitude modulation (AM) and frequency modulation (FM) to transport video over fiber. Why? Because, in many cases, these solutions still cost less than digital schemes. Still, fiber carries digitized video in numerous digital formats, ranging from nearly 1.5 Gb/s for a single digitized HDTV signal down to 9,600 Baud for highly compressed, low-resolution, low frame rate video signals.

Key Applications for Fiber Optic Video Transmission

Broadcast: Digital Video and High Definition Video

As the broadcast industry moves to digitized video and HDTV (high-definition television), or enhanced NTSC (National Television Standards Committee), the use of fiber optic technology becomes inevitable. This technology will revolutionize broadcast video in the same way that CD technology changed the audio industry. Figure 1.1 shows a typical HDTV transmitter.

Figure 1.1 – High Definition Serial Digital Component Video Transmitter
(Photo courtesy of Force, Inc.)

Fiber optic links can support both video and audio broadcast transmissions as well as data transmission. Video transport signal types include multichannel (4, 8, 12, 16, 40, 60, 80, and 110 channels are common), point-to-point RS-250, and digitized video (NTSC, CCIR 656, EU95,

SMPTE 259). Audio transport signal types include the multichannel audio snake, point-to-point CD quality (stereo), and digitized audio.

The critical fiber parameters for broadcast are light weight, lightning immunity, high bandwidth, long distance, and excellent signal quality. Actual applications include: electronic news gathering (ENG), signals to TV camera pan/tilt/zoom pedestals, multimedia distribution systems, campus video distribution systems, intra-studio broadcasting, and inter-studio broadcasting. A studio-to-transmitter link (STL) represents one example of a inter-studio broadcast link. This application could utilize equipment such as the transmitter shown in Figure 1.1. Figure 1.2 illustrates a typical studio-to-transmitter link. The ATSC encoder implements the digital compression essential to making HDTV transmission practical.

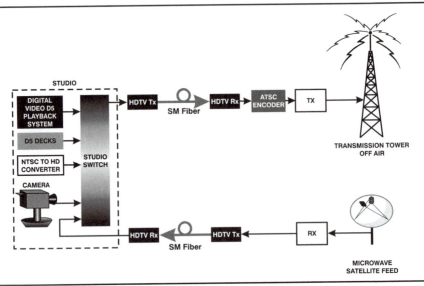

Figure 1.2 – Studio-to-Transmitter Link

Broadband CATV Transport

Once dominated by such transmission media as twisted pair, copper coaxial cable, satellite, and microwave transmission, broadband CATV networks now look to fiber for the transmission of radio frequency (RF) signals. This transition results from an increased consumer demand for new services, speed, bandwidth, and cost-containment.

While all-digital systems may ultimately prevail, they are still prohibitively expensive to install and operate for many applications. Recently, hybrid fiber/coax cable (HFC) CATV networks have gained acceptance as an alternative to copper-only systems, allowing for a more cost-effective transition. These permit CATV distributors to make the best use of both technologies. In areas of short transmission distance, a copper interface costs less than a fiber optic interface. In long transmission distances, copper not only costs more, but signal quality is often inadequate. HFC configurations, such as the one in Figure 1.3, allow a system design that accounts for both of these scenarios. CATV transmission is discussed in further detail in Chapter 15.

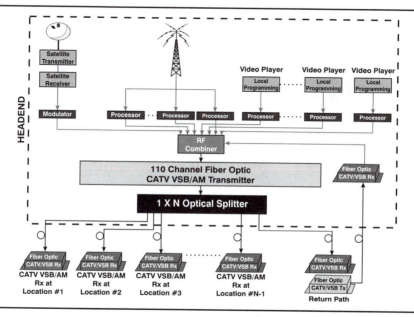

Figure 1.3 – CATV Video Distribution System

Fiber-to-the-Home and Fiber-to-the-Curb

Another telecommunications application gaining wide use is the subscriber loop, a circuit that connects a central office to subscriber telephones. With the high bandwidth of fiber, telephone companies could offer other services such as video and information services. Currently this technology also uses a hybrid fiber/coax distribution; however, future technology will attempt all-optical solutions.

For now, subscriber loops may be configured as fiber-to-the-curb (FTTC) and/or fiber-to-the-home (FTTH). As each name suggests, in FTTH systems, the transceiver is located inside the subscriber's home, while transceivers in a FTTC system stop at the curb, using copper coax cable to transmit from the external equipment to the subscriber's receiver. As video communications, fiber-to-the-curb, and fiber-to-the-home systems increase, the range of applications for this industry will only increase and diversify. Figure 1.4 illustrates the FTTH and FTTC topology.

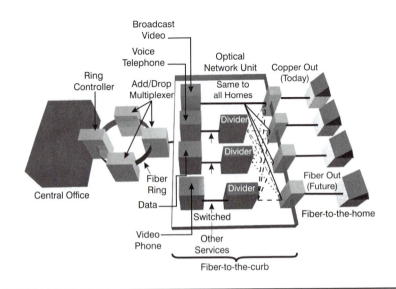

Figure 1.4 – Fiber-to-the-Curb and Fiber-to-the-Home Systems

High-resolution Imaging

Fiber optics can carry high-resolution video images encoded as RGB (red-green-blue) signals, with a bandwidth of over 350 MHz per color. The increased bandwidth and distance capability make this application useful in a number of applications, including medical imaging, computer worksta-tions, computer modeling, air traffic control remote imaging, flight simula-tion, telemetry, map making, high-end graphic design, and publishing. Table 1.1 outlines screen resolution, scan rate, and RGB bandwidth.

Table 1.1 – RGB Bandwidth and Screen Resolution

Resolution (Non-Interlaced)	Scan Rate (Hz)	Analog RGB Bandwidth (MHz)
640 x 480	60/72	18.4/22.1
800 x 600	60/72	28.8/34.6
1024 x 768	60/72	47.2/56.6
1280 x 1024	60/72	78.6/94.4
1600 x 1280	60/72	122.9/147.5
2560 x 2048	60/72	314.6/377.5

Distance Learning (Teleclassrooms)

Distance learning involves video/audio links that connect a teacher in one classroom to students in other classrooms. Communication is two-way by video cameras and audio systems connected via fiber optics. The advantages of fiber include no electromagnetic (EM) radiation, immunity to EM interference (EMI), long distance capability, and better signal quality. Figure 1.5 illustrates the dynamics of distance learning.

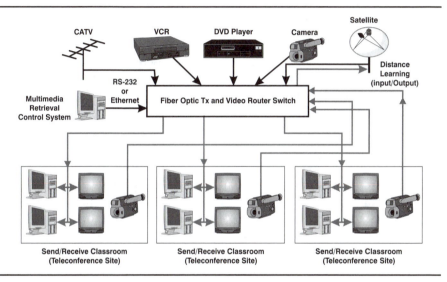

Figure 1.5 – **Distance Learning System Configuration**

Teleconferencing

Similar to distance learning, teleconferencing employs fiber optic systems to connect municipalities and other government units by both video and audio. An example of this, known as electronic magistrate, allows law enforcement officials to arraign suspects via video camera with an audio feed. Using this technology, officers can process suspects from remote sites rather than making a trip to the county seat, which is especially useful in rural communities. In addition, teleconferencing connects remote municipalities to the state seat of government and allows business conferences to be conducted face-to-face from a variety of remote locations.

The intersection of fiber optics and video transmission has only just begun. But both technologies have histories that begin in the eighteenth century. The next two chapters will briefly describe the development of these two technologies.

Chapter Summary

- Video signals differ from data signals in a number of ways: they require high transmission capacity; they include one or more associated audio channels; and the operating system must transmit a continuous, uninterrupted signal in order for proper reception.
- Early video signals traveled through the air using analog techniques that required a small amount of bandwidth (6 MHz).
- The telephony industry advanced techniques for digitizing voice signals.
- In the 1980s, MIT's Nicholas Negroponte developed a theory known as the "Negroponte Switch," which proposed that information once transmitted over the air would soon switch to wired architectures while wired services would move to a predominantly wireless architecture.
- Today, video transmission often uses optical fiber as a means of signal transport.
- Key fiber optic broadcast industry applications include digitized video, CATV transmission, fiber-to-the-curb, and fiber-to-the-home.
- Fiber optics transmit high-resolution images for CAD/CAM/CAE computer modeling, air traffic control remote imaging, flight simulation imaging, telemetry, map making, and high-end graphic design.
- Distance learning uses video/stereo audio links to connect classrooms in different locations and allows two-way video/audio contact between the location of the teacher and the locations of all remote classrooms.
- Teleconferencing uses the same approach as distance learning, connecting municipalities and other government units.

Chapter 2

A Brief History of Video and Video Transmission

Video transmission refers mainly to the visual elements of television transmission. However, the act of transmission, sending and receiving signals, over wire or radio waves, to convey information, news, and other types of communication, began with data and audio signals. Pioneers in television transmission adapted many of the techniques devised for telegraph and later telephone systems. Modern video transmission incorporates sound, and as a result of this shared development, the history of video cannot be fully understood without addressing the transmission of earlier signal types.

Wired Transmission: The Telegraph

Eighteenth century developments in the field of electricity eventually led to the nineteenth century invention of the electric telegraph, patented by Samuel Morse in 1837. Morse designed his telegraph to transmit Morse code, his alphanumeric system of dots and dashes. The first telegraph system in the United States, installed in 1843, spanned between Washington, D.C. and Baltimore, Maryland. Once completed, Morse's first transmission, "What hath God wrought!" crossed the 35 miles on May 24, 1844. The era of electrical communications transmission had arrived.

Not long after, scientists began exploring ways to double a wire's transmission capacity. Then, as now, the need for greater transmission capacity heavily influenced how the technology developed. Towards this goal, a German, Wilhelm Gintl, first described a duplex transmission system that allowed signals to be sent and received on the same line, doubling the line's capacity. In 1871, J.B. Sterns of the U.S. applied the principles of duplex transmission. Also in 1871, Frenchman Jean-Maurice-Émile Baudot devised a scheme he called multiplexing. This gave system designers the ability to share a single transmission line among a number of simultaneous users. (This scheme is still used extensively in video and data transmission and will be discussed in further detail in subsequent chapters.) In 1874, Thomas A. Edison patented a system of quadraplex transmission, in which two signals could be transmitted simultaneously in each direction on a single line. These and other achievements further expanded the era of the telegraph.

Then, in 1876, Alexander Graham Bell invented the telephone. Many expected the device, which allowed real-time, two-way voice conversations, to quickly replace the telegraph. The two technologies coexisted and even thrived on each other's technological advances, resulting in the growth of both industries into widespread communications networks. The era of the electric telegraph did not begin to decline until the end of World War II.

Wireless Transmission: The Radio

The nineteenth century also witnessed the development of radio transmission. This transmission technology took advantage of radio frequencies (RF) in the electromagnetic spectrum that allowed the signals to transmit across free space, unfettering transmission from the hard wires of the electric telegraph and the telephone. In 1888, Heinrich Hertz broadcasted and received the first transmitted radio signals. For Hertz, transmission distance was limited to a few meters in the laboratory. However, his experiments attracted the attention of Italian physicist Guglielmo Marconi. He repeated Hertz's experiment, ever increasing the transmission distance. By 1901, Marconi's radio transmission could cross the Atlantic Ocean.

In 1904, inventor Sir John Ambrose Fleming discovered the one-directional current affect between a positively biased electrode he called an anode, and a heated filament within a glass tube. He termed the device a diode for its two components. In laboratory experiments, he noticed that when he applied alternating current to the diode, only the positive halves of the current passed through the filament. Ambrose had stumbled upon a way to convert alternating current into direct current.

This interested American inventor Lee DeForest who placed an open-meshed grid between the anode and the filament to control the electron flow. DeForest called his invention the Audion Tube; the device caused a large change in voltage at the anode by applying a small change in voltage at the meshed grid. Thus, the radio signal could be amplified before entering the radio receiver, allowing weaker radio signals to be used in radio transmission. Figure 2.1 (next page) illustrates DeForest's invention.

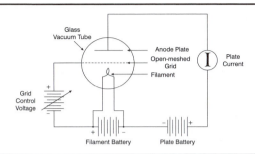

Figure 2.1 – DeForest's Audion Tube

These advancements led to the 1897 incorporation of the Wireless Telegraph and Signal Company, later renamed the Marconi Company, the first company created solely for the manufacture of radio apparatus. DeForest, still tweaking his Audion Tube, discovered its oscillating properties in 1912. By replacing the spark transmitter with an electronic tube oscillator, the device could generate very pure and stable radio signals. By 1910, Morse code transmissions between land and ships occurred daily, and the first land-to-aircraft transmission took place.

In 1915, DeForest sold the Audion Tube to the American Telegraph & Telephone company (AT&T). AT&T and DeForest used it to transmit the first speech radio transmission that same year, opening the door for commercial radio broadcasting. This achievement earned DeForest the moniker "the Father of Radio." The first commercial radio station, KDKA in Pittsburgh, Pennsylvania, went on the air on November 2, 1920. By 1922, 564 stations had received licenses to broadcast. This rapid growth quickly revealed a need for standardization, which the United States addressed in the Radio Act of 1927. The act formed the group, that would later become the Federal Communications Commission (FCC), to allocate separate wavelengths for broadcasters. The Radio Act also dissolved the threat of monopolies between broadcasters and radio manufacturers and led to the creation of four major networks: National Broadcasting Company (NBC), Columbia Broadcasting Company (CBS), Mutual Broadcasting System, which ceased broadcasting in 1999, and American Broadcasting Company (ABC).

Great Britain's radio broadcast history differs in that the original British Broadcasting Company, Ltd., created in 1922, was privately held. The Post Office of Great Britain, fearing commercialization of radio as well as interference with essential communications, formed the organization to encourage cooperation between radio manufacturers. On the recommendation of Britain's parliament, the private company was publicly incorporated as the

British Broadcasting Corporation (BBC), but the initial privatization allowed radio to develop in a more orderly fashion and provided an early need for standardization in the industry. Regardless of the early forms, however, radio broadcasting quickly became popular worldwide.

A Picture Is Worth 10,000 Words: Mechanical Television Systems

Ideas for transmitting visual images rather than audio signals began in the nineteenth century, but they required a number of technological advances. In 1875, George Carey of Boston, Massachusetts, proposed a television system that allowed the simultaneous transmission of every element in the picture over separate channels. In 1880, American, E.E. Sawyer, and Maurice LeBlanc in France, proposed the principle of image scanning whereby the image to be transmitted was scanned, line by line, frame by frame, relying on the human eye's insistence on order to reconstruct the individual elements as a single image.

The 1873 discovery that the element selenium (Se), had photoconductive properties, provided a much needed clue to the development of practical television. This discovery lead the German, Paul Nipkow, to patent a complete television system in 1884. Nipkow's system used a disk, pierced through with 18 square apertures arrayed in a spiral pattern around the disk, as illustrated in Figure 2.2.

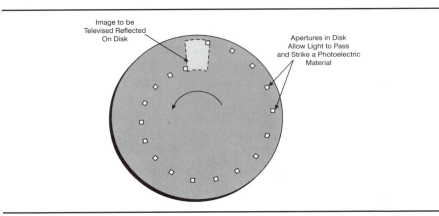

Figure 2.2 – Nipkow's Scanning Disk

The image to be televised was focused on the rotating disk; each rotation of the disk traced out successive lines, one beneath the other, until the entire image had been scanned. This sequence of lines entered a selenium-based photoelectric cell that translated the varying degrees of brightness into a varying sequence of electrical values. These values, which were transmitted single file, much like Morse's telegraph transmission, used a receiver that employed electrical impulses and a lamp to reproduce the original image. Rotation speed and the human eye allowed the image to be viewed as a whole rather than as the fragments that actually made up the image. The system required exact synchronization between the camera and receiver scanning speeds, a principle still fundamental to television systems.

Constantin Perskyi coined the term "television" at the 1900 Paris Exhibition International Electricity Congress; but still, real-world applications for the new word required more technological advances. One such advance, a cathode-ray tube with a fluorescent screen, emerged in 1897, developed by K. F. Braun of Germany. However, its usefulness for television systems went overlooked until 1907 when Russian Boris Rosing pointed out that the device would make a better television receiver. The amplifier described earlier, DeForest's Audion Tube, greatly advanced television research as well as revolutionizing radio transmission.

Advances in mechanical television systems continued into the early twentieth century. In the U.S., Charles Francis Jenkins achieved his first successful laboratory transmission in 1922, and by 1925 he achieved the first synchronized transmission of pictures and sound. Great Britain's John L. Baird gave a 1926 demonstration of "true" television transmission, using a mechanical system based on Nipkow's rotating scanner. At a rate of 30 lines repeating ten times per second, the picture flickered badly on the small receiver screen; however, television's birth as a practical technology stimulated further research. The higher scanning rates required for improved picture quality out-paced the mechanical system's ability to stay synchronized, requiring the development of an electronic approach. But a few more ground-breaking advances would still be needed.

Electronic Television Systems

A young, untrained inventor, named Philo T. Farnsworth had a lifelong fascination with electricity and electronics. After reading an article that proposed combining radio and motion pictures, Farnsworth, then age 14, dreamed up an idea to capture light in a jar and transmit it in a series of individual lines of electron beams. Each line of the image could be magnetically deflected, one line at a time, to form a moving picture. He called it the "image dissector" because it could dissect an image line by line with a pulsating electrical charge and then transmit these elements. Years later, living in Hollywood, California, Farnsworth developed a working model of the device with Cliff Gardner, his friend and brother-in-law, using money gained from private backers. Farnsworth applied for his first patent.

Farnsworth and Gardner also developed a receiver they called the "image oscillite," which allowed the image to be reconstructed. It took months to build their television system before it could be tested, but on September 7, 1927, Farnsworth's device transmitted and received a picture of a horizontal line that had been painted on a glass slide. When Gardner rotated the slide at the transmission end, viewers at the receive end saw the line rotate. The device worked. They continued to develop their electronic television system and filed patents on the technology. As publicity for the invention grew, Farnsworth, Gardner, and the original investors incorporated Television Laboratories in 1928. Figure 2.3 illustrates Farnsworth's image dissector.

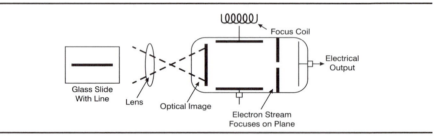

Figure 2.3 – Farnsworth's Image Dissector

As the news of Farnsworth's television system spread to the east coast, it caught the attention of David Sarnoff, the appointed vice president and general manager of Radio Corporation of America (RCA). Sarnoff learned of a fellow Russian, V. K. Zworykin, who had applied for a patent on what he called the iconoscope camera tube in 1923. His patent, unlike Farnsworth's was declined. Determined that RCA should have the patents on the next generation of transmission techniques, as the company had done with its radio patents, Sarnoff hired Zworykin to invent and patent the first television for RCA. In fact, Sarnoff first assigned Zworykin to visit Farnsworth to see what the California inventor created.

Zworykin constructed his own version of the television tube, the iconoscope, in 1932 while working at RCA. In an attempt to secure all patents to the technology, RCA contested Farnsworth's existing patents with the U.S. Patent Office. In the end, the Patent Office upheld Farnsworth's patent, but RCA continued to litigate through the appeals process, and while they could not sell their own version of the invention, as long as the patent was in litigation, neither could Farnsworth. RCA then designed the "Orthicon Tube," which they claimed as a unique invention, but in the process of trying to patent the Orthicon Tube, the Patent Office discovered several of Farnsworth's patented designs in RCA's new tube, and while they were allowed to patent the name, RCA could not patent the device. In the end, RCA would, for the first time in the company's history, pay royalties to Farnsworth for his inventions used in RCA televisions.

The Need for Television Standards

RCA's all-electronic television offered 120 lines initially. Continuing research, mainly in the RCA laboratories, increased scanning to 343 lines. By 1935, advances in electronic television came fast and furious. The need for standards, especially to define scanning line rates and frames per line, recognized as necessary by the BBC in 1931, became an issue in America. While worldwide standards never materialized, today, all countries adopt one of three standards: NTSC at 525 lines per picture and 30 pictures per second, PAL, or SECAM, both using 625 lines and 25 pictures per second.

In 1934, the Communications Act renamed the radio licensing committee the Federal Communications Commission (FCC). The FCC regulates U.S. interstate and international communications. Initially the scope of this regulation involved only radio, television, and wire, but today it includes satellite, cable, and wireless phone communications. This change resulted from the Telecommunications Act of 1996, the first update to the 1934 act. The FCC's current jurisdiction covers the 50 states, the District of Columbia, and U.S. territories. Among other tasks, the FCC regulates the radio frequency spectrum, issuing licenses to radio and televisions stations and wireless phone companies assigning each station or phone provider the use of a unique section of the frequency spectrum.

Monochrome Television

Figure 2.4 illustrates a monochrome TV transmitter. A TV camera, conceptually similar to Farnsworth's image dissector, scans and converts an image into an electrical signal. A sync generator provides the basic vertical and horizontal synchronization signals.

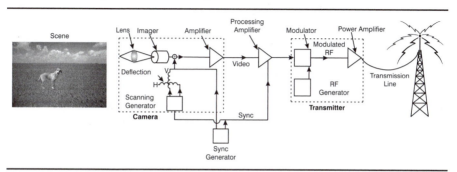

Figure 2.4 – Basic Monochrome TV Transmitter

The processed video signal generates a composite video signal, which the TV transmitter accepts. The TV transmitter contains an RF generator that creates the desired carrier frequency. The modulator multiplies the incoming video signal with the RF generator output. If present, audio signals would be FM modulated and put on a carrier above the main video carrier. The modulated RF signal is filtered to partially remove the lower sideband and then amplified prior to reaching the antenna.

Figure 2.5 shows a highly simplified block diagram of a TV receiver. The receiver amplifies the CATV input and then filters all but the desired channel frequency. The receiver detects the selected channel and restores the baseband composite video signal. The TV receiver also extracts sync information to drive the vertical and horizontal deflection coils. These coils steer the electron beam that is emitted at the back of the CRT. After the video signal is amplified, it modulates the CRT electron beam. The electron beam impinges on a phosphor-coated glass screen that emits light whose brightness corresponds to the strength of the electron beam.

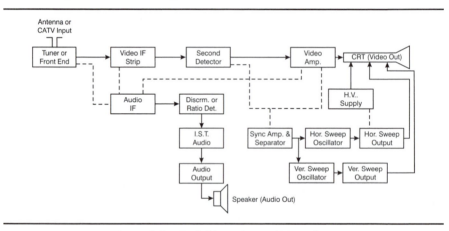

Figure 2.5 – Basic Monochrome TV Receiver

Color Television

By the 1950s, television technologically reached the next logical step — color television. Color transmission was by no means a new idea, having been proposed as early as 1904. England's John L. Baird gave the first practical demonstration of color television in 1928. The following year, American H.E. Ives and colleagues at Bell Laboratories transmitted 50-line color television images between New York City and Washington, D.C. In the mid-1930s, researchers described two basic approaches to transmitting color television signals. One method called for a sequential frame-by-frame transmission of three signals corresponding to red, green, and blue, the three primary colors. However, this approach had a number of drawbacks; it required an increased scan rate to avoid color flicker, and more importantly, it was incompatible with the black-and-white television receivers of the time. Georges Valensi of France pioneered a compatible color television technique. In 1938, he patented a method of transmission that would allow black-and-white receivers to correctly display color image transmissions in black-and-white. This premise became a keystone in the new technology.

Experiments in color television transmission occurred in both the United States and Great Britain. J.L. Baird and Peter Goldmark, a researcher at the CBS, both demonstrated sequential systems that used rotating color filters on the camera as well as the receiver. Both countries continued to develop this technology until the outbreak of World War II. All serious research into television stopped for the duration of the war.

In April 1946, CBS successfully transmitted the first color television signals from New York to Washington, D.C. and back. In September of the same year, CBS petitioned the FCC to adopt its television standard, "color-cast," and authorize CBS to transmit in the UHF or ultra high frequency portion of the spectrum. Only in this portion of the spectrum was there bandwidth sufficient to transmit color signals. However, the FCC found CBS's solution premature and refused to authorize CBS's use of the UHF. At the same time, researchers at RCA were developing a color television standard of their own. However, CBS was finally given the green light from the FCC in 1950. Television manufacturers uncertain about the future, debated about whether to build sets and converters that could receive the CBS colorcast. Only a year later, RCA proved its color system to the FCC, sparking a debate between the two broadcast giants that lasted until 1953, when the FCC reversed itself and embraced what we know as the RCA/NTSC color system.

The NTSC color system, formally adopted for all FCC approved television transmission in 1954, uses two interlaced transmitted images. Each interlaced image, or field, carries one half of the information required to create the full image. As we will see in later chapters, the first field carries the odd scan lines, and the second field carries the even scan lines. The brightness information, or luminance, is carried in the voltage level. The chrominance, or color information, is encoded in the phase of a 3.58 MHz carrier that is above the highest frequency of the luminance information, making the signal viewable on black-and-white television receivers as clearly as black-and-white transmissions. This standard differed from the phase alternation by line (PAL) and SECAM (système electronic couleur avec memoire) standards developed in Germany and France. These European standards aimed at reducing the color system's sensitivity to signal distortion. However, because NTSC used a 60 field frequency which the NTSC based on the 60 Hz power cycle used by the U.S., and PAL and SECAM systems used the European standard 50 field frequency, NTSC and PAL/SECAM are incompatible formats. Today, all countries broadcast using one of the three standards. Table 2.1 outlines the differences in these formats.

Table 2.1 – Comparison of NTSC, PAL, and SECAM

	NTSC	PAL	SECAM
Horizontal Lines per Picture	525	625	625
Transmitted Frames per Second	30	25	25
Number of Fields per Second	60	50	50

In 1956, WNBQ in Chicago, Illinois removed its black-and-white transmission equipment and replaced it with color equipment, becoming the first television station to broadcast all local programming in color. The Space Age, still in its infancy, quickly became a tool for television as early communications satellites, such as Telstar, were launched into space. By 1964, the FCC required all television manufacturer's to accept UHF channels, and in October of the same year, the world witnessed its first live satellite television program, the opening ceremonies of the 1964 Summer Olympics in Tokyo, Japan. NBC used its satellite, Syncom III, to complete the transmission link. Sales of color television sets became widespread in 1964. Despite the success of international transmission, the barrier of incompatible transmission standards remained.

The Telecommunications Act of 1996 and DTV/HDTV

The Telecommunications Act of 1996 represented the first overhaul of its predecessor, the Communications Act of 1934. Adopted by congress in January 1996, the Act was passed "To promote competition and reduce regulation in order to secure lower prices and higher quality services for American telecommunications consumers and encourage the rapid deployment of new telecommunications technologies." The act addressed competition in phone services, auctions to sell FCC-held open spectrum, and advances in television technologies.

The need to address incompatible global transmission standards, lead to the creation of digital television (DTV) standards. The Advanced Television Systems Committee (ATSC) developed this standard offering a number of advantages over the NTSC format. The DTV standard, which encompasses standard definition TV (SDTV), DTV, and high definition television (HDTV), offers 18 transmission options rather than the one 525 line, 30 frames per second rate of NTSC. DTV allows two types of scanning: progressive frame-by-frame scanning which creates a very clear picture but requires more bandwidth and can exhibit flicker due to the potentially lower frame rate; and interlaced, such as a transmission of NTSC. Table 2.2 describes the options available for DTV transmission.

Table 2.2 – Options for HDTV, DTV, and SDTV Standards

	Active Lines per Picture	Pixels per Line	Aspect Ratio	Field Rate*	Scanning Approach
HDTV	1080	1920	16:9	30	Progressive
HDTV	1080	1920	16:9	30	Interlaced
HDTV	720	1280	16:9	60	Progressive
DTV	720	1280	16:9	30	Interlaced
DTV/SDTV	480	704	4:3, 16:9	60	Progressive
SDTV	480	640	4:3	30	Interlaced

*Field rate has a number of steps between 23.976 and 60 fields per second depending on the transmission option.

The aspect ratio, which relates to the size of the screen, may be 16:9 for wide screen HDTV or 4:3, the aspect ratio used in current television sets and computer monitors. The digital domain simplifies the conversion of transmission formats and employs digital compression techniques, adding to the advantage of DTV standards. The HDTV standard allows for the clearest ever television transmission and reception, but the relatively high cost of an HDTV television currently prevents it from becoming as widely accepted as DTV. The FCC adopted this new digital standard in December 1996. Shortly thereafter, the FCC mandated that by 2006, all TV stations in the U.S. will be phased out or converted over to DTV stations broadcasting on newly assigned channels. At the same time, the freed space of the RF spectrum will be reassigned to other communications services such as wireless telephone transmission. By the end of 2001, more than 200 television stations had already added digital broadcast to their existing analog broadcast. Today networks broadcast most major network television shows using the HDTV standard, but local television stations and cable providers still broadcast NTSC standard video to the end user. But as with all new technologies, mass production will decrease the cost of HDTV televisions, making this technology as commonplace in the future as NTSC is today.

In issuing this mandate, the FCC has all but ordained the switch from conventional video transmission, to digital transmission. This greatly increases the opportunity for fiber and video to work together. Before delving into the methods for fiber optic video transmission, a brief history of fiber optic technology is in order.

Chapter Summary

- Samuel Morse patented the telegraph in 1837 as a device to transmit messages over wire using Morse code, his alphabet of dots and dashes.
- Thomas Edison patented quadraplex transmission, a system to send two signals simultaneously in each direction of a single line.
- Alexander Graham Bell invented the telephone in 1876, but it did not immediately replace the telegraph as was widely expected.
- In 1888, Heinrich Hertz first transmitted and received radio waves over short distances.
- Guglielmo Marconi sent the first transatlantic radio message in 1901.
- Lee DeForest, expanding on Sir John Fleming's diode, eventually creating the Audion Tube, a device that increased radio transmission distances by amplifying radio signals.
- AT&T and DeForest sent the first speech transmission in 1915.
- The first commercial radio station, KDKA in Pittsburgh, Pennsylvania, went on the air on November 2, 1920.
- The Radio Act of 1927 led to the creation of a wavelength licensing board that would later become the FCC, dissolved potential monopoly problems, and resulted in the creation of four major broadcast networks in the United States.
- In 1873, Paul Nipkow patented the first mechanical television system.
- Philo T. Farnsworth, with his brother-in-law, Cliff Gardner, demonstrated an all-electronic television system in 1927.
- The Communications Act of 1934 addressed the need for standardization in the broadcast industry.
- CBS demonstrated the first color television transmission in April 1946 using a system they called colorcast.
- In 1956 television station, WNBQ in Chicago, Illinois, became the first television station to broadcast all local programming in color.
- The Telecommunications Act 1996 represented the first update to the Communications Act of 1934.
- In December 1996, the FCC adopted a new digital television standard that encompasses SDTV, DTV, and HDTV and mandated all broadcasters to implement this standard by 2006.

Chapter 3

A Brief History of Fiber Optics

The principles guiding fiber optic transmission, be it video, audio, or data signals, occurred in the same time period as the development of radio transmission. As with the parallel technological advancements in radio transmission and television transmission, fiber optic transmission learned much from basic electronic transmission.

Early Developments in Light Transmission

In 1870, John Tyndall of England demonstrated the early principles of fiber optic transmission to the British Royal Society in London. He used a beam of light and a jet of water that flowed from one container to another. As water poured out through the spout of the first container, Tyndall guided a beam of sunlight through the path of water. The light, as seen by the audience, used internal reflection to follow a zigzag path inside the curved path of the water.

In 1880, William Wheeling obtained a patent for a light transfer method he called "piping light." Wheeling theorized that by reflecting the light from an electric arc to various pipes, he could illuminate several different rooms. However, Edison's successful incandescent light bulb all but eliminated the need for Wheeling's idea.

That same year, Alexander Graham Bell developed an optical voice transmission system he called a photophone. The photophone worked using mirrors that reflected sunlight onto a diaphragm that was attached within a mouthpiece. At the receive end, a selenium resistor mounted within a parabolic reflector connected to a battery that was, in turn, wired to a telephone receiver. Variations in the human voice caused the irradiated diaphragm to vibrate and cast differing light intensities which generated corresponding resistance changes in the selenium photoconductor. These altered the current that passed through the telephone receiver which then converted the light back into speech. Transmitting through free-space, the photophone could carry the human voice 200 meters. It took several more years before inventions to support this technology would develop, making the device impractical at the time of its invention. Nonetheless, Bell considered this invention to be superior to his own telephone because it did not need wires to connect the transmitter and receiver. In fact, this invention represents the world's first optical amplitude modulation (AM) audio link. Today, "free-space" optical links, similar in concept to Bell's photophone, find extensive use in metropolitan applications.

From Concept to Design

As with video transmission, fiber optic technology developed rapidly in the twentieth century. The fiberscope, the forerunner of modern laparoscopic devices, used the first practical all-glass fiber. It was devised in the 1950s by Brian O'Brien at the American Optical Company and Narinder Kapany (who coined the term "fiber optics") and colleagues at the Imperial College of Science and Technology in London. Early all-glass fibers experienced excessive optical loss, the loss of the light signal as it traveled the fiber, limiting transmission distances.

To correct this, motivated scientists developed glass fibers that included a separate glass coating. The innermost region of the fiber, or core, carried the light, while the glass coating, or cladding, prevented the light from leaking out of the core by reflecting the light within the boundaries of the core. Snell's Law explains this concept. It states that the angle at which light reflects as it passes from one material to another depends on the refractive indices of the two materials — in this case, the core and the cladding. Figure 3.1 illustrates the equations for Snell's Law.

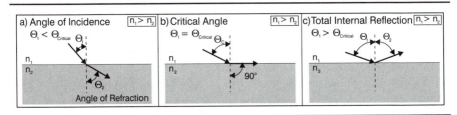

Figure 3.1 – Equations for Snell's Law

In Figure 3.1, the upper, lighter region of each frame indicates a higher refractive index than the lower, darker region. The refractive index of the upper region is designated n_1 while the lower region refractive index is n_2. Figure 3.1a shows a case where the angle of incidence is less than the critical angle. Note that the angle the light travels changes at the interface between the higher refractive index, n_1 region, and the lower refractive index, n_2 region. In Figure 3.1b, the angle of incidence has increased to the critical angle. At this angle the refracted light ray travels parallel to the interface region. In Figure 3.1c, the incidence angle has increased to a value greater than the critical angle. In this case 100% of the light reflects at the interface region.

The lower refractive index of the cladding (with respect to the core) causes the light to be angled back into the core, as illustrated in Figure 3.2.

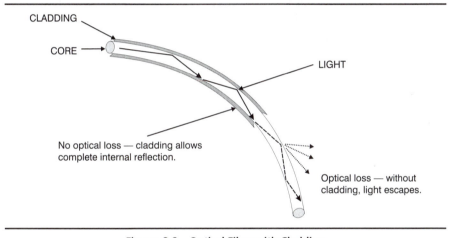

Figure 3.2 – Optical Fiber with Cladding

Advancements in laser technology next elevated the fiber optics industry. Only the light-emitting diode (LED) or its higher-power counterpart, the laser diode (LD), had the potential to generate large amounts of light in a spot tiny enough to be useful for fiber optics. As a Columbia University graduate student in 1957, Gordon Gould explored the idea of using lasers, describing them as an intense light source. In the research department at Bell Laboratories, Charles Townes and Arthur Schawlow lobbied for the use of lasers in scientific circles. Lasers went through several generations including the development of the ruby laser and the helium-neon laser in 1960. Semiconductor lasers, first realized in 1962, are widely used in fiber optics today.

Communications engineers quickly noticed the importance of lasers and their higher modulation frequency capability. Light has the capacity to carry 10,000 times more information than the highest radio frequency. Because environmental conditions such as rain, snow, hail, and smog disrupt laser light, scientists needed to find a transmission scheme other than free-space. In 1966, Charles Kao and Charles Hockham, working at the Standard Telecommunication Laboratory in England, presented optical fiber as an ideal transmission medium, assuming fiber attenuation (loss of signal strength) could be kept under 20 decibels per kilometer (dB/km). Optical fibers of the day exhibited losses of 1,000 dB/km or more. At a loss of 20 dB/km, 99% of the light would be lost over only 3,300 feet. In other words, only 1/100th of the transmitted optical power reached the receiver.

Intuitively, scientists theorized these optical losses resulted from impurities in the glass and not the glass itself. An optical loss of 20 dB/km was within the capability of the electronics and opto-electronic components of the day. In 1970, Drs. Robert Maurer, Donald Keck, and Peter Schultz of Corning succeeded in developing a glass fiber that exhibited attenuation at less than 20 dB/km, the threshold for making fiber optics a viable technology. Other advances of the day, such as semiconductor chips, optical detectors, and optical connectors initiated the true beginnings of the fiber optic communications industry.

Wavelength remains a significant factor in fiber optic developments. Figure 3.3 illustrates the wavelength "windows" as well as three curves.

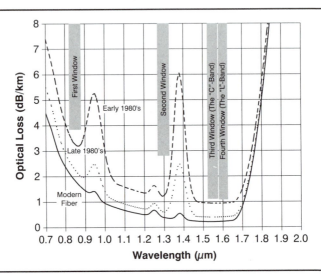

Figure 3.3 – Wavelength Windows in Optical Fiber

The top, dashed, curve corresponds to fiber used in the early 1980s; the middle, dotted, curve corresponds to late 1980s fiber; and the bottom, solid, curve corresponds to modern optical fiber. The earliest fiber optic systems were developed at an operating wavelength of about 850 nm. This wavelength corresponds to the so-called "first window" in a silica-based optical fiber. This window refers to a wavelength region that offers low optical loss. It sits between several large absorption peaks caused primarily by moisture in the fiber and Rayleigh scattering, the scattering of light due to the random fluctuations in the index of refraction, caused by the random structure of the glass itself.

The attraction to the 850 nm region came from its ability to use low cost IR LEDs and low-cost silicon detectors. As technology progressed, the first window lost its appeal due to its relatively high 3 dB/km loss limit. Most companies began to exploit the "second window" at 1310 nm with a lower attenuation of about 0.5 dB/km. In late 1977, Nippon Telegraph and Telephone (NTT) developed the "third window" at 1550 nm. It offered the theoretical minimum optical loss for silica-based fibers, about 0.2 dB/km.

These three wavelengths, 850 nm, 1310 nm, and 1550 nm, find use in many fiber optic installations, as do the visible wavelengths near 660 nm, which work in very low-end, short distance, systems. Each wavelength has advantages. Longer wavelengths offer higher performance, but always come with higher cost. Development of a "fourth window," near 1625 nm, will not offer lower optical loss than the 1550 nm window, but it may increase the bandwidth of long-length, multiple-wavelength communications system designs.

The International Telecommunications Union (ITU), an international organization that promotes worldwide telecommunications standards, has specified six transmission bands for fiber optic transmissions: the O-Band (original band — 1260 nm to 1310 nm), the E-Band (extended band — 1360 nm to 1460 nm), the S-Band (short band — 1460 nm to 1530 nm), the C-Band (Conventional Band — 1530 nm to 1565 nm), the L-Band (long band — 1565 nm to 1625 nm), and the U-Band (ultra band — 1625 nm to 1675 nm). A seventh band, not defined by the ITU, but used in private networks, runs around 850 nm.

Researchers have attempted to develop alternate fiber materials that could reduce cost or improve performance; however, like most of today's electronics, optical fiber remains silicon-based, although some alternative fiber materials do find specialized usage. For example, the short transmission capacity of plastic fiber makes it ideal for home theater installations where connections are made in a single stereo cabinet. Because of the plunging cost of glass fiber over the last decade, the drive to develop longer-distance plastic fiber has waned.

Fiber Optic Communications System

A general fiber optic communications system typically has three parts: the transmitter, which includes an encoder and a modulator; the transmission channel; and the receiver, which includes a demodulator and decoder, as illustrated in Figure 3.4. The term modem refers to a device that incorporates the modulator and the demodulator in a single package. Similarly, the word codec indicates a device that includes both the encoder and decoder.

Figure 3.4 – Basic Communications System

Three classes of communications systems exist. The first, simplex transmission, describes the fact that the information gets transmitted in only one direction, i.e., transmitter to receiver. The second, half-duplex transmission, describes a link that can transmit information in either direction, but only one channel at a time. A walkie-talkie is a good example of a half-duplex communication channel. In the third class, full-duplex transmission, both ends of the link contain a transmitter and a receiver, and information travels in both directions over two separate channels. A telephone represents a full-duplex communication channel. With the exception of teleconferencing and distance learning, most video transmission systems use simplex transmission.

All classes of communications systems require a transmission medium. Types of transmission media include electromagnetic waves ranging from low frequency RF to optical frequencies, which can be carried through free space or over cable or fiber; and sound waves, which use free space transmission. This book discusses transmission schemes for these media at length in Chapter 4. For now, suffice it to say that any transmission media will introduce some delay, distortion, noise, and/or interference, and the media generally represents the greatest limiting factor in any communications system.

Fiber Optic Components

The basic principles behind fiber optic transmission bear a strong resemblance to the concepts behind electronic transmission systems. Both systems contain three basic elements as illustrated in Figure 3.5 (next page).

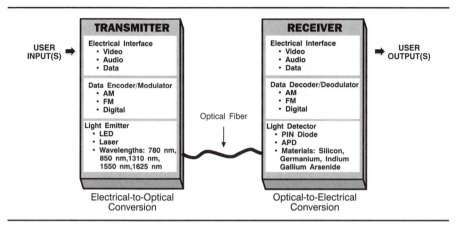

Figure 3.5 – Elements of a Fiber Optic Link

The transmitter in Figure 3.5 uses an electrical interface to encode the user's information through either amplitude modulation (AM), frequency modulation (FM), or digital modulation. This modulation occurs by changing the intensity of a light-emitting diode (LED) or a laser diode (LD). The wavelengths of these light sources range from 780 nm to 1625 nm for most fiber optic applications. The receiver uses either a PIN photodiode or an avalanche photodiode (APD) to decode the light signal back into electrical signals. Typically, manufacturers use silicon (Si), indium gallium arsenide (InGaAs), or germanium (Ge) to make these detectors. In some modern systems, an optical preamplifier precedes the photodetector to achieve improved received sensitivity. This will be covered in more detail in Chapter 16. The detected and amplified electrical signal is then sent through a data decoder or demodulator that converts the electrical signal back into the original input signal format. The third part of a link, the optical fiber, is an extremely thin strand of ultra-pure glass designed to transmit light signals from a transmitter to a receiver.

The fiber consists of three main regions. The core, at the center of the fiber, carries the light. It ranges in diameter from 9 microns (μm) to 100 microns in the most commonly used fibers. The cladding, surrounds the core, confining the light within the core. The cladding typically has a diameter of 125 microns. The core has a higher refractive index than the cladding, which allows for total internal reflection. Both the core and cladding are usually doped glass materials. The coating or buffer, typically a plastic material, provides protection and preserves the strength of the glass fiber. Usual diameters for the buffer are 250 microns, 500 microns, and 900 microns. Figure 3.6 shows the general cross-section of an optical fiber.

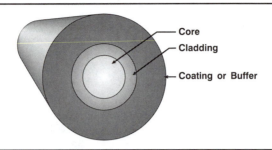

Figure 3.6 – Cross-section of an Optical Fiber

Applications for Fiber Optics

America's armed forces immediately took advantage of fiber optics to improve their communications and tactical systems. In the early 1970s, the U.S. Navy installed a fiber optic telephone link aboard the USS *Little Rock*. In 1976, the Air Force followed suit by developing its Airborne Light Optical Fiber Technology (ALOFT) program. By the mid-1980s FM video links, such as the ones shown in Figure 3.7, began to appear on Navy ships. The success of these applications spawned a number of military research and development programs to create stronger fibers, tactical cables, ruggedized, high-performance components, and numerous demonstration systems ranging from aircraft to undersea applications.

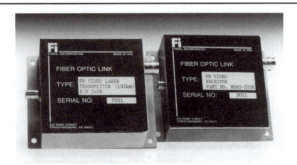

Figure 3.7 – FM Video Links Used on Navy Vessels in the 1980s
(Photo courtesy of Force, Inc.)

Soon after, commercial applications began to appear. The broadcast industry, always interested in better video transmission quality, embraced fiber optic video transmission. With its international viewing audience, networks broadcasting the Olympic games historically employed new technology. In 1980, broadcasters of the Winter Olympics, in Lake Placid, New York, requested a fiber optic video transmission system for backup video feeds. The fiber optic feed, because of its quality and reliability, soon became the primary video feed, making the 1980 Winter Olympics the first fiber optic television transmission. Later, at the 1994 Winter Olympics in Lillehammer, Norway, fiber optics transmitted the first ever digital video signal using the fiber video link shown in Figure 3.8, an application that continues to evolve today.

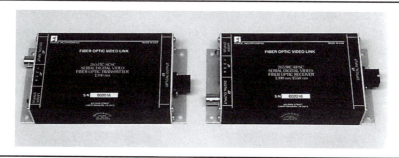

Figure 3.8 – Digital Video Link Used to Broadcast the 1994 Winter Olympics
(Photo courtesy of Force, Inc.)

The telecommunications industry, too, took advantage of new technology. In 1977, both AT&T and GTE created fiber optic telephone systems in Chicago and Boston respectively. Soon after, fiber optic telephone networks increased in number and reach. Network designers originally specified multimode graded-index fiber, but by the early 1980s, single-mode fiber operating in the 1310 nm and later the 1550 nm wavelength windows became standard. For example, by 1983, British Telecom's entire phone system used single-mode fiber exclusively. Computers, information networks, and data communications slowly moved to fiber, but today they too favor fiber's lighter weight cable, resistance to lightning strikes, and ability to carry more information faster and over longer distances.

In the mid-1980s, the United States government deregulated telephone service, allowing small telephone companies to compete with the giant, AT&T. Companies like MCI and Sprint led the pace in installing regional fiber optic telecommunications networks throughout the world. Existing natural rights of way, such as railroad lines and gas pipes, allowed these companies to install thousands of miles of fiber optic cable. This facilitated the deployment of these networks throughout the 1980s. With this boom, fiber transmission capacity struggled to keep up with the demand; fiber needed to go farther with greater capacity.

Thus began the "hero experiments," the cutting edge research that allows new technology to flourish. In 1990, Bell Labs sent a 2.5 Gb/s signal over 7,500 km without regeneration. The system, using a soliton laser and an erbium-doped fiber amplifier (EDFA), allowed the light pulse to maintain its shape and intensity. In 1998, Bell Labs' success went one better as researchers transmitted 100 simultaneous optical signals, each at a data rate of 10 gigabits (giga means billion) per second for a distance of nearly 250 miles (400 km). To increase the total data rate on one fiber to one terabit per second (10^{12} bits per second), this experiment used dense wavelength-division multiplexing (DWDM) technology, which allows multiple wavelengths to be combined into one optical signal. Figure 3.9 illustrates a basic DWDM system.

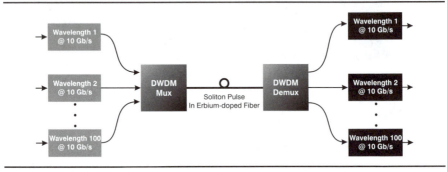

Figure 3.9 – Basic DWDM System Diagram

DWDM technology continues to develop as the thirst for bandwidth increases. Fiber's potential bandwidth, 50 terahertz or better, allows researchers to focus new technology on the move to optical networking and other applications. The FCC mandate to switch all broadcasting to DTV and HDTV standards gives researchers a challenge to develop fiber optic technology that can readily accommodate the requirements of these high definition standards.

Beyond television, however, consumers are pushing to have broadband services, including data, audio, and especially video, delivered to the home. Broadband service allows interactive communications for both consumers and businesses, bringing to reality interactive video networks, interactive banking and shopping from the home, and interactive distance learning. Video-on-demand hit a brick wall in coax cable that excelled at carrying the same signal to everyone, but failed as a means to route switched signals. That will not be true of the next generation of fiber optic technology. Video transmission and fiber optic technology are naturally suited to one another — color and light, the key components of both.

Chapter Summary

- John Tyndall first demonstrated that light could be transmitted within a stream of water in 1870.
- In 1880, Alexander Graham Bell developed an optical voice transmission system that represented the first optical AM transmission link.
- The fiberscope, developed in the 1950s, used an all-glass fiber to transmit images.
- Snell's Law describes total internal reflection, stating that light will be totally reflected at a boundary between a high refractive index and a low refractive index when the angle of incidence exceeds that critical angle.
- Optical fiber with cladding allowed researchers to reduce the optical loss compared to fibers with no cladding.
- Lasers and light-emitting diodes, used to transmit fiber optic signals, developed in the late 1950s and early 1960s.
- In 1970, scientists developed an optical fiber with an attenuation less than 20 dB/km, making fiber optics a viable technology.
- Fiber optic development is closely tied with the four wavelength windows in optical fiber: 850 nm, 1310 nm, 1550 nm, and 1625 nm.
- A general communications system includes a transmitter, a transmission channel, and a receiver.
- Transmission in communications systems may be simplex, half-duplex, or full-duplex.
- Simplex transmission communicates in one direction only.
- Half-duplex transmission can communicate in both directions, but only in one direction at a time.
- Full-duplex transmission can communicate bidirectionally at the same time using two channels.
- A fiber optic link uses a transmitter, an optical fiber, and a receiver.
- An optical fiber consists of the core, the area that carries the light; the cladding, which surrounds the core; and the buffer or coating.
- Real-world applications for fiber optic transmission were first developed for the military, with commercial applications following shortly afterward.
- U.S. deregulation of the big telephone companies led the way for smaller telecommunications companies to install an extensive network

of fiber optic lines by taking advantage of existing right of ways such as railroad tracks, and gas and utility lines.

- As demands for fiber optic transmission increased, "hero experiments" pushed the limits of optical fiber.

- One important hero experiment demonstrated the ability to transmit 100 signals over 250 km using DWDM technology, a technology undergoing aggressive development and deployment at this time.

- The FCC mandate to embrace DTV/HDTV makes the switch to fiber optic transmission inevitable.

- Broadband service allows the wide availability of consumer interactive communications such as interactive video networks, interactive home banking/shopping, and interactive distance learning.

Chapter 4

Overview of Fiber Optic Transmission Methods

Transmission Basics

Fiber provides a pipeline that can carry large amounts of data. Alternatives to fiber optics include over-the-air broadcast and hard-wired metallic wires carrying electrons. Figure 4.1 explains these transmission schemes.

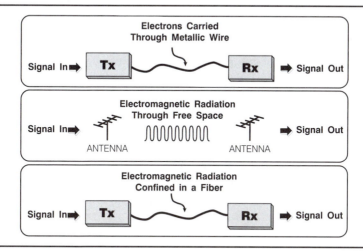

Figure 4.1 – Transmission Schemes

Metallic transmission uses a copper wire or coaxial cable to carry a modulated electrical signal. This allows the transmission of an unlimited number of private channels (assuming you have that much copper cable); however, each channel can carry only a limited amount of information due to the inherent characteristics of copper cable.

Free-space transmission represents how radio signals and over-the-air TV signals travel. It provides very large bandwidth capability as well as long distance capability, but this transmission scheme cannot offer private channels. Also, the free-space spectrum is a finite and costly commodity whose access is auctioned off by the FCC when new space becomes available. It cannot provide the millions of high-speed communication channels required by the global information age.

Waveguide transmission uses a waveguide (e.g., optical fiber) to confine the electromagnetic radiation (light) and moves it along a prescribed path. Optical fiber transmission offers high bandwidth and data rate, but it does not add clutter to the crowded free-space spectrum.

Modulation Schemes

A modulation scheme encodes, transmits, and decodes the information. Encoding information can improve the integrity of the transmission, allow more information to be sent per unit time, and in some cases, take advantage of some strength of the communication medium or overcome some inherent weakness. Modulating video signals can become complicated. Televisions use many horizontal lines to form a video image. The video signal contains the information to draw these lines, detailing whether parts of the line should be dark or light and how to display the colors. Sound is also encoded in the signal. Three basic techniques exist for transporting information such as video signals over optical fiber. Amplitude modulation (AM) includes baseband AM, RF carrier AM, and vestigial-sideband AM. Frequency modulation (FM) includes sine wave FM, square wave FM, pulse-frequency modulation, and FM-encoded vestigial-sideband. Table 4.1 outlines a comparison of these three formats.

Table 4.1 – AM, FM, and Digital Modulation

Parameter	AM	FM	Digital
Signal-to-Noise Ratio	Low-Moderate	Moderate-High	High
Performance vs. Attenuation	Sensitive	Tolerant	Invariant
Transmitter Cost	Moderate-High	Moderate	High
Receiver Cost	Moderate	Moderate-High	High
Receiver Gain Adjustment	Often Req.	Not Req.	Not Req.

Table 4.1 – AM, FM, and Digital Modulation (Continued)

Parameter	AM	FM	Digital
Installation	Adjustments Req.	No Adjustments Req.	No Adjustments Req.
Multichannel Capability	Good Capability Req. High Linearity Optics	Fewer Channels than AM	Good
Performance/Time	Moderate	Excellent	Excellent
Environmental Factors	Moderate	Excellent	Excellent

Figure 4.2 illustrates the basic operation of each of these techniques.

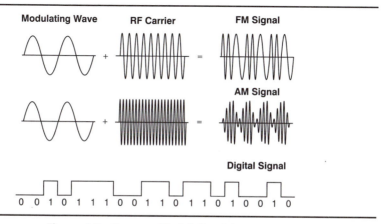

Figure 4.2 – Common Modulation Schemes

In this discussion of modulation techniques, the text will always refer to non-coherent optical systems, i.e., systems in which we manipulate only the intensity of the optical signal, not its frequency. Coherent schemes, which involve the direct modulation of the optical signal's frequency, are discussed more in Chapter 13. The frequency spectrum of simple, non-coherent baseband AM occupies the region from DC to about 5 MHz and requires the least bandwidth (using uncompressed digital encoding techniques). The RF carrier modulation spectrum is similar; it has been shifted to a non-zero frequency (F). This approach requires additional bandwidth and offers no advantage over baseband operation in a single channel per fiber system. However, it allows one to combine multiple channels onto a single fiber.

With vestigial-sideband AM, the spectrum again shifts to a non-zero frequency (F), and filtering removes most of the lower sideband. It allows for efficient use of the spectrum as compared to straight RF carrier AM, requiring about half the bandwidth per channel. The presence of harmonics yields the notable difference between sine wave FM, square wave FM, and pulse-frequency modulation. The square wave FM spectrum signal contains only odd-order harmonics. The pulse-frequency modulation spectrum contains all odd- and even-order harmonics yielding a cluttered spectrum poorly suited for multichannel stacking; however, it retains its value as a single-channel transmission scheme. (Refer to Figure 13.3 in Chapter 13.) Sine wave FM, RF carrier AM, and vestigial-sideband AM lack harmonics, making them suitable for multiple channel transmission. One can combine multiple channels for transmission over a single fiber by assigning different carrier frequencies to each video signal. The resulting sum of the modulated carriers yields a single composite electrical signal.

Video Quality Parameters

Dozens of parameters exist to describe the quality of a video signal. Common ones include signal-to-noise ratio (SNR), differential gain (DG), and differential phase (DP). The signal-to-noise ratio measures the clarity and crispness of the picture. A high SNR results in a sharp clear picture. Conversely, a low SNR results in a picture that displays "snow" or other interference. Differential gain measures the portion of the video signal that controls the brightness of any a given dot. A perfect video transmission link with zero DG distortion shows everything in the picture at the correct brightness while a video transmission link with a large amount of DG distortion shows incorrect shades of brightness. Differential phase measures the portion of the video signal that controls the color, hue, or shade. A video transmission link with no DP distortion displays all colors correctly, while large amounts of DP distortion displays incorrect colors.

Amplitude Modulation (AM)

The simplicity of amplitude modulation can result in low-cost hardware. In a baseband AM system, the input signal directly modulates the strength of the transmitter output. In the RF carrier AM technique, a carrier with a frequency higher than the frequency of the encoded information varies according to the amplitude of the encoded information. In a fiber optic system, the magnitude of the voltage input signal translates into a corresponding light intensity. AM modulation has two main drawbacks. First, the system requires highly linear optical components to prevent signal distortion as it travels through the communication link. Second, because varying the light intensity encodes the signal, the receiver cannot necessarily differentiate between intended signal level variations and the optical loss that occurs naturally in the fiber itself. For instance, providing a 100% maximum signal into the optical transmitter with 10 dB of optical loss between the transmitter and receiver, the receiver would indicate that the signal level is 10%. Figure 4.3 shows the basic transfer function of an AM system.

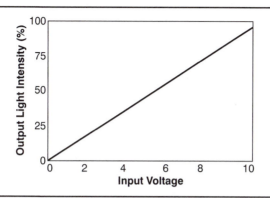

Figure 4.3 – AM System Transfer Function

The receiver cannot readily distinguish between changes in signal level and changes in optical loss due to the fiber. Compensating for this loss remains a challenge for fiber optic AM transmission; however, two solutions exist: one takes advantage of some property of the input waveform (for video, the amplitude of the sync pulse is invariant and can be used to distinguish optical loss from signal level variation); the other uses a technique that allows the receiver to interpret the signal level independently from optical loss. One accomplishes this by sending a pilot tone at a frequency that is above or below the frequency of the encoded information. The need for highly linear components can erase much of AM's advantage over other techniques because of the expense associated with obtaining highly linear LEDs or lasers. In spite of the difficulties mentioned above, AM systems represent the simplest and least expensive approach to encoding information for fiber optic transmission.

Frequency Modulation (FM)

Frequency modulation (FM) measures the received signal's timing information to recover the original signal. In addition, FM has immunity to amplitude variations caused by optical loss, one of fiber's weak points as a transmission medium. FM modulation centers around a high-frequency carrier. Differences in the signal amplitude change the frequency of the carrier instead of the amplitude. Another advantage of FM systems, seen in mathematical analyses, shows that the signal-to-noise ratio at the receiver can be improved by increasing the frequency deviation of the carrier. For example, assume that a transmitted video signal has a 5 MHz bandwidth. Using a 70

MHz carrier frequency and applying the video signal to produce a 5 MHz deviation, the receiver achieves about a 5 dB enhancement in its signal-to-noise ratio, compared to an AM system. If we increase the deviation of the carrier frequency to 10 MHz, then the improvement increases to 15.6 dB. Compared to AM, FM reduces the need for highly linear optical components, another important advantage.

Often, optical systems employing FM encoding refer to the technique as pulse-frequency modulation (PFM). This limits the FM signal by converting it to digital 0's and 1's before transmission. Generally the modulator is designed so that the pulse frequency increases as the input voltage increases. FM optical systems almost always require more complex electronic circuitry than AM optical systems, but often the total cost is comparable since lower-cost optical components can be used in the FM system. Figure 4.4 shows an FM receiver response.

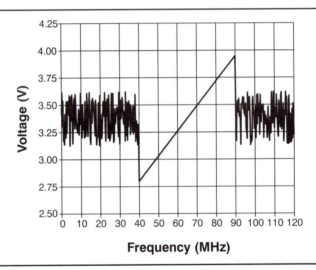

Figure 4.4 – FM System Receiver Response

Digital Modulation

Digital Basics

The bit (short for binary digit) is the basic unit of digital information. This unit has two values: one (1) or zero (0). The bit represents the electronic equivalent to the circuit being on or off, where zero = off and one = on. One-bit of information is limited to these two values, but using two bits of information allows the communication of more information, e.g., this scenario, 00 = off, 01 = on (dim), 10 = brighter, 11 = brightest. The more bits used in a unit, the more information can be sent. An 8-bit group is called a byte. A byte gives 2^8 or 256 different meanings to a pattern of ones and zeros. Each added bit doubles the number of possible combinations.

Digital systems can be illustrated by pulse trains such as the one seen in Figure 4.5. A pulse train represents the ones and zeros of digital information. The pulse train can depict high-voltage and low-voltage levels or the presence and absence of a voltage. In dealing with pulses, engineers must consider the shape of a pulse.

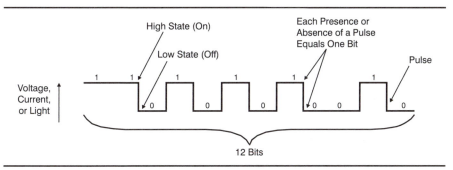

Figure 4.5 – Typical Pulse Train

Figure 4.6 illustrates the five main characteristics of a pulse. Amplitude is the height of the pulse. Rise time denotes the amount of time required to turn the pulse on and is typically the length of time required to go from 10% to 90% of amplitude. This sets the upper speed limit of the system, a critical factor.

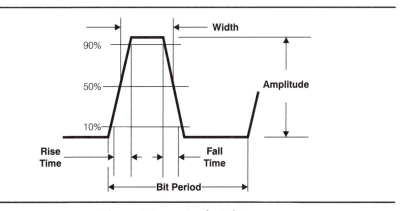

Figure 4.6 – Parts of a Pulse

The speed at which pulses turn off and on determines the fastest rate at which the pulses can occur. Fall time, as its name suggests, represents the time taken to turn the pulse off. Pulse width describes, in units of time, the width of the pulse at 50% of its amplitude. Bit period is the time required for the pulse to go through a complete cycle. Most digital systems are clocked; pulses must occur in the time allotted by the system for a bit period. The system clock, an unchanging pulse train, provides timing by defining the bit periods.

Digital Video and Audio

Digital can mean different things to video and CATV engineers, causing much confusion. The key types of digital video and audio are as follows:

- Uncompressed video and audio

- Lossless compression of video and audio

- Lossy compression of video and audio

- Complex digital modulation such as 64 QAM, 256 QAM, 16 VSB, 64 QPSK, etc.

- SONET, ATM or other telephony based standards

- SDV (serial digital video)

Uncompressed Digital Signals

Digitizing video follows the natural progression of video technology. A standard NTSC video signal has an analog bandwidth of 4.5 MHz. In the purest form of uncompressed digital video, the video signal sampling rate is four times the analog bandwidth (18 megasamples or Msamples per second) using an A/D converter with a resolution of 8 to 12 bits. This generates digital data rates of 144 Mb/s to 216 Mb/s. In most modern digital video applications, the video signals get encoded at the time of recording and decoded on playback. While this encoding method is not called compression, it does in fact reduce the digital data rate compared to pure uncompressed digital video. Depending on the digital format, the video signal will be sampled at 13.5 MSamples/second using one of the many existing standards such as 4:2:2, 4:1:1, or 4:2:0 sampling. In these sampling rates, the three numbers refer to the sample rate of the three common video components. These components are luminance (Y), a color value consisting of the red minus luminance (R-Y), and the color value of blue minus luminance (B-Y). These three components, Y, (R-Y), and (B-Y) are often referred to as "YUV." Chapter 11 will cover this in detail. In any case, these digital formats generate data rates from 135 Mb/s to 162 Mb/s. At the other end of the spectrum, a single uncompressed digitized HDTV video channel can generate serial data rates as high as 1,485 Mb/s.

A/D conversion allows for digital fiber optic video transmission. Figures 4.7 and 4.8 illustrate a digital optical transmission system for sending and receiving 16 uncompressed digitized video and audio signals. At the transmitting end, A/D converters encode the baseband video channels. Next, the digital channels are time-division multiplexed (TDM) and sent to the laser transmitter. The digital signal is converted into light pulses — on for a one and off for a zero.

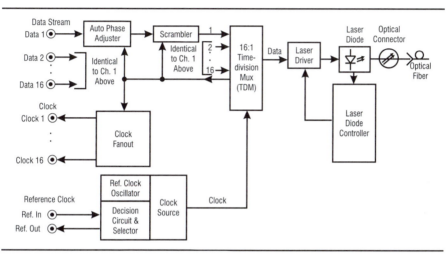

Figure 4.7 – Optical Tx Multiplexing and Sending 16 Digitized Video Signals

(Comlux® transmitter block diagram courtesy of Force, Inc.)

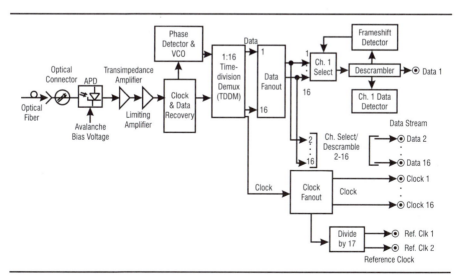

Figure 4.8 – Optical Rx Receiving and Demultiplexing 16 Digitized Video Signals

(Comlux® receiver block diagram courtesy of Force, Inc.)

At the receiving end, the light pulses are converted back into electrical pulses. The pulses are time-division demultiplexed (TDD) and sent through a digital-to-analog (D/A) converter. This converts the information back into a baseband video signal.

Analog-to-digital conversion requires three steps: sampling the signal at regular time intervals, quantizing the signal into discrete bins, and coding the quantized values into an appropriate binary code. Digital video transmission has several inherent advantages over analog transmission. Digital systems do not require more expensive, highly linear light sources, which allows a wide range of non-critical system operating parameters. In general, digital transmitters and receivers work with both single-mode or multimode fiber, and have a high immunity to noise. In addition, the system can retransmit a digital signal numerous times via optical regenerators without signal degradation.

Compressed Digital Signals

Video compression allows dramatic reduction of the bandwidth per video channel. We know that a single digitized video channel can generate serial data rates from 135 Mb/s for standard 4:2:2 digitized NTSC to 1,485 Mb/s for HDTV. Video compression keeps a single NTSC video signal from using 10 to 20 times more bandwidth than is needed to transmit a standard 6 MHz wide analog VSB/AM CATV channel. Thus, in order to simply *equal* the bandwidth of an analog channel, a digitized video signal requires a compression factor of 10 to 20.

Truly usable digitized video often requires further compression. Compression works by removing redundant information that may exist in the picture and by finding more efficient ways to encode elements in the picture. In many cases, compression algorithms take advantage of the way the human eye works by removing information less sensitive to the eye and preserving only the most critical features.

Compression algorithms may be described as lossless or lossy. A lossless compression algorithm does not degrade the picture in any way; the receiver can recover the original uncompressed image. Unfortunately, lossless compression algorithms can only achieve modest levels of compression, perhaps a factor of four. Lossy compression algorithms, on the other hand, can achieve very high levels of compression, but at a cost. The compression process permanently eliminates some picture information. Chapter 14 discusses compression algorithms in greater detail.

Comparison of Analog and Digital Video Signals

Analog describes the world we live in, where most variables (e.g., temperature, sound, color, etc.) exhibit a continuous range of difference. Sound varies in both amplitude and frequency; the human eye can perceive millions of color values between black and white. Consider a dimmer switch that adjusts the light within a certain range. The light levels vary over a wide continuous range. One can adjust the brightness anywhere from completely off to completely on. However, no human sense can distinguish a truly infinite range, and at some point, the two amplitudes appear identical. For the human ear, the smallest discernible unit is one decibel.

By contrast, digital implies distinct units. In a digital system all information exists in numerical values of digital pulses. In this example, consider a three-way lamp. One can set the lamp to low light level, high light level, and off. No levels exist between these three settings. Most electronic communication schemes rely on digital modulation.

Picture Quality versus System Noise in Analog and Digital Signals

Figures 4.9 and 4.10, on the following pages, show the degradation of an analog AM video signal and a digital video signal as the signal noise increases. In Figure 4.9 (next page), beginning at the upper left of the figure, SNR and picture quality are high. As the noise increases, the SNR steadily drops and more "snow" appears in the picture. Each picture to the right shows lower SNR with increasing snow until the picture is all snow. The SNR in this figure drops from about 50 dB in the upper left corner to 10 dB in the lower right corner.

Figure 4.10 (page 45) shows the degradation of a digital video signal as noise increases. At the upper left, the signal-to-noise ratio (SNR) is high and picture quality is high. As the noise increases, the picture quality holds steady and is not impaired until the SNR drops to a very low level, around 20 dB. At that point the picture quality drops rapidly.

In this case, the picture does not show "snow" as the SNR drops. Rather, because of the digital transmission scheme and the use of video compression the picture appears "blocky" and shows decreased resolution. As the SNR drops just a few more dB, the picture will either freeze to the last good frame or will go black entirely (illustrated).

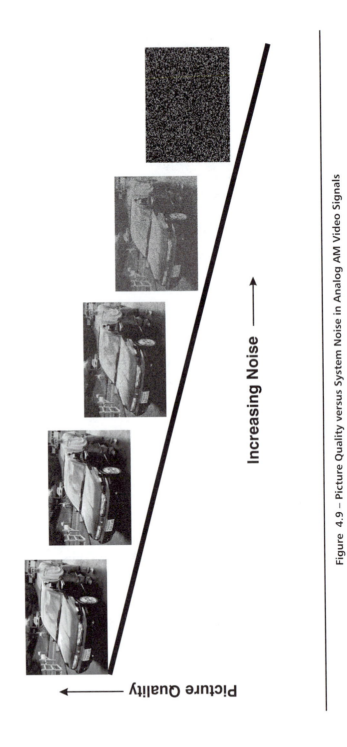

Increasing Noise →

← **Picture Quality**

Figure 4.9 – Picture Quality versus System Noise in Analog AM Video Signals

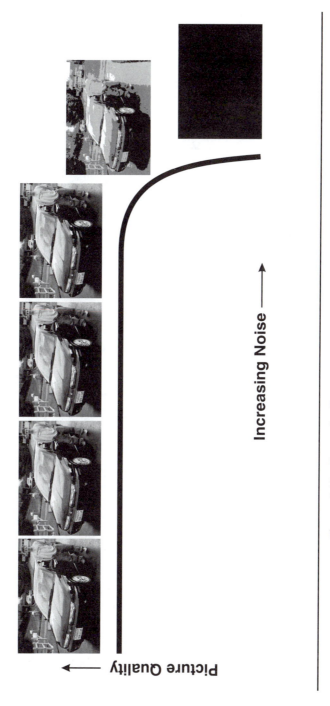

Figure 4.10 – Picture Quality versus System Noise in Digital Video Signals

Figure 4.11 compares FM, AM, and digital video links. At 0 dB optical loss, digital and AM modulation schemes have a higher than 70 dB signal-to-noise ratio, but at 3 dB of optical loss, the AM signal-to-noise ratio drops below the FM SNR.

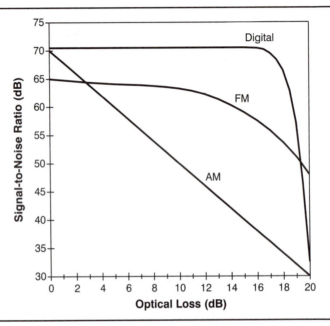

Figure 4.11 – FM Video Link versus AM Video Link

(FM data based on the performance of Force, Inc. fiber optic FM video links.)

The digital signal holds steady at around 71 dB from 0 dB of loss all the way out to 16 dB of optical loss. At a practical (and typical) optical loss of 10 dB, the FM link has a 13 dB signal-to-noise advantage and the digital signal has a 22 dB advantage over the AM link. The slope of the AM video link indicates that the signal-to-noise ratio drops 2 dB every time the optical loss increases by 1 dB. This contrasts to the digital and FM links that show nearly flat signal-to-noise ratio performance over the usable loss range. At the loss limit, the digital signal-to-noise ratio drops very rapidly. The FM SNR remains relatively constant at lower optical losses but typically follows the 2 dB drop per 1 dB optical loss at higher optical losses.

All three of these modulations schemes have different advantages and disadvantages in fiber optic video transmission. The modulation type used impacts many other system decisions, including the choice of optical fiber. The next chapter describes the characteristics of optical fiber and which fiber types work best in fiber optic video transmission.

Chapter Summary

- Transmission signals may use metallic wire, free space, or optical fiber to travel from point to point.

- Signal modulation involves encoding the signal, transmitting it, and decoding the signal at the other end of the transmission line.

- Three types of signal modulation include amplitude modulation, frequency modulation, and digital modulation.

- In baseband AM modulation, the input signal directly modulates the strength of the transmitter output.

- In RF carrier AM modulation, a carrier with a frequency higher than the frequency of the encoded information varies according to the amplitude of the encoded information.

- FM modulation centers around a high-frequency carrier; the frequency of the carrier changes according to the signal amplitude.

- In an analog AM video signal, decreased SNR will result in a gradually increasingly snowy appearance until the image completely degrades.

- In a digital video signal, decreased SNR does not affect picture quality until it falls below a certain threshold; at that point the picture quality drops off suddenly, and compression artifacts will appear as blocks in the picture.

- Pulse trains illustrate digital systems, representing the ones and zeros of digital information as high-voltage and low-voltage levels or the presence and absence of a voltage.

- The main parts of digital pulse are the amplitude, the rise time, the fall time, the pulse width, and the bit period.

- Types of digital video and audio include uncompressed, lossless compression, lossy compression, complex modulation schemes (e.g., 64 QAM, 256 QAM, 64 QPSK, etc.), telephony-based standards such as SONET and ATM, and serial digital video (SDV).

- Analog-to-digital conversion requires sampling the signal, quantizing the samples into discrete bins, and coding the quantized values.

- Sampling rates include three numbers, which correspond to the three common video components: luminance (Y), red minus luminance (R-Y), and blue minus luminance (B-Y).

- Examples of video sampling rates include 4:2:2, 4:1:1, and 4:2:0.

- Video compression reduces signal bandwidth by removing redundant information and efficiently encoding the elements in the picture.

- Lossless compression techniques do not degrade the picture quality in any way but can only achieve modest compression levels.

- Lossy compression techniques permanently eliminate picture information but can achieve very high compression levels.

- At 0 dB optical loss, digital and AM modulation schemes have an SNR higher than FM schemes, but at 3 dB of optical loss, the AM signal-to-noise ratio drops below the FM SNR.

- The modulation scheme selected for a fiber optic system can impact other elements of the overall system design.

Chapter 5

Characteristics of Optical Fiber

As countries continue to develop networks for global communication, fiber optics offers a method of transmission that allows for clearer, faster, more efficient communication than copper. A number of characteristics make optical fiber well-suited to video transmission. This chapter discusses the basics behind optical fiber transmission.

Principles of Operation

The principle of total internal reflection governs the operation of optical fiber. An image in a mirror represents only 90% of the reflected light. Total internal reflection reflects 100% of the light. Total internal reflection occurs because light travels at different speeds in different materials.

A dimensionless number called the index of refraction or refractive index, characterizes the different mediums through which the light travels. The index of refraction is the ratio of the velocity of light in a vacuum (c) to its velocity in a specific medium (v) as shown in Equation 5.1.

Eq. 5.1
$$n = \frac{c}{v}$$

One can observe the principle of total internal reflection when viewing a fish tank. Figure 5.1 (next page) shows the top view of a fish tank complete with an occupant and an observer.

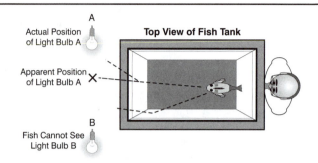

Figure 5.1 – Total Internal Reflection

(Illustration courtesy of Force, Inc.)

From a viewpoint behind the position of the fish, both the observer and the fish can see light bulb A. However, total internal reflection prevents the fish from seeing light bulb B. In this example, the water has a refractive index of 1.33, and the air has a refractive index of about 1.00. (Actually, the glass wall between the water and air has a refractive index of 1.45, but this doesn't materially affect the discussion.)

Light bends or refracts as it passes from a medium of one refractive index to a medium with a different refractive index. If light passes from a medium with a lower index of refraction to one with a higher index of refraction the light bends toward the normal, and if the light passes from a higher to lower index of refraction the light bends away from the normal. Snell's Law determines the amount of light that bends (Equation 5.2). Refer back to Figure 3.1 for the definitions of Θ_1, Θ_2, n_1, and n_2.

Eq. 5.2 $$n_1 \sin\Theta_1 = n_2 \sin\Theta_2$$

As the angle of incidence increases, the angle of refraction approaches 90°. The critical angle produces a 90° angle of refraction. Increasing the angle of incidence past the critical angle results in total internal reflection. In total internal reflection the angle of incidence equals the angle of reflection. Equation 5.3 calculates the critical angle.

Eq. 5.3 $$\Theta_c = \sin^{-1}\left(\frac{n_2}{n_1}\right)$$

Where:

n_1 = Refractive index of the core.
n_2 = Refractive index of the cladding.

Because the core of an optical fiber has a higher index of refraction than the cladding ($n_1 > n_2$), it allows total internal reflection to occur. Light entering the core of a fiber at an angle sufficient for total internal reflection travels down the core reflecting off the interface between the core and the cladding. Light that enters the fiber at an angle less than the critical angle refracts into the fiber's cladding and is lost.

An imaginary cone of acceptance with an angle alpha (α), determined by the critical angle, relates to a parameter called the numerical aperture (NA) of the fiber. NA describes the light gathering capability of fiber and is given as:

Eq. 5.4
$$NA = \sin\alpha = \sqrt{n_1^2 - n_2^2}$$
$$\text{and}$$
$$\alpha = \sin^{-1}\left(\sqrt{n_1^2 - n_2^2}\right)$$

To bring these parameters into perspective, it helps to calculate these fiber parameters. Assume that the fiber core refractive index is 1.47, and the cladding refractive index is 1.45.

So:

$n_1 = 1.47$
$n_2 = 1.45$

From Equation 5.5 we find the speed at which light travels in the fiber.

Eq. 5.5
$$v = \frac{c}{n} = \frac{(2.998 \cdot 10^8 \text{ m/s})}{1.47} = 2.039 \cdot 10^8 \text{ m/s}$$

We can invert this to find that it takes the light 4.903 ns to travel one meter in an optical fiber.

From Equation 5.6 we can calculate the critical angle, Θ_C:

Eq. 5.6
$$\Theta_c = \sin^{-1}\left(\frac{1.45}{1.47}\right) = 80.5°$$

From Equation 5.7 we can calculate the numerical aperture to be:

Eq. 5.7
$$NA = \sqrt{(1.47^2 - 1.45^2)} = 0.2417$$

Finally, from Equation 5.8 we can calculate angle α.

Eq. 5.8
$$\alpha = \sin^{-1}(0.2417) = 13.98°$$

Table 5.1 lists the refractive indices and propagation times of several materials. While the propagation times of optical fiber and copper coax cable appear almost identical, different factors determine these propagation times. In metallic cables, propagation delays depend on the cable dimensions and the frequency. The refractive index of the material used in optical fiber determines its propagation delay. Most applications do not suffer from absolute propagation time delay caused by fiber. However, system designs that involve sending many synchronous digital signals over separate fibers require that all signals arrive at roughly the same time. Another application concerning propagation time involves sending multiple signals over the same fiber using different wavelengths of light.

Table 5.1 – Refractive Index and Propagation Times for Various Materials

Medium	Refractive Index	Propagation Time
Vacuum	1.000	3.336 ns/m
Air	1.003	3.346 ns/m
Water	1.333	4.446 ns/m
Fused Silica	1.458	4.863 ns/m
Copper Coax Cable (RG-59/U)	N/A	5.051 ns/m

Propagation time through a fiber is calculated as follows:

Eq. 5.9
$$t = \frac{L \bullet n}{c}$$

Where:

t = Propagation time in seconds.
L = Fiber length in meters.
n = Refractive index of the fiber core (approximately 1.47).
c = Speed of light (2.998×10^8 meters/second).

Bandwidth Potential

While very high, fiber's potential bandwidth falls short of infinite. In single wavelength systems, chromatic dispersion limits the bandwidth. Operating a fiber at the zero-dispersion wavelength, also called the zero-dispersion point, with a monochromatic light source, yields a large fiber bandwidth. Figure 5.2 (next page) shows the bandwidth-distance product for a hypothetical single-mode fiber. The center wavelength for the light source lies on the x-axis. The figure shows three curves with FWHM giving values of 2 nm, 5 nm, and 10 nm. Full width half maximum represents the width of the spectral emission at the 50% amplitude points. The most narrow source shown, FWHM = 2 nm, offers a bandwidth-distance product of over 30,000 GHz•km at a center wavelength of 1310 nm, the fiber's zero-dispersion wavelength. As the center wavelength moves even a few nanometers from 1310 nm, the fiber's bandwidth-distance product drops dramatically. At a center wavelength of 1320 nm, the fiber's bandwidth-distance product has dropped by a factor of 30, to 1,000 GHz•km. Wider optical sources offer even lower bandwidth. Using a very narrow light source tuned exactly for the fiber's zero-dispersion wavelength would yield a bandwidth peak much higher than those shown in the plot.

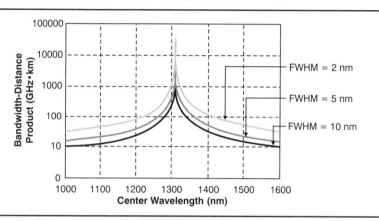

Figure 5.2 – Single-mode Fiber Bandwidth

Advantages of Optical Fiber

A fiber optic communication system holds many advantages over a copper wire system. While a simple two-strand copper wire can carry a low-speed signal over a long distance, it cannot send high-speed signals very far. Coaxial cables can better handle high-speed signals but still only over a relatively short distance. Copper cables can transmit AC or DC power in addition to communication signals, which fiber cannot, one advantage of copper cables. On the other hand, fiber optics holds an advantage over copper media in its ability to handle high-speed signals over extended distances. Other advantages of fiber optic transmission include:

• Immunity from Electromagnetic (EM) Radiation and Lightning: Made from dielectric (nonconducting) materials, EM radiation does not affect optical fiber. The electronics required at the end of each fiber, however, are still susceptible and require shielding. The military took advantage of fiber's immunity to EM radiation and lightning by exploring fiber's potential for secure communications. While fiber transmission itself is not inherently secure, it does not normally emit any readily detectable EM radiation. Commercial security and intelligent transportation systems enjoy fiber's lightning immunity, because these systems are deployed over a wide area making them susceptible to damage from lightning strikes and interference. Immunity from EM radiation is an important factor in choosing fiber to upgrade existing communication systems. The fiber can often make use of the same conduits that currently carry power lines, simplifying installation.

- Lighter Weight: This feature refers to the optical fiber itself. In real world applications, lighter fiber optic cables routinely replace heavier copper cables. For long distances, a complete fiber optic system (optical fiber and cable, plus the supporting electronics) also has a significant weight advantage over copper systems.

- Higher Bandwidth: Fiber has higher bandwidth than any alternative available. The CATV industry's copper cable supertrunks, due to limited bandwidth, required amplifiers every thousand feet or so. A modern fiber optic system can carry the same signals with similar or superior signal quality for 50 miles or more without intermediate amplification (repeaters). Most modern fiber optic communication systems utilize less than a few percent of fiber's inherent bandwidth.

- Better Signal Quality: Immunity to EM interference, lower loss per unit distance, and wider bandwidth makes signal quality substantially better compared to copper.

- Lower Cost: This has to be qualified. Fiber certainly costs less for long distance applications. However, copper cable costs less for short signal transmission distances. The fiber itself offers greater economy over copper, per unit distance, if bandwidth and transmission distance requirements are high. However, the cost of the electronics and electro-optics at the end of the fiber can be substantial. At today's copper prices, the cost of converting to optical fiber for very long distance links nearly equals the salvage value of the removed copper. A break-even distance acts as a gauge to determine the cost advantage of copper versus fiber. At distances shorter than the break-even distance, copper is cheaper and vice versa. In the mid-1980s the break-even distance was 10 km or more. Today, the break-even distance is often less than 100 meters. The reduced cost of fiber optic systems and components contributes to this cost reduction. Also, the cost of copper has increased over the same period of time.

- Easily Upgraded: The limitation of fiber optic systems today, and for years to come, is the electronics and electro-optics used on each end of the fiber. Fiber typically cannot use all of its transmission capability and high bandwidth. Future advances in electronics and electro-optics will interface seamlessly with fiber, particularly single-mode fiber.

- Ease of Installation: Despite the fears of newcomers to fiber optics, that glass breaks easily, glass fiber is actually many times stronger than steel. A good quality fiber optic cable incorporates strain relief materials as well as bend limiters that make the cable very hardy. Copper coax, is in fact, much more fragile than a fiber optic cable. Copper coax cables are prone to kinks and deformities that will permanently degrade the performance of the cable. Glass will not deform or kink, making it stronger than copper cable.

Key Fiber Types

In selecting the correct type of fiber for a given application, the system designer must consider several factors.

- Fiber core/cladding size (e.g., 50/125 μm)
- Fiber material and construction (e.g., glass core/glass cladding)
- Fiber attenuation measured in dB/km
- Fiber bandwidth-distance product measured in MHz•km
- Environmental considerations (e.g., temperature)

For fiber size, the first number listed (e.g., 50 or 62.5) represents the fiber core diameter in microns. The number after the slash is the cladding diameter, a key dimension when choosing a fiber optic connector. Fibers with the same cladding size can use the same size connectors. As for fiber construction, using fibers made from glass cores and glass cladding yields excellent performance at a reasonable cost. Figure 5.3 illustrates the most popular fiber sizes, giving one a visual feel for the relative core and cladding size. This allows one to identify an unknown fiber's core and cladding using a microscope. Descriptions for each fiber type follow.

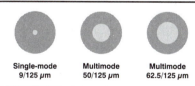

Single-mode
9/125 μm

Multimode
50/125 μm

Multimode
62.5/125 μm

Figure 5.3 – Popular Fiber Sizes

- 9/125 μm (SM): Used for high data rate and long distance applications.
- 50/125 μm (MM): Mainly used by military customers but experiencing a small comeback in commercial applications.
- 62.5/125 μm (MM): Very popular in most commercial applications; it has wide uses with low- to moderate-speed data links and video links.

Multimode Fiber

The first commercial fiber type, multimode fiber, carries numerous modes or light rays simultaneously through the waveguide. Modes result from the fact that light will only propagate in the fiber core at discrete angles within the cone of acceptance. This fiber type has a much larger core diameter, compared to single-mode fiber, allowing for the larger number of modes, and multimode fiber is easier to couple than single-mode fiber. Multimode fiber may be categorized as step-index or graded-index fiber.

Multimode Step-index Fiber

Figure 5.4 shows how the principle of total internal reflection applies to multimode step-index fiber. Because the core's index of refraction is higher than the cladding's index of refraction, the light that enters at less than the critical angle is guided along the fiber.

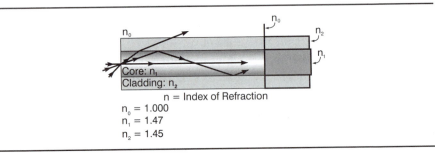

n = Index of Refraction
$n_0 = 1.000$
$n_1 = 1.47$
$n_2 = 1.45$

Figure 5.4 – Multimode Step-index Fiber

Three different rays of light are pictured traveling down the fiber. One mode travels straight down the center of the core. A second mode travels at a steep angle and bounces back and forth by total internal reflection. The third mode exceeds the critical angle and is refracted into the cladding and lost as it escapes into the air. Intuitively, it can be seen that the second mode travels a longer distance than the first mode, causing the two modes to arrive at separate times. This disparity between arrival times of the different light rays is known as dispersion, and the result is a muddied signal at the receiving end. Dispersion will be treated in detail later in this chapter; however, it is important to note that high dispersion is an unavoidable characteristic of multimode step-index fiber.

Multimode Graded-index Fiber

To compensate for the dispersion inherent in multimode step-index fiber, researchers developed multimode graded-index fiber. Graded-index refers to the fact that the refractive index of the core gradually decreases farther from the center of the core. The increased refraction in the center of the core slows the speed of some light rays, allowing all the light rays to reach the receiving end at approximately the same time, reducing dispersion.

Figure 5.5 shows the principle of multimode graded-index fiber. The core's central refractive index, n_A, is greater than that of the outer core's refractive index, n_B. As discussed earlier, the core's refractive index is parabolic, being higher at the center. As Figure 5.5 shows, the light rays no longer follow straight lines; they follow a serpentine path being gradually bent back toward the center by the continuously declining refractive index. This reduces the arrival time disparity because all modes arrive at about the same time. The modes traveling in a straight line are in a higher refractive index, so they travel slower than the serpentine modes. These travel farther but move faster in the lower refractive index of the outer core region.

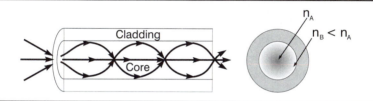

Figure 5.5 – Multimode Graded-index Fiber

Single-mode Fiber

Single-mode fiber allows for a higher capacity to transmit information because it can retain the fidelity of each light pulse over longer distances, and it exhibits no dispersion caused by multiple modes. Single-mode fiber also enjoys lower fiber attenuation (addressed in the next section), allowing more information to be transmitted per unit of time. Like multimode fiber, early single-mode fiber was generally characterized as step-index fiber, meaning the refractive index of the fiber core is a step above that of the cladding rather than graduated as it is in graded-index fiber. Modern single-mode fibers have evolved into more complex designs such as matched clad, depressed clad and other exotic structures. Figure 5.6 (next page) illustrates the path of a light ray through single-mode fiber.

Single-mode fiber has disadvantages. The smaller core diameter makes coupling light into the core more difficult and increases the tolerance demands for single-mode connectors and splices. In addition, 1550 nm systems may be susceptible to a number of relatively new, performance-limiting effects known as fiber nonlinearities. Modern single-mode fiber designs, discussed further in Chapter 6, addresses these nonlinearities.

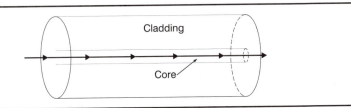

Figure 5.6 – Single-mode Fiber

Fiber Characteristics

Figure 5.7 considers attenuation, bandwidth-distance products, and power for three fiber sizes. Smaller numbers indicate the better fiber performance. Bandwidth-distance product represents the amount of information a single fiber can carry per second. Higher numbers indicate greater information carrying capacity. Power refers to the relative optical power that can be coupled into an optical fiber using an LED; 50/125 μm fiber is the reference. Looking at other fiber sizes, 62.5/125 μm fiber can couple 4.5 dB or 181% more power into the fiber than 50/125 μm fiber. Single-mode fiber would be about -13 dB relative to 50/125 μm fiber. However, easily coupled fibers tend to have poor bandwidth-distance products and attenuation rates.

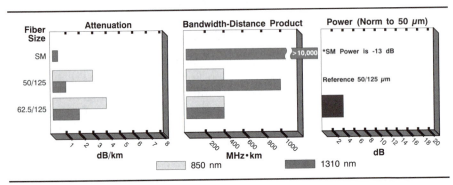

Figure 5.7 – Comparison of Optical Fiber Types

Operating wavelength directly influences fiber loss. Practical fibers have lower loss at 1550 nm and higher loss at 780 nm. Fiber bandwidth, another parameter, determines the maximum data rate. Table 5.2 shows the typical fiber optical loss at three fiber optic wavelengths. This data reflects the multiple levels of performance for each fiber size as given by a number of fiber manufacturers, listing the range of values seen in mainstream fibers.

Table 5.2 – Typical Fiber Loss

Fiber		Optical Loss (dB/km)		
Size	Type	850 nm	1310 nm	1550 nm
9/125 μm	SM	---	0.3-0.7	0.2-0.3
50/125 μm	MM	3.0-7.0	1.0-3.0	1.0-3.0
62.5/125 μm		3.0-7.0	1.0-4.0	1.0-4.0

Table 5.3 presents the bandwidth-distance product of the common fiber sizes at three fiber optic wavelengths, and Table 5.4 shows other miscellaneous fiber parameters.

Table 5.3 – Typical Fiber Bandwidth

Fiber		Bandwidth-Distance Product (MHz•km)		
Size	Type	850 nm	1310 nm	1550 nm
9/125 μm	SM	2,000	20,000+	4,000-20,000+
50/125 μm	MM	200-800	400-1,500	300-1,500
62.5/125 μm		100-400	200-1,000	150-500

Table 5.4 – Miscellaneous Fiber Parameters

Fiber Size	Numerical Aperture	Temperature Range	Min. Bend Radius
9/125 μm	0.14	-60 to +85°C	12 mm
50/125 μm	0.20	-60 to +85°C	12 mm
62.5/125 μm	0.275	-60 to +85°C	12 mm

Most optical fibers perform worse at low temperatures because the cable material becomes stiff and puts the fiber under stress. Other basic generalizations include:

- Larger core size fibers generally cost more.
- Larger core size fibers have higher loss (attenuation) per unit distance.
- Larger core size fibers have lower bandwidth.
- Larger core size fibers allow the use of lower cost light sources.
- Larger core size fibers typically use lower cost connectors.
- Larger core size fibers typically yield the lowest system cost (for short distance systems).

Optical Cables

Usually, manufacturers construct optical cables to the customer's specific application. However, all types of fiber optic cables contain common elements: the fiber housing, number of fiber's per cable, cable strength elements, etc. The fiber housing construction techniques include loose-tube or tight-buffer configurations. Loose-tube construction, used mainly in long distance applications and permanent installations, offers lower attenuation than tight-buffer, but a sharp cable bend may break the fiber. Loose-tube construction encloses the optical fibers in plastic buffer tubes filled with a water-impeding gel. A smaller, more flexible, tight-buffer cable better resists impact. In this cable design, the buffering material touches the fiber. This gives the cable high mechanical integrity in a small size, excellent in applications with space constraints.

A cable's fiber count affects its current and future usability. Fiber count considers the present and future end-user applications, the level of multiplexing, the number of routers used, and the network's physical topology. Fiber count in a fiber optic cable ranges from the simplest single-fiber construction to complex multifiber cables. Depending on the application, a variety of strength members can be designed into the cable construction, which allows the cable to withstand tension from 50-600 pounds for an extended period. The cable jacket, the final outer layer of the cable, may use a number of materials depending on the required mechanical properties, attenuation, environmental stress, and flammability. Table 5.5 lists the properties of common cable jacket materials.

Table 5.5 – Properties of Cable Jacket Material

Jacket Material	Properties
Polyvinyl Chloride (PVC)	Mechanical protection; different grades offer flame retardancy and outdoor use. Also for indoor and general applications.
Hypalon[®]	Can withstand extreme environments; flame retardant; good thermal stability; resistant to oxidation, ozone, and radiation.
Polyethylene (PE)	Used for telephone cables; resistant to chemicals and moisture; low-cost; flammable, so not used in electronic applications.
Thermoplastic Elastomer (TPE)	Low-cost; excellent mechanical and chemical properties.
Nylon	Used over single conductors to improve physical properties.
Kynar[®] (Polyvinylidene Fluoride)	Resistant to abrasions, cuts; thermally stable; resistant to most chemicals; low smoke emission; self-extinguishing. Used in highly flame retardant plenum cables.
Teflon[®] FEP	Zero smoke emission, even when exposed to direct flame. Suitable to temperatures of 200°C; chemically inert. Used in highly flame retardant plenum cables.
Tefzel[®]	Many of the same properties as Teflon; rated for 150°C; self-extinguishing.

Table 5.5 – Properties of Cable Jacket Material (Continued)

Jacket Material	Properties
Irradiated Cross-linked Polyolefin (XLPE)	Rated for 150°C; high resistance to environmental stress, cracking, cut-through, ozone, solvents, and soldering.
Zero Halogen Thermoplastic	Low toxicity makes it usable in any enclosed environment.
Kevlar, Hyplon, Tefzel, and Teflon are registered trademarks of E.I. Du Pont Nemours & Company. Kynar is a registered trademark of Pennwalt, Inc.	

Types of Fiber Optic Cables

The simplex cable contains a single fiber in the center. Duplex, two-fiber cables may appear circular, oval, or arranged zipcord fashion like an electrical cable. Figure 5.8 illustrates a zipcord cable.

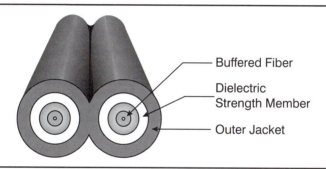

Buffered Fiber

Dielectric
Strength Member

Outer Jacket

Figure 5.8 – Duplex Zipcord Cable Construction

Complex cable assemblies include breakout (fanout) cables, composite cables, and hybrid cables. Breakout cables contain single-fiber or multifiber subcables, allowing access to individual fibers without the need for terminating patch panels. The cable industry disagrees about the exact definitions of composite cables and hybrid cables. For the sake of this discussion, composite cables mix both single-mode and multimode optical fiber in a single cable assembly, while hybrid cable describes a hybrid fiber/coax (HFC) cable that includes both optical fiber and copper cable in one cable assembly.

Both composite cables and hybrid cables offer the advantage of installation time and cost savings. However, these cables require application-specific custom manufacturing. Still, the increase in demand for the convergence of video, audio, and data transmission make these types of cables very attractive. Hybrid cables can also carry electrical signals, gaining them wide use in broadband CATV networks. Figure 5.9 shows a typical hybrid fiber/coax cable.

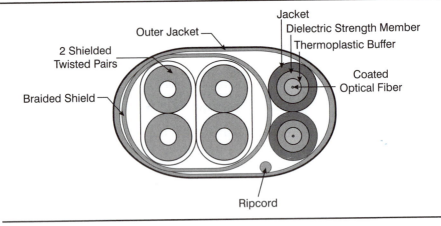

Figure 5.9 – Hybrid Fiber/Coax (HFC) Cable Construction

Cable Environments

Cable environment represents an important cable construction parameter. The least strenuous cable environments occur within computers, telephone switching systems, or distribution and splice organizers, although high stresses can occur due to small bend radii. The device itself protects these simple, low-cost cables. Intraoffice and intrabuilding cables, which get installed across a room, under a floor, between walls or above suspended ceilings, areas called plenum, must meet fire and electrical safety standards. The National Electrical Code lists three types of cable: nonconducting optical fiber general purpose cable (OFN), nonconducting optical fiber riser cable (OFNR), and nonconducting optical fiber plenum cable (OFNP). Cable manufacturers must submit the cable design to an independent test laboratory such as Underwriter's Laboratories (UL) in order to obtain an approval listing for their cables. Intraoffice and intrabuilding cables that meet these safety standards often take the name of their installation environment, the plenum. Intrabuilding cables have a breakout cable construction. The color coded subcables, divide the cable into individual fibers for distribution to separate end points in the office. Intraoffice cables tend to be of simpler construction, usually simplex or duplex cables.

Direct-burial cables require extra protection against moisture and temperature extremes, and they usually incorporate an extremely strong outer jacket to protect the cable from damage caused by digging or chewing rodents. Water-impeding gel protects the cable from moisture, a concern because long-term exposure to moisture will degrade the fiber's optical characteristics. Extremely cold temperatures compound this problem when the moisture expands as it freezes, applying stresses to the fiber that could cause microbends and increased optical loss.

Fiber optic cables intended for aerial installation must also handle environmental extremes. Aerial installation involves stringing the cable from building to utility pole or between utility poles. Generally, these cables are all-dielectric i.e., they contain no metal, preventing ground loops and providing lightning immunity. Within an aerial cable, strength members isolate the fibers from the stress on the cable, and the outer jacket material offers UV protection from the sun in addition to protection from moisture and temperature extremes. Indoor/outdoor cable features the materials needed to meet fire and electrical safety standards encased in a removable layer of outdoor jacket material.

Clearly, optical fiber offers a number of characteristics that make it naturally suitable to fiber optic video transmissions. But as bandwidth and data rates continue to climb, some of fibers shortcomings become noticeable. The next chapter describes the effects that limit optical fiber performance.

Chapter Summary

- Total internal reflection governs the operation of optical fiber.
- The index of refraction, or refractive index, characterizes the ratio of the velocity of the light in a vacuum to the velocity of light in a specific medium, such as air, water, or glass.
- Light will bend as it passes through a medium of one refractive index to a medium with a different refractive index.
- In optical fiber construction, the refractive index of the core exceeds the refractive index of the cladding, allowing total internal reflection to occur.
- Advantages of optical fiber transmission include: immunity from EM radiation, lighter weight cables, high transmission bandwidth, high signal quality, and easy installation and system upgrades.
- Factors for selecting optical fiber types include: fiber core/cladding size, fiber materials, fiber attenuation, fiber bandwidth-distance product, and environmental requirements.
- Optical cables contain one or more optical fibers surrounded by a strength element and a cable jacket.

- Cable construction types include tight-buffer, where the buffering material directly contacts the fiber, and loose-tube, which encloses the optical fiber in a buffer tube filled with a water-impeding gel.
- Fiber count affects an optical cable's current and future usability.
- Various cable jacket materials may offer flame retardancy, resistance to UV, resistance to cuts or abrasions, and other environmental considerations.
- Simplex cables contain a single optical fiber.
- Duplex, two-fiber cables, may be arranged in zipcord fashion like electrical cables.
- Breakout, or fanout, cables contain multiple subcables, allowing access to individual fibers without the need for separate patch panels.
- Composite cables contain both single-mode and multimode fiber subcables within a single cable jacket.
- Hybrid cables, also called hybrid fiber/coax (HFC cables) contain optical subcables as well as copper coax subcables.
- The installation environment of an optical cable represents an important parameter for cable construction.
- Intra-device environments, i.e., within computers, telephone switching systems, or distribution organizers, represent the least strenuous cable installation.
- Intraoffice and intrabuilding cables must meet National Electric Code safety standards for cable to ensure safe installation within a building's plenum.
- Direct-burial cables require extra protection to guard against moisture and temperature extremes, as well as a rugged cable jacket to protect from damage caused by digging or chewing rodents.
- Optical cables intended for aerial installation must handle environmental extremes such as temperature, UV exposure, and stress from wind or animals on the line.

Chapter 6

Fiber Limits

As data rates, transmission distances, number of wavelengths, and optical power levels surged to new levels, a number of nonlinear fiber effects suddenly became very important. In fiber's early days, problems centered around fiber attenuation and dispersion. As fiber performance increased, so did dispersion and another, less understood limit — fiber nonlinearities specifically linked to new field deployments (other than specialized applications such as undersea installations). These nonlinearities, as well as bandwidth limits, represent the fundamental mechanisms limiting optical fiber transmission.

Fiber Nonlinearities

The most common fiber nonlinearities include stimulated Brillouin scattering (SBS), stimulated Raman scattering (SRS), four wave mixing (FWM), self-phase modulation (SPM), and cross-phase modulation (XPM). Fiber nonlinearities arise from two basic mechanisms. The first, and most serious factor, results from the fact that the refractive index of glass varies with the optical power going through the material.

Figure 6.1 (next page) shows the relationship of the refractive index of silica versus optical power. Notice the relatively small magnitude of the change in refractive index; however, this change takes on importance in real systems where the interaction length may exceed hundreds of kilometers. The power dependent refractive index of silica gives rise to the SPM, XPM, and FWM nonlinearities. Scattering phenomena, the second set of mechanisms for generating nonlinearities, give rise to SBS and SRS.

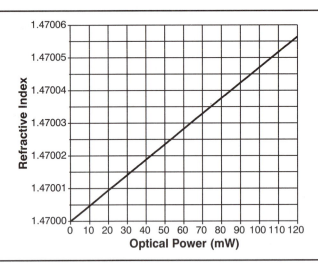

Figure 6.1 – Silica Refractive Index versus Optical Power

Stimulated Brillouin Scattering

Time-varying electric fields within a fiber interact with the acoustic vibrational modes of the fiber material, which in turn, scatter the incident light. This is known as Brillouin scattering. When the incident lightwave provides the source of the high intensity electric fields, the effect is known as SBS. The high power incident lightwave causes the refractive index of the fiber to vary periodically causing backreflection similar to the effect of Bragg gratings, a type of optical filter incorporated into optical fiber. As the input optical level increases beyond the SBS threshold, an increasingly larger portion of the light backscatters, creating an upper limit to the power levels that the fiber can carry. As the launch power increases above the threshold, the amount of backscattered light also increases. The precise threshold for the onset of the SBS effect depends on a number of system parameters including wavelength (the threshold is lower at 1550 nm than 1310 nm) and linewidth of the transmitter. Values of +8 to +10 dBm are typical for direct modulated optical sources operating at 1550 nm over standard single-mode fiber.

Stimulated Brillouin scattering (SBS) imposes an upper limit on the amount of usable optical power that can be launched into an optical fiber. The SBS effect has a threshold optical power; when optical power exceeds the SBS threshold, a significant portion of the transmitted light gets redirected back toward the transmitter. This limits the receiver's optical power, as well as causing problems associated with backreflection in the optical signals. The SBS process also introduces significant noise into the system, resulting in degraded bit error rate (BER) performance. High speed transmission systems that employ external modulators and continuous wave (CW) laser sources require strict control of SBS. It is also of vital importance to the transmission of 1550 nm CATV signals since these transmitters often have the very characteristics that trigger the SBS effect.

The SBS threshold strongly depends on the linewidth of the optical source; narrow linewidth sources have considerably lower SBS thresholds. Extremely narrow linewidth lasers (e.g., less than 10 MHz wide), often used in conjunction with external modulators, can have SBS thresholds of +4 to +6 dBm at 1550 nm. The SBS threshold increases proportionally as the optical source linewidth increases. Broadening the effective spectral width of the optical source minimizes SBS. See Chapter 15 for more details on the effects of SBS and countermeasures that can be taken to minimize the effect of SBS.

Stimulated Raman Scattering

Stimulated Raman scattering (SRS) has a high (1 Watt) threshold, making it less problematic than SBS. But real systems using EDFAs have higher optical output powers, and these will only go higher in the future. A fiber optic link that includes three such optical amplifiers will reach this limit since the limit drops proportionally by the number of optical amplifiers in series. SRS can cause scattering like SBS, but first the shorter wavelength channels are robbed of power, and that power feeds the longer wavelength channels. This resembles the operation of EDFAs where a 980 nm pump wavelength provides the energy that amplifies the signals in the longer wavelength, 1550 nm, region. Figure 6.2 shows the typical transmit spectrum of a six-channel DWDM system.

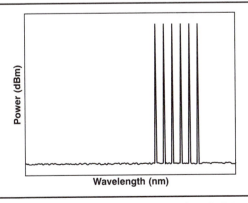

Figure 6.2 – 6 Channel DWDM Transmitted Optical Spectrum

All six wavelengths in the 1550 nm window have identical amplitudes. As Figure 6.3 illustrates, the short wavelength channels have a much smaller amplitude compared to the longer wavelength channels, the SRS effect.

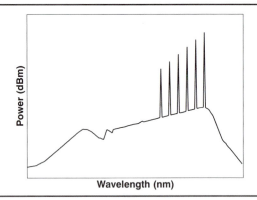

Figure 6.3 – SRS Effect on a 6 Channel DWDM Transmitted Optical Spectrum

Four Wave Mixing

Four wave mixing (FWM) usually occurs in fiber optic transmission systems carrying numerous simultaneous wavelengths (e.g., DWDM systems). Caused by the nonlinear nature of the fiber's refractive index, the FWM effect resembles composite triple beat (CTB), a distortion observed in CATV systems. CTB, like FWM, is classified as a third-order distortion phenomenon, also caused by nonlinearity, but typically this effect occurs in the electrical amplifier chain or one of the optical components, usually the laser. Third-order distortion mechanisms generate third-order harmonics in single-channel systems. In multichannel systems, third-order mechanisms generate third-order harmonics and a gamut of cross products, known as FWM products, which cause problems since they often fall near or on top of the desired signals. Two factors strongly influence the magnitude of the FWM products, referred to as the FWM mixing efficiency. The first factor, channel spacing, increases mixing efficiency dramatically as the channel spacing narrows. Fiber dispersion, the second factor, has the largest effect on mixing efficiency, close to the zero-dispersion point.

Self-phase Modulation

Figure 6.4 (next page) illustrates self-phase modulation. Like FWM, self-phase modulation (SPM) is due to the power dependency of the refractive index of the fiber core. It interacts with the chromatic dispersion in the fiber to change the rate at which the pulse broadens as it travels down the fiber.

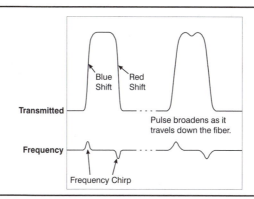

Figure 6.4 – Effects of SPM on a Pulse

Whereas increasing the fiber dispersion will reduce the impact of FWM, it will increase the impact of SPM. As an optical pulse travels down the fiber, the leading edge of the pulse causes the refractive index of the fiber to rise, resulting in a blue shift. The falling edge of the pulse decreases the refractive index of the fiber causing a red shift. These red and blue shifts introduce a frequency chirp on each edge which interacts with the fiber's dispersion to broaden the pulse. This increased SPM, however, can be minimized in dispersion-managed systems by alternating lengths of positive and negative dispersion fiber.

Cross-phase Modulation

Cross-phase modulation (XPM) involves two pulses of light, whereas SPM needs only one pulse. In XPM, these two pulses travel down the fiber, each changing the refractive index as the optical power varies. If these two pulses happen to overlap, they will introduce distortion into the other pulses through XPM. Increasing the fiber effective area will reduce XPM and all other fiber nonlinearities.

Summary of Fiber Nonlinearities

SBS

- Interaction between the incident lightwave and the acoustical vibration modes in the fiber causes SBS, which limits the amount of light that reaches the receiver.
- Above the SBS threshold, backscattered light increases dramatically, as does noise reaching the receiver.
- Fiber designs with larger effective areas have a higher SBS threshold, and the SBS threshold is lower at longer wavelengths.

- Threshold is directly proportional to the laser linewidth; direct modulation, dithering of a CW laser, or phase modulation of an external modulator all increase the effective area, raising the threshold.
- Without countermeasures, which can increase the SBS threshold in the 1550 nm region to +16 dBm, narrow linewidth laser sources in the 1550 nm region can face SBS at optical powers of +5 dBm.

SRS

- The SRS threshold power is about +30 dBm (1 Watt).
- SRS limits the amount of light that reaches the receiver above the threshold.
- Above the SRS threshold, SRS can rob power from shorter wavelength channels and feed that power to longer wavelength channels.
- Fiber designs with larger effective areas have a higher SRS threshold.

FWM

- FWM arises from the nonlinearity of the refractive index of optical fiber.
- FWM is a third-order distortion mechanism similar to CTB (composite triple beat) distortion in CATV transmission.
- FWM worsens as the fiber dispersion drops, and is worst at the zero-dispersion point. Higher chromatic dispersion results in less FWM.
- FWM is worst in WDM channel designs where the spacing is equal; unfortunately, equal channel spacing is the norm in standardized DWDM designs.
- FWM worsens as wavelengths are spaced closer together.
- Fiber designs with larger effective areas exhibit less FWM nonlinearity.

SPM

- SPM causes a frequency chirp on the rising and falling edges of an optical pulse, broadening the pulse.
- SPM affects a single light pulse traveling down the fiber.
- SPM acts along with chromatic dispersion to broaden pulses.
- Higher chromatic dispersion results in more SPM, but this can be negated in dispersion-managed systems.
- Fiber designs with larger effective areas have a higher SPM threshold.

XPM

- XPM causes multiple pulses traveling down the fiber to interact through their mutual effect on the refractive index of the fiber.
- Fiber designs with larger effective areas have a higher XPM threshold.

Dispersion

In the early years of fiber optics, most people assumed that fiber had infinite bandwidth and would meet mankind's communications needs well into the future. As transmission distances and bandwidth requirements increased, fiber optic researchers exploited additional wavelength "windows" to meet the increasing requirements. The third window, near 1550 nm, appeared to hold the answer. With losses of only 0.2 dB/km, it seemed adequate for any imaginable application. Millions of kilometers of fiber were installed around the world creating a high-speed communication network that would last for years. However, as data rates and fiber lengths increased, limitations due to fiber dispersion became unavoidable.

Anyone that has ever dealt with engineering problems understands trade-offs. The increase on the data rates and transmission lengths served to reveal important new characteristics of optical fiber. The first optical fiber type, step-index multimode fiber, had a huge problem with dispersion initially. Graded-index multimode fiber improved the situation a bit, but single-mode fiber eliminated severe multimode related dispersion. Engineers still had to overcome chromatic dispersion and polarization mode dispersion (PMD). Figure 6.5 shows the modal dispersion of multimode step-index fiber and graded-index fiber, as well as single-mode fiber.

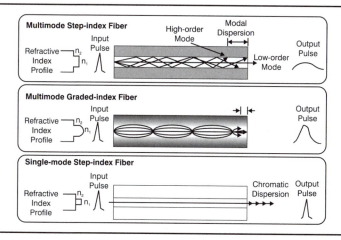

Figure 6.5 – Modal Dispersion

Chromatic Dispersion

Chromatic dispersion occurs because different wavelengths travel at different speeds within the same mode. Chromatic dispersion results from material dispersion, waveguide dispersion, or profile dispersion. In normal fibers, material dispersion and the zero-dispersion wavelength, where pulse broadening effects are minimized, occur near 1310 nm. In other fiber designs, the waveguide dispersion is tailored to shift the overall zero-dispersion wavelength to the 1550 nm region. These dispersion-shifted fibers are used in systems designed for long distance transmission in the C-band. Figure 6.6 shows chromatic dispersion along with its components, waveguide dispersion and material dispersion. In this example, chromatic dispersion goes to zero at a wavelength near 1550 nm, a characteristic of dispersion-shifted fiber. Zero dispersion occurs at 1310 nm in standard fiber.

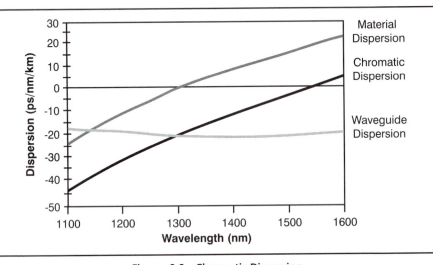

Figure 6.6 – Chromatic Dispersion

Lasers emit a range of optical wavelengths, and the speed of light in fused silica (fiber) varies with the wavelength of the light. Since a pulse of light from the laser usually contains several wavelengths, these wavelengths tend to get spread out in time after traveling some distance in the fiber. The refractive index of fiber decreases as wavelength increases, so longer wavelengths travel faster. As a result, the received pulse is wider than the transmitted one, or more precisely, is a superposition of the delayed pulses at the different wavelengths. Figure 6.7 (next page) illustrates the refractive index of fused silica as it changes with wavelength.

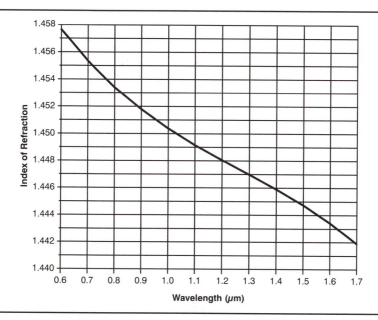

Figure 6.7 – Refractive Index of Fused Silica

To further complicate the situation, lasers, when they are being turned on, have a tendency to shift slightly in wavelength, effectively adding some FM modulation to the signal. This effect, called chirp, causes the laser to have an even wider optical line width. Non dispersion-shifted fiber at 1550 nm, which has the highest dispersion usually encountered in any real-world installation, exhibits the greatest distortion due to chirp in a transmission system.

Polarization Mode Dispersion

Polarization mode dispersion (PMD) represents another complex optical effect that can occur in single-mode optical fibers. Single-mode fibers support two perpendicular polarizations of the original transmitted signal. If a fiber were perfectly round and free from all stresses, both polarization modes would propagate at exactly the same speed, resulting in zero PMD. In the real world, fibers are not perfect, so the perpendicular polarizations may travel at different speeds and arrive at the end of the fiber at different times. The fiber is said to have a fast axis and a slow axis. The difference in arrival times, normalized with length, is known as PMD ($ps/\sqrt{km}$).

Excessive levels of PMD, combined with laser chirp and chromatic dispersion, can produce time-varying composite second order (CSO) distortion in AM video systems. The reduced picture quality manifests as a rolling or intermittent diagonal line across the TV screen. Like chromatic dispersion, PMD causes digital pulses to spread as the polarization modes arrive at their destination at different times. For digital high bit-rate transmission, this can lead to bit errors at the receiver or limit receiver sensitivity. Figure 6.8 illustrates this condition.

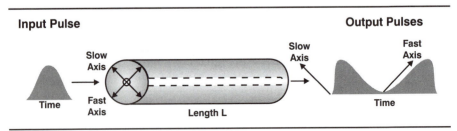

Input Pulse   **Output Pulses**

Figure 6.8 – Polarization Mode Dispersion

Calculating Dispersion

PMD generally represents a much smaller effect at any given data rate, so this section focuses on computing the effects of chromatic dispersion. Consider a non dispersion-shifted single-mode fiber, such as Corning SMF-28, the fiber type that represents the largest percentage of the installed fiber base. Its zero-dispersion wavelength lies between 1301 nm and 1321 nm, where it has very high bandwidth. However, the fiber attenuation in this range is about 0.35 dB/km. This attenuation limits transmission distances to perhaps 80 km. In the 1550 nm region, attenuation is only 0.2 dB/km, making operation in this window more desirable, because it would allow transmission to about 150 km. Equation 6.1 can be used to compute the dispersion of Corning SMF-28 single-mode fiber.

Eq. 6.1
$$D_\lambda = \frac{S_0}{4}\left(\lambda - \frac{\lambda_0^4}{\lambda^3}\right)$$

Where:

S_0 = 0.092 ps/(nm^2•km)

λ_0 = 1311 nm (Corning specifies λ_0 occurs between 1302 nm and 1322 nm. We have assumed an average value for this analysis.)

D_λ = Dispersion (ps/nm/km)

Figure 6.9 (next page) shows the behavior of Equation 6.1 over the wavelength range from 1250 nm to 1650 nm. Dispersion goes to zero at 1311 nm. At the 1550 nm window, dispersion is about 17 ps/nm/km. A laser with a spectral width of 1 nm will have dispersion at 17 ps/nm/km.

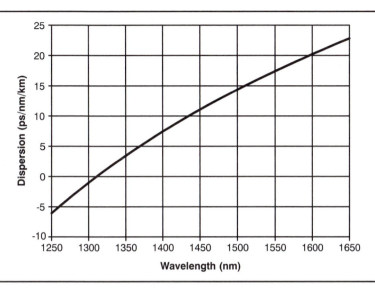

Figure 6.9 – Single-mode Fiber Dispersion

Dispersion Power Penalty

In digital transmission, one can use an optical attenuator to determine receiver sensitivity by increasing the attenuation between a fiber optic transmitter and receiver connected with a short length of fiber. Usually a given bit error rate (BER) defines the receiver sensitivity limit; typical bit error rates include 10^{-9} or 10^{-12}. Figures 6.10 and 6.11 illustrate a test setup for this measurement.

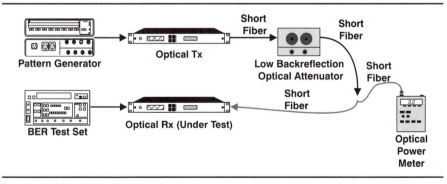

Figure 6.10 – Receiver Sensitivity with No Fiber Dispersion

(Illustration courtesy of Force, Inc.)

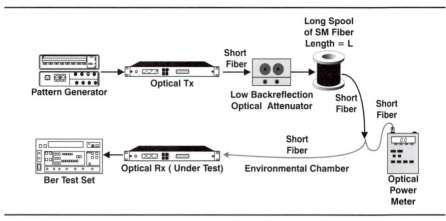

Figure 6.11 – Receiver Sensitivity with Fiber Dispersion
(Illustration courtesy of Force, Inc.)

The expected dispersion power penalty is given by a parabolic function of the ratio of symbol rate to dispersion-limited bandwidth times a coefficient "c" which relates to the roll-off of a raised cosine receiver response. To examine this in terms of dispersion power penalty versus total dispersion, we need to know the spectral width of the laser. For multilongitudinal-mode (MLM) lasers (e.g., Fabry-Perot type), the spectral width equals the root mean square spectral width. For single longitudinal-mode (SLM) lasers (e.g., distributed feedback lasers) the spectral width equals the width at the 20 dB down points divided by 6.07, the Gaussian spectral width at the 20 dB down point. Figure 6.12 shows the typical optical output spectrum of an MLM laser and the corresponding RMS spectral width.

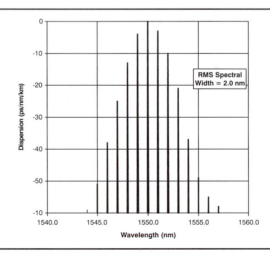

Figure 6.12 – MLM Laser Spectral Output

Figure 6.13 shows the typical optical output spectrum of an SLM laser and the spectral width.

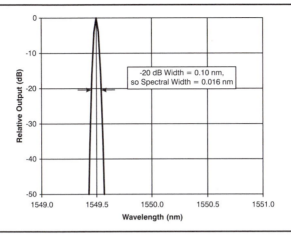

Figure 6.13 – SLM Laser Spectral Output

We will define ω to be the laser spectral width in nm as discussed above. τ will be the product of ω and D_λ discussed earlier. The constant "c" will equal 0.5. F_R will be the receiver data rate in bits per second. L will be the fiber length in km. F_F will be the bandwidth-distance product of the fiber in Hz•km. Fiber bandwidth "f" is given in Hz. dB_L will be the dispersion power penalty in decibels. The calculation is performed as follows:

$$\tau = \omega \cdot D_\lambda \qquad \text{ps/km}$$
$$f = 1n(4)/(\tau \cdot \pi) \qquad \text{Hz} \cdot \text{km}$$

Eq. 6.2
$$F_F = f/L \qquad \text{Hz}$$
$$\eta_L = c \cdot (F_R/F_F)^2$$
$$dB_L = 10 \cdot \text{Log} (1+\eta_L) \qquad \text{dB}$$

Figure 6.14 (next page) shows the dispersion penalty for a data link operating at the three data rates: 3.11 Gb/s, 1.55 Gb/s and 0.78 Gb/s. The laser is 0.1 nm wide with a center wavelength of 1550 nm and a fiber dispersion of 17 ps/nm/km. The maximum acceptable dispersion penalty is usually 2 dB. If the optical attenuation is kept low, a system may tolerate a larger dispersion penalty, but this action is not recommended. For the example shown in Figure 6.14, the maximum usable fiber length at a data rate of 3.11 Gb/s would be 85 km. At a wavelength of 1550 nm, the optical attenuation would be about 20 dB for that distance, much less than the 30 dB loss budget provided by many high-speed links. In this case, the fiber optic link would be said to be dispersion-limited.

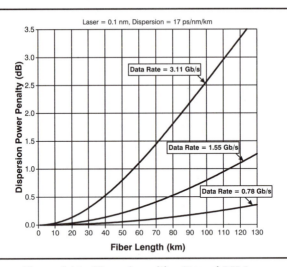

Figure 6.14 – Dispersion with a Normal DFB Laser

Figure 6.15 shows a second example with a more narrow line width laser. In this case, all conditions are the same except the laser spectral width is 0.05 nm. As a result, the dispersion penalty has dropped more than a factor of two compared to Figure 6.14. In this case, the dispersion penalty at a data rate of 3.11 Gb/s never reaches 2 dB, even at 130 km. The fiber optic link will, however, reach its optical attenuation limit near this distance. In this case, the fiber optic link is said to be attenuation-limited.

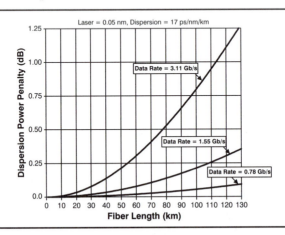

Figure 6.15 – Dispersion with a Narrow DFB Laser

To illustrate the impact of laser spectral width on the dispersion power penalty, Figure 6.16 shows the dispersion power penalty of a Fabry-Perot

(FP) MQW laser with a spectral width of 2 nm. Fiber dispersion is still 17 ps/nm/km and the operating wavelength is 1550 nm. In Figure 6.16, three lower data rates were chosen. Even so, the FP laser hits the dispersion penalty limit of 2 dB at a distance of 17 km at 780 Mb/s and 50 km at a data rate of 270 Mb/s. At both of these data rates, the data link is dispersion-limited. At a data rate of 100 Mb/s, the link is likely attenuation-limited.

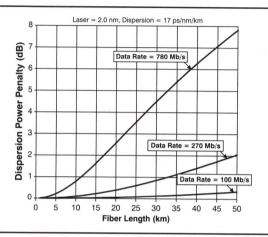

Figure 6.16 – Dispersion with a FP Laser

Modern fiber designs, now available, offer lower dispersion. Figure 6.17 shows the dispersion characteristics of the four key types of optical fiber being deployed in the 1550 nm window at this time.

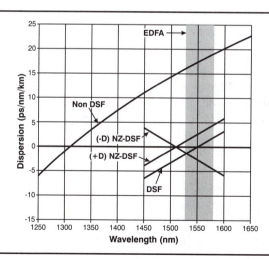

Figure 6.17 – Dispersion of Single-mode Fiber Types

Figure 6.17 also shows a shaded area referred to as the EDFA window. System designers today have begun to exploit the EDFA window for DWDM (dense wavelength-division multiplexing) systems. This window is rapidly expanding to both shorter and longer wavelengths.

- Non DSF: The oldest type of single-mode fiber, non dispersion-shifted fiber, is designed to have zero dispersion near 1310 nm.
- DSF: The second major single-mode fiber type, dispersion-shifted fiber, has very low attenuation and dispersion in the 1550 nm window. However, this fiber's popularity has dimmed in the recent explosion in DWDM, because when it is used to transmit multiple close wavelength, nonlinearities near the zero-dispersion point cause problems.
- (+D) NZ-DSF: Similar to the DSF, this fiber type has a zero-dispersion wavelength intentionally placed outside of the 1550 nm window. The fiber has a positive dispersion slope versus wavelength.
- (-D) NZ-DSF: Similar to (+D) NZ-DSF type, the dispersion slope is negative versus wavelength. Alternating segments of (+D) NZ-DSF and (-D) NZ-DSF fiber types allows one to gain an overall near-zero dispersion.

Laser Types to Counter Dispersion

Based on what we saw in Figures 6.14, 6.15 and 6.16, the line width of the laser is critical in limiting the magnitude of the dispersion power penalty. As is usual with engineering problems, the lowest cost laser has the widest line width and thus the largest dispersion power penalty. The four key laser classes are:

- Fabry-Perot (FP)/multi-quantum well (MQW): This low-cost laser also has the worst dispersion power penalty because of its wide optical line width, typically 1-4 nm. (Note: Laser line width is often referred to in MHz or GHz, rather than nm. The conversion factor is 1 nm = 125 GHz at λ = 1500 nm. So, a FP laser has a line width of 125-500 GHz).
- Standard DFB: Standard DFB lasers have laser line widths on the order of 0.1 nm, or 12 GHz. At gigabit data rates, this can seriously limit transmission quality over 50 km.
- Screened DFB: This is basically the same laser design as the standard DFB; however, it has very narrow line width, typically in the 0.01 to 0.05 nm range (1-5 GHz). This allows the link to reach much longer distances at gigabit data rates.
- External modulator/DFB: This is the best solution available at this time. A very narrow line width laser (1-2 MHz or 0.000008-0.000016 nm) operates in a CW (continuous wave) mode. This also eliminates any chirp effects that increase the laser line width even further. An external

modulator turns the laser on and off, acting as an electronic shutter. External modulators are available for digital and analog applications and are capable of data rates to 40 Gb/s and analog bandwidths of 20 GHz or more. However, the narrow line width sources can stimulate a host of additional fiber nonlinear effects, especially SBS or stimulated Brillouin scattering.

- VCSELs: The vertical cavity surface-emitting laser is the newest laser structure. The VCSELs emit light vertically, as the name suggests, and has a vertical laser cavity. These MQW devices emit light in layers only 20-30 atoms thick. Bragg-reflectors with as many as 120 mirror layers form the laser reflectors. Small size and highly efficient mirrors keep the lasing threshold current very low, below 1 mA. VCSELs also exhibit a high efficiency slope. Manufacturing techniques make VCSELs ideal for applications that require an array of devices. VCSELs are relatively low cost, lower power devices intended for short distance applications. They are most common at shorter wavelengths, e.g., 850 nm.

EDFAs

Erbium-doped fiber amplifiers (EDFAs) are mentioned here because they are often used in very long-haul fiber optic systems. In these systems, EDFAs are placed at intermediate positions to boost the signal before it becomes too small to recover. Since EDFAs do not add or subtract any measurable amount of dispersion to the system, the transmitter at the beginning of a long link sets the maximum transmission distance, regardless of how many EDFAs are used between the transmitter and receiver.

Dispersion Compensation

We have learned about the major types of dispersion in single-mode fiber, the major types of single-mode fiber, and techniques for calculating the impact of dispersion on link performance. Now we need to learn about other passive components that will allow us to minimize the effects of dispersion. Generally they consist of an element with the opposite dispersion of that in the fiber. These dispersion-compensating modules (DCM) are usually nothing more than a long spool of fiber with the opposite dispersion characteristics, which can be purchased with specified amounts of dispersion, e.g., -1,000 ps/nm. Unfortunately, they introduce considerable optical loss in the system, often 8 dB or more.

DCMs may be used in conjunction with 3-port devices called circulators, such as the one illustrated in Figure 6.18. Light enters the circulator in port 1 and outputs only to port 2. The light travels through the DCM, reflects off of the reflector and reenters port 2, which outputs the light to port 3 only. With this technique, the light has traveled through the DCM twice, using only half as much fiber to get the same compensating effect.

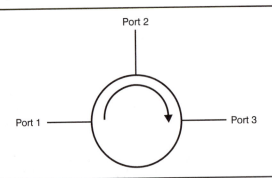

Figure 6.18 – DCM Using a Circulator

Circulators also work with devices called Bragg grating reflectors. These devices connect to port 2 of the circulator, and do not require a separate reflector. The Bragg grating reflectors again introduce the opposite dispersion to clean up the signal. Currently they only operate over a very narrow range of wavelengths, perhaps a few nanometers. Figure 6.19 shows another dispersion compensation technique, alternating lengths of (+D) NZ-DSF and (-D) NZ-DSF fiber. While imperfect over the entire band, this scheme reduces dispersion by an order of magnitude or more. Both techniques yield very low dispersion, making them usable for DWDM applications.

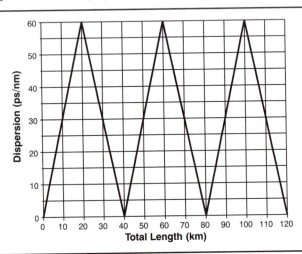

Figure 6.19 – DCM Using Alternating NZ-DSF Fiber Types

Dispersion Summary

- Most fiber installed before 1988 was non DSF type, which has high dispersion at 1550 nm, but works well for DWDM applications because it avoids many of the worst fiber nonlinearities.
- NZ-DSF fiber type has much lower dispersion in the 1550 nm band.
- The optimum new fiber installation would consist of alternating lengths of (+D) NZ-DSF and (-D) NZ-DSF, yielding low overall dispersion, required by DWDM applications.
- The use of narrow linewidth lasers reduce the dispersion power penalty.
- Long distance fiber optic transmitters specify a level of dispersion tolerance in ps/nm, which can be determined by dividing this number by the dispersion of the fiber in ps/nm/km.

We know that the type of light source can contribute to dispersion and fiber nonlinearities in an optical system. The next chapter will describe the light sources as well as light detectors that fiber optic systems utilize.

Chapter Summary

- The power-dependent refractive index of silica creates fiber nonlinearities that can severely limit capacity in a transmission system.
- Fiber nonlinearities include: stimulated Brillouin scattering (SBS), stimulated Raman scattering (SRS), four wave mixing (FWM), self-phase modulation (SPM), and cross-phase modulation (XPM).
- SBS has a threshold which, when exceeded, redirects a large portion of the transmitted light back to the transmitter, introducing noise, degrading the BER performance and saturating the receiver, which reduces the amount of usable optical power that a fiber can handle.
- Brillouin scattering occurs when time-varying electric fields within a fiber interact with the acoustic vibrational modes of the fiber, causing incident light to scatter.
- The exact threshold for SBS depends on system parameters such as wavelength and transmitter linewidth; typical threshold values include +8 to +10 dBm for direct modulated optical sources and +4 to +6 dBm for external modulated optical sources.
- Narrow linewidth sources have considerably lower SBS thresholds than wide linewidth sources.
- SRS has a higher threshold than SBS, around 1 Watt, making it less problematic than SBS in most cases, but fiber optic spans that use multiple EDFAs may be affected by SRS.
- In stimulated Raman scattering, the short wavelengths are robbed of power feeding the long wavelengths.

- Four wave mixing occurs in systems that carry numerous simultaneous wavelengths such as DWDM systems, and resembles CTB in that it is a third-order distortion which can generate third-order harmonics and cross-products that may fall on or overlap the original signals.
- SPM interacts with chromatic dispersion in the fiber core to broaden the width of the pulse as it travels down the fiber.
- Cross-phase modulation, which involves two pulses of light, interacts with the fiber core in the same way as SPM.
- Chromatic dispersion limits fiber's bandwidth potential.
- Narrow light sources can reduce a system's chromatic dispersion.
- Polarization mode dispersion (PMD) results from the differing arrival times of light pulses with different polarizations.
- Excessive PMD, combined with laser chirp and chromatic dispersion, causes CSO distortion in AM video systems.
- To calculate dispersion power penalty, we must first know the spectral width of the laser being used.

Chapter 7

Electro-optic and Opto-electronic Devices

As the title of this chapter suggests, the ability to convert electrical signals into an optical domain, and vice versa, forms the basis for fiber optic transmission. True of any system design, both the light emitters (electro-optic devices) and light detectors (opto-electronic devices) offer a variety of performance parameters that require careful consideration.

Light Emitters

Light emitters, a key element in any fiber optic system, convert an electrical signal into a corresponding light signal. The efficiency of this conversion process produces very little heat compared to the heat generated by incandescent lights. This component's characteristics often dictate the final performance limits of a given fiber optic link, as well as the system cost. Two types of light emitters find widespread use in modern fiber optic systems: laser diodes (LDs) and light-emitting diodes (LEDs). LEDs are usually specified as surface-emitters or edge-emitters. Laser diodes may be Fabry-Perot (the name refers to the mirrored surfaces on the ends of the laser cavity), distributed feedback (DFB), or, more recently, the vertical cavity surface-emitting laser (VCSEL).

Theory of Operation

Laser diodes and LEDs operate on the principle of the p-n semiconductor junction found in transistors and diodes. When an n-type and a p-type semiconductor are placed together, the excess electrons from the n region move over into the p region to fill the holes left by the deficiency of electrons in the p-type material. When the number of electrons accumulates to the point of repelling each other, the electrons stop moving into the p-type area. This buildup of charges creates a potential that prevents a current from flowing through the junction. Placing a potential across the p-n junction counteracts the internal potential enough to allow current to pass. In direct semiconductors designed for optics, the electrons lose an amount of energy, called bandgap energy, corresponding to a property of the semiconductor material. This energy is released as photons that have a wavelength related to the bandgap energy.

Light Emitter Performance Characteristics

Several key characteristics of LEDs and lasers determine their usefulness in a given application. These are:

- Peak Wavelength: The source emits the most power at its peak wavelength. It equates to the wavelengths transmitted with the least attenuation through optical fiber. Common peak wavelengths occur near 780 nm, 850 nm, 1310 nm, 1550 nm, and 1625 nm.
- Spectral Width: The emitted light spans a range of wavelengths, known as the spectral width, centered at the emitter's peak wavelength.
- Emission Pattern: A source's emission pattern directly influences the amount of light that can be coupled into the optical fiber. The size of the emitting region should correspond to the diameter of the fiber core.
- Power: The output power of the source must provide sufficient power to the detector at the receiving end after fiber attenuation, coupling losses and other system constraints have been taken into consideration. Lasers offer a higher output power than LEDs.
- Speed: A light source must turn on and off fast enough to meet the bandwidth limits of the system. The source's rise time or fall time, the time required to go from 10% to 90% of peak power, governs the speed of a system. Lasers have faster rise and fall times than LEDs.

Spectral Characteristics

Figure 7.1 (next page) illustrates the spectral characteristics of LEDs and lasers, given in FWHM. FWHM stands for full width half maximum, a measure of the width of the optical spectrum taken at the point where the intensity falls to half of the maximum value. An 850 nm surface-emitting LED has a FWHM of 60 nm, which usually dramatically limits the achievable bandwidth of such devices because of the high dispersion of the fiber 850 nm. A surface-emitting 1310 nm LED has an even wider spectrum with a typical FWHM of single-mode SM fiber since the fiber dispersion is zero near 1310 nm. This wider spectrum causes increased dispersion and also poses difficulties in WDM systems. A 1550 nm surface-emitting LED would even be wider. An edge-emitting 1310 nm LED has a more compact spectrum with a typical FWHM of about 50 nm.

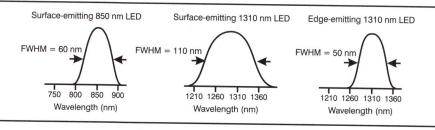

Figure 7.1 – LED Optical Spectra

Figure 7.2 illustrates similar information for two types of laser diodes. The graph on the left shows a 1310 nm Fabry-Perot laser. The laser emits light at a number of discrete frequencies. Unlike a helium-neon (HeNe) laser which emits a single line at 633 nm, Fabry-Perot lasers are multimode lasers in that they emit light at multiple, closely spaced wavelengths simultaneously. This wider spectrum causes some dispersion in the fiber, but it minimizes modal noise, common in multimode fibers, which occurs when the optical power propagates through mode-selective devices, such as connectors and splices.

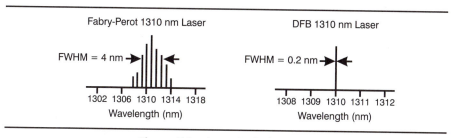

Figure 7.2 – Laser Optical Spectra

Modal noise, caused by constructive and destructive interference of the light, causes the sparkled laser spot common to HeNe lasers. Highly coherent diode lasers produce a similar speckle pattern inside an optical fiber. Connectors and discontinuities in the fiber disturb this pattern, resulting in a sharp increase in system noise. Multimode lasers work better with multimode fiber since they demonstrate less coherence and produce a lower contrast speckle pattern. The DFB laser is almost perfectly coherent, emitting a single frequency, like the HeNe laser, making it prone to modal noise.

Light-emitting Diodes

LEDs are made of several layers of p-type and n-type semiconductors. A p-n junction generates the photons, and several p-p and n-n junctions direct the photons to create a focused emission of light. The p-p and n-n junctions direct the light by providing changes in the index of refraction. Two main types of LEDs currently in use include surface-emitters and edge-emitters.

Layers of semiconducting material that emit light in a 180° arc comprise the construction of surface-emitters LEDs. This emission pattern limits coupling efficiency to the fiber, reducing overall power, but these devices offer high reliability and low cost. Edge-emitters confine the light to a narrow beam, comparable to the size of the optical fiber core, directed from the side of the emitter. This allows for higher output power as well as easier coupling to the fiber; they are also faster than surface-emitting LEDs. LEDs, although able to operate in extreme temperature ranges (-55°C to +125°C), can experience drift in the optical output power as temperature varies. Shorter wavelength LEDs exhibit less drift over temperature. An 850 nm LED may only drift -0.03 dB/°C, while a 1310 nm LED may drift three to five times as much. Also, surface-emitting LEDs have greater stability over temperature than edge-emitting types. In all cases, the optical power drops as the temperature increases. Temperature also affects the peak emission wavelength. Most LEDs exhibit a 0.3 nm/°C to 0.6 nm/°C drift in the peak emission wavelength as temperature varies. Multi-wavelength systems need light emitters that have a stable operating temperature to prevent crosstalk, the interference of one channel on another. Figure 7.3 illustrates LED behavior over four temperature ranges.

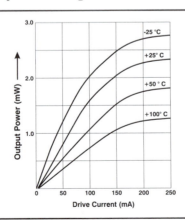

Figure 7.3 – Typical LED Behavior versus Temperature

LEDs turn on much faster than they turn off, due to their long carrier recombination lifetimes, which can be in the tens of nanoseconds range. LED drive circuits can apply quick reverse bias to the LED as it turns off. This sweeps the carriers out of the active region. Most commercial LEDs have a top-end bandwidth of 100-200 MHz, limiting them to low-speed applications. The wider spectral bandwidth of LEDs causes more dispersion in the optical fiber, which severely limits the optical signal's maximum transmission distance. Figure 7.4 shows several examples of typical packaged LEDs.

Figure 7.4 – Typical Packaged LEDs

(Photo courtesy of PD-LD, Inc.)

Analog LED Drive Circuits

Figure 7.5 shows three analog LED drive circuit configurations.

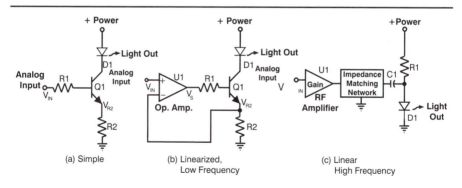

Note: Most VCSELs can use the same drive circuits as LEDs

Figure 7.5 – Analog LED Drive Circuits

Circuit 7.5a shows a common configuration. The first circuit uses a transistor, Q1, and a few resistors to convert an analog input voltage into a proportional current flowing through the LED, D1. Also referred to as a transconductance amplifier, this configuration converts a voltage into a current. Current drives LEDs; their output light equates proportionally to the drive current, not the drive voltage. In this circuit, voltage drop across an LED remains relatively constant at about 1.5 Volts as the drive current varies. LEDs tolerate a peak drive current of about 100 mA.

Circuit 7.5a works as follows: the small resistor, R1, prevents oscillations in Q1. The input voltage, V_{IN}, appears on the base of Q1. The voltage at the emitter of Q1, V_{R2}, equals the base voltage minus 0.6 Volts. Since these base and emitter voltages only differ by a DC offset voltage, the AC portion of the base equals that of the emitter. Now the emitter voltage V_{R2} causes a current equal to $V_{R2}/R2$ to flow through R2. Because of the way transistors operate, the Q1 collector current approximately equals the Q1 emitter current. [To be precise, the collector current equals $\beta/(\beta+1)$ times the emitter current. The transistor current gain, β (beta), is usually 10 to 100.] Putting this all together, we find that the LED current, and thus the output light, relates to the input voltage V_{IN} as follows:

Eq. 7.1
$$I_{D1} = \left(\frac{(V_{IN}-0.6)}{R2}\right) \cdot \left(\frac{\beta}{(\beta+1)}\right)$$

Base capacitance varies with the base voltage, introducing nonlinearities that limit the circuit's linearity, a drawback to the circuit in Figure 7.5a. The circuit shown in Figure 7.5b eliminates most of the nonlinearities associated with Q1. In this case, U1 forms a feedback loop that drives the base of Q1 such that V_{R2} equals V_{IN}. U1 even takes care of the 0.6 Volt base to emitter drop associated with Q1. In this case, LED current, and thus the output light, relates to the input voltage V_{IN} as follows:

Eq. 7.2
$$I_{D1} = \left(\frac{V_{IN}}{R2}\right) \cdot \left(\frac{\beta}{(\beta+1)}\right)$$

The circuit shown in Figure 7.5b still experiences some lesser nonlinearities associated with Q1, but these do not represent the limiting factor. This circuit can only achieve a bandwidth of about 10-100 MHz, limited by the delay associated with the feedback signal in the servo loop formed by U1. The circuit in Figure 7.5b works well for applications transmitting a DC coupled analog signal.

Figure 7.5c shows the highest performance analog LED drive circuit. In this case resistor R1 supplies the DC current to D1. The current equals the voltage drop across R1 divided by the resistance of R1. In some cases, a constant current source or a network that includes temperature compensation may replace R1. A wideband RF amplifier, U1, serves two purposes. First it amplifies V_{IN} to allow the use of a small input signal. Second, it isolates the LED from the input circuit, allowing precise impedance matching at the input, V_{IN}, which reduces reflections. The output of U1 is usually 50 Ohms or 75 Ohms. A typical LED may have an input impedance ranging from 5 Ohms to 10 Ohms. An impedance matching network is inserted between the amplifier and D1 to properly adapt the impedance. Capacitor, C1, serves to block any DC level associated with the output of the matching network. This circuit will drive LEDs to their highest possible frequencies, perhaps 500 MHz. Circuit 7.5c usually delivers the highest possible linearity. In this case, the LED, D1, usually limits performance.

New, low-cost lasers, vertical cavity surface-emitting lasers (VCSELs), may use the same drive circuits as LEDs. Like LEDs, VCSELs have very stable characteristics over temperature and usually do not include a rear facet monitor photodiode commonly used with lasers. Most VCSELs run at a maximum drive current of 12 mA. However, VCSELs manufactured to date have very poor analog characteristics, making them unsuitable for even the least demanding analog applications. Perhaps future VCSELs will have better linearity, but currently they appear unsuited for analog applications. (These lasers are discussed further later in this chapter.) Figure 7.6 shows the typical analog behavior of a VCSEL.

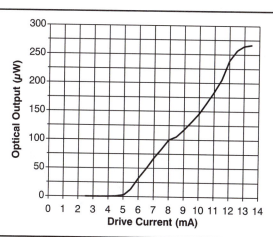

Figure 7.6 – VCSEL Response to an Analog Drive Circuit Using Multimode Fiber

Digital LED Drive Circuits

A digital drive signal raises no concern about LED linearity; the LED is either on or off, but the circuit must allow the LED to reach maximum speed. Figures 7.7a, 7.7b, and 7.7c show three popular digital LED drive circuits. The first circuit, shown in Figure 7.7a, represents a simple series drive circuit. The input voltage is applied to the base of transistor, Q1, through resistor, R1. The transistor will either be off or on. With Q1 in the off condition, no current will flow through the LED, and it will emit no light. When transistor, Q1, is on, the cathode (bottom) of the LED is pulled low. Transistor, Q1, pulls its collector down to about 0.25 Volts. Again, the current equals the voltage across resistor R2 divided by the resistance of R2. The voltage across R2 equals the power supply voltage less the LED forward voltage drop and the saturation voltage of the drive transistor.

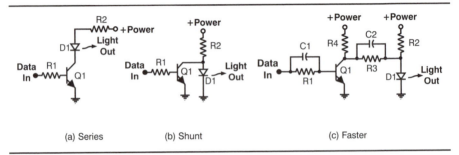

(a) Series   (b) Shunt   (c) Faster

Figure 7.7 – Digital LED Drive Circuits

These circuits offer the key advantage of a low average power supply current. If one defines the peak LED drive current as I_{LEDmax} and assumes that the LED duty cycle is 50%, then the average power supply current equals only $I_{LEDmax}/2$. Further, the power dissipates as $(I_{LEDmax}/2) \cdot V_{SUPPLY}$ where V_{SUPPLY} is the power supply voltage. The power dissipated by the individual components, the LED, transistor and resistor R1, equals the voltage drop across each component multiplied by $(I_{LEDmax}/2)$.

Low speed represents the key disadvantage of the circuit shown in Figure 7.7a, and this type of drive circuit rarely finds use in systems with data rates above 30-50 Mb/s. Two design methods will allow for low power dissipation. The circuit could use a high-efficiency LED and reduce I_{LEDmax} to the lowest possible value, but a second method, reducing the duty cycle of the LED to a low value, usually results in larger gains.

The second LED drive circuit, shown in Figure 7.7b, offers much higher speed capability. It uses Q1 to quickly turn the LED off. This circuit, known as a shunt drive circuit, will drive the LED several times faster than the series drive circuit shown in Figure 7.7a because it allows greater drive symmetry. In Figure 7.7b, resistor, R2, provides a positive current to turn on the LED. Typically, R2 would be in the 40 Ohm range. This makes the turn-on current about 100 mA peak. Transistor Q1 provides the turn-off current.

When saturated, transistor Q1 will have an impedance of a few Ohms. This provides a much larger discharging current, allowing the LED to turn off quickly. Power dissipation typically more than doubles in a shunt drive circuit compared to the series drive circuit. In fact, the circuit draws more current and power when the LED is off than when the LED is on! The exact power dissipation can be computed by first analyzing the off and on state currents and then combining the two values using information about the operating duty cycle.

Figure 7.7c shows a variation on the shunt drive shown in Figure 7.7b. Two additional resistors and two capacitors further increase the operating speed. Capacitor C1 improves the turn-on and turn-off characteristics of transistor Q1 itself. Care should be taken to keep the value of C1 low to prevent overdriving and damaging the transistor base. The additional components, resistors R3 and R4, and capacitor C2 provide overdrive when the LED is turned on and underdrive when the transistor is turned off. The overdrive and underdrive accelerates the LED transitions. Typically, the RC time constant of R3 and C2 approximately equals the rise or fall time of the LED itself.

Figure 7.8 shows the response of an LED to a digital modulation signal. drive circuits more sophisticated than the one shown in Figure 7.7c generated the electrical signal shown. Starting at time zero, the digital signal goes to a logic level "1." The strong overshoot seen on the electrical drive signal may be twice the steady state logic "1" drive current, and it accelerates the turn-on time or rise time of the LED. Even so, we see that the optical output lags behind the electrical signal.

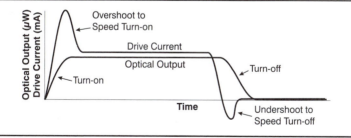

Figure 7.8 – LED Response to a Digital Modulation Signal

Typical values for very high-performance LEDs and drive circuits would be 0.7 ns rise time of the electrical signal and 1.5 ns optical rise time. Later, when the digital signal goes back to a logic "0," we see the same process repeated. The strong undershoot component of the electrical signal acts to accelerate the turn-off of the LED and serves to reverse bias the LED, sweeping out the carriers. Even so, typical values for turn-off times are 0.7 ns for the electrical signal and 2.5 ns for the optical signal. Note that while in a logic "0" state, the drive current does not quite go to zero. Most circuits provide a small amount of pre-bias current, a few percent of the peak drive current, to keep the LED forward biased and improve dynamic response.

All of these techniques increase the operating speed of the LED and drive circuit to about 270 Mb/s. Numerous laboratory tests and prototype circuits have achieved rates to 500-1,000 Mb/s, but none of these have made it into mass production. Typically, these levels of performance require a great deal of custom tweaking on each part to achieve the high data rates.

Laser Diodes

Two main types of laser diode structures include Fabry-Perot (FP) and distributed feedback (DFB). DFB lasers offer the highest performance levels and also the highest cost of the two types. They emit nearly monochromatic light (i.e., they emit a very pure single color of light) while FP lasers emit light at a number of discrete wavelengths. DFB lasers lend themselves to the highest speed digital applications and for most analog applications because of their faster speed, lower noise, and superior linearity.

Fabry-Perot lasers include buried hetero (BH) and multi-quantum well (MQW) types. BH and related styles ruled for many years, but MQW types have moved to the foreground. They offer significant advantages over all former types of Fabry-Perot lasers, including lower threshold current, higher slope efficiency, lower noise, better linearity, and much greater stability over temperature. As a bonus, excellent performance margins allow for higher MQW laser yields, reducing laser cost.

Most laser diodes incorporate a rear facet photodiode to provide real-time monitoring of the laser output, necessary because the laser threshold current changes with temperature, as does slope efficiency. One exception, vertical cavity surface-emitting lasers (VCSELs), have very stable characteristics over time and often omit monitor photodiodes.

While usually more affordable, the noise and slow speed of FP devices limits their usability. DFB lasers exhibit a high signal-to-noise ratio, making them quieter devices, as well as a narrow spectral width, making them suitable for very high data rates. Expressed as relative intensity noise (RIN) in units of dB/Hz, good Fabry-Perot devices offer laser noise levels of -125 to -130 dB/Hz while a good DFB laser can have RIN values below -155 dB/Hz. DFB lasers designed for continuous wave (CW) operation can have RIN values below -170 dB/Hz. To convert RIN values into a resultant signal-to-noise ratio, take the absolute RIN value and subtract $10 \bullet \text{Log}_{10}$ (BW) where BW is the bandwidth of interest in Hertz. A laser RIN of -130 dB/Hz with a system bandwidth of 1 MHz, allows for the signal-to-noise ratio of the laser's optical signal to be 70 dB. Figure 7.9 shows the typical construction of a laser diode. The laser diode chip emits light in two directions. Useful output emits from one end of the laser chip while light from the other end strikes an angled large area photodiode, reducing backreflections into the laser cavity.

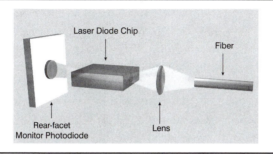

Figure 7.9 – Laser Construction

(Illustration courtesy of Force, Inc.)

Analog Laser Drive Circuits

Figure 7.10 shows two circuit configurations used to drive lasers for analog applications. The first circuit shown in 7.10a offers moderate linearity and good performance in frequencies up to 500 MHz.

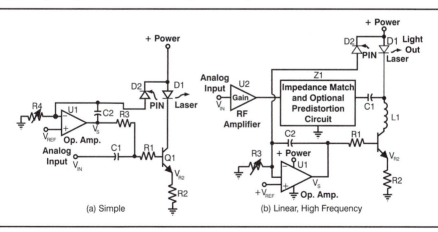

Figure 7.10 – Analog Laser Drive Circuits

The analog signal path includes C1, R1, Q1, R2, and D1, the laser diode. Q1 acts as a transconductance stage, voltage in and current out. C1 passes only the AC portion of the analog input signal. R1, usually only a few tens of Ohms, squelches any possible oscillations in Q1. The AC portion of analog input voltage V_{IN} appears at the base of Q1 and at the emitter of Q1. The AC voltage at the emitter of Q1, V_{IN}, is imposed across R2 to create a modulation current $V_{IN}/R2$. U1 supplies DC current to the laser through R3 and R1. U1 creates a servo loop that maintains a constant photodiode current through the rear facet monitor PIN diode. Circuits such as the one shown in Figure 7.10a indirectly maintain constant laser optical output. The rear facet monitor PIN diode receives light from one end of the laser chip while the other end of the chip illuminates the optical fiber. While the light in the fiber correlates to light in the monitor PIN diode, it never matches exactly at all output and environmental conditions, a phenomenon called tracking error. In this discussion, however, we will refer to the servo circuit as a circuit that maintains constant optical output.

The constant optical output servo circuit works as follows: the inputs of the opamp, U1, are both at V_{REF}. In the absence of any current from D2, a current equal to $V_{REF}/R4$ will flow out of the negative (-) input of U1. This current causes the output of U1, V_S, to increase linearly as C2 charges up. As V_S increases, the DC current flowing into the base of Q1 increases, which increases the collector and laser current as $V_S/R2$. As the laser current increases, the light output increases, which generates an increasing current out of rear facet monitor PIN diode, D2.

The output of U1 will continue to increase until the current out of D2 exactly matches the current $V_{REF}/R4$. As the temperature of the laser increases, it requires more current to maintain the same optical output. In response, the output of U1 increases to keep the current out of D2 equal to the current $V_{REF}/R4$. R4, usually an adjustable resistor, allows the circuit to set the average laser output to a specific value.

The more advanced circuit, shown in 7.10b, offers good to excellent linearity at very high frequencies (GHz). The analog signal path only involves U2, Z1, C1, and the laser diode, D1. In this circuit, amplifier U2 provides input matching, gain and isolates the laser from outside conditions. The impedance matching block, Z1, can take on many forms. At a minimum, it interfaces the output of the amplifier U2, usually 50 or 75 Ohms, to the laser that has an impedance ranging from 5 Ohms to 25 Ohms. In some cases, the laser package incorporates this impedance matching.

Predistortion Circuits

For the most demanding linear applications, Z1 can also contain a predistortion circuit, which dramatically improves the linearity of lasers for applications such as 110 channel CATV VSB/AM links. The constant optical output servo circuit works the same as the one shown in Figure 7.10a.

While modern DFB lasers exhibit good linearity, they often fail to handle demanding multichannel applications. Figure 7.11 illustrates the response of an analog laser drive circuit with no predistortion circuit.

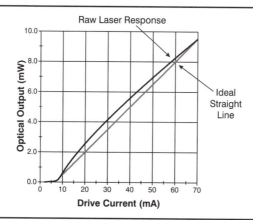

Figure 7.11 – Analog Laser Response without Predistortion

By comparison, Figure 7.12 illustrates the gain achieved with a predistortion circuit in the laser analog drive circuit.

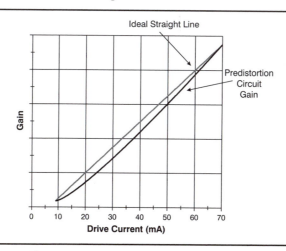

Figure 7.12 – Gain of the Predistortion Circuit

Digital Laser Drive Circuits

Figure 7.13 shows two common discrete component circuit configurations used to drive lasers for digital applications. In reality, because of the high demand for digital laser drivers, there exists a wide variety of ICs

designed for this function. We cover the discrete component circuit configurations in detail because they illustrate the most commonly used principles
in commercially available laser driver ICs.

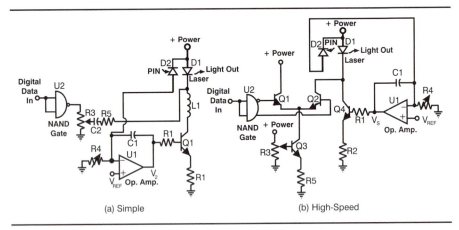

(a) Simple   (b) High-Speed

Figure 7.13 – Digital Laser Drive Circuits

The relatively simple circuit shown in Figure 7.13a finds use at frequencies up to several hundred megahertz. "Digital data in" takes a relatively
simple path. The NAND gate, U2, buffers the signal and provides fast and
consistent edges. Potentiometer R3 adjusts the amplitude of the laser's
incoming digital signal, an adjustment, usually referred to as a modulation
depth adjustment. Capacitor C2 allows the AC component of the "digital
data in" to pass and blocks any DC component.

This circuit, like nearly all digital laser drive circuits, cannot handle a
DC component in the "digital data in" signal. That means that the "digital
data in" signal must always have transitions present. Resistor R5 provides
some impedance matching into the laser. R5 feeds directly into the cathode
of the laser D1. Inductor L1 provides DC bias to the laser and also allows
the AC component of the "digital data in" signal to reach the laser. The rear
facet monitor photodiode, D2, outputs a current proportional to the laser
output. The current out of D2 goes to a servo loop to ensure that the average optical output of D1 remains constant. U1 forms the heart of the servo
loop. Capacitor C1 configures U1 as an integrator. The +input of U1
remains at some positive voltage, V_{REF} which usually lies midway between
ground and +power.

Potentiometer R4 adjusts the average optical output power of the laser
D1. It does so by sinking a current out of the –input of U1. This negative
current causes the output of U1, referred to as V_2, to increase. As V_2
increases, transistor Q1 turns on. This causes an increasing current to flow

through L1 and thus D1. As the current through D1 increases, the average optical output of D1 increases, which likewise increases the current from D2, the rear facet monitor photodiode. This action continues until the current out of D2 exactly matches the current being sinked by potentiometer, R4. R4, usually referred to as the "power adjust" in digital laser drive circuits, sets the rear facet monitor photodiode current. In reality, the average optical output power and the rear facet monitor photodiode current are almost equivalent. They differ only by a laser characteristic known as tracking error. Three components in the circuit, C2, L1, and C1, limit the low-frequency, and thus, low data rate operations. As a rule of thumb, a digital laser driver circuit should handle frequencies as low as 1/100th of the design data rate. So a laser driver designed to handle a 622 Mb/s data rate must also handle frequencies as low as 6.22 MHz.

The more complex circuit shown in Figure 7.13b allows very high, multi-gigabit speeds. Other than the omission of L1, the servo loop portion of the circuit matches the circuit in Figure 7.13a. In this circuit, Q4, a very fast, low capacitance transistor, replaces L1. Ideally its collector will appear as a current source and will not interfere with the modulation signal. Potentiometer R4 sets the rear facet monitor photodiode current or average optical output power.

The "digital data in" signal first goes through the NAND gate, U2, as in the first circuit. However, this circuit incorporates a NAND gate with the differential outputs of U2 to drive a transistor-based differential amplifier consisting of Q1 and Q2. Transistor Q3 forms a constant current source. Potentiometer R3 sets the current flowing in the collector of Q3. This current determines the amount of modulation current that gets switched to the laser in response to ones and zeros. As the outputs of U2 switch back and forth, the modulation current from the collector of Q3 oscillates between the +power line (by Q1) and the laser, D1, (by Q2). The digital laser drive circuit must avoid saturation, which slows the circuit down. Q1, Q2, and Q3 all operate in a linear mode in circuit 7.13b, allowing them to operate at very high speeds.

VCSELs

The first commercialized laser chips, edge-emitters, output laser light from the edges, and the laser cavity ran horizontally along the laser's length. In the laser structure of the vertical cavity surface-emitting laser (VCSEL), the laser cavity runs vertically. Figure 7.14 illustrates the structure of a VCSEL, whose principles of operation closely resemble those of conventional edge-emitting semiconductor lasers. At the heart of the VCSEL, an electrically pumped gain region, also called the active region, emits light.

Layers of varying semiconductor materials above and below the gain region create mirrors. Each mirror reflects a narrow range of wavelengths back into the cavity causing light emission at a single wavelength.

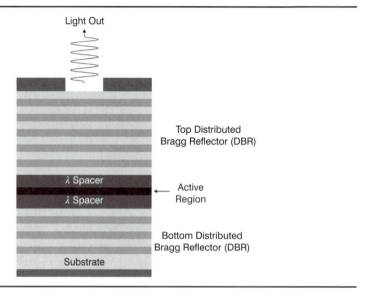

Figure 7.14 – Basic VCSEL Structure

VCSELs incorporate the structure of a multi-quantum well device, and lasing occurs in layers only 20-30 atoms thick. Distributed Bragg reflectors (DBRs), with as many as 120 layers of mirrors, form the laser reflectors. Because of the small size of the VCSELs and the high efficiency of the mirrors, VCSELs can achieve low threshold current, below 1 mA. VCSELs also exhibit a very high slope efficiency. Early multimode devices have an optical output of several milliwatts at a drive current of 12 mA and a typical slope efficiency of 200 μW/mA.

The stable transfer function of a VCSEL (light out versus drive current) allows stability over a wide temperature range, a feature unique to these laser diodes. Many manufacturers recommend that VCSELs operate at a current of 12 mA and even omit the customary monitor photodiode. Earlier laser types generally used cleaved ends of the laser chip to form reflectors; however, these reflectors rarely reflected more than 35% of the light. VCSELs use DBRs formed of a hundred or more alternating layers of material that efficiently reflect light at a specific wavelength. A more efficient reflector allows the light intensity to build up at lower drive levels.

VCSELs have several advantages over edge-emitting lasers. Manufacturers create edge emitters on a substrate from which the emitter must be cut before packaging and testing. This process can cost more than the laser diode itself, with no guarantees the laser will pass the tests. Because VCSELs emit light vertically from their surface, manufactures can test them while still on the "wafer" of substrate material (illustrated in Figure 7.15), which saves time and money. Compared to edge emitters, VCSELs have a narrower, more circular light beam, simplifying coupling to the fiber. Lower output power and the short wavelength capabilities of today's VCSELs limits their usefulness in some applications. However, their cost advantage makes them an attractive option for other applications.

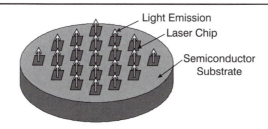

Light Emission
Laser Chip
Semiconductor Substrate

Figure 7.15 – VCSEL Wafer

VCSELs are ideal for applications that require arrays of devices. For example, one could create a linear array of lasers for use with ribbon optical fiber. This allows the formation of multiple parallel data links, useful where 8-bit bytes of data must be moved from point to point. Conventional solutions involve serializing the bytes, transmitting them over a single fiber, and then reconstructing the parallel bytes at the receive end. VCSEL arrays and ribbon fiber permit transmission of each of the eight bits with its own laser and fiber. This simplifies the electronics at each end, allowing for much higher data rates.

Light Detectors

Light detectors perform the opposite function of light emitters, converting the optical signals back into electrical impulses used at the receiving end of the fiber optic data, video, or audio link. The commonly used semiconductor photodiode produces current in response to incident light, i.e., light striking the photodiode creates a current in the external circuit. Absorbed photons create electron-hole pairs. For each electron-hole pair created, an electron flows as current in the external circuit. Like light emitters, detectors operate on the principle of the p-n junction. An incident photon striking the diode gives an electron in the valence band sufficient energy to move to the conduction band, creating a free electron and a hole. If the creation of these carriers occurs in a depleted region, the carriers separate and create a current. As they reach the edge of the depleted area, the electrical forces diminish and current ceases. While p-n diodes make poor fiber optic detectors (due to the small detecting region), PIN photodiodes and avalanche photodiodes (APDs) compensate for the drawbacks of the p-n diode.

Important Detector Parameters

Capacitance

Capacitance depends on the active area of the device and the reverse voltage across the device. A small active diameter reduces capacitance. However, as the active diameter decreases, it becomes difficult to align the fiber to the detector. The fact that photodiode response slows down at the edges of the active area complicates the situation. Illuminating the edges of the detector slows response and increases edge jitter. To minimize this effect, designers illuminate only the center region of the active area.

Responsivity

The ratio of current output to optical input defines the responsivity of a photodetector. With other factors equal, the higher the responsivity of the photodetector, the better the receiver sensitivity. Since responsivity varies with wavelength, it is specified either at the wavelength of peak responsivity or at a wavelength of interest. Responsivity is important because it defines the relationship between optical input and electrical output. The theoretical maximum responsivity is about 1.05 A/W at a wavelength of 1310 nm. Commercial 1310 nm InGaAs detectors provide typical responsivity of 0.8 to 0.9 A/W. Figure 7.16 shows the responsivity of three popular detector materials used in fiber optics versus wavelength. The dotted line is the maximum theoretical responsivity at each wavelength or 100% quantum efficiency.

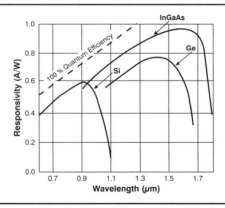

Figure 7.16 – Typical Spectral Response of Various Detector Materials

Response Time

Response time represents the time needed for the photodiode to respond to optical inputs and produce an external current. The combination of the photodiode capacitance and the load resistance, along with the design of the photodiode, determines the response time. As with light emitters, detector response time is specified as rise time or fall time, and it is usually measured between 10% and 90% amplitude points. The response time of a diode relates to its usable bandwidth.

The design of the photodiode as well as its application parameters influence detector response time. For instance, the size of a detector (active area, usually expressed as a diameter in mm or μm) directly influences its capacitance. The applied reverse voltage decreases the capacitance and speeds response. The impedance that the detector operates into also affects the response time. Equation 7.3 gives -3 dB frequency of a detector.

Eq. 7.3
$$f_{-3dB} = \frac{1}{(2 \cdot \pi \cdot R \cdot C)}$$

Where:

R = Impedance that the detector operates into.
C = Capacitance of the detector.

Equation 7.4 estimates the 10-90% rise or fall time of the detector.

Eq. 7.4
$$\tau = 2.2 \cdot R \cdot C$$

Equation 7.5 relates rise and fall time to -3 dB bandwidth.

Eq. 7.5
$$\tau = \frac{0.35}{f_{-3dB}} \quad \text{or} \quad f_{-3dB} = \frac{0.35}{\tau}$$

Consider a high-speed detector with a capacitance (C) of 0.5 pF operating into an impedance (R) of 50 Ohms. This detector would exhibit a rise time of 55 ps and a -3 dB frequency of 6.4 GHz. Keep in mind that other detector factors could limit the performance to lower values. The calculated values should be considered the best that could be achieved.

Edge Effect

Detectors only provide fast response in their center region, an often overlooked property of the detector. The outer regions of the detector exhibit a phenomenon aptly called edge effect, and it impacts the detector's response in two ways. First, the detector edge has a higher responsivity compared to the center. This causes problems when aligning a fiber to the detector. When using a continuous wave light source, the operator will almost always be fooled into aligning the fiber to the edge of the detector, not the center, because of the higher responsivity. To avoid this, use an oscilloscope and align the detector to the fiber with a high frequency square wave light source to identify the cleanest edges. Using a frequency of 1 MHz or higher usually allows the detector edge effect to be avoided during fiber alignment. Figure 7.17a shows the response of a detector when properly aligned to the fiber, while Figure 7.17b illustrates the response of an improperly aligned detector exhibiting edge effect.

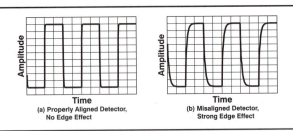

Figure 7.17 – Edge Effect

Dark Current

Dark current can be a deceptive term. It implies that the detector somehow manages to create an electrical current in the absence of light. Dark current actually refers to the small current that flows through the detector because of the intrinsic resistance of the detector, also called shunt resistance. The applied reverse voltage causes this current. Temperature sensitivity will double the dark current every 5°C to 10°C, contributing to detector noise and creating difficulties for DC coupled amplifier stages.

Linearity and Backreflection

PIN diodes operate as linear devices. However, for the most demanding applications, such as multichannel CATV links, one must take special care to reduce distortion to very low levels. Analog PIN detectors often have distortion products below -60 dBc. Reducing detector backreflection requires special care in analog applications. Generally, the angle-polished fiber couples to the detector at a perpendicular angle. Low-backreflection detectors may be tilted by 7° to 10° as shown in Figure 7.18.

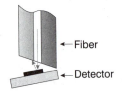

Figure 7.18 – Low Backreflection Detector Alignment

Aligning a fiber to a low-backreflection, low-distortion PIN diode can be trickier than aligning a fiber to a laser diode. The alignment procedure must account for clean detector response to eliminate the edge effect, low backreflection, high responsivity, high linearity, and low noise. Typical test fixtures used for this detector alignment display all five parameters at once. Figure 7.19 shows two packaged low backreflection photodiodes.

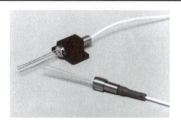

Figure 7.19 – Low Backreflection Photodiodes
(Photo courtesy of PD-LD, Inc.)

Noise

Noise and distortion degrade a signal as it travels through a fiber optic link. Distortion is a deterministic process that, in principle, can be corrected. Noise, however, is a random process that permanently degrades the signal. Noise appears in all elements of a communication system; however, it critically affects the receiver, which must interpret an already weak signal. Higher signal strength at the transmitter reduces the impact of transmitter noise compared to the attenuated receiver signal.

Two types of noise affect detectors: shot noise and thermal noise. Shot noise results from the process of creating the current, which uses a set of discrete occurrences rather than a continuous flow. The creation of more or fewer electron-hole pairs fluctuates the current, creating shot noise. The increase in bandwidth and current creates more noise. Shot noise can also occur in dark current environments.

A second type of noise, thermal noise, arises from fluctuations in the load resistance of the detector. Thermal energy gives the electrons mobility in the resistor. At any given moment, the net movement toward one electrode or the other generates random currents that add to and distort the signal current from the photodiode. Shot noise and thermal noise exist in the receiver independent of the arriving optical power. For adequate receiver operation, the signal power should be at least ten times that of the noise power for digital systems and as much as 100,000 times larger for AM systems.

PIN Photodiode

A p-n diode's deficiencies correspond to the small depletion area (active detection area); many electron-hole pairs recombine before they can create a current in the external circuit. In the PIN photodiode, the depleted region is made as large as possible. A lightly doped intrinsic layer divides the more heavily doped p-types and n-types. In the absence of light, PIN photodiodes behave electrically like an ordinary rectifier diode. If forward biased, they conduct large amounts of current. The forward turn-on voltage relates to the energy gap of the detector. For silicon, this energy gap is around 1.1 eV (electron Volts). For InGaAs, the energy gap is 0.77 eV and for germanium, the energy gap is around 0.65 eV.

PIN detectors operate in two modes: photovoltaic and photoconductive. Photovoltaic mode, which applies no bias to the detector, slows the operation of the detector. The detector output voltage is approximately logarithmic to the input light level; however, real-world fiber optic receivers never use the photovoltaic mode. Photoconductive mode applies a reverse bias, providing output that is highly linear with the input light power. PIN detectors can be linear over seven or more decades of input light intensity. Figure 7.20 shows the cross-section and operation of a PIN photodiode.

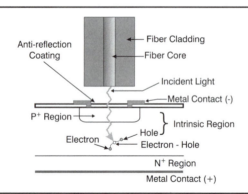

Figure 7.20 – Cross-section and Operation of a PIN Photodiode

Avalanche Photodiode

In APDs, primary carriers, the free electrons and holes created by absorbed photons, accelerate, gaining several electron Volts of kinetic energy. A collision of these fast carriers with neutral atoms causes the accelerated carriers to use some of their own energy to help the electrons break out of the valence shell. Additional free electron-hole pairs, called secondary carriers, appear. The process, called collision ionization, creates these secondary carriers. As primary carriers create secondary carriers, the secondary carriers themselves accelerate and create new carriers, a collective process known as photomultiplication. Figure 7.21 illustrates a cross-section and operation of an avalanche photodiode (APD).

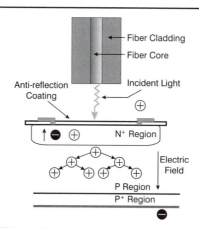

Figure 7.21 – Cross-section and Operation of an APD

The inherent gain provided by APDs simplifies the electronics amplifier chain. However, APDs require high-voltage power supplies for their operation, ranging from 30 or 70 Volts for InGaAs APDs to over 300 Volts for Si APDs. This, plus the requirement for temperature compensation, adds circuit complexity. Because of poor linearity, APDs find use mainly in digital systems. The added circuit complexity and the high operating voltage make APDs less reliable than PIN detectors, thus PIN detectors are the first choice for most deployed low-speed systems or short-haul applications. At multigigabit data rates or long-haul applications, however, APDs rule supreme.

Comparison of PIN Photodiodes and APDs

As with light emitters, one must consider how the detector couples to the fiber. Manufacturers package detectors and light emitters the same way, using microlensed devices or pigtailing the device to a short length of fiber. Table 7.1 offers a comparison of PIN photodiodes and APDs.

Table 7.1 – Comparison of PINs and APDs

Parameter	PIN Photodiodes	APDs
Construction Materials	Silicon, Germanium, InGaAs	Silicon, Germanium, InGaAs
Bandwidth	DC to 40+ GHz	DC to 40+ GHz
Wavelength	0.6 to 1.8 μm	0.6 to 1.8 μm

Table 7.1 – Comparison of PINs and APDs (Continued)

Parameter	PIN Photodiodes	APDs
Conversion Efficiency	0.5 to 1.0 Amps/Watt	0.5 to 100 Amps/Watt
Support Circuitry Required	None	High Voltage and Temperature Compensation
Cost (Fiber Ready)	$1 to $500	$100 to $2,000

Understanding Specifications

One must understand the theory of light emitters or detectors in order to apply them successfully. However, interpreting and understanding the specifications of a specific device is a bit of an art and takes some practice to perfect. The example below describes a detector; however, we can roughly equate the light emitter specifications. The detector in the example is a 75 μm InGaAs detector with a fiber pigtail. Table 7.2 lists the detector's performance specifications.

The specifications listed in Table 7.2 usually describe real-life application conditions. In this case, the table tells us that the parameters listed are at an operating temperature of +25°C and a reverse bias voltage of 5 Volts. It is important to understand what such a statement doesn't say as well as what it does say. It doesn't say what happens if you operate the detector at higher or lower temperatures or at reverse voltages other than 5 Volts. While one would normally assume that the parameters would be relatively stable over a wide range of temperatures and reverse bias voltages, such an assumption can, on occasion, backfire.

Table 7.2 – Detector Performance Specifications

Parameter		Min.	Typ.	Max.	Units
Conditions (unless noted) T = 25°C, V_R = 5 V. All specifications are without connector.					
Responsivity	1550 nm	0.90	1.00		A/W
	1310 nm	0.83	0.90		A/W
Distortion Product[1] (IM_2)			-80	-70	dBc
Backreflection				-50	dB
Dark Current				0.9	nA
Capacitance[2]			0.25	0.35	pF
Bandwidth[3]			3.5		GHz
Fiber Pigtail Length SM Fiber 900 μm Buffer, 8.7/125 μm		0.9		1.1	m

1. IM_2 measured at V_R = 12 V, P_{avg} = 0 dBm, MI = 0.7, R_{load} = 50 Ohms, f_1+f_2 = 850.25 MHz, f_1-f_2 = 50.25 MHz.
2. Measured with case grounded.
3. -3 dB point into a 50 Ohm load.

Responsivity comes first in Table 7.2. Responsivity defines the light to current transfer function of the detector. For instance, at 1310 nm the minimum responsivity is listed as 0.83 A/W. That means that if we illuminate the detector with 1 mW (0 dBm) of light, it will output 0.83 mA of current. The table lists the minimum and typical responsivity of the detector at the most popular wavelengths of 1310 nm and 1550 nm. The minimum values can be considered guaranteed minimum values. However, the conditions for the table that state that the parameters are "without connector." If the connector adds 0.5 dB of loss, then the effective responsivity of the detector drops to 0.80 A/W minimum at 1550 nm and 0.74 A/W at 1310 nm. For light emitters a corresponding specification, output power, determines how much the emitter can give off, which must be an amount sufficient to meet the detector's responsivity.

Detectors intended for linear applications must have a distortion product specification, IM_2, such as this one listed as -50 dB typical. Again, beware of typical specifications; they are not guaranteed. There is no standard way to specify or test IM_2, so we need to refer to footnote 1 to see how IM_2 was determined. In this case, the detector was reverse biased at 12 Volts and 0 dBm (1 mW) of light impinged on the detector. The modulation index (MI) of the two test tones was 0.7. Frequencies of 400 MHz and 450.25 MHz were used to test the detector. While this test does reveal some information about the linearity of the detector, it is of little value if the detector is used for an AM CATV application. AM CATV systems may have more than 77 analog channels, and this data cannot be reliably extrapolated for this number of channels. To work around this, designers should seek out a detector that is specified for AM CATV applications and has linearity expressed in terms of CSO (composite second order) and CTB (composite triple beat).

The table specifies backreflection tolerance as -50 dB maximum, which works well in most scenarios but represents the minimum requirement for high performance AM CATV systems. The dark current is specified at 0.9 nA maximum. Keep in mind this is at +25°C and 5 Volts reverse bias. The dark current will increase with temperature and reverse bias voltage. The capacitance is listed as 0.25 pF typical and 0.35 pF maximum with the case grounded (see footnote 2). Again the 0.35 pF value should be used in a design analysis. The bandwidth of the detector at +25°C and 5 Volts reverse bias is listed as 3.5 GHz typical. Again, no guarantees here. Finally, the fiber pigtail ranges in length from 0.9 to 1.1 meters. Light emitter parameters would include operating wavelength, spectral bandwidth, threshold current, operating current, and beam divergence angle.

Table 7.3 lists the limits beyond which the detector will be damaged or destroyed. Normally a design would not push a detector to these limits, as doing so risks premature failure in service. The detector can withstand a reverse voltage of 20 Volts and a maximum reverse current of 5 mA in normal operation. This indirectly implies (using the responsivity in Table 7.2) that the maximum light input is slightly higher than 5 mW (+7 dBm). The detector can also sustain a maximum forward current of 5 mA. It is not normal to forward bias a detector. The forward voltage required to achieve a forward current of 5 mA is probably less than 0.5 Volts.

Table 7.3 – Detector Absolute Maximum Ratings

Parameter	Rating	Units
Reverse Voltage[1]	20	V
Reverse Current[1]	5	mA
Forward Current[2]	5	mA
Power Dissipation	50	mW
Operating Temperature	-25/70	°C
Storage Temperature	-40/85	°C

1.   Under reverse bias, current at which device may be damaged or destroyed.
2.   Under forward bias, current at which device may be damaged or destroyed.

The next parameter, power dissipation, is limited to 50 mW. This further constrains the maximum light input for high reverse voltages. For instance, if the reverse voltage is 20 Volts, the maximum reverse current must be reduced to 2.5 mA to avoid exceeding the power dissipation limit. This would correspondingly limit the maximum input light to a bit over 2.5 mW (+4 dBm).

Finally, the maximum operating and storage temperatures are listed. The detector's materials or fabrication techniques usually limit the maximum storage temperature. In light emitters, absolute maximum ratings include the device case temperature, the operating temperature, optical power output, reverse voltage, and storage temperature.

In most cases the analysis goes beyond the two tables of data presented here. Most components will include graphs that describe the performance over a wider range of conditions. Figure 7.22 shows one type of performance graph that describes a typical detector.

There are no easy shortcuts to reading and understanding the specifications for a detector or light emitter. The system designer must carefully read and understand every parameter of both the light emitter and the detector to ensure that they really understand the devices sufficiently to incorporate

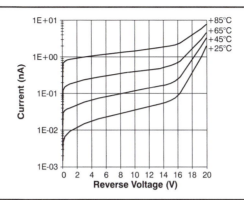

Figure 7.22 – Dark Current versus Temperature and Reverse Bias Voltage

them into a design. Light emitters and detectors form the basis for all fiber optic transmission devices. However, other elements must be present to make these work for fiber optic video transmission. The next chapter will cover other basic optical components that make up a complete system for fiber optic video transmission.

Chapter Summary

- Light emitters, such as light-emitting diodes (LEDs) or laser diodes (LDs), convert an electrical signal into a corresponding light signal.
- Light emitters operate on the principle of the p-n semiconductor junction found in transistors and diodes, where an n-type and a p-type semiconductor placed together, causes excess electrons from the n region to move to the p region, allowing the flow of electrons.
- Key light emitter characteristics include: peak wavelength, spectral width, emission pattern, power, and speed.
- Light emitters with a wide spectral width have more problems with dispersion than emitters with a narrow spectral width.
- LEDs may be surface-emitters or edge-emitters; surface-emitters offer high reliability and low cost while edge-emitters allow for higher output power and easier fiber coupling.
- Laser diodes include Fabry-Perot (FP) and distributed feedback (DFB) types.
- Temperature can affect the peak emission wavelength of a light emitter.
- LEDs and laser diodes may use analog drive circuits or digital drive circuits to match a given application.

- In lasers, predistortion circuits dramatically improve linearity, allowing long-distance transmission.
- Vertical cavity surface-emitting lasers (VCSELs) use an active electrically pumped gain region to emit light.
- VCSELs use the same drive circuits as LEDs, and they exhibit high stability over a wide temperature range.
- Light detectors, such as PIN photodiodes and avalanche photodiodes (APDs), convert optical signals into corresponding electrical signals.
- Key detector parameters include: capacitance, responsivity, response time, edge effect, dark current, linearity, backreflection, and noise.
- PIN photodiodes uses an intrinsic region between the p region and the n region, which allows for a large depletion area.
- Fiber optics use PIN photodiodes in photoconductive mode, which applies a reverse bias to provide a highly linear output.
- APDs use photomultiplication to create a current flow, giving them inherent gain, an advantage over PIN photodiodes.
- When specifying components, the typical specification is rarely the guaranteed specification; therefore, designers should use minimum or maximum specifications where available.

Chapter 8

Basic Optical Components

In addition to the light sources and detectors used in fiber optic systems, all fiber optic transmission systems require other basic optical components, including optical connectors, splices, splitters, and wavelength-division multiplexers (WDMs).

Optical Connector Basics

The term interconnection device refers to any mechanism or technique used to join an optical fiber to another fiber or to a fiber optic component. Optical connectors represent the most common interconnection device. While difficulty in using early connector designs initially delayed the commercialization of fiber optics, today's designs have become mature, and highly reliable devices. Each connector type exhibits different characteristics, advantages, disadvantages, and performance parameters, but all retain same four basic components.

- Ferrule: Usually constructed of metal, ceramic, or plastic, the ferrule, which acts as a fiber alignment mechanism, holds the optical fiber in place within the connector. The hollow center of the ferrule exceeds the diameter of the fiber cladding, and the fiber end face aligns flush with the end of the ferrule.
- Connector Body: Also called the connector housing, the connector body secures the ferrule. Constructed of metal or plastic, the connector body includes one or more assembled pieces which hold the fiber in place. Strength members and cable jackets are bonded and/or crimped to the connector body. The ferrule extends past the connector body to slip into the coupling device.

- Cable: Attached to the connector body, the cable acts as the point of entry for the fiber. Normally, a strain-relief boot adds extra strength to the junction between the cable and the connector body.
- Coupling Device: Many fiber optic connectors do not use the male-female configuration common to electronic connectors. Instead, a dual female coupling device such as an alignment sleeve mates the male connectors. Similar devices, known as feed-through bulkhead connectors, may be installed in fiber optic transmitters and receivers.

Some connectors incorporate a modified end face polishing method called PC (physical contact). The PC uses a curved polish and forced mating of the connector end faces to dramatically reduce system backreflection. This eliminates the glass-air-glass interface found in non-PC connectors and further reduces the backreflection. Another variation, polishing a 5° to 15° angle on the end face, achieves low backreflection; however, angled physical contact (APC) connectors require special bulkhead couplings to properly align the connectors so that the surfaces touch. Names that imply low backreflection include PC, UPC, Super-PC, and Super Polish. Today's connector designs tend to be push-pull types, which offer fast connection times and allow increased packing density because this design requires less finger access. These connectors have also focused on minimizing installation time (onto the fiber), reducing insertion loss, and addressing backreflection more completely than in earlier designs.

Types of Fiber Optic Connectors

There are many fiber optic connector types available but only the few, listed in Table 8.1, are widespread.

Table 8.1 – Connector Types

Connector	Insertion Loss	Repeatability	Fiber Type	Applications
FC	0.50-1.00 dB	0.20 dB	SM, MM	Datacom, Telecommunications
LC	0.15 dB (SM) 0.10 dB (MM)	0.20 dB	SM, MM	High-density Interconnects
MT Array	0.30-1.00 dB	0.25 dB	SM, MM	High-density Interconnects

Table 8.1 – Connector Types (Continued)

Connector	Insertion Loss	Repeatability	Fiber Type	Applications
SC	0.20-0.45 dB	0.10 dB	SM, MM	Telecommunications
SC Duplex	0.20-0.45 dB	0.10 dB	SM, MM	Datacom
ST	Typ. 0.40 dB (SM) Typ. 0.50 dB (MM)	Typ. 0.40 dB (SM) Typ. 0.20 dB (MM)	SM, MM	Inter-/Intra-building, Security, Navy

- FC: (Also available as FC/PC and FC/APC.) The FC connector features a flat end face on the ferrule that provides "face contact" between joining connectors. The FC represents a very good second generation connector design with very good features and performance but relatively high cost. It offers excellent single-mode and multimode performance. FCs are still widely used for analog systems or high bit-rate systems, such as CATV systems, where backreflection management is important. FC/PC connectors incorporate a "physical contact" curved polished fiber end face that greatly reduces backreflections.
- LC: Developed for premise wiring applications, the LC connector uses a body similar to the RJ-45 telephone style housing and a 1.25 mm diameter ferrule with a diameter half that of most fiber optic connector ferrules.
- MT Array: This connector works with ribbon fiber, allowing a single connector to be used with four, eight, ten, or twelve fibers. The connector itself is slightly larger than a standard SC connector. It can be used with single-mode or multimode fiber. Single-mode options include several levels of PC polishing (offering different levels of backreflection) as well as APC. This allows for significantly higher packing density compared to all other connector types discussed above.
- SC and SC Duplex: The SC (subscription channel) connector uses a locking push-pull mechanism that gives an audible click when inserted or removed. This pull-proof design prevents rotational misalignment, and decouples the ferrule from the cable and the connector body when stress is applied. A duplex version of the SC connector, gaining popularity in networks, allows full-duplex transmission. Suitable for single-mode and multimode fibers, the SC, also available in an APC

configuration, offers excellent packing density as well as exceptional performance, and cost.

- ST: This predominantly multimode connector type features a spring loading twist-and-lock bayonet coupling that keeps the fiber and ferrule from rotating during multiple connections. The cylindrical ferrule may be made of plastic, ceramic, or stainless steel. ST connectors offer very good features, cost, and performance. The bayonet coupling makes this connector popular in applications with high vibration and shock levels.

Care of Fiber Optic Connectors

In order to grasp the small size of a fiber optic connector core, think of a human hair with an average diameter of 50-75 μm. Single-mode fibers, by comparison, average core diameters of only 8-9 μm in diameter, six to nine times smaller! A dust particle only 1 μm in diameter landing on the core of a single-mode fiber can cause up to 1 dB of loss. Larger dust particles (9 μm or larger) can completely obscure the core of a single-mode fiber. Therefore, fiber optic connectors need to be cleaned *every* time they are mated.

Unprotected connector ends can experience damage by impact, such as hitting the floor, by airborne dust particles, or excess humidity or moisture. When not in use, a protective cover should go over the fiber optic connector. Most connector manufacturers provide some sort of protection boot. The best protectors cover the entire connector end, but most boots generally involve simple close-ended tubes that fit snugly over the ferrule only. Many of these tight fitting plastic ferrule protection boots contain jelly-like contamination (most likely mold release) that adheres to the sides of the ferrule. A blast of cleaning air or a quick dunk in alcohol will not remove this residue. This jelly-like residue can combine with common dirt to form a sticky mess that causes the connector ferrule to stick in the mating adapter. Often, the stuck ferrule will break off as one attempts to remove it, so always thoroughly clean the connector before mating, even if it was cleaned before the protection boot was installed.

The Effects of High Optical Power

High optical power levels can cause potentially catastrophic damage to optical fibers and connectors, an often overlooked factor in discussions about handling and caring for optical fibers and connectors. Most designers tend to think of the power levels in optical fibers as relatively insignificant. However, a few milliwatts at 850 nm will do permanent damage to a retina. Today, optical amplifiers can generate optical powers of 1 Watt of more into a single-mode fiber. This becomes quite significant when one considers that the optical power is confined in the optical core only a few microns in diameter. Power densities in a single-mode fiber carrying an optical power of 1 Watt (+30 dBm) can reach 3 megawatts/cm^2 or 30 gigawatts/m^2! To put it in everyday terms, sunlight at the surface of the Earth has a power density of about 1,000 Watts/m^2. Most organic materials will combust when exposed to radiant energies of 100 kilowatts/m^2. Clearly, power densities of 30 gigawatts/m^2 deserve attention.

Effects on Optical Connectors

One should never clean an optical connector attached to a fiber that is carrying light. Optical power levels as low as +15 dBm, or 32 milliwatts, may cause an explosive ignition of the cleaning material when it contacts the end of the optical connector, destroying the connector. Typical cleaning materials, such as tissues saturated with alcohol, will combust almost instantaneously when exposed to optical power levels of +15 dBm or higher. The micro-explosions at the tip of the connector can leave pits in the end of the connector and crack the connector's surface, destroying its ability to carry light with low loss. Figure 8.1 shows an optical connector that has been heavily damaged by high optical power levels. Usually the damage is limited to less severe pitting.

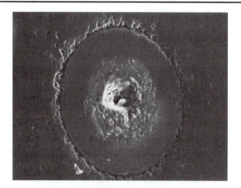

Figure 8.1 – Connector Damaged by High Optical Power
(Photo courtesy of Dr. D.D. Davis.)

The Fiber Fuse

At high optical power levels (around 1 Watt), another damage mechanism has been observed which can result in the catastrophic destruction of the fiber core over many kilometers. This phenomenon is characterized by the propagation of a bright visible light in the fiber starting from the point of initiation and moving toward the laser source at about 1 meter per second. The term "fiber fuse" has been used because of the similarity in appearance to a burning fuse. The fiber fuse can be initiated by contact with the end of the fiber, or by localized heating of the fiber. It has also been observed to initiate spontaneously from mechanical splices, probably due to contamination on the surfaces. Figure 8.2 shows the setup required to observe the fiber fuse in action.

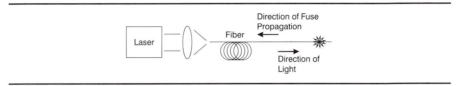

Figure 8.2 – Fiber Fuse Mechanism

Thermally induced absorption generates the fiber fuse mechanism. Normally, an optical fiber's absorption is extremely low, usually less than 0.25 dB/km. However, if the temperature of the glass exceeds 1,100°C, absorption increases dramatically to over 1,000 dB/km. The absorbed laser energy, which represents about 3×10^6 W/cm^2 of power density in the fiber core, creates a plasma that absorbs most of the optical energy. The adjacent region of the fiber also heats to the point where its absorption increases, and the fuse propagates toward the laser source. Unless a small air gap in a connector impedes the fiber fuse, it will continue to burn, destroying the entire length of fiber back to the transmitter. Figure 8.3 shows a dramatic example of the core of a single-mode fiber destroyed by a passing fiber fuse.

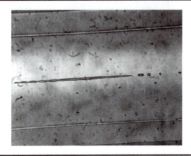

Figure 8.3 – Effect of a Fiber Fuse on a Single-mode Fiber Core
(Photo courtesy of Dr. D.D. Davis.)

Experiments have shown that the velocity of fuse propagation depends on the power level. Fibers which have been subjected to the fiber fuse appear normal on the outside, but microscopic inspection of the core reveals severe damage in the form of periodic bubbles or long non periodic filaments; evidence of melting and reforming of the glass as the fuse passes.

Fiber Optic Connector Cleaning Technique

Required Equipment and Technique

- Lens-grade, lint-free tissue, such as the type sold for eyeglasses.
- Denatured alcohol. (Alcohol other than denatured alcohol contains mineral oil and is not suitable for cleaning connectors.)
- 30X microscope.
- Canned dry air.

1. Verify the fiber attached to the connector is not carrying optical power.
2. Fold the tissue twice, so it is four layers thick.
3. Saturate the tissue with alcohol.
4. To clean the sides of the connector ferrule, place the connector ferrule in the tissue, and apply pressure to the sides of the ferrule. Rotate the ferrule several times to remove all contamination from the ferrule sides.
5. Move to a clean part of the tissue, making sure it is still saturated with alcohol and four layers thick. Put the tissue against the end of the connector ferrule. Put your fingernail against the tissue directly over the ferrule. Scrape the end of the connector until it squeaks. It will sound like a crystal glass that has been rubbed when it is wet.
6. Use the microscope to verify the quality of the cleaning. Repeat the steps with a clean tissue until the connector end face appears clean in the microscope.
7. Mate the connector immediately! Do not let the connector collect dust.
8. Pressurized air can be used to remove lint or dust from the port being mated with the connector. Never insert any liquid into the ports.

Handling

1. Never touch the fiber end face of the connector.
2. Cover connectors not in use with protection boot provided. However, remember to thoroughly clean the ferrule end BEFORE mating it to the intended unit.
3. Index-matching gel, a gelatinous substance that has a refractive index close to that of the optical fiber, may not be recommended. One example, glycerin, will reduce connector loss and backreflections. However, any index-matching gel may collect dust or abrasives that can damage the fiber end faces. It may also leak out over time, increasing backreflections.

Splicing

Splices are a means of permanently connecting two fibers. Typically, a splice joins lengths of cable outside buildings, while connectors join the ends of cables inside buildings. Splices offer lower cost, lower attenuation, and lower backreflection than connectors. Two types of splices include fusion splices and mechanical splices, such as capillary splices.

Fusion Splicing

Fusion splicing involves butting two cleaved fiber end faces together and heating them until they melt together or fuse. A fusion splicer controls the alignment of the two fibers, keeping losses as low as 0.05 dB. Fusion splicers have a relatively high cost, but they offer many features such as an electric arc welder to fuse the fibers, alignment mechanisms, a camera or binocular microscope to magnify the alignment by 50 times or more, and instruments to check the optical power through the fibers both before and after fusing. Figure 8.4 illustrates the operation of a typical fusion splicer.

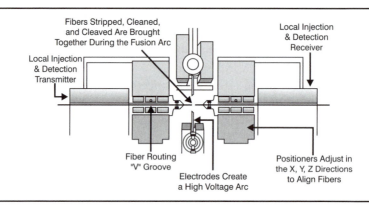

Figure 8.4 – Typical Fusion Splicer

Optical Couplers and Splitters

Fiber optic couplers either split optical signals into multiple paths or combine multiple signals onto one path. The number of input and output ports, expressed as an N x M configuration, characterizes a coupler. The letter N represents the number of input fibers, and M represents the number of output fibers. Many configurations for fused couplers exist, but they commonly use even multiples of two (2 x 2, 4 x 4, 8 x 8, etc.).

The simplest couplers are fiber optic splitters. These devices possess at least three ports but may have more than 32 for more complex devices. A simple 3-port device, also called a tee coupler, can be thought of as a directional coupler. The three ports include a common fiber and two input or output ports. A typical application involves injecting light into the common port and splitting it into two independent legs (the output ports). The coupler manufacturer determines the ratio of the distribution of light between the two output legs. Popular splitting ratios include 50%-50%, 90%-10%, 95%-5% and 99%-1%; however, almost any custom value can be achieved. (These values are sometimes specified in dB values.) For example, using a 90%-10% splitter with a 50 μW light source, the outputs would equal 45 μW and 5 μW. However, excess loss, a parameter shared by couplers and splitters, dictates a lower total output compared to the input. Excess loss figures range from 0.05 dB to 2 dB for different coupler types.

An interesting property of splitters involves their symmetry. For instance, if the same coupler injected 50 μW into the 10% output leg, only 5 μW would reach the common port. Table 8.2 gives the typical split ratios and insertion losses for modern single-mode couplers. Insertion loss is equal to the sum of the excess loss and $10 \bullet \text{Log}_{10}$ of the split ratio for each leg.

Table 8.2 – Typical Single-mode Fiber Insertion Losses

Split Ratio (%)	Typical Insertion Loss (dB)
50/50	3.1/3.1
45/55	3.6/2.7
40/60	4.1/2.3
35/65	4.7/2.0
30/70	5.4/1.7
25/75	6.2/1.4
15/85	8.4/0.8
10/90	10.2/0.6
5/95	13.2/0.4
10/45/45	10.5/4.0/4.0
20/40/40	7.3/4.5/4.5
30/35/35	5.4/4.8/4.8
40/30/30	4.1/5.4/5.4
50/25/25	3.1/6.2/6.2
60/20/20	2.3/7.2/7.2
70/15/15	1.7/8.5/8.5
80/10/10	1.0/10.5/10.5
25/25/25/25	6.4/6.4/6.4/6.4

Common applications for couplers and splitters include:
- Local monitoring of a light source output (usually for control purposes).
- Distributing a common signal to several locations simultaneously. An 8-port coupler allows a single transmitter to drive eight receivers.

- Creating a linear, tapped fiber optic bus. Here, a 95%-5% splitter would allow receivers in the bus to tap a small portion of the energy while the bulk of the energy continues down the main trunk.

Optical couplers find wide use in applications that require links other than point-to-point links. This includes bidirectional links and local area networks (LAN). In LAN applications, either a star topology or a bus topology incorporates couplers. In a star topology, stations branch off from a central hub, much like the spokes on a wheel. This allows easy expansion of the number of workstations; changing from a 4 x 4 to an 8 x 8 doubles the system capacity. The star coupler divides all outputs, allowing all stations to hear each other. These devices have many ports (usually a power of two), commonly as many as 32 or 64. Star couplers allow the creation of a large party-line circuit wherein many connected transceivers can communicate with each other, assuming the network adopts a protocol to prevent two or more transceivers from communicating simultaneously. Large insertion loss, (typically 20 dB for a 64-port device) and the need for complex collision-prevention protocol represent the biggest disadvantages of the star coupler. Figure 8.5 shows typical star and tee couplers, discussed next.

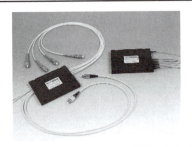

Figure 8.5 – Star and Tee Couplers
(Photo courtesy of Hopecom, Inc.)

Bus topology utilizes a tee coupler to connect a series of stations that listen to a single backbone of cable. In a typical bus network, a coupler at each node splits off part of the power from the bus and carries it to a transceiver in the attached equipment. In a system with N terminals, a signal must pass through N-1 couplers before arriving at the receiver. Loss increases linearly as N increases. A bus topology may operate in a single direction or a bidirectional or duplex configuration. In a unidirectional setup, a transmitter at one end of the bus communicates with a receiver at the other end. Each terminal also contains a receiver. Duplex networks add a second fiber bus or use an additional directional coupler at each end and at each terminal. In this way, signals flow in both directions. Figure 8.6 illustrates the differences in a unidirectional bus and a duplex bus.

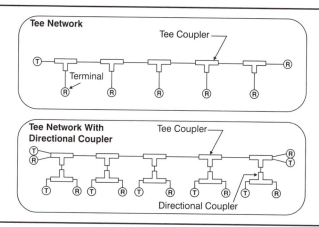

Figure 8.6 – Tee Network Configurations

As requirements for increased transmission capacity changed, the fiber optics industry responded with wavelength-division multiplexing (WDM), which sends two or more distinct signals per fiber. Like the simple splitter, WDMs typically have a common leg and a number of input or output legs. They lack the splitting loss common in splitters, but WDMs also exhibit the same range of excess loss. Figure 8.7 shows two WDMs allowing bidirectional data transmission over a single fiber. The type of data does not matter. One could be a video signal, the other an RS-232 data stream. Alternatively, both signals could be video signals or high-speed data signals at 2.488 Gb/s.

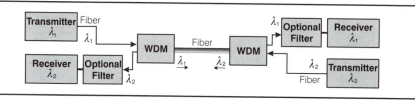

Figure 8.7 – Bidirectional WDM Application

Crosstalk and channel separation represent two important considerations in a WDM device. Crosstalk, also called directivity, refers to port-to-port separation of each demultiplexed channel. Crosstalk specifications express how well a coupler maintains this port-to-port separation. Channel separation describes a coupler's ability to distinguish wavelengths. Widely separated wavelengths allow light to travel in either direction without the penalty found in splitters.

Understanding Specifications

As with emitters and detectors, successful fiber optic system design and maintenance requires learning how to read and understand specifications for passive optical components such as couplers and WDMs. While most fiber optic component suppliers have honest reputations, published data sheets often contain specifications that involve some degree of specsmanship, "how to lie with statistics," or lack of knowledge by the vendor.

Table 8.3 – WDM Coupler Specifications

Item	Unit	Parameter	
Wavelength	nm	1310 nm and 1550 nm	
Bandwidth	nm	± 20	
Grade	N/A	A	B
Max. Insertion Loss	dB	0.7	1.1
Min. Wavelength Isolation	dB	32	26
Typ. Isolation in a ± 10 BW	dB	40	34
Max. Temperature Coefficient	dB/°C	0.003	
Operating Temperature	°C	-40 to ~+75	
Storage Temperature	°C	-40 to ~+85	
Package Dimensions	m	100 x 80 x 10	
Typ. Reliability (MTBF)	Years	125	

Table 8.3 outlines some typical WDM coupler specifications. The first line indicates that the WDM operates at nominal wavelengths of 1310 nm and 1550 nm. The second line lists the bandwidth as ±20 nm. From here on, the remaining specifications are valid only for wavelengths between 1290-1330 nm and 1530-1570 nm. The coupler will operate outside these bounds, but the listed specifications will not necessarily apply.

Moving down the table, the manufacturer offers two grades of the WDM, A and B. Grade A, the better grade unit, will cost more. However, it also offers better performance. The table lists the maximum insertion loss as 0.7 dB and 1.1 dB respectively for grades A and B. This important spec has an impact on WDM system design, which must consider the maximum expected loss for each element in the optical signal path. The next specification, minimum wavelength isolation, dictates that unwanted wavelengths in the system will attenuate 32 dB for grade A and 26 dB for grade B. This represents the amount of isolation that the system designer should expect, assuming the designer stays within the valid wavelength bands.

The next line, typical isolation in ± 10 nm bandwidth, gets designers in trouble. Table 8.3 lists typical isolations of 40 dB and 34 dB. Notice two critical points about this specification. First, the bandwidth has been restricted to half of the originally promised ± 20 nm. Second, and most important, this line lists a typical value, not a guaranteed value. Many designers working with typical values usually run into system problems.

The maximum temperature coefficient lists 0.003 dB/°C for both grades. Below that, the specified operating temperature range is -40°C to +85°C, a span of 125°C. Multiplying the span by 0.003 dB/°C gives a value of 0.375 dB. This value presents a possible point of confusion. Usually this temperature coefficient applies to the insertion loss. In this example, nothing tells the designer whether or not the maximum insertion loss specifications include the 0.375 dB temperature coefficient, requiring some clarification by the vendor.

The next specification, storage temperature, allows a wider temperature range than that of the operating temperature. In this case, the WDM can withstand temperatures in storage that are 10°C higher than during operation. Exceeding a unit's specified storage temperature may cause permanent and irreversible damage to the WDM. The next line gives the package dimensions as 100 x 80 x 10 mm. To verify that the configuration of the unit meets the application's requirements, seasoned designers always insist on seeing a drawing. The last specification, typical reliability, lists 125 years. Again, this represents a typical specification, not a guaranteed specification. The coupler may fail in a year or even a week. Look for guaranteed minimum and maximum specifications when possible.

In addition to these components, some important optical concepts must be understood in order to design a high quality transmission system. The next chapter reveals the nature of light and other advanced concepts that will impact design considerations.

Chapter Summary

- An interconnection device joins an optical fiber to another fiber or a fiber optic component.
- All optical connectors include a ferrule, which holds the fiber in place; a connector body, which secures the ferrule; the cable, which attaches to the connector body and acts as a point of entry for the fiber; and a coupling device which allows the interconnection to take place.
- Connector end faces may offer modified polishing techniques including physical contact (PC) that forces the connector end faces together, or angled physical contat (APC) connectors, which offer low backreflection.
- Types of fiber optic connectors include FC, LC, MT array, SC, and ST.

- The diameter of a dust particle may be larger than the diameter of a fiber core, requiring careful cleaning of all connectors before they are mated in a fiber optic system.
- Splices differ from optical connectors in their permanence.
- Fusion splicing butts together the ends of two cleaved fibers and heats them until they fuse together into a single fiber, usually using a complex fusion splicer to align the fibers, minimizing optical loss.
- Optical splitters or couplers split or join multiple optical signals for transmission on one fiber.
- Coupler and splitter manufacturers set the splitting ratio for each port of the device; 50%-50%, 90%-10%, 95%-5%, and 99%-1% represent the most common splitting ratios available.
- Optical couplers find extensive use in point-to-multipoint applications including many types of networks.
- Network topologies requiring optical couplers/splitters include the bus topology, the ring topology, and the star topology.
- WDM components allow two or more optical signals to be combined for transmission on one fiber and separate the composite signal back into two or more signals of different wavelengths at the receiving end.
- Successful fiber optic system design requires a strong understanding of the manufacturer's specifications used to select the system components.
- To avoid under-specifying the system, a designer should look for guaranteed minimum and maximum specifications and avoid designing the system based on typical specifications only.

Chapter 9

Important Advanced Optical Concepts

The Nature of Light

In order to understand some of the more complex components used in modern, high-performance, fiber optic transmission systems, one should understand the nature of light. Light properties, not obvious in our daily lives, prove vital to the success of many modern fiber optic components. Light travels as an oscillating wave of electric and magnetic fields. (It can also act like a particle, but that is not pertinent to this discussion.) Two phenomena affect the behavior of light: interference and polarization.

Interference

Many fiber optic components use interference including fiber Bragg gratings, optical filters built directly into the fiber; lithium niobate modulators, used to modulate the laser externally rather than by directly, and many types of bulk filters, devices used in wavelength-division multiplexing. Two types of interference include constructive and destructive interference.

Figure 9.1 (next page) illustrates the first type, constructive interference. The top two curves represent two electrical fields of two light waves traveling along the same path. The distance between the crests or troughs of the waves defines the light's wavelength. The two light waves shown are also "in phase." This means the peaks and the valleys of the two waveforms align perfectly. Constructive interference dictates that two in-phase light waves with the same wavelength produce a single light wave with an amplitude equal to the sum of the amplitudes of the two original light waves.

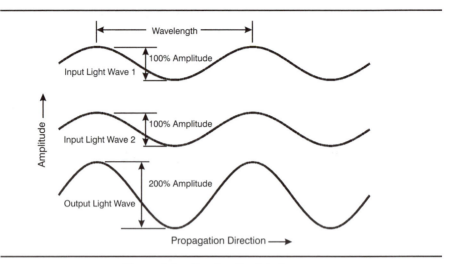

Figure 9.1 – Constructive Interference

Light waves that are "out of phase" react differently, causing destructive interference, illustrated in Figure 9.2. In this case, the two input light waves almost cancel each other out, resulting in an output light wave that is only 17% of the original amplitude. The resultant amplitude would go to zero if the two input light waves were exactly out of phase.

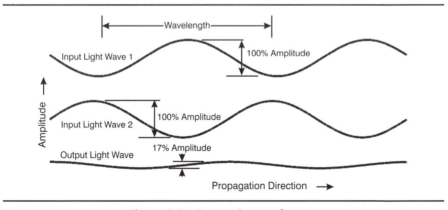

Figure 9.2 – Destructive Interference

Interference usually occurs when a light wave combines with a delayed version of the same light wave. This principle governs lithium niobate modulators, optically transparent crystals with the ability to change the delay of light in response to a change in an applied electric field.

Polarization

Light waves travel along vector fields, two planes separated by 90°. Figure 9.3 shows a polarized light wave traveling along the X axis. It consists of two components; the component labeled E represents the varying electric field and is known as the E-vector. The component labeled B represents the varying magnetic field and is known as the B-vector. The axis of the E-vector governs the plane of polarization. In this case, the light wave shown is vertically polarized because the E-vector runs along the vertical axis. A jumble of horizontally and vertically polarized light waves traveling together comprises an unpolarized light wave.

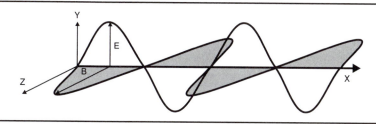

Figure 9.3 – Light Wave Showing E and B Vectors

Polarized sunglasses utilize this principle. Their design allows the passage of only one polarization of light. Most reflected light has a horizontal polarization. The sunglasses have vertically polarized lenses, which block horizontally polarized reflection.

The Electromagnetic Spectrum

The electromagnetic spectrum organizes light into frequencies (wavelengths), including the small band of visible light, near-infrared light, the fiber optic wavelengths, and all other transmission frequencies. Fiber optic wavelengths are measured in nanometers (the prefix nano meaning one billionth) or microns (the prefix micro meaning one millionth). Figure 9.4 illustrates the electromagnetic spectrum.

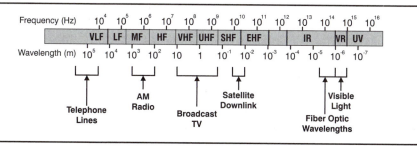

Figure 9.4 – Electromagnetic Spectrum

Wavelengths for fiber optic applications can be broken into two main categories: near-infrared and visible. Visible light, as defined by the human eye, ranges in wavelengths from 400 to 700 nanometers (nm) and does not present many uses in fiber optic applications because of the high optical loss at these wavelengths. Near-infrared wavelengths, used heavily in modern fiber optic systems, range from 700 to 1,700 nanometers.

Photons, Electrons, and Counting Statistics

Electromagnetic theory tells us that radio waves and light waves are merely different manifestations of the same phenomenon. Both radio waves and light waves are described by Maxwell's Equation. Both light and radio waves can be thought of as waves or particles, photons in this case. For the purposes of this discussion, we will use the photon description. Photons can be thought of as little packets of energy. Light photons have much higher energy levels than radio wave photons; therefore, at an equivalent power level, more radio wave photons would exist compared to light wave photons. To understand the implications, a few simple calculations (nothing rigorous) can convey some general principles.

Assume that a transmitter generates 1 milliwatt (mW) of radio waves at a frequency of 1 MHz, or 1,000 kHz. That radio wave will have a wavelength of about 300 meters, a typical number for an AM radio station. Now refer to Appendix F, Table F.2, "Conversion Factors." At a frequency of 1 MHz, the energy carried by each photon, equals 4.136×10^{-9} eV. We also see that 1 eV equals 1.602×10^{-16} mW/s. So for every second, the 1 mW radio wave equals to 6.242×10^{15} eV. Dividing that result by the energy carried by each photon, we see that the transmitter emits 1.509×10^{24} photons per second.

Now assume that a laser generates 1 milliwatt (mW) of light at a frequency of 193 THz, equivalent to a wavelength of 1550 nm, a typical wavelength used in a modern long-haul fiber optic transmission system. Per Table F.2, at a frequency of 193 THz, the energy carried by each photon would equal 0.798 eV. We also see that 1 eV equals to 1.602×10^{-16} mW/s. Again, for each second, our 1 mW light wave equals 6.242×10^{15} eV. Dividing that result by the energy carried by each photon, we see that the laser emits 7.822×10^{15} photons per second. Clearly, the light source emits 193 million times fewer photons per second than the radio transmitter at the same exact output power level.

The randomness with which radio transmitters or lasers emit photons creates shot noise. Associated with the lower photon count, shot noise represents one of the more significant sources of noise in a fiber optic system. We know the long-term average number of emitted photons, but we cannot predict with certainty how many photons the light source would emit each picosecond. Ignoring any random phenomena, we might confidently predict that the source emits 7,822 photons each ps. However, since each photon emission is a random event, the variation will be roughly proportional to the square root of the number of photons. [The square root of the mean is referred to as one sigma (σ) or one standard deviation.] This would be true about 68% of the time. If we used three times the square root of the count, three sigma (3σ), the result would then be true 99.7% of the time. For the purpose of this discussion we will use the square root which will yield an answer that is true 68% of the time. So in the case of the laser discussed above, we could correctly say that the light source emits 7,822 ±88 photons each second. The ±88 photon variation (square root of 7,822) will appear to the receiver as shot noise. Thus the signal (7,822) to noise (88) ratio (SNR) would only be 7,822/88 or 88:1, equivalent to 39 dB.

Figure 9.5 shows the probability of a given photon count per ps from our laser. The radio transmitter emits 1.509×10^{12} photons each ps. The statistical variation for this case, the square root of the number of photons, equals 1.228×10^{6} photons. So we can say that each ps, we expect our radio transmitter to emit 1.509×10^{12} ±1.228×10^{6} photons. In this case, the SNR is much higher, 1.228×10^{6}:1, equivalent to 122 dB. Clearly, one can achieve a much higher SNR with a radio signal versus a light signal at the same power level. This would also allow us to receive a radio signal at a dramatically lower power level than could be achieved with a light receiver.

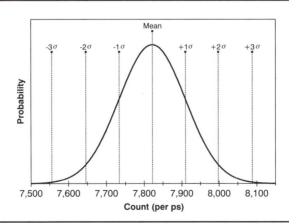

Figure 9.5 – Probability of a Given Photon Count from a Laser

This discussion pertains to fiber optic AM video transmission, discussed in Chapter 12, and fiber optic CATV transmission, covered in detail in

Chapter 15. In most practical cases, shot noise in the incoming light will limit the receiver's output SNR. Therefore, one must increase the amount of light at the receiver input in order to raise the SNR.

Counting statistics, commonly encountered in public opinion polls, offer an interesting analogy to the shot noise in a communications system. For example a given opinion poll may have a margin of error of ±3%. If we apply the principles we used to derive shot noise, we can readily determine the number of people polled. An error margin of ±3% implies that the "SNR" is 1/0.03 or 33.3:1. The square of 33.3 is the number of people that were polled, 1,100 in this case. In reality, the pollsters probably talked to 1,000 people. If a poll had an error margin of ±5%, the "SNR" would be 1/0.05 or 20:1 implying that they polled 400 people. One rarely sees a poll with an error margin less than ±3% because of the cost of polling so many people. To reach an error margin of ±2%, you would have to poll 2,500 people, and you would have to poll 10,000 people to reach an error margin of ±1%. Few pollsters will spend ten times as much time effort to decrease the error margin from ±3% to ±1%.

Backreflection

Excessive backreflections in the fiber plant degrade the performance of all laser-based fiber optic links. The only question becomes how much backreflection affects the link's performance? Backreflections hurt the performance of a link because the reflected light gets into the laser cavity, disturbs the standing optical wave, and creates noise. As a result, many high-end lasers incorporate optical isolators. In some cases, lasers incorporate dual isolators offering 50 dB or more reduction in backreflections. (One would think that a double-isolated laser would be immune to backreflections, but this is not the case.) The noise generated by backreflections reaching the laser represents only one possible source, in many cases a minor source of noise because of the widespread use of optical isolators.

Interferometric interference noise (IIN) offers a more significant source of noise in a modern fiber optic system. This noise is generated by Fabry-Perot cavities created between multiple reflecting elements in the fiber plant, usually fiber optic connectors or splices. The technology for modern splices has advanced, making fiber optic connectors the main source of IIN. To address backreflection, the fiber optic industry first introduced PC (physical contact) polished connectors and later angled physical contact (APC) connectors. The APC connectors especially go a long way toward eliminating any concerns about connector-related backreflections. Figure 9.6 illustrates the generation of AM noise by an FP cavity.

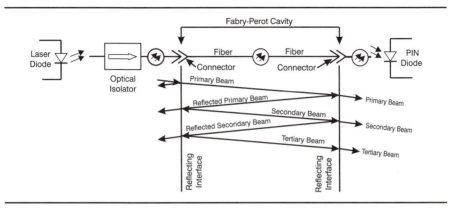

Figure 9.6 – Generation of AM Noise by a Fabry-Perot Cavity

A link's susceptibility to backreflections depends on the type of signal carried by the fiber optic link. Broadband analog links such as multichannel CATV links show the susceptibility. Figure 9.7 illustrates the effects of back-reflection on a single-channel broadband analog fiber optic link incorporating an isolated DFB laser and transmitting a single 100 MHz tone.

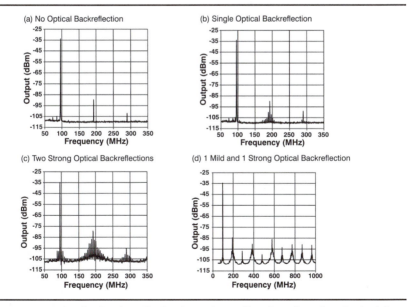

Figure 9.7 – Backreflection in a Single Channel Broadband Analog Fiber Optic Link

Figure 9.7a shows a single transmitted tone. The noise floor is about 76 dB below the carrier and the second and third harmonics are 56 dB and 68 dB down. Figure 9.7b shows the effects of a single weak backreflection. The noise floor goes to about 75 dB and the relative amplitude of the third harmonic increases by 3 dB. In Figure 9.7c, two strong backreflections have been added. The noise floor has now increased by about 14 dB and the second and third harmonics are now 44 dB and 60 dB down. Multiple sidebands have formed around the fundamental signal as well as the second harmonic. Figure 9.7d looks at the same basic data over a wider frequency range. The periodic nature of the noise floor indicates the presence of backreflections. The spacing between the peaks in the noise floor relates to the physical distance, and thus the time delay, between the reflecting elements in the system. Figure 9.8 shows the effects of backreflection on a multichannel link.

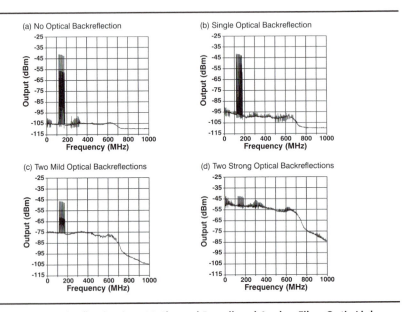

Figure 9.8 – Backreflection in a 10 Channel Broadband Analog Fiber Optic Link

Figure 9.8a shows the signal through a 10-channel broadband analog link with minimal backreflections. The CNR is 65 dB and the second harmonic is 60 dB down. Figure 9.8b shows a single added backreflection. The noise floor increases 5 to 10 dB. In Figure 9.8c, two moderate backreflections are added to the optical path. The noise floor has increased dramatically to reduce the CNR from 65 dB originally to about 28 dB. In Figure 9.8d, two strong backreflections are added to the optical path. The signal, with a CNR of 10 dB is almost totally lost in the noise floor.

Relative Intensity Noise (RIN)

Optical fiber itself can generate noise. This noise, known as fiber-induced RIN (relative intensity noise) or double Rayleigh scattering, usually only concerns analog systems. Some of the scattered light travels back through the fiber where it again scatters and changes direction, emerging from the fiber together with the desired signal. A large separation between the scattering events causes a time delay between the signal and the double-scattered light (much longer than data pulses). The beating (constructive and destructive interference) between the signal and the multiple scattered light causes noise and distortion at the receive end. Figure 9.9 illustrates fiber RIN.

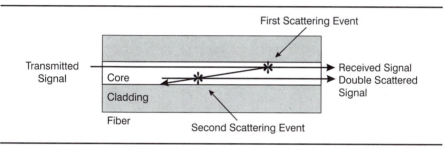

Figure 9.9 – Fiber RIN

Crosstalk

Crosstalk describes the phenomenon where information from one channel leaks into another channel. This occurs commonly with electrical cables where magnetic and electric fields from one cable can couple into nearby electrical cables; however, optical fibers do not exhibit crosstalk. While infinitesimal amounts of light can leak out of an optical fiber, light will not couple into nearby optical fibers without a very special set of conditions. However, crosstalk can occur in WDM elements and through nonlinearities in optical fiber.

Figure 9.10 (next page) shows the insertion loss of a WDM. At 1310 nm insertion loss is less than 1 dB, while at 1550 nm it exceeds 28 dB. The 1550 nm channel shows similar behavior. This means that the rejection of the unwanted signal is only 28 dB down optically from the desired channel. Translating that into RF terms, the interfering signal will be 56 dB down (2 dB RF for each 1 dB optical) from the desired signal, inadequate isolation for video signals.

Video systems require 35 dB minimum isolation, preferably 40 dB or higher, to achieve the optical rejection of unwanted signals. Referring to Figure 9.10, note that only the exact center of the unwanted wavelength

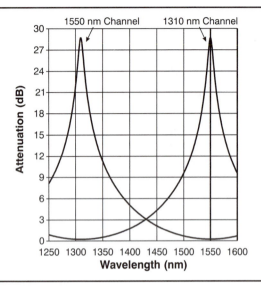

Figure 9.10 – Characteristics of a Fused Fiber WDM

achieves 28 dB of rejection. Figure 9.11 shows details of the rejection of the 1310 nm channel near 1550 nm.

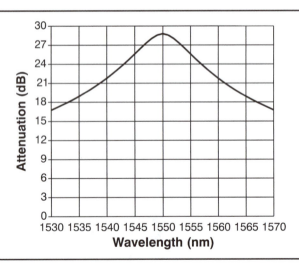

Figure 9.11 – Rejection of the 1310 nm Channel Near 1550 nm

The rejection at a wavelength of 1550 nm is 28.5 dB. However if the wavelength varies only 5 nm to 1545 nm or 1555 nm, the rejection drops to 25.5 dB. The typical wavelength tolerance of many lasers is ±20 nm, in which case the rejection would drop to 16.5 dB. Clearly the characteristics of the WDM and laser wavelength variation must be taken into account when estimating the rejection of a WDM in a real system.

Nonlinearities associated with optical fiber also produce crosstalk in a fiber optic system. Because the refractive index of the fiber's core varies according to the light intensity, nonlinearities known as four-wave mixing, and cross-phase modulation could result. These factors usually only affect high launch power systems (>+10 dBm), long distance systems (>100 km), or systems that contain many closely-spaced wavelengths.

All of these factors have the potential to impact the transmission system. In addition, the principles of light govern the operation of fiber optic transmitters, receivers, and their close cousin, the transceiver. The next chapter discusses these devices in detail.

Chapter Summary

- Light properties vital to fiber optic transmission do not appear in everyday life.
- Two types of interference include constructive and destructive interference.
- In constructive interference, the combined amplitude of two waves, in phase, exceeds the amplitude of the original waves.
- Out-of-phase light waves demonstrate destructive interference where the two waves cancel each other out, reducing the signal.
- Polarization describes the fact that the two components of a light wave travel in two planes separated by 90°, allowing one plane of light to be filtered from the light wave if needed.
- Polarized sunglasses use the principle of polarization by blocking one half of the light wave, reducing glare.
- The electromagnetic spectrum includes visible and invisible frequencies.
- According to the Electromagnetic Theory, radio waves and light waves can be described by Maxwell's Equation, and may be considered waves or particles, also called photons.
- Photons can be considered packets of energy, but light photons have much higher energy levels than radio photons.
- Because light photons have higher energy levels, a light source, i.e., a laser or LED, emits fewer photons than a radio transmitter; however this low photon count contributes to shot noise in the fiber optic system.

- Backreflection greatly reduces the performance of laser-based transmitters because the light reflected back into the laser cavity disrupts the original transmitted light.
- Backreflection noise generated by Fabry-Perot cavities between connections, called interferometric interference noise (IIN), impairs a system's performance.
- A link's susceptibility to backreflections depends on the type of transmitted signal.
- Multichannel analog CATV video links are highly susceptible to the effects of backreflections.
- The optical fiber itself generates relative intensity noise (RIN) via double Rayleigh scattering.
- Crosstalk describes the fact that information on one channel may leak into another channel.
- Fiber nonlinearities may also contribute to crosstalk.

Chapter 10

Transmitters, Receivers, and Transceivers

Modern fiber optic transmission systems can be extraordinarily complex as the data rates, channel counts, and transmission distances increase. However, as previously discussed, the basic elements of fiber optic transmission include the transmitter (Tx) that allows for data input and outputs an optical signal, the optical fiber that carries the data, and the receiver (Rx) that decodes the optical signal to output the data.

Basics of a Transmitter

The transmitter in Figure 10.1 uses an electrical interface to encode the data using one of the three modulation schemes previously discussed: amplitude modulation, frequency modulation, and digital modulation. The electrical-to-optical conversion occurs via either a light-emitting diode or a laser diode. Common wavelengths of these light sources range from 850 nm to 1625 nm for most fiber optic applications.

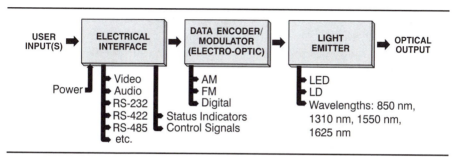

Figure 10.1 – Parts of a Fiber Optic Transmitter

A fiber optic transmitter may operate as a stand-alone device, or it may be integrated into a larger system. Figure 10.2 shows a photo of a typical stand-alone transmitter intended for AM CATV signals. This particular module uses a 1310 nm DFB laser to transmit CATV (multiple channel video) signals using AM techniques. In this case, the unit provides the optical output on connector J1. Connector J2 provides the RF connection to input AM CATV signal. DC power to the unit enters on connector J3 and provides several status output signals. Connectors J4 and J5 connect to an RS-485 control bus, which allows remote status and control access to the module. On the left side of the module, two visual indicators give a quick assessment of the unit's status.

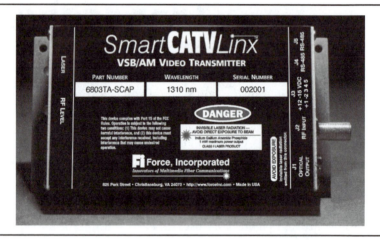

Figure 10.2 – Typical Fiber Optic Transmitter
(Photo courtesy of Force, Inc.)

The warnings below the manufacturer's part number and serial number indicate several things. The verbiage on the left side of the label tells the user that the device complies with FCC regulations regarding EM emissions. The "Danger" label, on the right, required by the Food and Drug Administration (FDA), warns the user that the product contains a laser that emits invisible radiation which may harm the human eye. (The FDA regulates laser-based products for all applications, originally stemming from the development of laser-based medical tools.) All fiber optic laser emissions are invisible to the human eye, and one should never look into the optical output port of a transmitter to "see if it is putting out light."

Basics of a Receiver

Fiber optic receivers, as illustrated in Figure 10.3, decode light signals back into electrical signals using either a PIN photodiode or an avalanche photodiode. Typically, these detectors are made from silicon, indium gallium arsenide, or germanium. Optical-to-electrical conversion uses the same modulation scheme as the transmitter, allowing the receiver to output the original video, audio, or data input.

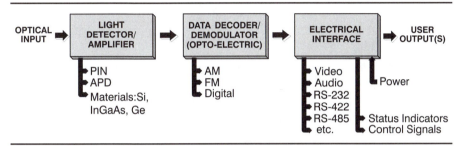

Figure 10.3 – Parts of a Fiber Optic Receiver

Like a transmitter, fiber optic receivers can be stand-alone devices or integrated devices. Figure 10.4 shows a photo of a typical stand-alone receiver intended for AM CATV signals.

Figure 10.4 – Typical Fiber Optic Receiver
(Photo courtesy of Force, Inc.)

This particular receiver uses an InGaAs PIN detector to receive the AM CATV signals. A highly linear impedance matched amplifier follows the PIN detector. Push-pull amplifiers are commonly used to achieve adequate levels of second-order distortion. High IP3 amplifiers minimize third-order distortion. In this case, the unit provides the optical input on connector J1. Connector J2 provides the RF connection to output the received AM CATV signal. Connector J3 is used to apply DC power to the module and also provides several status output signals. Connectors J4 and J5 connect to an RS-485 control bus which allows remote status and control access to the module. On the left side of the module, two visual indicators give a quick assessment of the unit's status.

Note that the receiver omits the warnings shown on the transmitter. Receivers, as passive devices, do not emit anything, including FCC-banned EM emissions. In addition, receivers contain detectors, not lasers, negating the need for FDA laser warnings on the label. However, the optical fiber which connects to the receiver has an optical output that can damage the human eye if the transmitter is in use. Again, do not look into the fiber end to see if it carries light. Instead, use an optical power meter, such as the one in Figure 10.5, to verify the optical output.

Figure 10.5 – Optical Power Meter
(Photo courtesy of Force, Inc.)

Basics of a Transceiver

A fiber optic transceiver combines a fiber optic transmitter and a fiber optic receiver into a single package. In some cases, the transceiver includes additional features such as open fiber output control, which reduces the laser output to eye-safe levels if the system loses contact with the mating transceiver. Some transceivers may also incorporate a WDM so that a single fiber can support bidirectional communication.

Small size (referred to as a footprint) usually dictates the use of a transceiver rather than a separate transmitter and receiver. The market currently offers a wide selection of open standard fiber optic transceivers, although nearly all handle digital data transmission only. Figure 10.6 illustrates a typical fiber optic transceiver.

Figure 10.6 – Typical Fiber Optic Transceiver
(Photo courtesy of Optical Communication Products, Inc.)

Understanding Specifications

Data sheets for fiber optic transmitters, receivers, and transceivers offer a number of key specifications for a fiber optic transmitter and fiber optic receiver that could be part of a fiber optic transceiver. Table 10.1 lists the performance parameters of the transmitter section, Table 10.2 lists the performance parameters of the receiver section, and Figure 10.7 shows a typical recommended application circuit for a fiber optic transceiver such as the one in Figure 10.6.

Table 10.1 – Typical Specifications for a Fiber Optic Transmitter

Laser Transmitter Characteristics (T= 0°C to +70°C, 50% Duty Cycle) Long Reach 1310 nm (MLM) FP Laser						
Parameter	**Symbol**	**Minimum**	**Typical**	**Maximum**	**Unit**
Wavelength	λ	1293	1310	1334	nm
Spectral Width[1]	$\Delta\lambda$			1.8	nm
Output Power[2]	P_O	-4.0	-1.6	+2.0	dBm
Extinction Ratio		11			dB
Data Rate		550	622	650	Mb/s
Rise/Fall Time (10%-90%)	$T_r\,T_f$			0.7	ns

Table 10.1 – Typical Specifications for a Fiber Optic Transmitter (Continued)

Laser Transmitter Characteristics (T= 0°C to +70°C, 50% Duty Cycle) Long Reach 1310 nm (MLM) FP Laser					
Parameter	**Symbol**	**Minimum**	**Typical**	**Maximum**	**Unit**
Random Jitter[3]				0.12	ns
Supply Voltage	V_{CC}	4.75	5.0	5.25	V
Supply Current	I_{CC}			135	mA
1. FWHM 2. Measured average power coupled into single-mode fiber. The minimum power specified is at Beginning-of-Life (BOL). 3. RMS value.					

The table header indicates that the transmitter section uses a "long reach" 1310 nm Fabry-Perot (FP) laser. Furthermore, the specifications listed in the balance of Table 10.1 are valid for ambient temperatures ranging from 0°C to +70°C and for a 50% duty cycle. The 50% duty cycle requirement causes serious limitations for serial digital video (SDV) applications because the nature of SDV requires long strings of zeros and ones, violating the 50% duty cycle specification.

The table lists wavelength first. In this case, the wavelength ranges from 1293 nm to 1334 nm, while 1310 nm represents the typical wavelength. This data does not provide any clues to how the wavelength will vary versus temperature or time, only that it will be somewhere within the specified window. The range of wavelengths can cause the fiber's optical loss to vary by a significant amount compared to the value published for 1310 nm. Next, the table gives a spectral width of 1.8 nm maximum. Footnote 1 tells us that the spectral width parameter is FWHM (Full Width Half Maximum). As we learned in an earlier chapter, the spectral width will lead to chromatic dispersion which will limit the bandwidth of the fiber and distort the pulses. The next specification, output power, can range from -4.0 dBm (0.4 mW) to +2.0 dBm (1.6 mW). The ramifications of this will become apparent shortly when we examine the receiver performance characteristics. The table lists an extinction ratio of 11 dB, meaning that the light level associated with a logic "1" is 11 dB (12.5 times) larger than the light level associated with a logic "0." The transmitter's data rate must fall between 550 Mb/s and 650 Mb/s, though the device was designed for an operating data rate of 622 Mb/s.

The rise/fall time parameter of 0.7 ns refers to the rise and fall time of the optical output signal. Usually this parameter refers to the 10% to 90% transition time. Occasionally, some vendors will use the 20% to 80% transition time. This leads to specifications that appear more favorable but do not actually improve performance. The next parameter is random jitter at 0.12 ns. According to footnote 3 this is an RMS number. This figure gives a measure of how "clean" the transition edges will be. Last, the table lists the supply voltage and supply current for the transmitter. This current will need to be added to the receiver current listed in the next table.

Table 10.2 lists the typical specifications for a fiber optic receiver. The table header tells us that the following performance parameters are valid only at +25°C. This immediately creates a disconnect with the transmitter, which specified a much wider temperature range. The wavelength range of the receiver is listed as 1,200 nm minimum to 1,550 nm maximum. We see from these numbers that the receiver operates with the full range of wavelengths generated by the transmitter.

Table 10.2 – Typical Specifications for a Fiber Optic Receiver

Receiver Characteristics (T= 25°C)					
Parameter	**Symbol**	**Minimum**	**Typical**	**Maximum**	**Unit**
Wavelength	λ	1200		1550	nm
Average Optical Sensitivity[1]	P_{MIN}	-28	-30		dBm
Average Max Input Power[1]	P_{MAX}			-5	dBm
Data Rate		100		700	Mb/s
Rise/Fall Times	$T_r T_f$			0.7	ns
Data Dependent Jitter				0.19	ns
Supply Voltage	V_{CC}	4.75	5.0	5.25	V
Supply Current	I_{CC}			145	mA
1. Specified in average optical input power and measured at 622 Mb/s and 1310 nm wavelength with 2^{23-1} PRBS.					

The next parameter, average optical sensitivity, is listed as -28 dBm minimum and -30 dBm maximum. For design purposes, we must use the minimum -28 dBm value in order to perform a worst case analysis. Unfortunately, this sample specification omits the BER that corresponds to the optical sensitivity. While we may guess that a BER of 10^{-9} is probably implied, it is important to recognize that this is only a guess. Next, the average maximum input power equals -5 dBm (0.32 mW). Referring back to Table 10.1, we see that the transmitter optical output power ranges from -4 dBm (0.4 mW) to +2 dBm (1.6 mW). This poses a serious problem for our system design. A low-loss optical fiber connecting the transmitter to the receiver will overdrive the receiver with too much optical power, causing errors or complete signal disruption. To avoid this, one must guarantee an optical loss of at least 7 dB between the transmitter and receiver. This reduces the transmitter maximum output of +2 dBm (1.6 mW) to -5 dBm (0.32 mW) to stay within the maximum limits of the receiver.

The average optical sensitivity, -28 dBm minimum, along with the minimum transmitter output power, implies a maximum optical loss between the transmitter and receiver of 24 dB (-4 dBm minus -28 dBm). However since we earlier determined a minimum optical loss of 7 dB, the optical dynamic range will be 17 dB (24 dB minus 7 dB). Therefore, a working data link requires at least 7 dB of optical loss between the transmitter and receiver and a maximum of 24 dB of optical loss. If a system designer overlooks the minimum optical loss or assumes that the transmitter outputs more than the specified power, the fiber optic link may not operate because of insufficient optical input to the receiver.

The next parameter listed, the data rate, has a minimum of 100 Mb/s and a maximum of 700 Mb/s. Two different receiver characteristics set these limits. The upper frequency limit of the detector, the preamplifier, and the digitizing circuitry set the maximum data rate limit. It relates, somewhat, to the rise and fall times that will be discussed next. One can intentionally limit the maximum data rate by limiting the preamplifier bandwidth. Excessive bandwidth will introduce excess noise, which will reduce the receiver sensitivity. Low bandwidth causes the receiver to produce large amounts of data dependent jitter (DDJ). The coupling capacitors between stages in the receiver typically set the minimum data rate. The coupling capacitors allow high frequency information to readily pass, but will block low frequency information. As a good rule of thumb, the -3 dB cutoff frequency set by these coupling capacitors must be at least 1/100th of the lowest transmitted data rate. In the case of this receiver, the -3 dB frequency must be less than 1 MHz. Digitized video signals, in order to successfully pass the pathological test codes associated with the standards, require a very low -3 dB frequency, sometimes below 1 kHz.

Table 10.2 cites the rise and fall times as 0.7 ns. When a data sheet specifies the rise and fall times with no other explanatory text, one usually assumes that the specification refers to the 10% to 90% rise or 90% to 10% fall time. For a system where a single pole dominates in setting the rise and fall time, the equivalent frequency is 0.35 divided by the rise or fall time, in this case, 500 MHz.

We alluded to data dependent jitter in our discussion of the maximum data rate and the bandwidth of the various elements in the receiver. A data stream can contain a wide range of frequency components. Consider a data stream running at 1 Gb/s. The fastest frequency component arises when one transmits alternating ones and zeros, in this case 500 MHz. If the data stream is modified so that there are alternating pairs of ones and zeros transmitted, the frequency drops to 250 MHz and so on. Longer consecutive ones and zeros result in ever lower frequencies. The analog portion of the receiver, usually the detector and the preamplifier, must have relatively flat frequency response over the full range of expected frequency components in order to have low data dependent jitter. This particular receiver has 0.19 ns of data dependent jitter. Last the table lists the power supply parameters. The receiver requires a steady supply voltage between +4.75 Volts and +5.25 Volts with a maximum power supply current of 145 mA.

Any application diagrams that a manufacturer may provide should be studied carefully. For example, Figure 10.7 shows the nine electrical pins of a fiber optic transceiver as well as the recommended way to connect those pins. In this diagram, pins 1 and 9 are ground, pins 5 and 6 are used to apply V_{CC}. While not explicitly shown, one of those two pins probably powers the transmitter section while the other powers the receiver section. The manufacturer recommends considerable bypassing and isolation on these power lines. The 10 μF capacitors take care of the low frequency noise. The inductor, "L," blocks high frequency noise and the 0.1 μF capacitors shunt any high frequency noise to ground and also provide a stable power supply to the transceiver during quick transients.

Pins 7 and 8 apply the data being transmitted to the transceiver. The transceiver requires a differential data signal as noted by TRANSMIT DATA and $\overline{\text{TRANSMIT DATA}}$. The receive data on pins two and three is also a differential data signal as noted by RECEIVE DATA and $\overline{\text{RECEIVE DATA}}$. When receiving light above a specific threshold, Pin 4 indicates the requirement of a 10 kOhm resistor to ground for proper operation.

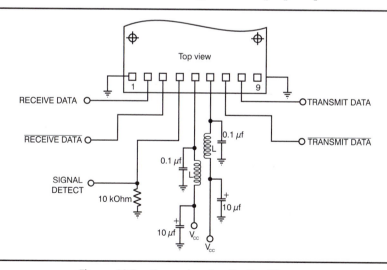

Figure 10.7 – Transceiver Application Diagram

Developing Specifications

A number of important points must be covered when specifying a fiber optic transmitter, receiver or transceiver. Table 10.3 outlines a fiber optic checklist, which helps address all the parameters in a logical manner.

Table 10.3 – Fiber Optic System Checklist

Optical Characteristics	
Fiber Type	SM, MM, 50/125 μm, MM, 62.5/125 μm typical.
Wavelength (nm)	Specify primary, secondary, other.
Attenuation (dB/km)	Specify attenu.ation @ 780 nm, 850 nm, 1310 nm, 1550 nm, or 1625 nm
Connector Type	ST, SC, SC/APC, FC, FC/APC typical.
End-to-End Optical Loss	Specify minimum and maximum loss values.
Types of Signals to Be Transmitted	
Analog Systems	Specify bandwidth (MHz), low frequency response (MHz), system SNR (dB), and the linearity requirements, which include differential gain (%), and differential phase (°).
Digital Systems	Specify coding scheme (NRZ, RZ, or Other); bit error rate (typically 10^{-9}, 10^{-10}, or 10^{-12}); and logic format (TTL, ECL, PECL, or other).
Other Transmission Specifications	Minimum, average, and peak required receiver optical input powers (dBm); maximum, average, and peak allowable receiver optical input power (dBm); and receiver dynamic range (dB).
Physical and Electrical Requirements	
Available Space for Equipment	Defines transmitter and receiver maximum length, width, and height.
Terminal Connections, Type and Number	RS-232, BNC, RCA, F, or other connection types typical. Specify number of each type in the system.
Packaging Requirements	Stand-alone package, PCB board mount package, rack-mount package (specify rack units or RU).
Power Supply Voltage	Specify voltages in AC (V) or DC (V) as well as frequency (Hz).
Power Supply Current	Specify current draw (mA), and power (W).
Equipment Location	Building, equipment closet, outside. Also specify distance between locations and cable routing requirements (intraduct, plenum, buried, aerial, etc.).
Operating Temperature Range	Specify a minimum and maximum operating temperature range.
Storage Temperature Range	Specify a minimum and maximum storage temperature range.

The design of fiber optic devices will greatly impact its usability in a given fiber optic system. In fiber optic video transmission, the nature of video and the nature of light have many parallels, but fiber faces a few challenges as well. The next chapter will discuss in detail the nature of video signals, and how their inherent characteristics define the advantages and challenges of using fiber optic transmission systems.

Chapter Summary

- Fiber optic transmitters use an electrical interface to encode data, and act as an electrical-to-optical converter.
- Transmitters may encode data using amplitude modulation, frequency modulation, or digital modulation.
- Common transmission wavelengths include 850 nm, 1310 nm, 1550 nm, and recently, 1625 nm.
- Fiber optic receivers act as optical-to-electrical converters, using the same modulation scheme as the transmitter, to change the received optical signal back into its original electrical video, audio, or data format.
- Transmitters and receivers may be stand-alone devices or integrated components of a system.
- Transmitters may require labels that state FCC emissions compliance and/or warn the user that the transmitter contains a laser.
- All fiber optic wavelengths are invisible to the human eye and may cause permanent damage on exposure, so one should use an optical power meter to verify optical output.
- Transceivers include a transmitter and a receiver in a single package.
- Some transceivers offer additional features, such as an open fiber output control, which reduces laser output to eye-safe levels, or a WDM to allow bidirectional communication on one fiber.
- Key specifications for transmitters include: wavelength, spectral width, output power, extinction ratio, data rate, rise/fall time, random jitter, power supply voltage, and power supply current.
- Key specifications for receivers include: wavelength, average optical sensitivity, average maximum input power, data rate, rise/fall time, data dependent jitter, power supply voltage, and power supply current.
- Key specifications for transceivers includes the parameters used by transmitters and receivers.

- A manufacturer's applications diagrams can convey much about the operation of a device, including how to make connections, and what types of bypassing and isolation the power lines may require.
- To develop specifications for a given application, one must consider optical requirements, the type of signal being transmitted, and the physical and electrical requirements and restrictions of the application.
- Fiber type, wavelength, attenuation, connector type, and end-to-end optical loss define the optical requirements of a given application.
- The specifications required in system design vary depending on whether the system is analog or digital.
- Physical requirements determine the overall size of the equipment as well as its location in the installation.

Chapter 11

The Nature of Video Signals

Video signals are exquisitely complex waveforms that encode several types of information about a scene. Typically a scene is scanned at the transmit end and converted into a number of lines or pixels per scene. The lines from the decomposed scene can be thought of as a series of pixels. Generally, a series of lines comprises a TV signal, while computer displays use a pixel-based configuration.

General Characteristics of all Video Formats

A usable video waveform conveys the following information:
- Brightness (luminance) of each pixel
- The color (hue) of each pixel
- Color saturation information
- Precise location of the pixel on the display

Of course, to keep the image's appearance smooth and continuous, each scene or frame must display a great number of pixels. In addition, in order to avoid flicker, the video signal must display a large number of images each second. Most human observers will not see flicker if the number of frames displayed each second exceeds approximately 48 frames. A motion picture film, for instance, shows 24 frames each second, but the light flashes twice for each frame making it appear like 48 frames per second. NTSC displays 60 images each second. It's like watching a slide show that advances very quickly.

NTSC

An NTSC frame consists of 525 lines, of which 486 are visible. The vertical retrace interval hides the remaining lines. An NTSC signal uses the unviewable lines for blanking, the time allotted to allow the electron beam from the lower right corner of the TV back to deflect back to the upper left corner in preparation for the next frame. In order to conserve bandwidth, the architects of the NTSC system chose to send only half of a frame, called a field, at a time. NTSC uses an interlaced scanning system to assemble two consecutive fields, field 1 and field 2, into a full frame. This trick reduces the required bandwidth by a factor of two without introducing the flicker caused by transmitting 30 full frames per second. Figure 11.1 shows the NTSC interlaced scanning pattern.

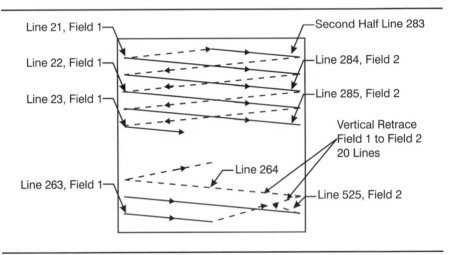

Figure 11.1 – Interlaced Scanning

Field 1 is displayed first starting with line 21. At the end of line 21, the image is momentarily blanked, and the horizontal retrace occurs (shown as a dashed line), resetting at the start of line 22. This continues to line 263. Halfway through line 263 the image is blanked, and the vertical retrace interval starts (shown as a dashed line). The image resets to the top center of the screen in preparation for field 2, which starts at the middle of line 283. Line 284 is positioned midway between lines 21 and 22, thus the term interlaced. This continues to line 525 when the vertical retrace interval starts in preparation for the next field 1. At 525 lines per frame, 30 frames per second, the image uses approximately 15,750 lines per second. (The exact frame rate, 29.97 frames per second, yields 15,734 lines per second.) Each line takes about 63.5 microseconds to draw.

Perception of flicker depends primarily upon two conditions: the brightness level of an image and the relative area of an image in a picture. The 30-Hz transmission rate for a full 525-line television frame compares to the highly successful 24-frame-per-second rate of motion-picture film. However, at the higher brightness levels produced on television screens, if all 486 lines (525 minus blanking lines) of a television image were presented sequentially as single frames, viewers would observe a disturbing flicker in picture areas of high brightness. Motion-picture projectors flash twice per frame to reduce the flicker effect. Interlaced scanning reduces video bandwidth compared to progressive scanning which scans the image in one frame. Progressive scanning of 525 lines would require completion in 1/60th second to achieve the same level of flicker perception, doubling the bandwidth for an equivalent number of pixels per line.

Modern TV Systems

Three main television standards exist throughout the world today. NTSC, written by the National Television Standards Committee, is the oldest existing standard, developed in the USA. First used in 1954, this standard consists of 525 lines and 60 fields per second. It may sometimes be referred to as "Never Twice the Same Color." Only two types of NTSC exists, known as NTSC-M and NTSC-N.

SECAM (système electronique pour couleur avec memoire) was developed in France and first used in 1967. It uses a 625-line, 50-field-per-second display and may be referred to as "Something Essentially Contrary to the American Method" or "Second Color Always Magenta!" Different types of SECAM use different video bandwidth and audio carrier specifications. VHF uses types B, D, K1, and L; UHF uses types G, K1, K, and L. These different types are generally not compatible.

PAL, an acronym for Phase Alternating (by) Line, was developed in the United Kingdom and Germany in 1967. It also uses a 625-line, 50-frame display. Proponents call it "Perfection At Last." Due to the cost of the enormous circuit complexity, critics often refer to it as "Pay A Lot." Different types use different video bandwidth and audio carrier specifications. Common types are B, G, and H; less common types include D, I, K, N, and M. As with SECAM, the different types are generally not compatible. These main TV systems have subtle and arguable differences. All the existing standards represent a compromise, and many efforts have been made over the years to address the shortcomings in each of the systems.

NTSC/525 — The Advantages

- Higher frame rate of 60 fields per second reduces visible flicker.
- Versatile color edits: NTSC allows the ability to edit any field without disturbing the color signal.
- Less inherent picture noise: Almost all pieces of video equipment achieve better signal to noise characteristics in NTSC/525 format than in PAL/625 format.

NTSC/525 — The Disadvantages

- Lower number of scan lines reduces clarity on large screen TVs, and makes the line structure more visible.
- Smaller luminance signal bandwidth: The use of a relatively low frequency (3.58 MHz) color subcarrier makes picture defects such as moire, cross-color, and dot interference more pronounced due to the greater likelihood of interaction between high-frequency elements in the monochrome picture signal and the lower color subcarrier frequency.
- Susceptibility to hue fluctuation: Variations in the color subcarrier phase cause shifts in the displayed color, requiring TV receivers to have a hue adjustment to compensate.
- Lower gamma ratio: The gamma value for NTSC/525 is set at 2.2 as opposed to the slightly higher 2.8 defined for PAL/625. This means that PAL/625 can produce pictures of greater contrast.
- Many NTSC TV receivers feature undesirable automatic features such as an auto-tint circuit to make hue fluctuations less visible to uncritical viewers. This circuit changes all colors approximate to flesh tone into a "standard" flesh tone, hiding the effects of hue fluctuation; these TVs cannot correctly display a certain range of color shades.

PAL/625 — The Advantages

- PAL's greater number of scan lines, 625, offers more picture detail.
- Wider luminance signal bandwidth: Placing the color subcarrier at 4.43 MHz allows the reproduction of a larger bandwidth of monochrome information, compared to NTSC/525, without interference effects.
- Stable hues: The reversal of subcarrier phase on alternate lines allows phase error correction by an equal and opposite error on the next line.
- Higher gamma ratio: The gamma value for PAL/625 is set at 2.8 as opposed to the lower 2.2 figure of NTSC/525. This permits a higher level of contrast than on NTSC/525 signals.

PAL/625 — The Disadvantages

- More flicker: The lower frame rate, 50 fields per second, makes flicker more noticeable on PAL/625 transmissions. This is more apparent for people accustomed to viewing NTSC/525 signals.
- Lower signal-to-noise ratio: The higher bandwidth requirements cause PAL/625 equipment to exhibit a slightly worse signal-to-noise performance than its equivalent NTSC/525 version.
- Loss of color editing accuracy: Due to the alternation of the phase of the color signal, it only reaches a common point once every eight fields/four frames. This reduces the accuracy of edits to only ±4 frames (8 fields).
- Variable color saturation: PAL achieves accurate color through cancelling out phase differences between the two signals, and the act of cancelling out errors reduces the color saturation while holding the hue stable. The human eye is far less sensitive to saturation variations than to hue variations, making this very much the lesser of two evils.

SECAM/625 — The Advantages

- SECAM's greater number of scan lines, 625, offers more picture detail.
- Stable hues and constant saturation: SECAM shares with PAL the ability to render images with the correct hue, and goes a step further in ensuring consistent saturation of color as well.

SECAM/625 — The Disadvantages

- Greater flicker as with PAL/625.
- Because studios cannot mix two synchronous SECAM color signals, most SECAM TV studios originate in PAL and must be transcoded into SECAM prior to broadcasting.
- Patterning effects: The FM subcarrier causes patterning effects even on non colored objects.
- Lower monochrome bandwidth: Because one of the two color subcarriers sits at 4.25 MHz (in the French version), SECAM carries a lower-bandwidth monochrome signal.
- Incompatibility between different versions of SECAM: SECAM is at least partially politically inspired and has a wide range of variants, many of which are incompatible with each other. For example, French SECAM uses FM subcarrier, and SECAM-M uses an AM subcarrier.

NTSC, PAL, and SECAM Formats Compared

Several international standards exist which specify the audio and video components of a waveform for use with television and video monitors that use a subcarrier for color or chrominance information. North America and Japan use the NTSC format, and European nations use either PAL or SECAM video formats. Table 11.1 compares the various video levels. Newer standards specify a voltage amplitude of 0.714 Volts, defined as 100 IRE units, between the blanking level and the white level for the video portion of the waveform (blanked video signal). The black to blank level (typically referred to as the setup), which shuts off the beam during the retrace time, varies between the formats. The total amplitude is about 140 IRE units for NTSC and 100% for PAL and SECAM, measured from sync tips to reference white for monochrome, with a saturated subcarrier. RS-170, an older standard, does not include a subcarrier for chrominance information. Computer graphics commonly use the RS-343A standard. Like RS-170, the standard does not use a subcarrier for color or chrominance information. Rather, three separate signals (red, green, and blue) are generated, each containing intensity and blanking information. Typically, only the green channel contains sync information.

Table 11.1 – Video Format IRE and Voltages

Standard	Video Output Levels	Value	Volts
Monochrome RS-343A	Blank to White	100 IRE	0.714 ± 1
	Blank to Black	7.5 ± 5 IRE	typ. 0.054
	Blank Level		0
	Blank to Sync	typ. 40 IRE	-0.286± 0.05
Monochrome RS-170	Blank to White	100 IRE	1.0 ± 0.05
	Blank to Black	7.5 ± 5 IRE	typ. 0.075
	Blank Level		0
	Blank to Sync	40 ± 5 IRE	typ. -0.4
NTSC RS-250C	Blank to White	100 IRE	0.714
	Blank to Black	7.5 ± 2.0 IRE	typ. 0.054
	Blank Level		0
	Blank to Sync	40 ± 5 IRE	typ. -0.286
PAL	Blank to White	70%	typ. 0.700
	Blank to Black	0%	0
	Blank Level		0
	Blank to Sync	-30%	typ. -0.300

Table 11.1 – Video Format IRE and Voltages (Continued)

Standard	Video Output Levels	Value	Volts
SECAM	Blank to White	70%	typ. 0.700
	Blank to Black	0%	0
	Blank Level		0
	Blank to Sync	-30%	typ. -0.300

Figure 11.2 illustrates a composite video waveform, showing the levels as given in Table 11.1.

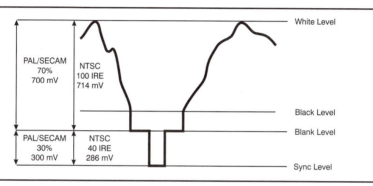

Figure 11.2 – Composite Video Waveform

Other items of interest when comparing the various video formats are the number of lines per frame, field frequency, and normal video bandwidth as listed in Table 11.2.

Table 11.2 – Comparison of Video Format Field Frequencies

	NTSC	PAL	SECAM
Number of Lines per Frame	525	625	625
Field Frequency	60	50	50
Luminance Bandwidth (MHz)	4.2	5	6
Chrominance Subcarrier (MHz)	3.58	4.43	4.3 to 4.4
Chrominance Bandwidth (MHz)	0.5 to 1.5	1.3	1.3

Since chrominance subcarrier formats generate output levels between blank and sync levels (to generate color burst information during the back porch time, explained later in this chapter), the sync and blank control inputs to most digital-to-analog converters cannot be used in such applications. The 20 IRE gap between sync and the most negative color burst level represents a 15% loss in gray-scale range just to encode the sync.

Table 11.3 provides a listing of the various video formats and the countries that use those standards at the time of this writing.

Table 11.3 – Countries and Television Formats

Format	Countries
NTSC-M	Antarctica, Antigua, Antilles, Aruba, Azores (U.S. Armed Forces), Bahamas, Belgium (U.S. Armed Forces), Belize, Bermuda, British Indian Ocean Territory (AF Diego Garcia TV – AFRTS), Burma, Cambodia, Canada, Cayman Islands, Chile, Colombia, Costa Rica, Cuba, Curacao, Diego Garcia, Dominica, Dominican Republic, Ecuador, El Salvador, Galapagos Islands, Germany (U.S. Armed Forces), Greenland (U.S. Armed Forces), Grenada, Guam, Guatemala, Haiti, Honduras, Jamaica, Japan, Johnstone Island, Korea (South), Leeward Islands, Marshall Islands, Mexico, Micronesia, Midway Island, Montserrat, Myanmar, Netherlands (U.S. Armed Forces), Nicaragua, North Mariana Island, Okinawa, Palau, Panama, Peru, Philippines, Puerto Rico, St. Grenadine, St. Kitts, St. Lucia, St. Vincent, Samoa (Eastern), Suriname, Taiwan, Tonga, Trinidad & Tobago, Turks & Caicos Islands, United States of America, Venezuela, Virgin Islands (U.S. and British), Yemen, Vietnam
NTSC-N	Barbados, Bolivia
PAL	Isle of Man, Sri Lanka
PAL-B	Abu Dhabi, Afghanistan, Algeria, Andorra, Australia, Azores, Bangladesh, Bhutan, Brunei Darussalam, Cameroon, Canary Islands, Cook Islands, Croatia, Easter Island, Estonia, Ethiopia, Equatorial Guinea, Gambia, Ghana, Gibraltar, Greece, Greenland, Fernando Po, Fiji, Finland, Indonesia, Laos, Madeira, Maldives, Mozambique, Nepal, New Zealand, Nigeria, Norfolk Island, Norway, Pakistan, Qatar, Saba and Sarawak, Samoa (Western), Seychelles, Slovakia, Sudan, Syria, Tanzania, Yemen
PAL-B/G	Albania, Austria, Bahrain, Bosnia, Cambodia, Cape Verde, Crete, Cyprus (Turkish), Czech Republic, Denmark, Dubai, Faroe Island, Germany, Hungary, Iceland, India, Israel, Italy, Jordan, Kampuchea, Kenya, Kuwait, Lebanon, Latvia, Liechtenstein, Lithuania, Luxembourg, Macedonia, Malawi, Malaysia, Malta, Montenegro, Netherlands, Norway, Oman, Papua New Guinea, Portugal, San Marino, Sao Tome, Saudi Arabia, Serbia, Sierra Leone, Singapore, Slovenia, Somalia, Spain, Sri Lanka, Swaziland, Sweden, Switzerland, Thailand, Turkey, Uganda, United Arab Emirates, Vatican, Yugoslavia, Zambia, Zimbabwe
PAL-B/H	Belgium, Liberia, Slovenia
PAL-D	China (People's Republic), Tibet
PAL-D/K	Estonia, Korea (North), Poland, Romania, Rwanda, Slovakia
PAL-G	Monaco, Syria
PAL-I	Angola, Ascension Islands, Botswana, Falkland Islands (Las Malvinas), Guinea (Bissau), Hong Kong, Ireland, Lesotho, Macao, Namibia, South Africa, United Kingdom, Zanzibar
PAL-K1	Niger
PAL-M	Brazil
PAL-N	Argentina, Aryenuna, Paraguay, Uruguay

Table 11.3 – Countries and Television Formats (Continued)

Format	Countries
SECAM-B	Afghanistan, Egypt, Equatorial Guinea, Estonia, Iraq, Lebanon, Mauritania, Mauritius, Morocco, Slovakia, Syria, Tunisia
SECAM-B/G	Cyprus, Guyana (Republic), Iran, Libya, Luxembourg, Saudi Arabia, Tunisia
SECAM-D	Bulgaria, Congo (People's Republic), Korea (North), Mongolia, Vietnam
SECAM-D/K	Argentina, Armenia, Azerbaijan, Belarus, Benin, Botswana, Burkina Estonia, Faso, Georgia, Kazakhstan, Kyrgyzstan, Latvia, Lithuania, Moldova (Moldavia), Russia, Rwanda, Slovakia, Tajikistan, Turkmenistan, Ukraine, Uzbekistan
SECAM-G	France (French Forces TV), Monaco
SECAM-K	Benin, Reunion, Zaire
SECAM-K1	Burundi, Central African Republic, Chad, Comoros, Cote D'Ivoire (Ivory Coast), Dahomey, Djibouti, Gabon, Guadeloupe, Guinea (Republic), Guyana (French), French Polynesia, Madagascar, Mali, Martinique, Mayotte, New Caldonia, Polynesia, St. Pierre Miquelon, Senegal, Society Islands, Tahiti, Togo, Wallis and Futuan, Upper Volta
SECAM-L	France, Luxembourg, Monaco

What Do the Specs Mean?

Literally dozens of specifications indicate the performance of a video signal, but this book will only cover few of the most important parameters. Figure 11.3 shows a single horizontal line of video including a sync pulse, a color burst signal, and the video information. The line ends at 63.5 μs and shows the leading edge of the next sync pulse.

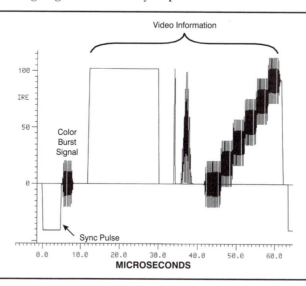

Figure 11.3 – Typical NTSC Composite Test Signal

Figure 11.4 shows an NTSC line of video in more detail. This figure focuses on the first third of the line to see the sync pulse, color burst, and other control features.

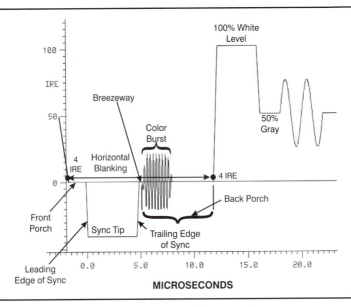

Figure 11.4 – Detail of an NTSC Line

The short zero IRE interval before the sync pulse is called the "front porch." The front porch starts when the video signal drops below four IRE. The leading edge of the sync pulse occurs at time zero. The sync tip (the top of the sync pulse) persists for about 4.75 μs followed by the trailing edge of the sync pulse. Another short zero IRE interval called the "breezeway" occurs after the sync pulse. The color burst signal, a 3.58 MHz sine wave, occurs next. The NTSC specification requires eight to eleven cycles of the waveform to be present. Another zero IRE interval follows the color burst. As soon as the level exceeds four IRE the waveform is then interpreted as actual video information. The time interval from the start of the breezeway to the point where the level exceeds four IRE is called the "back porch." The horizontal blanking interval consists of the entire interval from the start of the front porch of the sync pulse to the point where the video level exceeds four IRE.

Figure 11.5 (next page) shows an overview of the NTSC vertical sync mechanism which is considerably more complex than the horizontal sync mechanism. The lowest waveform represents the location of the vertical sync. The third and fourth waveforms show the inverted horizontal sync from Figure 11.4. Note that the horizontal sync shifts slightly from field 1 to field 2. This accounts for the fact that the interlaced fields shift by half of a line. The first and second lines show the actual vertical sync pulse pattern. There are subtle differences between the pattern of the pulses associated with the vertical sync for field 1 and field 2, which identify both fields.

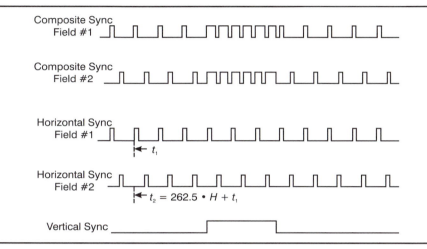

Figure 11.5 – Detail of a Vertical Sync Mechanism for NTSC

Figure 11.6 shows the signal processing steps used to derive the various drive and sync signals from a 3.579545 MHz crystal. These frequencies are synchronized to the composite video signal to allow accurate decoding.

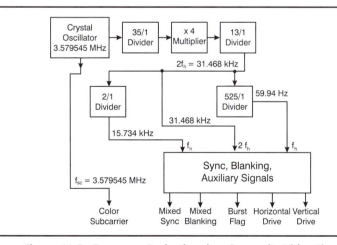

Figure 11.6 – Frequency Derivations in a Composite Video Signal

Typical NTSC Test Signals

Figure 11.7 shows one popular NTSC signal, the composite test signal. The start of the waveform resembles the structure associated with the horizontal blanking discussed in Figure 11.4. The first video feature in the composite test signal is a 100 IRE white reference level. This allows one to set video levels and measure short time and line time distortions. The next feature, the 2T pulse, can indicate the presence of short time distortions (pulse-to-bar ratio and K-factor measurements). The 12.5T pulse determines chrominance-to-luminance gain and delay. The last feature in the composite test signal is a modulated staircase which measures differential gain and differential phase.

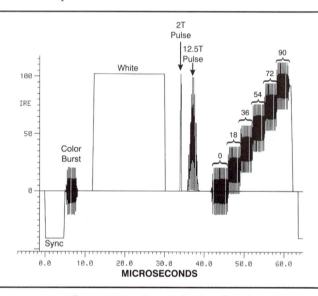

Figure 11.7 – Composite Test Signal

Another popular test signal, the combination test signal, starts out with the familiar horizontal blanking features followed by a 100 IRE white reference level. Next a series of six sine wave bursts with 50 IRE amplitude at frequencies of 0.5 MHz, 1.0 MHz, 2.0 MHz, 3.0 MHz, 3.58 MHz, and 4.2 MHz occurs. These six sine wave bursts measure the frequency response flatness of the system. The last three sine wave bursts, referred to as the "pink panther," have amplitudes of 20 IRE, 40 IRE, and 80 IRE. They measure chrominance nonlinear phase and gain as well as chrominance-to-luminance intermodulation. Figure 11.8 (next page) illustrates the combination test signal.

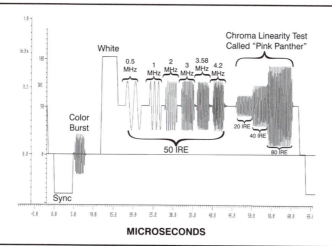

Figure 11.8 – Combination Test Signal

The next three figures show the effects of distortion or degradation on these same idealized video waveforms. Figure 11.9 shows the composite test signal with line time distortion. Note that the top of the white reference level slopes downward. This causes what should be a solid white bar to gradually change to light gray as the line is drawn on the monitor.

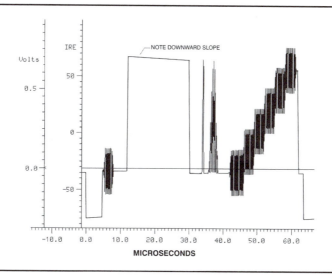

Figure 11.9 – Example of Line Time Distortion

Figure 11.10 shows the effect of field time distortion using a time frame of 30 ms. Only two complete fields, the levels of the sync pulse and back porch, are shown. Ideally these should be at levels of -40 IRE and zero IRE. The actual values range from correct, to about 12 IRE, too high. This distorts the brightness of the image from the top to the bottom of the screen.

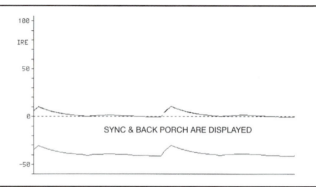

Figure 11.10 – Field Time Distortion

Figure 11.11 illustrates a very noisy version of the combination test signal. An AM fiber optic video link transmitted this signal, with a great deal of optical loss between the transmitter and the receiver. This loss translates into noise that results in a low signal-to-noise ratio, about 40 dB, in the link, which manifests itself as a "snowy" picture.

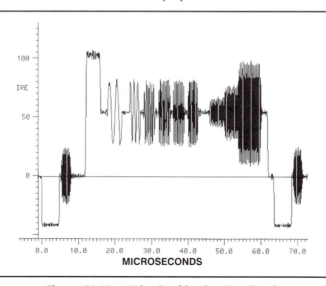

Figure 11.11 – Noisy Combination Test Signal

The last important NTSC test signal, the color bar test pattern in Figure 11.12, allows precise adjustment of the video monitor. Many instances of "bad" video can be traced to an improperly adjusted monitor.

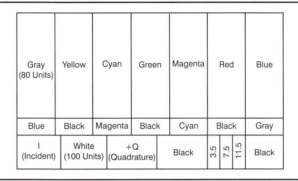

Gray (80 Units)	Yellow	Cyan	Green	Magenta	Red	Blue
Blue	Black	Magenta	Black	Cyan	Black	Gray
I (Incident)	White (100 Units)	+Q (Quadrature)	Black	3.5 7.5 11.5		Black

Figure 11.12 – Standard Color Bar Pattern

How to Adjust a Color Monitor

Without proper adjustment, a monitor will display an inferior picture. Follow the steps below to adjust a video monitor or TV.

1. Power the monitor or TV and allow the device to warm up.
2. Lower the lights in the room to eliminate any reflections in the monitor.
3. Display the color bars on the TV or monitor.
4. Set the contrast control, also called "picture," to its midpoint.
5. Turn the chroma control, also called "color," all the way down until the color bars are shades of black and white.
6. Locate the three narrow PLUGE bars (Picture LineUp Generating Equipment), and the numbers representing IRE units. Adjust the brightness control until the middle (7.5 units) PLUGE bar is not quite visible. The lightest PLUGE bar on the right (11.5 units) should be barely visible. If the 11.5 units PLUGE bar is not visible, turn the brightness up until it becomes visible.
7. Set the contrast control to the proper white level by turning the contrast completely up until the white bar (100 units) blooms and flares. Turn the contrast down until this white bar just begins to change.

Introduction to Digital Television (DTV)

The Evolution from Analog to Digital

For many years broadcasters have used digital techniques for devices such as timebase correctors, frame synchronizers, and special effects mixers. This created a problem with an analog-based signal; each time the system used one of these digital signal processing units, it had to use analog-to-digital (A/D) and digital-to-analog (D/A) conversion processes. These conversions affected signal quality and also added cost. As the suite of digital signal processing units increased to include still stores and complex computer-generated graphics, it started to make more sense to keep the video and audio signal in the digital domain to avoid multiple the A/D and D/A conversions. Today, digitized video signals allow the delivery of up to 500 digitally compressed television channels by satellite.

Four Video Formats

Television systems fit one of four categories: NTSC/PAL/SECAM; RGB/ Y, R-Y, B-Y, $4f_{sc}$; and 4:2:2 (CCIR.601) as shown in Table 11.4.

Table 11.4 – Classification of Four Video Formats

	Composite	Component
Analog	NTSC, PAL, SECAM	RGB (Y, R-Y, B-Y)
Digital	$4f_{SC}$	4:2:2 (CCIR.601)

The table shows the classification of these four video formats. Composite analog signals include NTSC, PAL, and SECAM. One signal encodes both luminance and the color information, so the composite signal requires only one piece of coaxial cable for distribution. RGB, which drives computer monitors, uses a component analog format. The format $4f_{SC}$ is a common composite digital format, and 4:2:2 is a common component digital format and serves as the basis of most digital video techniques in use today.

Inevitably, the process of encoding causes some loss of picture quality. Let us look first at component television, which represents how a video signal starts out in the camera. The component signals RGB (red, green, and blue), or luminance (Y) and color difference signals (R-Y, and B-Y) require three separate coax transmission cables. This yields the highest possible video quality, but it is inconvenient. In addition, all of these analog signals can pick up noise and may experience nonlinearities which lead to signal degradation. Noise pickup and distortion accumulate in analog systems, slowly degrading the signal as it is processed multiple times. Digital technology keeps television pictures clean, even through multigeneration recording and transmission, one of DTV's key advantages. One can digitize either composite or component signals.

Digitizing Composite Video

An analog composite video signal, whether NTSC, PAL or SECAM, starts with the black level at 0 mV and climbs up to 700 mV or 714 mV at peak white. Consider a video signal starting at black level on the left of the

TV screen and rising to peak white at the right-hand side. A waveform monitor will show a smooth slope. Now, when digitizing the waveform, take eight samples of the analog level, representing 89.3 mV each. When we try to reproduce this slope from the digitized information using only eight levels the slope becomes a coarse staircase! Therefore, it requires many more than eight levels of the analog video signal to digitize a signal for faithful reproduction.

A digital signal, represented by one bit, has two levels, on and off. A 2-bit word can have 2^2, or four levels. A 4-bit signal has 2^4 (16) levels, and so on. Digitized video signals often use ten bits. A 10-bit digital video word contains samples from 2^{10} levels, or 1,024 discrete video levels, making each step now approximately 0.714 mV. This reduces the size of each stair step and allows us to generate a fairly accurate reproduction of the smooth ramp. Sampling theory requires digitizing the analog video signal at a rate at least twice as high as the highest frequency in the analog video signal. In reality, setting the sampling rate to a higher value than the theoretical minimum simplifies the design of the required filters. Composite digital television often uses a clocking frequency of four times the subcarrier frequency ($4f_{SC}$). NTSC uses a color subcarrier frequency of 3.58 MHz, and PAL uses a frequency of 4.43 MHz. So for an NTSC signal, we take samples at 14.3 MHz (4 x 3.58 MHz), while in PAL, $4f_{SC}$ we take samples at 17.7 MHz.

Component Digital Video

The CCIR.601 standard defines a scheme for digitizing component video signals. Component video has no subcarrier, and it uses a sampling, or clocking, frequency of 13.5 MHz for both the 525 and 625-line worlds. The luminance channel (Y) is sampled at 13.5 megasamples per second (MS/s), and each of the two, less detailed chrominance (color difference channels) (R-Y) and (B-Y) are sampled at half that rate, 6.75 MS/s. If 13.5 MHz is four times the frequency of some imaginary subcarrier (at 3.375 MHz), then 6.75 MHz would be two times the same frequency. The ratio of 13.5 MS/s and the two chrominance sampling frequencies of 6.75 MS/s to the imaginary subcarrier frequency of 3.375 MHz is known as 4:2:2 digital component television. If you add these three frequencies together [13.5 MHz for luminance, 6.75 MHz for the (R-Y) chrominance channel, and 6.75 MHz for the (B-Y) chrominance channel] you get 27 MHz, a very important number, as the majority of digital work is currently based on 27 MHz, which generates 27 million 10-bit words each second. With this international standardization, the only significant difference between NTSC and PAL that remains in the component digital world is the number of TV lines, 525 versus 625.

Figure 11.13 illustrates the digital chrominance-luminance sampling used in 4:2:2, 4:1:1, and 4:2:0 formats. In 4:2:2, each square, whether empty or filled with a gray circle represents a single pixel where luminance (Y), or pixel brightness, is sampled 13.5 million times each second. The color, chrominance, is only sampled every other column in the 4:2:2 sampling scheme. So half of the color detail is thrown away and the same color is used for two columns when the image is reconstructed.

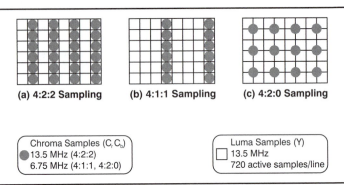

(a) 4:2:2 Sampling   (b) 4:1:1 Sampling   (c) 4:2:0 Sampling

Chroma Samples (C_r C_b)
● 13.5 MHz (4:2:2)
  6.75 MHz (4:1:1, 4:2:0)

Luma Samples (Y)
□ 13.5 MHz
  720 active samples/line

Figure 11.13 – Chrominance-Luminance Sampling

Figure 11.13b shows the 4:1:1 sampling scheme. Like 4:2:2, the luminance is sampled every pixel at a 13.5 MHz rate. In 4:1:1, the chrominance is only sampled every 4th column, effectively discarding 75% of the color information. The last method, 4:2:0, shown in Figure 11.13c, is widely used in consumer applications. Again, the luminance is sampled 13.5 million times each second. The chrominance is sampled at one-fourth the rate of the luminance, or 3.375 MHz for C_r and 3.375 MHz for C_b, the same as 4:1:1 sampling. While 4:2:0 has the same chrominance sampling rate as 4:1:1, it can be seen in Figure 11.13c that 4:2:0 sampling provides balanced bandwidth in the horizontal and vertical directions, whereas 4:1:1 chrominance sampling has four times higher vertical resolution than horizontal resolution.

Serializing and Deserializing

Now that we can generate 27 million 10-bit words each second, the next question becomes: How do we send these digital signals down cables? We could send all ten bits down ten pairs of wires in a parallel cable in much the same way as a home computer uses a parallel port to communicate with the printer. Ten parallel paths offer fast communication, but the need to route and distribute these signals throughout a broadcast studio makes this solution impractical. Further research led to the development of serializer and deserializer chip sets. The serializer and deserializer chip sets take the 27 million 10-bit words each second and convert them into a single bit stream at 270 Mb/s and back again. The NTSC serial bit rate becomes 10 bits/word x 14.3 MWords/s or 143 Mbits/sec (177 Mbits/sec in PAL), and for 4:2:2 component it is 270 Mbits/sec.

SMPTE document 259M defines this bit rate, described as a serial digital interface (SDI). (The SMPTE 259M document actually covers both 4:2:2 and $4f_{SC}$, but the term SDI is commonly becoming associated with component serial digital interface. We shall use SDI to refer to a component serial interface.) The SDI (component) signal carries clean video and it is much easier to route around the TV studio.

Digitizing Video Signals

Movies and television have always sought to provide the human observer with a convincing representation of reality. What viewers perceive to be continuously moving pictures actually contain sequences of still photographs. The pictures change often enough to convince the eye that the image is real, continuous movement. Television draws only half of the picture (a field), relying on the persistence of human vision to create the illusion of a complete moving picture, when actually only three electron beams in a cathode ray tube move. Nevertheless, viewers find the results quite acceptable.

A digital video signal, while free of noise and very robust, occupies too much bandwidth for economical tape or disk recording or transmission over the air. With the advent of digital television, engineers have had to devise more tricks to compress digital video. Fortunately, most television pictures contain a lot of repetitive detail in plain backgrounds, blue sky, and common successive frames. A digital signal can discard this detail without the eye noticing, a process called digital video compression.

JPEG, MPEG, and MPEG-2

The computer industry used lossless data compression techniques for many years to pack more data onto hard disks and increase transmission speed over modems. Lossless compression techniques, as the name implies, can restore a compressed data file to its exact initial uncompressed state. Unfortunately, lossless data compression techniques do not work well with video and data since they may only compress the data by a factor of two or four times. Video, unlike computer data, could tolerate a lossy compression algorithm because of the redundancies that exist in any picture. The computer industry first came up with the Joint Photographic Experts Group (JPEG) standard for compressing high-resolution digital still pictures. The

Moving Picture Experts Group (MPEG) was formed in 1988 to determine international standards for the digital compression of moving pictures.

Computer imaging now uses motion JPEG and MPEG techniques, and they can be very cost-effective for disk recording, CD-ROMs, etc., but neither offer optimum results for broadcasting. What has emerged, however, is MPEG-2 (an ISO/IEC ratified standard). The industry adopted this standard very quickly, driven by the strong desire to provide viewers with a huge choice of programs delivered direct-to-home (DTH) via satellite or cable TV, using set-top decoders. MPEG-2 encoding is based on an integrated circuit chip set pioneered by C-Cube Microsystems. Compression techniques continue to evolve, but regardless of whether or not the system offers the ultimate method of compression for digital video, television engineers cannot afford to ignore MPEG-2 as a widely accepted data-reduction system.

The Challenge of Compression

As the purist will testify, one cannot compress video to any extent with a lossy compression algorithm, without throwing away something and reducing the picture quality. Fortunately, however, the human visual system can be easily fooled. One can achieve impressive results by choosing compression techniques that selectively discard information the eye is unlikely to notice. Two basic types of digital video compression techniques include spatial compression, e.g., discrete-cosine transform (DCT), and temporal compression, which includes encoding changes between frames, as well as motion estimation and compensation. JPEG uses only spatial encoding, MPEG uses both spatial and temporal encoding.

Each digital television picture contains a finite number of pixels, as listed in Table 11.5.

Table 11.5 – Bit Rates for the Active Part of a Digital Video Signal

Format	Pixels x Lines x Frames x Bits	Serial Bit Rate
NTSC	720 x 486 x 29.97 x 16	167.8 Mb/s
PAL	720 x 576 x 25 x 16	165.9 Mb/s

Conventional 4:2:2 NTSC and PAL television contains 720 pixels along the active part of each horizontal line. NTSC uses 486 active lines/frame (576 active lines in PAL) and 30 frames/sec (25 in PAL). Each pixel is made up of eight bits for luminance (brightness) and four bits each for the two color-difference signals (R-Y and B-Y, also known as C_r and C_b), for a total of 16 bits.

MPEG-2 reduces these bit rates primarily in two areas of the motion picture: the information in each frame (spatial — relating to space, e.g., a blue sky), and details that do not change from frame to frame (temporal — relating to time). This compression technique encompasses multiple levels from compressed data rates of less than 4 Mb/s through conventional TV at 6 to 15 Mb/s and high-definition television operating at up to 80 Mb/s. Table 11.6 shows the levels supported by MPEG-2.

Table 11.6 – MPEG-2 Profiles and Levels

Level	Data Rate	Spatial Resolution Layer	Profiles					
			Simple	Main	SNR	Spatial	High	
High	80 Mb/s	Enhancement	1920 x 1152				1920 x 1152	Lines x Pixels
			60				60	Frames/Sec
		Lower					960 x 576	Lines x Pixels
							30	Frames/Sec
High - 1440	60 Mb/s	Enhancement		1440 x 1152		1440 x 1152	1440 x 1152	Lines x Pixels
				60		60	60	Frames/Sec
		Lower				720 x 576	720 x 576	Lines x Pixels
						30	30	Frames/Sec
Main	15 Mb/s	Enhancement	720 x 576	720 x 576	720 x 576		720 x 576	Lines x Pixels
			30	30	30		30	Frames/Sec
		Lower				352 x 288		Lines x Pixels
						30		Frames/Sec
Low	4 Mb/s	Enhancement		352 x 288	352 x 288			Lines x Pixels
				30	30			Frames/Sec
		Lower						Lines x Pixels
								Frames/Sec

MPEG-2 also provides flexibility in the type of compression used for each level. Compression types, known as profiles, may vary from use of the full 4:2:2 signal at the high end to the elimination of complete frames at the simple end. Encoders can vary considerably depending on the application, so details of the encoding scheme must be transmitted along with the data to enable the decoder to reconstruct the signal. In this way encoder designs can handle the various levels using different profiles while keeping the cost of the decoders to a minimum for the desired application. Most commercial broadcasters uses the main profile at the main level (MP@ML).

Layers and Scalability

One of the most ingenious features of MPEG-2 is its ability to transmit video signals of widely ranging quality. A relatively inexpensive MPEG-2 decoder can reconstruct a useful picture by using only part of the encoded video bitstream, the rest of the data being reserved for quality enhancements. Coded video data consists of a series of video bitstreams called layers. The first layer, the base layer, can always be decoded independently. The other layers are called enhancement layers.

Enhancement layers may be used for spatial, temporal, and other scalable extensions. Scalable video has two layers of coded video data, whereas a non scalable video bitstream contains only one layer. Scalability makes the video more resilient to transmission errors. Critical base layer information uses the transmission paths with the best error performance while the enhancement layer data can use a channel with inferior error performance.

Video Bitstream

The video bitstream is made up of blocks of pixels, macroblocks (MB), pictures, groups of pictures (GOP), and video sequences, as follows in ascending order: block, macroblock, slice, picture, group of pictures, video sequence. Figure 11.14 illustrates the video bitstream. The smallest element, a block, consists of eight lines by eight pixels per line (8 x 8). Blocks are grouped into macroblocks (MB), according to one of the MPEG-2 predefined profiles. The 4:2:0 macroblock format has four blocks for luminance, one block for C_r, and one block for C_b. The 4:2:2 MB format has four luminance blocks, two C_r blocks, and two C_b blocks. The 4:4:4 has four luminance blocks, four C_r blocks, and four C_b blocks.

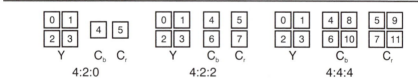

Figure 11.14 – Macroblock Structures

A 4:2:2 MB will contain eight blocks (8 x 8 x 8 = 512 pixels). Slices, strings of macroblocks arranged horizontally along the raster, can vary in length from a minimum of one macroblock to a maximum of one line. Pictures and groups of pictures will be examined during our discussions about temporal compression.

Temporal Compression

Temporal compression minimizes the duplication of data contained in successive pictures by transmitting motion vector data and some difference information, rather than the whole picture over again. To facilitate motion predicting, MPEG-2 separates the video into three types of pictures: I (Intracoded) pictures, P (Predictive coded) pictures, B (Bidirectionally interpolated) pictures. I-pictures, the key reference for the other two picture types, use spatial compression to compress the information in a single chosen field or frame. Temporal compression achieves bit rate reduction by noting changes between fields and converting them into motion vectors, which are encoded into data for later interception by the decoder. Changes are transmitted in the form of P-pictures and B-pictures. P-pictures are predicted directly from the previous I-picture. B-pictures are derived using either I-picture or P-picture information and these reference sources may be either ahead of or behind the B-picture. Hence the term bidirectional interpolation.

The three types of pictures are transmitted sequentially in a group of pictures (GOP), as shown in Figure 11.15; an I-picture always appears first (shaded gray in the figure). A GOP typically contains 12 pictures, but some encoders can detect changes between successive fields. If the change is substantial, the encoder assumes that the scene has changed and forces a new I-picture. This causes the sequence to start over again. The GOPs are sent in a video sequence that contains data defining picture size, rates, and quantization matrices. The video sequence and all elements, down to the slice size, provide unique start codes to facilitate detection by the decoder. Compression ratios of up to 10:1 can still be achieved using JPEG. MPEG-2 can achieve compression ratios in the order of 25:1and is considered a distribution-quality compression format.

Figure 11.15 – Typical Group of Pictures (GOP)

Spatial Compression

The word spatial refers to the space in a single picture. Spatial compression minimizes the duplication of data in each picture. The technique achieves bit rate reduction by first transforming the video data from the space and time domain into the frequency domain using the discrete-cosine transform (DCT) method (a trigonometric formula derived from Fourier analysis theory, which is described further in Chapter 15) and then applying quantization and variable length coding techniques to reduce the bit rate. Figure 11.16 illustrates a typical video encoder block diagram.

Figure 11.16 – Digital Video Encoder

A time-based device, such as a waveform monitor, normally displays video. However, to accomplish data reduction, we must transform the video data into the frequency domain. DCT transforms the data in each block of 8 x 8 pixels into blocks of 8 x 8 frequency coefficients. In the frequency domain, low frequencies represent most of the noticeable high energy picture elements while higher frequencies represent the less important details (Figure 11.17). So far in the encoding process, we have discarded no bits.

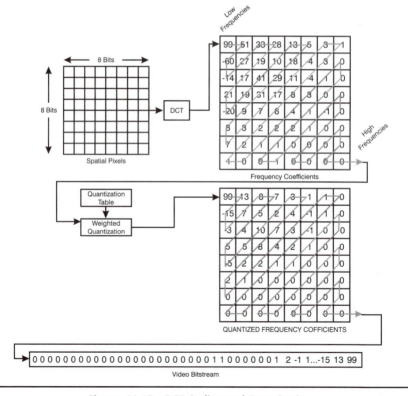

Figure 11.17 – DCT Coding and Quantization

After DCT encoding, the data is subjected to a quantization process, weighted to reduce data in the high frequency areas, where the eye is less sensitive. We use more bits per pixel to quantize the important low-frequency coefficients and fewer bits per pixel for the high-frequency coefficients. We quantize the DC components at ten bits; coarser quantization of very low frequencies cause the blocks themselves to become visible in the pictures as we will see shortly. To create the compressed video bitstream, the 64 frequency coefficients are scanned in a zig-zag fashion from top left to bottom right and, as can be seen from Figure 11.17, strings of zeros represent the high-frequency areas.

We achieve further data reduction by transmitting only the number of zeros instead of the usual values of the coefficients. The last stage in the spatial compression process employs variable length coding (VLC). VLC assigns shorter code words to frequently occurring events and longer code words to less frequent events; it is also reversible. JPEG and MPEG systems use these methods of spatial compression for bit rate reduction.

Figures 11.18a and 11.18b show the results of very high compression of an image. Figure 11.18a shows the uncompressed image. In Figure 11.18b, the 8 x 8 DCT algorithm has been applied and the compression level has been set very high. This discards almost all of the high-frequency information resulting in very visible 8 x 8 blocks and poor image quality.

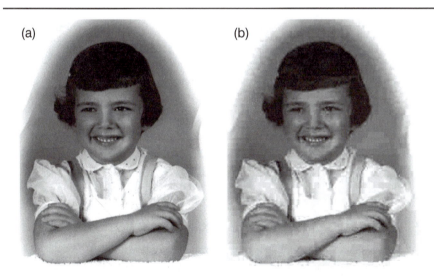

(a)   (b)

Figure 11.18 – An Uncompressed Image versus a Highly Compressed Image Showing Visible 8 x 8 Blocks

Program Streams and Transport Streams

After compressing the video, the audio, video, and system information is multiplexed together. This technique normally uses two audio/video multiplexers. One takes the video and audio packetized elementary streams (PES) and produces the program stream, and the other uses the same data to generate the transport stream. Figure 11.19 shows how this process works. Robust transmission paths normally carry program streams where errors are less likely to occur. The program stream data packets may vary in length and can contain a relatively large number of bytes.

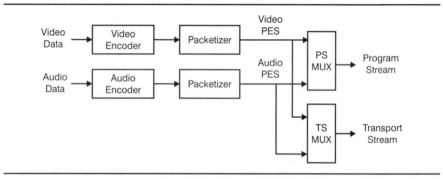

Figure 11.19 – Audio and Video Multiplexing

A transport stream, on the other hand, can contain one or many programs with one or many independent time bases, allowing the multiplexing of multiple TV channels. Transport stream packets find use where errors will most likely occur, and they are always 188 bytes in length. Figure 11.20 illustrates this transport stream.

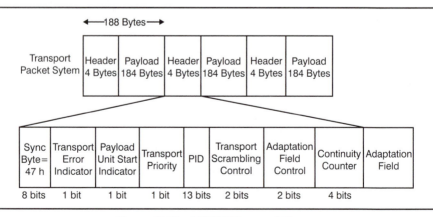

Figure 11.20 – MPEG-2 Transport Stream

MPEG-4 and Future Directions

Any future that involves digitized video will clearly use video compression. While MPEG-2 is a very successful protocol, it does not always give the best possible results. Newer algorithms offer the potential for better quality at the same data rate or even lower data rates, with the same quality. MPEG-4, a newly developed standard, uses a technique called wavelets rather than the 8 x 8 DCT algorithm. The wavelet technique tends to produce compressed images with less visible artifacts than the 8 x 8 DCT technique. As computers and related chips become faster, it will be possible to implement and deploy ever more complex video compression algorithms.

Component Analog Video Formats

Recent trends for video formats have moved to component analog video (CAV) formats, much like the RGB format used in most computer graphics systems. Table 11.7 summarizes the major video equipment CAV formats currently in use. These values use the standard color saturation level of 75%, the common limit to the amplitude range of the chrominance subcarrier in the NTSC format.

Table 11.7 – Component Analog Video Formats

Format	Video Output Function	Signal Amplitude (Volts)	Comments
GRB	G, R, B	+0.700 +0.300	At 100% saturation, 0% setup three wire = (G+sync), (R+sync), (B+sync)
Betacam (1)	Y Sync R-Y, B-Y	+0.714 -0.286 ± 0.350	At 75% saturation, 7.5% setup on Y only three wire = (Y+sync), (R-Y), (B-Y)
Betacam (1)	Y Sync CTDM R-Y CTDM B-Y Sync	+0.714 -0.286 ± 0.350 ± 0.350 -0.630	At 100% saturation, 7.5% setup on Y only two wire = (Y+sync) [CTDM (R-Y), (B-Y+sync)]
MII (2)	Y Sync R-Y B-Y	+0.700 -0.300 ± 0.324 ± 0.324	At 100% saturation, 7.5% setup on Y only three wire = (Y+sync) CTCM (R-Y), (B-Y+sync)
MII (2)	Y Sync CTCM R-Y CTCM B-Y Sync	+0.700 -0.300 ± 0.350 ± 0.250 -0.650	At 75% saturation, 7.5% setup on Y only two wire = (Y+sync), CTCM (R-Y), (B-Y+sync)

Table 11.7 – Component Analog Video Formats (Continued)

Format	Video Output Function	Signal Amplitude (Volts)	Comments
SMPTE	Y Sync PB PR	+0.700 -0.300 ± 0.350 ± 0.350	At 100% saturation, 0% setup three wire = (Y+sync), PB, PR
(1) Trademark of Sony Corporation. (2) Trademark of Matsushita Corporation.			

GRB is the matrix decoded version of NTSC with sync added to all three channels, which may be extended to 700 mV gray scale at 100% saturation with a PLUGE offset for monitor black/white adjust. Reversal of the non complex RGB to GRB format is consistent with the green signal corresponding to the Y or luminance signal in the other color difference (B-Y and R-Y) formats. Betacam and MII are popular Sony and Matsushita formats. Each format comes in a 3-wire or 2-wire version and involves the component time-division multiplexed CTDM (3-wire) or CTCM (2-wire) nomenclature. The Society for Motion Picture and Television Engineers (SMPTE) and the European Broadcasting Union (EBU) have adopted their own color difference formats to remove brand name association. Most CAV formats sample the color difference components at half the rate or bandwidth of the luminance signal (the common 4:2:2 hierarchy, not to be confused with the RS-422 interface). Most CAV formats do not use the 7.5 IRE setup used in NTSC, which represents a 7.5% loss in dynamic range. Consequently, the newer CAV standards (GRB and SMPTE/EBU) call for no setup pedestal.

Up to this point, this book has covered the basic principles of both video transmission and fiber optic transmission. The next chapter will describe in detail methods of amplitude modulated fiber optic video transmission.

Chapter Summary

• All video formats convey information about the brightness of each pixel, the color of each pixel, the color saturation, and the precise location of each pixel on the display.

• Three main television standards used throughout the world today are NTSC, PAL, and SECAM.

• NTSC uses an interlaced scanning pattern that scans 525 lines per frame, 30 frames per second, offering a higher frame rate to reduce visible flicker, versatile color edits, and less inherent picture noise; however, the low number of scan lines reduces clarity, a smaller luminance signal bandwidth increases the likelihood of picture defects, and this format can experience phase shifts in the displayed color.

- PAL formats use a greater number of scan lines, giving the picture greater clarity, and they have a wider luminance signal bandwidth, a high gamma ratio, and stable hues; on the other hand, the lower frame rate increases visible flicker, lowers signal-to-noise ratio, decreases color editing accuracy, and varies color saturation.
- SECAM has stable hues, and constant saturation, and the higher scan line rate increases clarity, but SECAM also experiences increased visible flicker, patterning effects caused by the FM subcarrier, and low monochrome signal bandwidth.
- Key features of various video formats include: frame rate, field rate, aspect ratio, color system, scan lines, subcarrier frequency, and applicable TV standard.
- Worldwide, nations uses two versions of NTSC, one of 14 versions of PAL, or one of eight versions of SECAM.
- A typical line of an NTSC video composite test signal includes a sync pulse, a color burst signal, and the actual video information.
- A composite test signal offers a white reference level at 100 IRE that allows one to set video levels and measure short time distortion and line time distortion, a 2T pulse that detects short time distortion, a 12.5T pulse, which determines chrominance-luminance gain and delay, and a modulated staircase that measures the signal's differential gain and differential phase.
- Line time distortion causes the white bar of a color bar pattern to gradually turn to light gray as the line is drawn on the monitor.
- Field time distortion shifts each field away from its ideal level.
- Digital video signals fall into one of a number of categories: analog composite NTSC/PAL/SECAM; digital composite $4f_{sc}$; analog component RGB, Y, R-Y, B-Y; and digital component 4:2:2.
- Component signals have no subcarrier, unlike composite signals.
- Digital video compression removes repetitive detail from successive frames in a video signal to reduce the required bandwidth.
- Motion JPEG and MPEG techniques find extensive use in computer imaging.
- MPEG-2 offers broadcast quality video transmission.
- Two digital video compression techniques include spatial encoding, usually a discrete cosine transform, and temporal encoding which involves encoding changes between frames, and motion estimation and compensation.
- JPEG uses only spatial encoding while MPEG uses both spatial and temporal coding.

- MPEG-2 covers data rates of 4 Mb/s to 15 Mb/s for conventional signals and up to 80 Mb/s for HDTV operation and can transmit signals of varying quality using layers; the base layer which contains the essential information can be decoded independently from the enhancement layers which add details to the image.

- A coded video signal with only one layer is said to be non scalable while a signal with two or more layers is considered scalable.

- A digital video bitstream is made up of blocks of pixels, macroblocks (MB), groups of pictures (GOP), and video sequences.

- A block in a digital video bitstream contains eight lines by eight pixels per line (8 x 8).

- Blocks are grouped into macroblocks based on one of the MPEG-2 predefined profiles: 4:2:0, 4:2:2, or 4:4:4.

- Temporal compression minimizes the duplication of data contained in successive frames by transmitting motion vector data and some difference information, rather than repeating the entire image.

- MPEG-2 divides the video bitstream into three different types of signals to achieve temporal compression: intracoded (I) pictures, predictive (P) coded pictures, and bidirectionally (B) interpolated pictures, which are transmitted sequentially in a group of pictures, which typically includes twelve pictures, the first of which is always an I picture type.

- Spatial compression achieves bit reduction by transforming the video data from the space and time domain into the frequency domain using a discrete cosine transform (DCT) method and then applying quantization and variable length coding techniques.

- In the quantization step, DCT uses more bits per pixel to quantize the important low-frequency coefficients and fewer bits per pixel for the high-frequency coefficients; DCT components are normally quantized at 10-bits because at a coarser bit rate, the 8 x 8 blocks become visible in the pictures.

- The high-frequency coefficients are scanned from top left to bottom right, allowing further data reduction by transmitting only the number of zeros in the stream, and not the usual coefficient values.

- Variable length coding assigns shorter code words for frequently occurring events and longer code words for less frequent events.

- Once the video is compressed, the video, audio, and system information must be multiplexed into a program stream carrying data packets of varying lengths of information, and a transport stream which is always 188 bytes in length.

Chapter 12

Video Over Fiber Using AM Techniques

Amplitude modulation represents the simplest technique for encoding any type of signal. In a baseband system, the input signal directly modulates the strength of the transmitter output. In the RF carrier AM technique, a carrier, with a frequency much higher than the encoded information, varies according to the amplitude of the information being encoded. In a fiber optic system, the magnitude of the voltage input signal directly translates into a corresponding light intensity.

Basics of AM

We know that a video signal contains a range of levels from black to white that equals 140 IRE units. This IRE amount corresponds to 1.0 Vp-p. Thus, one IRE unit equals about 7.14 mV$_{p-p}$. A picture containing only black levels will only be 40 IRE units high, or about 0.286 V$_{p-p}$ (refer back to Figure 11.2). Using a simple AGC to output 1.0 V$_{p-p}$ yields a severely distorted output waveform for an all-black picture. The sync-pulse, usually 40 IRE units high, will become 140 IRE high, and most monitors cannot interpret the signal, making this approach useless.

Successful AM transmission requires a more sophisticated circuit that analyzes the input waveform and sets the sync pulse level to 40 IRE units. In this approach, the circuit has to know what picture format to expect: NTSC, PAL, or another type. A circuit designed to work with NTSC may not be compatible with other formats. Figure 12.1 shows a typical fiber optic AM video transmitter and receiver.

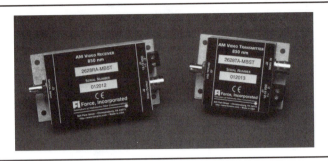

Figure 12.1 – Fiber Optic AM Video Link

(Photo courtesy of Force, Inc.)

In an AM system, the received signal amplitude directly reflects the link loss. This dictates that the AM link must possess gain control at the receiver. Recovered baseband video has difficulty implementing an automatic gain control (AGC) and may require a manual control. This complicates the installation of some AM links, requiring the user to inject a test signal from an oscilloscope to set the correct receiver gain level. Manual gain control does not allow the link to automatically adapt to changes in the link loss due to fiber degradation or transmitter power variations. In addition, mating and demating optical connectors will also change the received optical power. Ideally, a practical AM system requires an AGC such as the one illustrated in Figure 12.2.

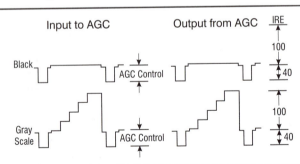

Figure 12.2 – Sync Pulse Level AGC

Linear Amplifiers and Noise Figure

All AM systems must use highly linear amplifiers throughout the signal path. Any deviation from linearity will cause distortion of the AM signal.

We will deal with the deleterious effects of nonlinearity at several other points in this book. The key amplifier parameters for consideration include: gain, linearity, bandwidth, and noise figure.

Gain (G, measured in units of dB) determines the increase in the signal's amplitude. Linearity measures how much the amplifier distorts the signal, and its effects can be complex. By specifying the linearity in a way that directly relates to the type of signals and its application, one can estimate the amplifier's distortion on the signal. Linearity can be expressed in many ways, including IP3, (third order intercept), P_{1dB} (1 dB compression point), CSO (composite second order), and CTB (composite triple beat).

Bandwidth describes the range of amplified frequencies from lowest to highest. Bandwidth denotes the frequencies at which the response drops by 3 dB. This causes the amplitude to drop to 70.7% of its maximum value, often an unacceptable value for video applications. Some high performance video amplifiers will specify bandwidth as the frequency where the response drops by 0.1 dB or less. A 0.1 dB drop means that the amplitude will only drop to 98.9% of its maximum value. The noise figure (NF) may also be expressed as equivalent noise input (ENI).

Amplifier Noise Calculation

Noise figure, a commonly used and misunderstood parameter, adds to the confusion of understanding noise calculation in an amplifier. Consider an isolated amplifier such as the one illustrated in Figure 12.3.

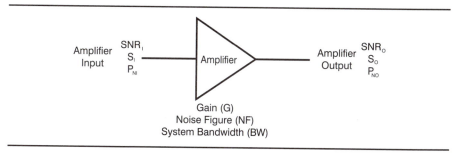

Figure 12.3 – Amplifier Noise Calculation

As we know, the amplifier itself exhibits three main characteristics; gain (G), noise figure (NF), and bandwidth (BW). The input signal has a level S_I and a signal-to-noise ratio SNR_I. The amplifier noise figure (NF) can also determine the effective noise that is present at the input of the amplifier, P_{NI}. Conversely, SNR_O represents the signal-to-noise ratio at the output of the amplifier. It will always be less than SNR_I due to the noise added by the amplifier. The output signal level is S_O and the noise at the output of the amplifier due to the amplifier itself is P_{NO}. P_{NO} is P_{NI} times the gain (G) of the amplifier.

Most texts indicate that the signal-to-noise ratio degrades by the noise figure (NF) when the signal goes through an amplifier. This misleading explanation conflicts with other formulae that show that the first amplifier in the chain as dominating SNR degradation. The noise figure tells us how much worse the amplifier noise is compared to a perfect Johnson noise source. A Johnson noise source can be thought of as an ideal resistor. Resistors generate noise because their atoms move in response to the ambient temperature. The equation for Johnson noise is:

Eq. 12.1
$$V_{Noise} = (4 \cdot k \cdot T \cdot R \cdot B)^{1/2}$$

Where:
k = Boltzmann's Constant = 1.38×10^{-23} (J/K)
T = Temperature (K)
B = Bandwidth (Hz)
R = Resistance of the Noise Source (Ohms)

The power due to V_{Noise} is P_{Noise} (note the equation takes into account the maximum power transfer between equal impedances, thus the $4 \cdot R$ factor in the denominator):

Eq. 12.2
$$P_{Noise} = \frac{V_{Noise}^2}{4 \cdot R} = k \cdot T \cdot B$$

P_{Noise} will have a value of -173.9 dBm at room temperature for a bandwidth of 1 Hz.

Noise in an amplifier or fiber optic link is often expressed in terms of noise figure NF (f). Other related terms are the noise factor (F) and noise temperature (T_N). Noise factor F is related to noise figure f as follows:

Eq. 12.3
$$f = Log_{10}(F)$$

The noise temperature T_N relates to the noise factor F as follows:

Eq. 12.4
$$T_N = 290 \cdot (F-1)$$

Figure 12.4 shows the relationship between noise temperature, noise factor, and noise figure for noise figures from 0 dB to 6 dB. The equation for amplifier output noise due to the amplifier alone is:

Eq. 12.5
$$P_{NO} = 10 \cdot Log_{10}(k \cdot T) + 10 \cdot Log_{10}(B) + G + NF$$

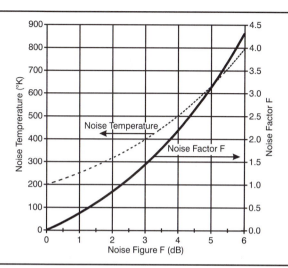

Figure 12.4 – Noise Temperature, Noise Factor, and Noise Figure

Where $k = 1.38 \times 10^{-20}$ mW/°K (Boltzmann's Constant)

Eq. 12.6 $P_{NO} = -173.9 + 10 \bullet Log_{10}(B) + G + NF$

For VSB/AM video, bandwidth equals 5 MHz, so:

Eq. 12.7 $P_{NO} = -106.9 + G + NF$

and

Eq. 12.8 $P_{NI} = -106.9 + NF$

Let's calculate a few examples. In all cases, assume the following:
Amplifier Gain, G = 34 dB
Noise Figure, NF = 7 dB
Amplifier Output Noise, P_{NO} = -65.9 dBm = 2.57×10^{-7} mW
Amplifier Input Noise, P_{NI} = -99.9 dBm = 1.02×10^{-10} mW

Amplifier Noise Calculation — Example 1

If the input signal is -26 dBm = S_I and input SNR is 55 dB then:
S_I = -26 dBm
P_{NI} = -99.9 dBm
S_N (noise on input signal) = -81 dBm = 7.94×10^{-9} mW

Eq. 12.9
$$\text{Total Noise} = \sqrt{(1.02 \bullet 10^{-10})^2 + (7.94 \bullet 10^{-9})^2}$$
$$= 7.941 \times 10^{-9} \text{ mW}$$
$$= -80.99 \text{ dBm}$$

Eq. 12.10 $-99.9 \text{ dBm} = 1.02 \cdot 10^{-10} \text{ mW}$

So in Example 1, the output carrier-to-noise ratio equals 54.99 dB.

Amplifier Noise Calculation — Example 2

If the input signal is -36 dBm = S_I and input SNR is 55 dB then:
S_N (noise on input signal) = -91 dBm = 7.94×10^{-10} mW

Eq. 12.11

$$\text{Total Noise} = \sqrt{(1.02 \cdot 10^{-10})^2 + (7.94 \cdot 10^{-10})^2} = 8.035 \cdot 10^{-10} \text{ mW} = -90.95 \text{ dBm}$$

So in Example 2, the output signal-to-noise ratio equals:
(-36-(-90.95)) = 54.95 dB.

Amplifier Noise Calculation — Example 3

If the input signal is -46 dBm = S_I and input SNR is 55 dB then:
S_N (noise on input signal) = -101 dBm = 7.94×10^{-11} mW

Eq. 12.12

$$\text{Total Noise} = \sqrt{(1.02 \cdot 10^{-10})^2 + (7.94 \cdot 10^{-11})^2} = 1.29 \cdot 10^{-10} \text{ mW} = -98.9 \text{ dBm}$$

So in Example 3, the output signal-to-noise ratio equals:
(-46-(-98.9)) = 52.9 dB.

Amplifier Noise Calculation — Example 4

If the input signal is -51 dBm = S_I and input CNR is 55 dB then:
S_N (noise on input signal) = -106 dBm = 2.51×10^{-11}

Eq. 12.13

$$\text{Total Noise} = \sqrt{(1.02 \cdot 10^{-10})2 + (2.51 \cdot 10^{-11})^2} = 1.05 \cdot 10^{-10} \text{ mW} = -99.9 \text{ dBm}$$

So in Example 4, the output signal-to-noise ratio equals:
(-51-(-99.8)) = 48.8 dB.

Figure 12.5 shows the signal-to-noise ratio of the amplifier used in Examples 1 through 4 above. The figure also shows the noise on the input signal and the noise due to the amplifier at the amplifier input. The output SNR only starts to drop when the noise on the input signal becomes comparable to the noise due to the amplifier at the amplifier input.

Clearly, noise figure becomes a serious issue at very low input signal levels. At higher input levels, the noise of the amplifier has an almost negligible

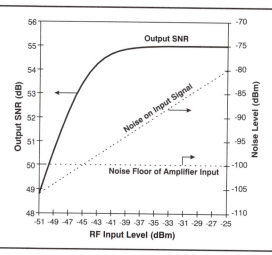

Figure 12.5 – Plot of SNR for Examples 1 through 4

effect. Conventional wisdom suggests that the noise figure of the first amplifier is the most important. As the signal amplification increases through each amplifier, the impact of the noise figure declines. The effective noise figure of a chain of amplifiers is given by the Friis equation. Figure 12.6 shows a chain of three amplifiers.

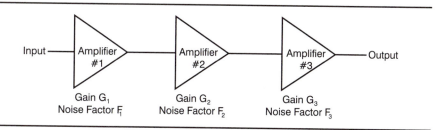

Figure 12.6 – Cascade of Three Amplifiers

Equation 12.14 gives the Friis formula for computing the effective noise factor F of the cascade of amplifiers shown in Figure 12.6.

Eq. 12.14
$$F = F_1 + \frac{F_2 - 1}{G_1} + \frac{F_3 - 1}{G_1 \cdot G_2} + \frac{F_4 - 1}{G_1 \cdot G_2 \cdot G_3} + \ldots$$

CNR and SNR

In video transmission, the difference between CNR (carrier-to-noise ratio) and SNR (signal-to-noise ratio) represents a confusing point. Both ratios measure the strength of the desired video signal versus the unwanted noise associated with all electronic signals. CNR is usually used to describe the performance of broadcast VSB/AM video signals such as those associated with over the air TV broadcast or CATV signals. Table 12.1 shows a highly subjective interpretation of CNR.

Table 12.1 – Subjective Interpretation of CNR Measurements

CNR	Subjective Interpretation
<38 dB	Poor
38-42 dB	Fair
42-47 dB	Good
>47 dB	Excellent

CNR is computed by measuring the peak amplitude of the video carrier and the RMS noise floor. The CNR is then computed as:

Eq. 12.15 $CNR = 20 \cdot Log_{10}(S_1/N_1)$

Where:

S_1 = Peak amplitude of the video carrier (mV)
N_1 = RMS Noise floor (in a 4 MHz bandwidth)

Figure 12.7 shows what this measurement might look like on a spectrum analyzer display. The measurement is made between the peak of the video carrier and the average of the noise floor. Usually the noise is measured in a 30 kHz bandwidth so that the minimum noise point can be located between the video and audio carriers. Once the minimum noise floor is located, it is converted to a 4 MHz bandwidth by adding 21.25 dB. [That is $10 \cdot Log_{10}(4,000\ kHz/30\ kHz)$.] Various factors actually make the noise measurement a bit more complex including imperfections in the filters used to measure the noise as well as noise associated with the measuring equipment itself.

SNR, usually associated with baseband analog video signals such as the A/V signals output by a VCR or cable box, measures the peak video amplitude to the total weighted noise. It is computed as follows:

Eq. 12.16 $SNR = 20 \cdot Log_{10}(S_1/N_1)$

Where

S_1 = Peak amplitude of the video signal (mV)
N_1 = Integrated weighted noise

The weighting function accounts for the way human vision interprets noise at different frequencies. A human observer will be less critical of high frequency noise compared to low frequency noise, thus, the weighting func-

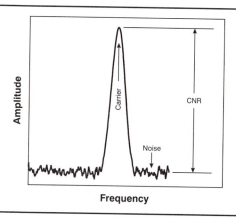

Figure 12.7 – CATV CNR as Displayed on a Spectrum Analyzer

tion reduces high frequency noise. Commonly used NTSC weighting functions include NTC-7 weighting and unified weighting, which is often used in conjunction with low-pass filters. For a video signal that has uniform noise across the 6 MHz channel, a 5.0 MHz low-pass filter will improve the SNR by about 1.0 dB, and improvement with the 4.2 MHz low-pass filter is about 1.5 dB. The NTC-7 weighting function improves the SNR by about 5.8 dB, and the unified weighting function improves the SNR by about 6.0 dB. For video signals that have more high-frequency noise, such as a signal transported over a fiber optic FM video link, the weighting function will give an even larger improvement. Table 12.2 shows typical video SNRs and their qualitative assessments.

Table 12.2 – Subjective Interpretation of SNR Measurements

SNR	Subjective Interpretation
40-47 dB	Poor to Fair
47-51 dB	Good
51-55 dB	Very Good
>55 dB	Excellent

The simplicity and cost-effectiveness of amplitude modulation make it a good choice for many fiber optic video transmission systems. However, not all types of signals do well with this technique. The next chapter details frequency modulation, another, more complex, and in some applications, more preferred method of modulating video signals.

Chapter Summary

- AM is a simple modulation scheme that usually allows for overall low system cost.
- In AM, the optical link loss directly affects the received signal amplitude, requiring an automatic gain control at the receive end in order to restore the original signal amplitude.
- Linear amplifiers allow AM transmission systems to maintain linearity, which eliminates distortion.
- Key parameters for linear amplifiers include: gain, linearity, bandwidth, and noise.
- Amplifier noise figure (NF) can be used to determine the effective noise that is present at the input of an amplifier.
- In an amplifier, the output signal-to-noise ratio will only begin to drop off when the noise on the input signal compares to the noise due to the amplifier at the input.
- Carrier-to-noise ratio (CNR) and signal-to-noise ratio (SNR) may get confused, but CNR usually describes broadcast VSB/AM performance while SNR is usually associated with baseband analog video signals.
- CNR is computed by measuring the peak amplitude of the video carrier and the RMS noise floor.
- SNR is a measure of the peak video amplitude to the total weighted noise.
- The weighting function adjusts for the way human vision interprets noise at different frequencies.

Chapter 13

Video Over Fiber Using FM Techniques

We've examined AM transmission. Now the discussion turns to frequency modulation (FM). This scheme simplifies video transmission in some ways, while complicating it in other ways.

Basics of FM

Frequency modulation uses the instantaneous amplitude of a modulating signal (voice, music, data, etc.) to directly vary the frequency of a carrier signal. Modulation index beta (β) describes the ratio of maximum frequency deviation of the carrier to the maximum frequency deviation of the modulating signal.

FM General Equation

In an intensity-based system, the modulation index measures how much the modulation signal affects the light output. To determine this value, let the carrier be $x_c(t) = A_c \cdot \cos(\omega_c t)$, and the modulating signal be $x_m(t) = \beta \cdot \sin(\omega_m t)$.

So the modulation index is:

Eq. 13.1 $$\beta = \left(\frac{\Delta\omega}{\omega_m}\right) = \frac{\text{maximum carrier frequency deviation}}{\text{modulation frequency}}$$

Narrowband FM (NBFM)

Narrowband FM is defined as the condition where β is small enough to make all terms, after the first two in the series expansion of the FM equation, negligible.

Narrowband approximation is not an absolute limit and could be higher than: $\beta = \Delta\omega/\Delta_m < \approx 0.2$. The bandwidth (BW) of the resultant FM signal is shown in Equation 13.2.

So:

Eq. 13.2 $$BW \text{ (Hz)} = 2 \cdot \omega_m$$

Wideband FM (WBFM)

Wideband FM is defined as when a significant number of sidebands have significant amplitudes and its bandwidth are given as:

Eq. 13.3 $$BW \text{ (Hz)} = 2 \cdot \Delta\omega$$

Carson's Bandwidth Rule

Carson's bandwidth rule, proposed by J.R. Carson in the 1920s, defines the approximate bandwidth requirements of system components for a carrier signal that is frequency modulated by a continuous or broad spectrum of frequencies, wideband FM, rather than a single frequency. This amounts to a good approximation for both very small and very large β:

Eq. 13.4 $$BW \text{ (Hz)} = 2(\Delta\omega + \omega_m) = 2 \cdot \omega(1 + \beta)$$

When the modulation is a sinusoidal signal, suppression may occur in the carrier and certain sideband frequencies. Zero crossings of the Bessel functions, $J_n(\beta)$, occur where the corresponding sideband, n, disappears for a given modulation index, β. The composite spectrum for a single tone consists of lines at the carrier and upper and lower sidebands, with amplitudes determined by the Bessel function values at those frequencies, as shown in Figure 13.1 (next page).

Figure 13.1 shows the behavior of the zero through third-order Bessel function, $J_n(\beta)$. At low values of β, the amplitude of the carrier frequency (n=0) dominates. In Figure 13.1, when β reaches a value of 1.0, the first-order sidebands (n=1) are about 60% of the carrier amplitude and the second-order sidebands (n=2) are about 15% of the carrier amplitude. The higher order sidebands comprise less than a few percent of the carrier.

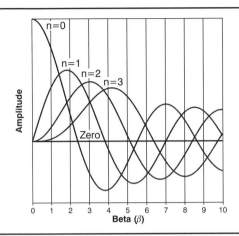

Figure 13.1 – FM Bessel Functions

Figures 13.2a through 13.2e show the amplitude of the carrier and the various sidebands as β increases from zero (no modulation) to five. Note that Figure 13.2d is a special case. At a β of 2.405, the carrier frequency completely disappears leaving only the sidebands. This is often used to precisely calibrate FM modulators. By the time the β reaches 5.0, the sideband structure is very wide and quite complex.

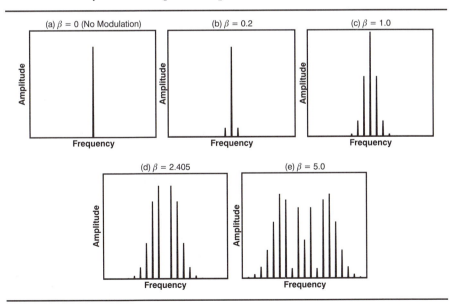

Figure 13.2 – FM Sidebands

The Advantages and Limitations of FM versus AM

A comparison of the frequency spectra of various AM and FM modulation schemes allows a clearer understanding of their differences, as illustrated in Figure 13.3. Simple baseband AM (Figure 13.3a) occupies the region from DC to 5-10 MHz. This technique requires the least overall bandwidth. The RF carrier modulation spectrum (Figure 13.3b) resembles simple baseband; the frequency spectrum has shifted to some non-zero frequency (F). This requires additional bandwidth and offers no advantage over baseband operation in a single-channel system. However, it does allow one to combine multiple channels onto a single fiber. With vestigial-sideband AM, the spectrum (Figure 13.3c) again shifts to a non-zero frequency (F), and filtering removes most of the lower sideband. It allows the spectrum to be used with much more efficiently than straight RF carrier AM, requiring half the bandwidth per channel.

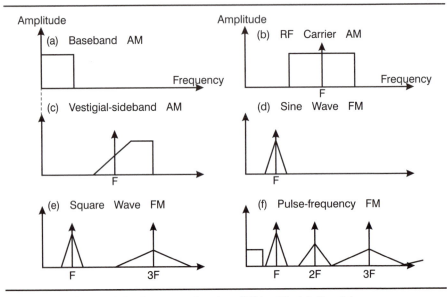

Figure 13.3 – Frequency Spectra of Video Modulation Schemes

Single Channel FM Video Transmission

Three basic types of FM modulation, sine wave FM, square wave FM, and pulse-frequency modulation, can transport video over optical fiber. The presence of harmonics differentiates between sine wave FM (see Figure 13.3d), square wave FM (see Figure 13.3e), and pulse-frequency FM (see

Figure 13.3f). The square wave FM spectrum signal contains all odd-ordered harmonics. The pulse frequency FM spectrum contains all odd- and even-ordered harmonics. This yields a cluttered spectrum poorly suited for multiple channel stacking. However, it retains value as a single-channel transmission scheme. Figure 13.4 shows a typical single channel FM video transmitter and receiver.

Figure 13.4 – Single Channel FM Video Link

(Photo courtesy of Force, Inc.)

Multichannel FM Video Transmission

RF carrier AM, vestigial-sideband AM and sine wave FM are best suited for multiple channel transmission, because they lack harmonics. Assigning different carrier frequencies to each video signal allows for the transmission of combined channels over one optical fiber. The sum of the resulting modulated carriers yields a single composite electrical signal. It is this composite electrical signal that modulates the intensity of the optical emitter (laser or LED). Figure 13.5 illustrates the spectrum of a 4-channel sine wave FM system. In this case, the four channels occupy the frequencies of 70 MHz, 90 MHz, 110 MHz, and 130 MHz.

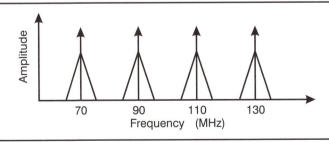

Figure 13.5 – A 4-Channel Sine Wave FM System

Achievable Performance Levels

Whereas in an AM system the received signal amplitude directly reflects the link loss, FM modulation and demodulation provides a properly recovered signal level independent of link loss and the input video format. Signal level varies only by component tolerances in the transmitter and receiver. The output level typically equals the input level ±20%. This reduces long-term maintenance and ensures proper performance and consistent quality over the duration of the link's life.

Under similar conditions, FM signal-to-noise ratio will exceed AM signal-to-noise ratio. The performance of each modulation scheme relates the video signal-to-noise ratio to the fiber optic link's carrier-to-noise ratio. The FM beta (β) represents unity for this comparison; a larger β results in improved SNR performance. Table 13.1 compares the estimated SNR for an AM versus FM scenario, summarizing the factors contributing to the overall SNR performance. It also describes each modulation scheme with a single factor relating the video SNR to the fiber optic link carrier-to-noise.

Table 13.1 – Signal-to-Noise Ratio (SNR) AM versus FM

Baseband AM Modulation		Square Wave FM Modulation	
Picture is 0.7 of 1.0 V_{P-P} Penalty: $20 \cdot Log_{10}(0.7)$	-3.01 dB	Picture is 0.7 of 1.0 V_{P-P} Penalty: $20 \cdot Log_{10}(0.7)$	-3.01 dB
TV Weighting Benefit	+7.40 dB	TV Weighting Benefit	+7.40 dB
N/A		For one channel, the carrier amplitude is 100% modulated. The improvement due to FM (β = 1) is Benefit	+3.52 dB
Light modulation is restricted to 50% to obtain adequate linearity. Benefit: $20 \cdot Log_{10}(0.5)$	-6.02 dB	For linearity, FM demands less than AM. Assume 100% modulation. Penalty: $20 \cdot Log_{10}(1.0)$	0.0 dB
Total (SNR-CNR)	**-1.63 dB**	**Total (SNR-CNR)**	**+7.91 dB**

The FM equation (valid only for CNRs that are above the FM threshold) is defined as:

Eq. 13.5

$$SNR = 1.5 \cdot \beta^2 \cdot CNR$$

Additional improvements would be obtained for β values ranging from one to ten as shown in Table 13.2 (next page).

Table 13.2 – β Improvement versus SNR

β	SNR Improvement
1	0 dB
2	12 dB
5	25 dB
10	40 dB
ΔF = Peak Deviation in FM Output; f_m = Baseband Bandwidth	

Of course, increased bandwidth becomes the penalty for larger β values. With all other factors equal, FM typically maintains an 8 dB advantage over AM. This translates into longer distance links, more loss margin, higher picture quality, or some combination of the three. However, this overlooks the effects on picture quality caused by nonlinearities in the link.

FM transmission requires more bandwidth than AM, a key disadvantage. If one considers an NTSC video signal with a 5 MHz bandwidth allotment, then a baseband AM system only requires 5 MHz of bandwidth. However, an FM system requires at least seven times this bandwidth for a total of 70 MHz to accommodate the 70 MHz FM carrier. This, in turn, requires higher bandwidth from the electro-optical components and the associated electrical components.

A good quality 62.5/125 μm multimode fiber has a bandwidth-distance product of at least 400 MHz•km. Thus the carrier frequency of 70 MHz becomes a factor at a distance of 5 km or longer. In applications that use 850 nm LEDs, the carrier frequency can cause dispersion at transmission distances beyond 1.5 km. Multimode fiber, used with an 850 nm LED, exhibits very high dispersion.

FM Video Link Performance

Figure 13.6 (next page) shows the typical architecture of an FM video link. The top of the figure illustrates an FM transmitter. In this design, the FM modulator centers around 70 MHz with a deviation of 10 MHz. Once through the modulator, the comparator converts the analog signal to a digital signal, and the fiber optic digital transmitter converts the signal into light pulses. The FM video receiver operates in the reverse manner, converting the digital signal to an electronic signal. The FM demodulator decodes the signal and then removes the carrier frequency components using a low pass filter.

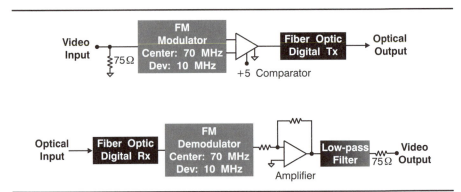

Figure 13.6 – FM Video Link

Figure 13.7 illustrates the performance achieved by a fiber optic video link showing signal-to-noise ratio of the video signal versus fiber length in meters. The signal quality remains constant up to 9,000 meters of fiber and rolls off to 16,000 meters where it drops below the minimum specification of 48 dB signal-to-noise ratio.

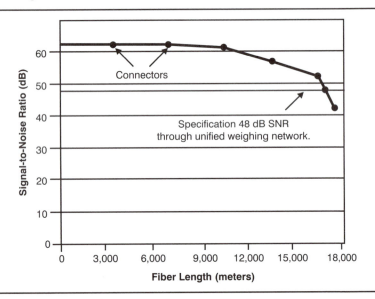

Figure 13.7 – SNR versus Fiber Length

(Data based on the performance of Force, Inc. fiber optic FM video links.)

Unconventional FM Modulators

Laser chirp can be used to create a super wideband FM modulator that would allow, for instance, the conversion of the complete CATV spectrum (40 MHz to 860 MHz) to an FM signal that is 5 GHz wide. Figure 13.8 shows the basic technique. Laser #1 directly modulates with the wideband AM signal. Laser #2 operates at a constant current. A fiber optic coupler mixes the outputs of the two lasers, modulating the frequency, and thus wavelength, of the light. This is often referred to as a coherent transmission scheme.

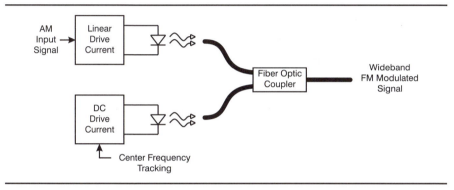

Figure 13.8 – Wideband FM Modulator

Frequency modulation offers a number of advantages over amplitude modulation, but tomorrow's fiber optic video transmission will require much more bandwidth and data rate capacity. The next chapter discusses digital modulation, the scheme that finds use in today's high-end and tomorrow's standard video transmission systems.

Chapter Summary

- Frequency modulation uses the instantaneous amplitude of a modulating signal such as voice, video, music, etc., to directly vary the frequency of a carrier signal.
- Narrowband FM is the condition where beta is small enough to make all but the first two terms of the FM equation negligible.
- Wideband FM is defined as the instance when a significant numbers of sidebands have significant amplitudes.
- Carson's bandwidth rule, devised by J.R. Carson in the 1920s, gives a means to approximate both very small and very large beta values.
- Three types of FM modulation include sine wave FM, square wave FM, and pulse-frequency modulation.

- Pulse-frequency modulation is poorly suited for multiple channel transmission schemes but offers an effective scheme for single-channel transmission.
- Sine wave FM is well-suited to multichannel transmission because the scheme lacks harmonics.
- FM modulation and demodulation provides a correctly recovered signal level independent of link loss and input video format.
- FM signal-to-noise ratios typically exceed AM signal-to-noise ratios under similar operating conditions.
- Increasing FM beta values will improve SNR but also increases the required bandwidth.
- An FM video transmitter modulates an incoming signal then outputs the signal as light pulses.
- An FM video receiver demodulates the signal and converts the light pulses back into electrical signals.
- Laser chirp can be used to create a wideband FM modulator.

Chapter 14

Video Over Fiber Using Digital Techniques

The FCC has set the year 2006 as the deadline for broadcasters to switch from standard definition television (SDTV) to digital TV (DTV) and high definition television (HDTV). Among the many advantages of this transition, transmission distance and repeaters (signal regenerators) do not affect the quality of digitized video. A visit to any major broadcast industry trade show, such as those sponsored by the National Association of Broadcasters (NAB) or the Society of Motion Picture and Television Engineers (SMPTE), reveals that cameras, tape decks, mixing boards, matrix switches, effects boxes, etc. operate in digital format.

Basics of Digital Modulation

Fiber optics plays a big part in the move to the new television standards, providing an excellent means of signal transport by offering the bandwidth required for these standards. Currently, analog video signals can be carried over relatively long lengths of coax cable. With a bandwidth of only 4.5 MHz, analog signals do not tax the limited bandwidth of coax cable, but even so, coax cable introduces a great deal of frequency dependent distortion requiring an equalization network. A digitized video signal's increased bandwidth usurps coax's ability to carry the new signal.

A standard NTSC video signal typically requires a serial bit rate of 143.2 Mb/s. By contrast, high-end HDTV standards require serial bit rates of 1,485 Mb/s. Coax cable can carry such high-speed digital data streams short distances, typically 300-600 meters for NTSC and 30-60 meters for HDTV. Fiber optics, on the other hand, can easily carry the full range of digital signals up to tens of thousands of meters. Figure 14.1 shows a typical digital fiber optic video receiver.

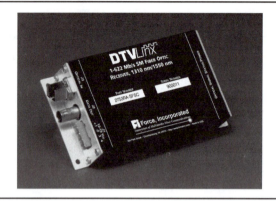

Figure 14.1 – Fiber Optic Digital Video Receiver

(Photo courtesy of Force, Inc.)

Digitized Video Formats and Data Rates

Several standards exist or have been proposed for digitized video transmission. All result in a serial digital data stream. Table 14.1 lists the key standards.

Table 14.1 – Digitized Video Standards

Standard	Sample Rate	Word Rate	10-Bit Serial Data Rate
NTSC	14.318 MHz	14.318 M/s	143.18 Mb/s
PAL ($4f_{sc}$)	17.7 MHz	17.7 M/s	177 Mb/s
SMPTE 259M (4:2:2)	13.5 MHz	27 M/s	270 Mb/s
CCIR 656	13.5 MHz	27 M/s	270 Mb/s
EU95	72 MHz	144 M/s	1440 Mb/s
SMPTE 292M	74.25 MHz	148.5 M/s	1485 Mb/s

The first four standards represent those used today. Several European community development programs have focused on EU95, a digitized HDTV standard. Compared to analog video's 4.5 MHz bandwidth, the bandwidth required by these standards staggers the mind. Figure 14.2 compares the bandwidth of a typical copper coax cable and fiber optic cables, showing the frequency response of copper coax cable, multimode fiber, and single-mode fiber.

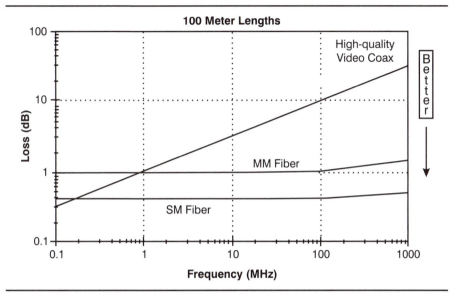

Figure 14.2 – Comparison of Copper Coax and Fiber Bandwidth

Serial Data Transmission Formats and Standards

Table 14.2 describes standards used to convert a video signal from analog to digital. The standards describe the scale factors, word formats, overall data structure, and the line serial data rate for coaxial cable transport.

Table 14.2 – Serial Digital Video Formats

Standard	Picture Aspect Ratio	Sample Rate	Word Rate	Line Serial Date Rate
SMPTE 259M Level "A" (NTSC)	4 x 3	14.318 MHz	14.318 M/s	143.18 Mb/s
SMPTE 259M Level "B" (PAL $4f_{sc}$)	4 x 3	17.7 MHz	17.7 M/s	177 Mb/s
SMPTE 259M Level "C" (4:2:2)	4 x 3	13.5 MHz	27 M/s	270 Mb/s
SMPTE 259M Level "D" (4:2:2)	16 x 9	18.0 MHz	36 M/s	360 Mb/s
ITU-R601, CCIR 656	4 x 3	13.5 MHz	27 M/s	270 Mb/s
EU95	16 x 9	72.0 MHz	144 M/s	1440 Mb/s
SMPTE 292M	16 x 9	74.25 MHz	148.5 M/s	1.485 Gb/s

Several new SMPTE standards define the resolutions required for digital broadcasting and HDTV. SMPTE 292M resembles SMPTE 259M but includes much higher data rates and addresses fiber optic specifications. The full bandwidth HDTV 1.485 Gb/s data rate allows copper coaxial cable to transmit up to 100 meters, while fiber can transmit more than 100 kilometers. Fiber optics can also transmit SMPTE 310M for HDTV formats using MPEG-2 data compression at rates up to 40 Mb/s. Digital broadcasters use both SMPTE 292M and 310M signals in their fiber optic studio-to-transmitter links (STL). Table 14.3 lists the key parameters of the serial digital data link associated with these SMPTE standards.

Table 14.3 – Signal Levels and Specifications for SMPTE 259M, 292M, and 310M

Parameter	259M Requirement	292M Requirement	310M Requirement
Input/Output Load	75 Ohm	75 Ohm	75 Ohm
Electrical Return Loss	>15 dB from 5 MHz to F_{CLOCK} (Max. 360 MHz)	>15 dB from 5 MHz to F_{CLOCK} (Max. 1.485 GHz)	>30 dB from 100 kHz to F_{CLOCK} (Max. 70 MHz)
Data Amplitude (Into 75 Ohms)	800 mV ±10% p-p	800 mV ±10% p-p	800 mV ±10% p-p
DC Offset	0.0 ± 0.5 Volts	0.0 ± 0.5 Volts	0.0 ± 0.5 Volts
Rise/Fall Times (20-80%)	0.4 ns to 1.50 ns	≤ 270 ps	0.4 ns to 5.0 ns
Jitter & Distortion	<±250 ps	≤ 135 ps	2 ns p-p Max.
Electrical Connector	BNC	BNC	BNC

Table 14.4 lists the key parameters involved with the serial digital data link associated with SMPTE 259M, which describes how to serialize data or send it over copper or fiber cable.

Table 14.4 – SMPTE 259M

Parameter	Requirement
Input/Output Impedance	75 Ohm
Return Loss (Electrical)	15 dB Minimum
Data Amplitude (Into 75 Ohms)	800 mV ±10% peak-peak
DC Offset	±0.5 Volts
Rise/Fall Times (20-80%)	<1.50 ns
Jitter & Distortion	<±250 ps
Electrical Connector	BNC

The broadcast industry currently uses equipment that works with SMPTE 259M, including a compatible fiber optic link that interfaces with both copper and fiber cables.

Datacom versus Telecom Fiber Optic Links

The telecom industry developed the first, most common type of high-speed data link. Telecom links, usually optimized for a single data rate, focus on reliability and very long distance performance. Emphasis on these factors reduces the importance given to bit error rate (BER), jitter, and wide data rate capability. Fiber optic links developed for telecom applications often boast a BER of 10^{-9}. In a telephone conversation, this corresponds to a single audible "click" every 4.4 hours.

The datacom industry developed a second type of high-speed link. In datacom links, a BER of 10^{-9} means one error per second for a computer-to-computer link running at 1 gigabaud, which can be disastrous to a computer. Most datacom applications demand minimum BER of 10^{-12} or 10^{-15}. Encoding data with parity bits or checksum words corrects bit errors that may have a detrimental impact on datacom applications. Table 14.5 shows the required BER for various digitized video formats and conditions.

Table 14.5 – Effect of BER on Digital Video Formats

Standard	1 Bit Error/ Frame	1 Bit Error/Sec	1 Bit Error/Hr	1 Bit Error/Day
NTSC	2.1×10^{-7}	7.0×10^{-9}	1.9×10^{-12}	8.1×10^{-14}
PAL ($4f_{SC}$)	1.7×10^{-7}	5.7×10^{-9}	1.5×10^{-12}	6×10^{-14}
SMPTE 259M (4:2:2)	1.1×10^{-7}	3.7×10^{-9}	1.0×10^{-12}	4.3×10^{-14}
CCIR 656	1.1×10^{-7}	3.7×10^{-9}	1.0×10^{-12}	4.3×10^{-14}
EU95	2.1×10^{-9}	7.0×10^{-10}	1.9×10^{-13}	8.1×10^{-15}
SMPTE 292M	2.0×10^{-9}	6.7×10^{-10}	1.8×10^{-13}	7.8×10^{-15}

Jitter has less impact on telecom links since they often run at a single data rate with a 50% duty cycle of short run lengths. Datacom on the other hand expects a given fiber optic link to handle a range of data rates and coding schemes. This expectation does not allow for a 50% duty cycle, making the effects of jitter more apparent. Data block-coded by 4B5B has an average duty cycle varying from 40% to 60%. Lastly, telecom links usually transmit to distances up to 100 km without repeaters compared to a typical datacom application transmission distance.

The broadcast industry appears to more closely fit the requirements of the datacom industry than the telecom industry, especially regarding low bit error rates. Table 14.6 (next page) provides a detailed comparison between the fiber optic link requirements for the telecom, datacom, and broadcast industries.

Table 14.6 – Comparison of Telecom, Datacom, and Broadcast Requirements

	Distance	Optical Loss	Wavelength	Allowable Jitter	Data Rate Range	BER
Telecom	Up to 100 km	High	1310/1550 nm	High	Narrow	$< 10^{-9}$
Datacom	0.1 to 20 km	Low to Moderate	850/1310 nm	Low	Wide	$<10^{-12}$
Broadcast	0.1 to 20 km	Low to Moderate	850/1310/1550 nm	Low	Wide	$<10^{-12}$

Wavelengths and Optics for Digitized Video

Like many fiber optic applications, the most popular transmission wavelengths and laser types include 1310 nm and 1550 nm. Because of the high modal noise associated with 780-850 nm, lasers have difficulty achieving reliable bit error rates of 10^{-12} to 10^{-15}. Links using 1310 nm or 1550 nm Fabry-Perot lasers can meet all broadcast industry requirements at very attractive prices. In addition, they can handle all projected broadcast industry serial data rates on multimode fiber up to distances of 700 meters and on single-mode fiber up to 60 km. With standards still emerging for digitized video, users must consider versatile fiber optic links.

Light-emitting diodes (LEDs) may transmit serial data rates up to 270 Mb/s, and a few laboratory demonstrations suggest the capability of operating speeds to 500 Mb/s or even 1 Gb/s. However, these transmitter sources must be hand "tweaked," prohibiting them from reaching volume production. In addition, the wider spectral width of LEDs greatly reduces fiber's overall bandwidth.

Optical Fiber and Connector Types for Digitized Video

Two main fiber types dominate the U.S. market today: multimode fiber and single-mode fiber. Laser-based gigabit fiber optic data links can operate over multimode graded-index fiber for distances up to 700 meters and data rates to 1,485 MBaud, the maximum data rate associated with HDTV. At data rates below 500 Mb/s, distances can exceed 5 km. Single-mode fiber is the most widespread. The use of single-mode fiber removes the bandwidth and distance limitations associated with multimode fiber. Single-mode fiber allows distances of 10-15 km using 1310 nm and 40-60 km using 1550 nm DFB lasers. A variety of optical connector types work well with the requirements of the broadcast industry, including the ST connector, popular for multimode fiber applications, the SC/APC connector, and the FC/APC connector, both of which work well in single-mode applications.

Digitized Video Transmission Performance

The broadcast industry will not fully switch to fiber optics until copper fails to do the job. Complete deployment of digitized video will increase fiber usage. As mentioned, copper coax systems transmit standard video signals up to thousands of meters, but they only transmit a few hundred meters at digitized NTSC rates and only tens of meters at digitized HDTV rates. Broadcast studios may not locate video processing equipment within that working distance, requiring optical fiber. Figure 14.3 shows the typical eye diagram associated with copper-based serial digital transmission over 100 meters and at a data rate of 270 Mb/s, digitized 4:2:2.

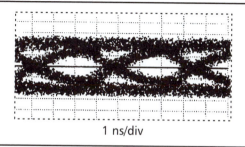

1 ns/div

Figure 14.3 – Eye Pattern for 100 m, Copper Coax, 270 Mb/s.

Figure 14.4 shows the clear advantage of fiber optics in an eye diagram associated with fiber optic serial digital transmission over 11,121 meters at a data rate of 531 Mb/s, about twice that of digitized 4:2:2.

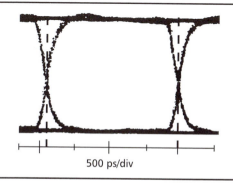

500 ps/div

Figure 14.4 – Eye Pattern for 11,121 m, SM Fiber, 531 Mb/s.

(Courtesy of Force, Inc.)

The eye diagram associated with the copper coax resembles that of an an unequalized cable. The use of cable equalization would reduce this distortion, which results from different amounts of attenuation used for different frequency components in the waveform, as well as the different delays associated with these frequency components. This distortion results in intersymbol interference. In other words, the data bits will overlap and smear together.

Fiber optics possesses bandwidth hundreds or thousands of times larger than copper coax cable, greatly reducing the problem. Properly designed fiber optic links require no equalization. This reduces setup time and the skill required to establish a working link. In other words, it may actually be easier to install a fiber optic link than a serial copper coax link.

In 1994, the Winter Olympics in Lillehammer, Norway utilized digitized video transmission, the first major application for this technology. Norwegian television selected fiber optic connections between the outside broadcast (OB) units at some venues located 15-20 km away. Several venues, for events like downhill skiing and ski jumping, required more connections, and the terrain made microwave links unusable. In addition to serial digital video links, this first-of-its-kind transmission used state-of-the-art technology such as low backreflection SC connectors, and 1310 nm/1550 nm wavelength-division multiplexing.

Compressed Digital Video

Advantages and disadvantages surround digital compression. However, it seems that the advantages outweigh the disadvantages. The disadvantages arise from the visual artifacts that remain in a digitized NTSC signal at DS3 rates, a compression ratio of 4:1. Moreover, studio transmission may not use digital compression, preferring a lossless compression algorithm which may achieve only a 2:1 compression ratio and retain high data rate requirements.

Modern digital video formats almost always incorporate some form of digital video compression (DVC). For years digital "NTSC-like" video required a bit rate of approximately 100 Mb/s. DVC technology can reduce the required bit rate to less than 5 Mb/s. This compression requires complex digital signal processing and large-scale circuit integration, but advances in chip and microprocessor design have made inexpensive implementation of the compression algorithms feasible.

Bit rate and quality determine the level of compression complexity used. Each degree of complexity removes different types of redundancy from the video image. The image is broken into 8 x 8 blocks of pixels. By comparing different blocks and transmitting only the differences, known as differential pulse-code modulation (DPCM), one can greatly reduce the bit rate with no degradation of quality. The viewer cannot see much of the information within each block. Vector quantization (VQ) or discrete-cosine transform (DCT) techniques can eliminate bits corresponding to these imperceptible details. This intraframe coding can result in a factor of 20 reduction in the bit rate, although the evaluation of image quality becomes subjective. Finally, stationary images or moving objects do not require constant retransmission of every detail. Recent developments in motion compression techniques eliminate these interframe redundancies. Combinations of these techniques have resulted in coders that convert NTSC-like video (100 Mb/s uncompressed) into a few megabits per second and HDTV images (1 Gb/s uncompressed) into less than 20 Mb/s.

Figure 14.5 shows an example digital video compression using a technique that analyzes the differences between successive frames. Figure 14.5a shows frame one of a two frame sequence. Initially, the system must transmit all of the first frame. Frame one shows a vacant dirt farm field. In Figure 14.5b, frame two, a dog appears on the scene. By analyzing the differences between frame one and frame two we can greatly reduce the amount of information that needs to be sent. Figure 14.5c shows the difference between the two frames. Since only the dog changes, the system only needs to transmit the dog.

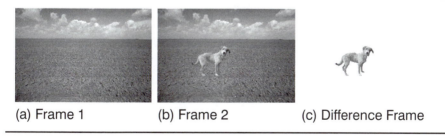

(a) Frame 1   (b) Frame 2   (c) Difference Frame

Figure 14.5 – Example of Interframe Difference Analysis

Several techniques exist for transmitting DVC signals. One method uses time-division multiplexing (TDM) and digital light wave systems. Another uses each channel to modulate an RF carrier and transmit via analog light wave systems. Numerous applications exist for both alternatives. TDM systems for DVC are no different from any other digital transmission system.

The use of RF techniques offers an additional level of RF compression, wherein the use of advanced multilevel modulation formats maximize the number of bits per Hertz of bandwidth.

QAM Encoding

Quadrature amplitude modulation (QAM) represents one example of multilevel digital-to-RF conversion. For example, 64 QAM uses eight amplitudes and eight phase levels and requires only 1 Hz for five bits of information. As the number of levels, and the number of bits per Hertz, increases, the CNR of the channel must increase to maintain error-free transmission. A 64 QAM channel requires a CNR of approximately 30 dB. Figure 14.6 illustrates a synopsis of the bandwidth and CNR requirements for FM, VSB/AM, and DVC.

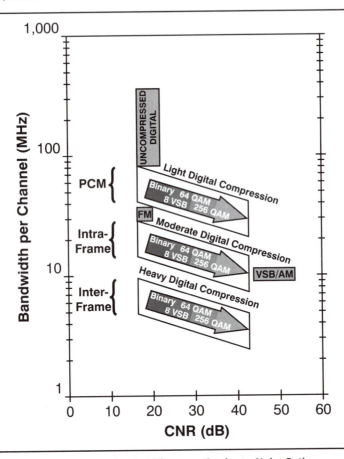

Figure 14.6 – Bandwidth versus Carrier-to-Noise Ratio

VSB/AM requires high CNR but low bandwidth. FM is the opposite. Digital video can occupy a wide area, depending on the degree of digital and RF compression. The combination of DCV and QAM offers the possibility of squeezing a high-quality video channel into 1 MHz of bandwidth, with a required CNR of 30 dB. This drastic improvement over VSB/AM or FM will tremendously impact the future of video transmission systems.

Digital modulation carries a number of advantages over other fiber optic modulation schemes. The future of video transmission ultimately includes digital transmission as the best means of sending the huge amounts of data required. This is especially true of CATV transmission that will advance the reality of broadband interactive services to the home. The next chapter describes high performance CATV transmission in greater detail.

Chapter Summary

- The broadcast industry is beginning to embrace the emerging technologies of digitized video and high-definition television.
- Digitized video requires more bandwidth than AM or FM, making optical fiber a better choice for transmission than coax cable.
- A number of digitized video standards exist, including: SMPTE 259M, SMPTE 295M, CCIR 656, and EU95.
- The frequency response of single-mode fiber is greater than that of multimode fiber or coax cable, exhibiting the lowest signal loss of the three.
- Broadcast fiber optic links require link parameters usually associated with high-speed datacom applications.
- Transmission wavelengths of 1310 nm and 1550 nm are the most widely used in digitized video transmission.
- Single-mode fiber and SC/APC or FC/APC connectors are most frequently employed when transmitting digitized video.
- A comparison of eye diagrams of digitized video signals over copper coax cable and single-mode optical fiber illustrate the performance advantages of fiber over copper.
- The use of digital compression has a number of disadvantages, such as visual artifacts in the received picture; however, compression technologies will be incorporated into the new transmission scheme when HDTV becomes the standard.
- Digital video compression (DVC) can reduce the required bit rate from 100 Mb/s to 5 Mb/s.
- Bit rate and signal quality determine the level of compression complexity used by a given system.

- Differential pulse-code modulation (DPCM) breaks an image into 8 x 8 blocks of pixels, compares the blocks, and transmits only the differences in the blocks.
- Quadrature amplitude modulation (QAM) represents a multilevel digital-to-RF conversion.
- The improvement of QAM transmission over VSB/AM transmission or FM transmission will tremendously impact the future of video transmission systems.

Chapter 15

High Linearity CATV Fiber Optic Systems

Fiber optics distribute CATV signals over large geographic areas with higher quality video and lightning immunity. However, CATV systems carrying 100 or more predominantly analog channels demand a linear system. In a truly linear system, the system's output is directly proportional to the system's input. However, in reality, most systems exhibit some degree of nonlinearity. The biggest challenge usually lies with the laser diode. Its light-to-current (LI) curve is usually close to a straight line above the threshold current but is never perfectly straight. These deviations from linear operation creates problems in systems that demand high linearity. Figure 15.1 illustrates a typical light-to-current curve.

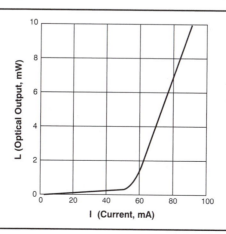

Figure 15.1 – Typical Light-to-Current Curve

Fourier Synthesis

Before we can fully understand the challenges facing high linearity CATV systems, we must first understand some basics about Fourier series and how distortion arises and manifests itself. The process of Fourier synthesis, using Fourier's theorem, demonstrates this concept. A periodic signal can be described by a Fourier decomposition as a Fourier series, in other words, as a sum of sinusoidal and cosinusoidal oscillations. By reversing this procedure, a periodic signal can be generated by superimposing sinusoidal and cosinusoidal waves. The general function is:

Eq. 15.1 $$X(t) = \frac{\alpha_0}{2} + \sum_{\kappa=1}^{\infty} (\alpha_\kappa COS(\kappa \omega_0 t) + b_\kappa SIN(\kappa \omega_0 t))$$

Where:

$\omega_0 = 2\pi \bullet F$
F = Frequency (Hz).

Fourier series offers a powerful and simple method for determining how distortion relates between the time domain and frequency domain in a fiber optic CATV system. The Fourier series of a square wave is:

Eq. 15.2 $$X(t) = SIN(\omega_0 t) + \frac{1}{3} SIN(3\omega_0 t) + \frac{1}{5} COS(5\omega_0 t) - \ldots$$

or

Eq. 15.3 $$X(t) = COS(\omega_0 t) - \frac{1}{3} COS(3\omega_0 t) + \frac{1}{5} COS(5\omega_0 t) - \ldots$$

The Fourier series of a saw-toothed wave is:

Eq. 15.4 $$X(t) = SIN(\omega_0 t) + \frac{1}{2} SIN(2\omega_0 t) + \frac{1}{3} SIN(3\omega_0 t) + \ldots$$

Assume that we wish to transmit a single pure tone with a frequency F of $1/(2\pi)$ Hz and amplitude $a_1 = 1$, a pure sinusoidal wave. If we transmit this signal through an AM CATV link that has perfect linearity, then the signal at the receiver will contain only frequency F. However, in the presence of any distortion in the AM CATV link, other frequency components, integer multiples of F, will appear. This will also distort the time domain, and a pure sinusoidal waveform will no longer be seen.

Let's look at the effects of the two most common type of nonlinearities that can occur in AM CATV links and see the effects on the time domain and frequency domain response.

Even and Odd Harmonics

Distortions to linear signals in the time domain may be considered asymmetrical or symmetrical distortions that lead to even-order or odd-order harmonic distortion. Figure 15.2a offers an example of an asymmetrical distortion that results from biasing a laser diode too close to its threshold point. At high input levels, the output follows the input in a linear fashion. When the input drops below about 25% of full scale, the output flattens out either as the laser nears or drops below the threshold current.

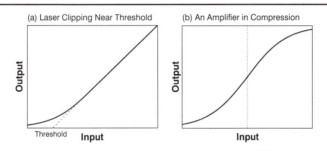

(a) Laser Clipping Near Threshold   (b) An Amplifier in Compression

Figure 15.2 – Asymmetrical and Symmetrical Distortion

The symmetrical distortion shown in Figure 15.2b exists in all modern RF amplifiers. Once the input to an amplifier reaches a certain point, the output goes into compression and no longer follows the input signal in a linear way. This type of distortion is usually symmetrical around the central point, shown as a vertical dotted line in the figure. Figure 15.3 shows the frequency domain implications of asymmetrical, even-order distortion, illustrating the fundamental (input) frequency and also the second and fourth harmonics. Adjustments to the phase of the second and fourth harmonics causes flattening of the bottom of the combined waveform, so it corresponds to the curve shown in Figure 15.2a.

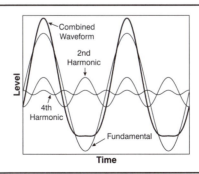

Figure 15.3 – Even-order (Asymmetrical) Waveform Distortion

Figure 15.4 shows the time domain implications of symmetrical, odd-order distortion, illustrating the fundamental (input) frequency and also the third and fifth harmonics. Adjustments to the phase of the third and fifth harmonics causes the same flattening of the top and bottom of the combined waveform corresponding to the curve shown in Figure15.2b.

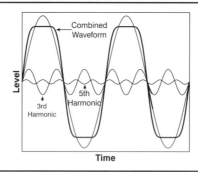

Figure 15.4 – Odd-order (Symmetrical) Waveform Distortion

CATV Lasers

High Linearity Lasers

Over the years, laser manufacturers have developed chip designs that have ever improving linearity. Today one can buy 10 mW (+10 dBm) lasers that can handle 77 or more analog channels and deliver CSO and CTB better than -55 dB. There is a price (literally) to pay for this performance. High linearity lasers require extensive screening that results in low yields. One must match a custom-tuned predistortion circuit to each high linearity laser in order to achieve high performance.

Predistorted Lasers

As we saw earlier, any slight deviation from a purely linear transfer function will cause distortion and harmonics. Chapter 7, Figure 7.11 gave an example of a slightly nonlinear laser, and Figure 7.12 showed the response of a predistortion circuit used on that laser shown. Complex predistortion circuits have a wide number of adjustments for the amplitude and phase of counter harmonics, the delay of the correction signals, frequency flatness and much more. Each laser has its own custom-tuned predistortion board. Low yield during initial screening, the labor required to tune the circuit, and low yield after mating the circuit to the laser make these devices expensive. Regardless, today, predistorted high linearity lasers deliver more than 20 mW (+13 dBm) with 77 or more analog channels and provide CSO and CTB better than -63 dB.

CSO and CTB

Figure 15.5 shows the RF spectrum of a CATV channel. Three main features include the video carrier, 1.25 MHz above the start of the 6 MHz channel slot; the color subcarrier, located 3.58 MHz above the video carrier; and the audio carrier, located 4.5 MHz above the video carrier. The noise between the peaks indicates an unmodulated video channel.

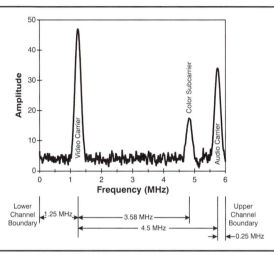

Figure 15.5 – CATV Channel and Carriers

Figure 15.6 shows the same unmodulated CATV channel with four additional peaks present.

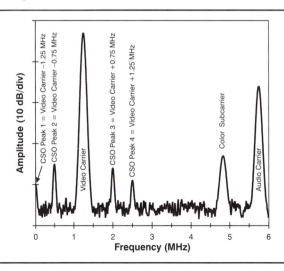

Figure 15.6 – CATV Channel CSO

These peaks result from CSO distortion. CSO peaks usually show up at four distinct frequencies: ±0.75 MHz and ±1.25 MHz around the video carrier. A given channel may show one, two, three or all four of these peaks. The peak with the largest amplitude is the reported peak. The peaks located 0.75 MHz and 1.25 MHz above the video carrier frequency generally do the most harm. Because the CSO peaks below the video carrier frequency are out-of-band, they have less of an impact on the picture quality. Severe CSO distortion may cause additional peaks to appear. Generally, one of the original four CSO peaks will still retain the largest amplitude.

Figure 15.7 shows the same unmodulated CATV channel; however, an additional peak has appeared directly beneath the video carrier peak resulting from CTB distortion. To view the distortion, one must switch off the CATV channel under observation. In cases of severe CTB distortion, additional peaks may appear. Generally, the original CTB peak under the video carrier will still retain the largest amplitude.

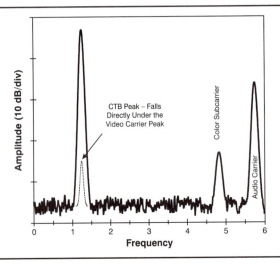

Figure 15.7 – CATV Channel CTB

CSO and CTB Beat Products

High linearity fiber optic CATV links face the challenging task of transmitting more than 100 analog video channels. Each of these channels consists of three relatively strong carriers, the video carrier, color subcarrier, and audio carrier. Any nonlinearity in the transmission path will cause the creation of new beat frequencies. Some of these new frequencies will be simple harmonics, but far more will result from interactions between several of the original carriers. Two key types of distortion will result, CTB and CSO.

Figure 15.8 shows the number of CTB beat products that result in CATV systems with 40, 60, 77, 85, and 110 channels. For a 40 channel CATV system (up to about 330 MHz), the maximum number of CTB beat products is 479 at a frequency of 217.25 MHz. For a 60 channel CATV system (up to about 450 MHz), the maximum number of CTB beat products is 1,184 at a frequency of 277.25 MHz. For a 77 channel CATV system (up to about 550 MHz), the maximum number of CTB beat products is 2,019 at a frequency of 325.25 MHz. For an 85 channel CATV system (up to about 600 MHz), the maximum number of CTB beat products is 2,487 at a frequency of 355.25 MHz. For a 110 channel CATV system (up to about 750 MHz), the maximum number of CTB beat products is 4,259 at a frequency of 433.25 MHz. Notice how quickly the number of CTB beat products increases with the increase in channel loading. The channel in the middle of the frequency band represents the worst case channel for CTB.

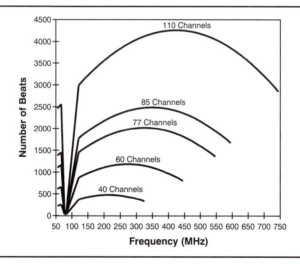

Figure 15.8 – Number of CTB Beat Products

Figure 15.9 (next page) shows the number of CSO beat products that result in CATV systems with 40, 60, 77, 85, and 110 channels. For a 40 channel CATV system (up to about 330 MHz), the maximum number of CSO beat products is 25 at a frequency of 77.25 MHz. For a 60 channel CATV system (up to about 450 MHz), the maximum number of CSO beat products is 45 at a frequency of 77.25 MHz. For a 77 channel CATV system (up to about 550 MHz), the maximum number of CSO beat products is about 62 at a frequency of 77.25 MHz. For an 85 channel CATV system (up to about 600 MHz), the maximum number of CSO beat products is 70 at a frequency of 77.25 MHz. For a 110 channel CATV system (up to about

750 MHz), the maximum number of CSO beat products is 95 at a frequency of 77.25 MHz. Notice that the number of CSO beat products increases more slowly than CTB as the channel loading increases. In most real world channel loadings, channel 5 represents the worst case channel for CSO, with channel 6 a close second, a result of the fact that channels 5 and 6 are not spaced the same way as the other channels.

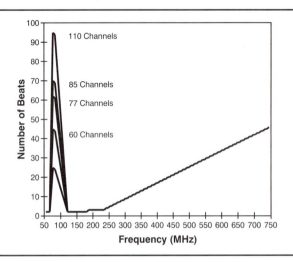

Figure 15.9 – Number of CSO Beat Products

Noise Power Ratio (NPR) Testing

Fiber optic CATV links can be grouped into two types, forward path and return path links. Forward path links carry video and audio signals from the headend to the consumers. Return path links carry signals, usually data signals, in the opposite direction, from the consumer to the headend. While CNR, CSO, and CTB commonly characterize and specify forward path links, another parameter, noise power ratio (NPR), often characterizes return path links. NPR, a powerful test technique, takes into account the CNR as well as the distortion introduced by the link.

Figure 15.10 shows the typical input signal used to perform NPR testing. This input signal, formed by applying a deep notch filter (at 22 MHz in this figure) to a broadband white noise source, results in white noise with a narrow, quiet area. This input signal passes through the fiber optic link. At the output of the fiber optic receiver, the deep notch at 22 MHz may fill in by two different processes: noise in the fiber optic transmitter or noise in the fiber optic receiver. Distortion products such as the second harmonic of noise near 11 MHz will fall in the notch, as well as the third harmonic of noise near 7.33 MHz, and various intermodulation products. The NPR measurement resembles a signal-to-noise+distortion measurement (called SINAD) often used on audio equipment.

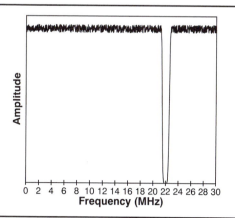

Figure 15.10 – NPR Testing — Input Signal

Figure 15.11 illustrates the response of two separate output filters used to perform the NPR measurement. The left peak, near 10 MHz, measures the gain of the fiber optic link, giving the output signal level. The right peak, near 22 MHz, measures the noise and distortion that fall in the deep notch. The 22 MHz bandpass filter is more narrow than the deep notch in the noise. The NPR equals the ratio of the total energy through the 10 MHz bandpass filter divided by the total energy through the 22 MHz filter.

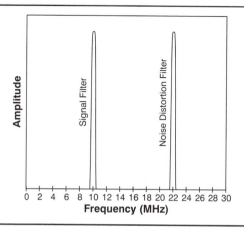

Figure 15.11 – Output Filters

Figure 15.12 shows the NPR testing result from a typical fiber optic link. At low RF input levels, noise in the notch determines the NPR. As the input RF level increases, the NPR flattens out and reaches a peak. As the level increases further, the NPR starts to drop as the result becomes dominated by distortion products filling up the deep notch. The optimum RF input range lies in the region around the peak in the NPR curve.

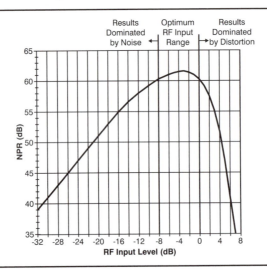

Figure 15.12 – NPR Testing — Results

External Modulators

Most early fiber optic transmitters used directly modulated lasers. However as data rates increased and transmission span lengths grew, wavelength chirp, caused by turning a laser on and off, limited data rates. Wavelength chirp widens the effective spectral width of the laser which causes dispersion problems. Reducing this dispersion requires a laser source with no wavelength chirp and a narrow linewidth. External modulation, which allows the laser to be turned on continuously, achieves this effect because modulation occurs outside of the laser cavity. An external modulator functions much like an electrically activated shutter. As analog devices, external modulators allow the amount of light passed to vary from some maximum amount (P_{MAX}) to some minimum amount (P_{MIN}).

Lithium Niobate Amplitude and Phase Modulators

The popularity of lithium niobate ($LiNbO_3$) as a material used in external modulators results from its low optical loss and high electro-optic coefficient. This coefficient refers to the electro-optic effect, when the refractive index of the material changes in response to an applied electric field. The refractive index of the material causes light to travel at a speed inversely proportional to the refractive index of the material. Thus if we could suddenly increase the refractive index of a material, we could slow the light beam down and vice versa. Figure 15.13 shows the block diagram of a typical external modulator.

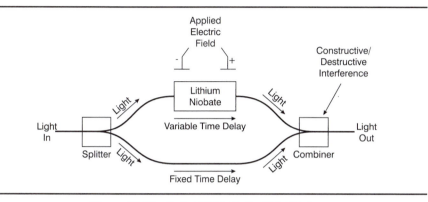

Figure 15.13 – Basic LiNbO$_3$ Optical Modulator

The light enters the external modulator via the input fiber. First, an optical splitter splits the light onto two fibers. The top fiber path travels through a length of LiNbO$_3$ crystal. The light in the bottom fiber experiences a fixed delay. After the light travels through the lithium niobate crystal and the fixed length of fiber, an optical combiner merges the two fiber paths. The light travels through identical path legs. The speed at which light travels through any medium depends on the refractive index of the material. A higher refractive index results in slower light speed. An equal time delay through the fixed fiber and the LiNbO$_3$ crystal will produce in-phase light when it reaches the output optical combiner. Referring to the nature of light as described in Chapter 9, we see that since the light waves in both legs are in phase, they will constructively add to form the maximum possible output. The refractive index and the speed of light change as the applied voltage changes. When the speed changes enough to delay the light by half of one wavelength, the light will be out of phase when it reaches the output 3 dB coupler. Now the light will exhibit destructive interference, yielding the minimum possible output.

Figure 15.14 shows the response of the basic lithium niobate optical modulator. For analog operation, V_0 represents one possible bias point. Digital operation could use typical operating points of $-V\pi/2$ and $+V\pi/2$.

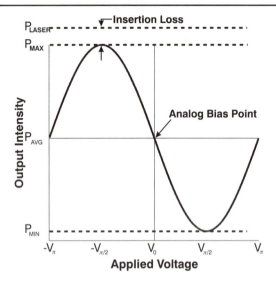

Figure 15.14 – Operating Curves for a Typical Lithium Niobate Modulator

Figure 15.15 shows the simplest type of external modulator, a phase modulator. The phase modulator has a single optical input of polarization-maintaining (PM) fiber and a single optical output of PM or single-mode fiber. In a simple phase modulator, two electrodes surround the waveguide. The bottom electrode is grounded while an outside voltage signal drives the top electrode. As the voltage on the top electrode changes, the refractive index of the waveguide changes accordingly, alternating the light as the refractive index rises and falls. While this modulates the phase of the light, the output intensity remains unchanged.

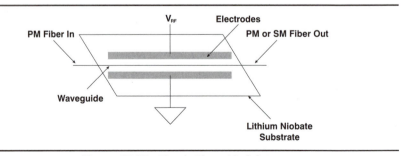

Figure 15.15 – Simple Phase Modulator

Digital versus Analog Operation

In simple applications, an external modulator transmits a digital data stream. The drive voltage toggles between $-V_{\pi/2}$ and $V_{\pi/2}$. This causes the output intensity to swing from maximum to minimum utilizing maximum modulation depth.

External modulators may also transmit analog signals, but in this case, they require extensive stabilization and linearization. Stabilizing the bias point at exactly the 50% point minimizes that second-order distortion. However, a third-order distortion remains. A small drive signal may yield a response that does not require linearization. For CATV applications sending 80 or 110 channels, applying predistortion to the signals removes third-order distortion effects.

CATV Detectors

APDs operate in a nonlinear fashion, making inherently linear PIN detectors suitable for applications such as multichannel CATV. PIN detectors represent one of the most linear EO or OE components available, often displaying excellent linearity over six decades or more light intensity. However, to work in high channel count CATV applications, PIN detectors must achieve exceptional levels of linearity. The best detectors have a small (75 μm or less) diameter, low series resistance, and very high shunt resistance. The small detector size usually indicates low capacitance, which will yield high bandwidth and low noise. (The capacitance of the detector introduces a zero in the response of the receiver, which tends to emphasize high frequency noise.) Low series resistance allows the detector to operate at high light levels without distortion and improves linearity over a wide range of light levels. High shunt resistance reduces leakage current (also called dark current), which reduces noise and also improves linearity, especially at lower light levels. A CATV PIN diode must have five characteristics:

1. Good linearity
2. Low backreflection
3. High responsivity
4. Flat frequency response
5. Low noise

Some parameters are a function of the design, but the detector packaging and the fiber's alignment to the detector influence them as well. Using an angle polished fiber pigtail, and off-setting the detector from the fiber minimizes backreflections. (Refer back to Figure 7.18.) Detector manufacturers align analog detectors at test stations that simultaneously test and display all five critical parameters in real time. The operator or automated alignment station will then search for an alignment that satisfies the performance criteria for all five parameters. Detectors rated for analog applications cost more because they require more manufacturing (alignment) time, more screening time at the chip level, more test time to achieve the required performance, and lower yield, since not all detectors will achieve the desired performance level for all parameters.

CATV Receivers

A CATV receiver starts with a CATV detector described earlier. Figure 15.16 shows a typical CATV receiver in photoconductive mode. The PIN detector will be reverse biased with a voltage sufficient to fully deplete the intrinsic region. The voltage must be large enough to minimize the effects of the series resistance at high light levels. On the other hand, if the voltage is too high, the detector will have excessive dark current which will increase the noise.

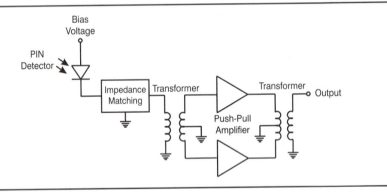

Figure 15.16 – CATV Receiver

Detectors can also operate at zero voltage bias, called the photovoltaic mode, but this is usually only useful in specialized applications, such as optical power meters, which must accommodate a wide range of input light levels with high accuracy. Detectors operating in the photovoltaic mode have very slow response and very poor analog characteristics.

A PIN detector operating in the photoconductive mode, with a 377 Ohm impedance, looks very much like an ideal current source. However, 377 Ohms does not match with amplifiers that will typically have a 75-Ohm impedance. In order to obtain maximum power transfer, one must include an impedance-matching network that matches 377 Ohms to 75 Ohms. This creates up to 7 dB of essentially noise-free gain. After the impedance-matching network, a transformer changes the single-ended signal to a balanced signal. This balanced signal is fed to a pair of matched amplifiers in a push-pull configuration. A second transformer combines all of the amplifier outputs to create a single-ended signal. The push-pull amplifier minimizes second-order distortion. The amplifiers must maintain a high IP3 in order to minimize third-order distortion.

CATV Transmission Systems

Fiber optic CATV system designs include the high split or fanout configuration. In the fanout configuration, a single transmit site broadcasts to a large number of receive sites, sometimes using dedicated fibers or incorporating fiber sharing. In the linear bus configuration, a single transmit site feeds only a single fiber. At each site, fiber optic splitters tap off a portion of the light, allowing most of it to continue down the fiber bus.

Cable systems began as strictly copper systems; however, hybrid fiber/coaxial cable (HFC) networks have become widespread in the CATV industry. This network uses a fiber optic trunk line as the backbone and coaxial cable lines for the drops to individual sites. As mentioned, copper cable's prevalence has declined as bandwidth demands make optical fiber the only choice. Passive components such as signal dividers, signal combiners, and taps create multiple paths in the network allowing greater coverage for more users. Amplifier stations placed at intervals along these paths recover the attenuated signal's strength. Figure 15.17 illustrates a CATV headend.

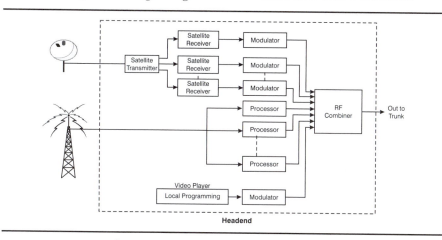

Figure 15.17 – CATV Headend Block Diagram

Trunks cascade one after another to cover greater distances. Feeder reach directly from the trunk to uniformly cover smaller areas, and the drop covers the final short-distance connection to the individual receiver, i.e., the cable customer's television. Signals come from many sources including satellites and distributed from the headend of the system. The signals are amplified and converted to the desired television channel frequency before distribution to the cable system.

A few years ago, many predicted the demise of AM CATV, but AM CATV fiber optic links continue to thrive. For many years, 1310 nm dominated CATV transmission. Much refinement went into the lasers to improve their linearity, lower their noise and increase their output power. Today, optical output powers exceed 20 mW (+13 dBm), and linearity supports 110 channels. The recent popularity of 1550 nm allows transmission distance to increase from 20-30 km to 60-140 km.

1310 nm Systems

Before 1980, coax cable ruled most CATV systems. These systems involved large numbers of RF amplifiers spaced every 1,000-2,000 feet. Figure 15.18 shows a typical pre-fiber CATV architecture.

Headend   RF Amplifiers Spaced Every 1,000-2,000 Feet (Coax Cable)

Figure 15.18 – Typical Pre-Fiber CATV Architecture

In the early 1980s the CATV industry began using direct modulated 1310 nm VSB/AM links for "supertrunks," as shown in Figure 15.19. This configuration reduced the overall number of cascaded amplifiers by transporting a high-quality replica of the headend signals deep in the distribution system

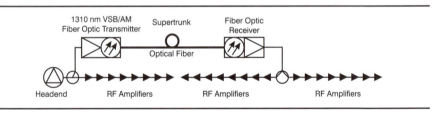

Figure 15.19 – Early Fiber Optic CATV Architecture

Hybrid Architectures

Figure 15.20 shows the use of multichannel digital systems to perform headend consolidation in the early 1990s. In this configuration, high quality signals transported by a multichannel digital system from a master headend replace a separate headend. The system also incorporates fiber supertrunks to reduce amplifier cascades, making the cost savings quite significant with this approach.

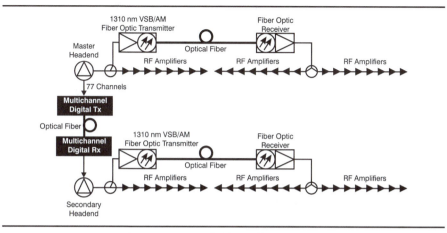

Figure 15.20 – Hybrid CATV Architecture

1550 nm Systems

High performance, externally modulated 1550 nm VSB/AM transmitters and erbium-doped fiber amplifiers (EDFAs) changed the hybrid CATV architecture in the mid 1990s. The current evolution of the CATV distribution system includes copper coax, fiber supertrunks, multichannel digitized transport, and a new element, externally modulated 1550 nm VSB/AM fiber optic links. Increasingly, 1550 nm VSB/AM links carry signals between headend sites over long distances with EDFA boosters along the way. The 1550 nm VSB/AM transmitter utilizes an external modulator and a 1550 nm laser operating in the continuous wave (CW) mode with a very narrow linewidth, often less than 1 MHz. This corresponds to an optical linewidth less than 10^{-4} nm, allowing the dispersion of the most common type of installed fiber, non dispersion-shifted fiber (NDSF), to be largely ignored. Dispersion of NDSF is about +17 ps/nm/km.

The system shown in Figure 15.21 incorporates optical splitters and EDFAs. The CATV industry has embraced EDFAs, whose invention also enabled the DWDM explosion. Most EDFAs exhibit good linearity and a low noise figure so the CATV video channel payload suffers minimal degradation. When using externally modulated 1550 nm transmitters, the system may require EDFAs because of the relatively low (+7 dBm) optical output power of externally modulated transmitters. The EDFA can boost this output to over +20 dBm (100 mW), allowing wide split ratios and/or long distance transmission. By contrast, the optical output of direct modulated 1310 nm transmitters usually ranges up to +12 dBm (16 mW) without amplification. Recently, the availability of praseodymium-doped fiber amplifiers (PDFAs) allows the amplification of 1310 nm signals up to +16 dBm (40 mW) or more. These amplifiers have a relatively narrow, but adequate, operating wavelength range, usually 1305 nm ±5 nm, and they also perform well with analog multichannel signals, such as CATV signals.

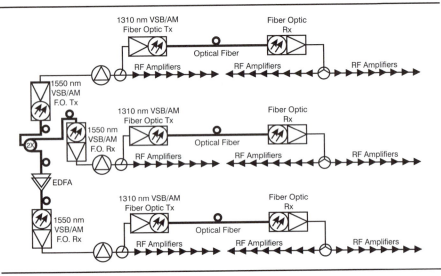

Figure 15.21 – Hybrid 1310/1550 nm CATV Architecture

To date, CATV systems have not employed Raman optical amplifiers. Raman amplifiers differ from conventional EDFAs in that the amplification does not take place in a module, it takes place in the transmission fiber itself. A common topology places a Raman pump laser at the receive end of the fiber and launches optical power back towards the transmitter. The Raman pump laser wavelength is typically about 40 nm less that the wavelength intended for amplification. As the forward traveling signal encounters the reverse traveling Raman pump signal, the forward signal robs energy from the Raman pump signal, and is thus amplified. Future CATV systems may employ Raman amplifiers to further stretch the maximum transmission distance.

Limiting Factors to CATV VSB/AM System Performance

Fiber nonlinearities dominate the performance of 1550 nm VSB/AM links. Stimulated Brillouin scattering (SBS) represents the most serious effect. Fiber-induced relative intensity noise (RIN) also limits the maximum practical operating distance of VSB/AM links. Optical backreflections in the fiber plant represent another factor that renders the signal unusable. Other more complex factors, such as the interaction between self-phase modulation (SPM) and fiber dispersion, can cause the CSO to degrade rapidly over long fiber lengths. Laser clipping, caused by the RF input signal driving the laser below its threshold, is yet another factor that can limit CNR, CSO, and CTB performance.

Stimulated Brillouin Scattering (SBS)

Stimulated Brillouin scattering (SBS), also discussed in Chapter 6, "Fiber Limits," imposes an upper limit on the amount of optical power that can be launched into an optical fiber. The SBS effect has a threshold optical power, which, when exceeded, redirects a significant fraction of the transmitted light toward the transmitter. Figure 15.22 illustrates the SBS effect.

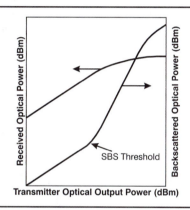

Figure 15.22 – SBS Effect

The resulting saturation of optical power reaches the receiver, and problems associated with optical signals being reflected back into the laser also develop. In addition, the SBS process introduces significant noise into the system, resulting in degraded BER performance in digital systems and degraded CNR in analog systems. One approach for broadening linewidth involves externally modulating the transmitter, while spreading out the linewidth by adding a very small AC modulation signal to the DC current source used to drive the laser itself. This broadens the spectral linewidth of the transmitter and increases the threshold for the onset of SBS. This option also increases the dispersion susceptibility of the transmitter, primarily a concern when operating at 1550 nm over non dispersion-shifted single-mode fiber. Practical implementations of SBS suppression circuitry based on laser drive dithering can increase the SBS threshold by 5 dB.

Phase dithering the output of the external modulator also increases the SBS threshold. In this case, a high frequency signal, usually twice that of the highest frequency being transmitted, gets imposed onto both output legs of the external modulator. This modulates the phase of the light, effectively spreading out the spectral width. Figure 15.23a shows the optical spectra of an VSB/AM transmitter without phase dithering. The central carrier exceeds the SBS threshold, causing serious system degradation.

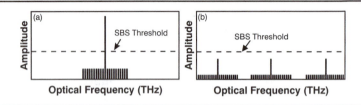

Figure 15.23 – Optical Spectra of a VSB/AM Transmitter

In Figure 15.23b, a high frequency dither signal has been applied to the phase modulation input of the external modulator. All of the lines now lie well below the SBS threshold. Practical implementations of SBS suppression circuitry can increase the SBS threshold to about +16 dBm. This option also increases the dispersion susceptibility of the transmitter, primarily a concern when operating at 1550 nm over non dispersion-shifted single-mode fiber. Adding EDFAs in the signal path also decreases the SBS threshold. The SBS threshold for a system containing N amplifiers is the threshold without amplifiers in mW divided by N. This can result in very low SBS thresholds that can seriously impair system performance.

CSO Distortion

Self-phase modulation (SPM) also has the potential to cause distortion in 1550 nm CATV VSB/AM fiber optic links, assuming that the system uses NDS fiber, which has dispersion of about 17 ps/nm/km at 1550 nm. The interaction between SPM and the dispersion of the fiber causes CSO distortion. SPM does not affect 1310 nm systems since the dispersion of NDS fiber is near zero at 1310 nm. However, it severely affects broad spectrum transmitters, especially in direct modulated transmitters. Use of dispersion-compensating modules (DCMs) can largely eliminate CSO distortion. DCMs consist of fixed lengths of special fiber that have dispersion opposite to that of normal NDS fiber. The DCM fiber has very high dispersion enabling a short length of fiber to correct a long length of NDS fiber. Bragg gratings also perform dispersion compensation.

Fiber-induced Relative Intensity Noise (RIN)

Fiber-induced relative intensity noise (RIN) limits the maximum practical operating distance of analog multichannel links. Figure 15.24 shows its impact on a 1550 nm externally modulated VSB/AM link.

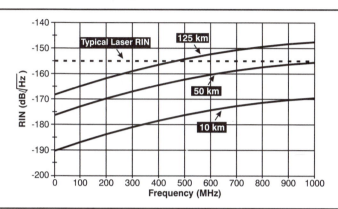

Figure 15.24 – Fiber RIN at 1550 nm

Interference effects caused by Rayleigh scattering create fiber RIN. In an analog system, these reflections constructively and destructively interfere with the forward propagating light. Any phase noise in the transmitted signal gets converted to AM noise by this process. Typical laser noise in such a system is -155 dB/Hz$^{1/2}$. In long links, e.g., 125 km, the fiber-induced RIN exceeds the laser noise above frequencies of 450 MHz. That means that the CNR performance of the link will degrade compared to shorter distances.

Backreflection

The impact of backreflections on a signal has been discussed at length in Chapter 9. The advent of APC connectors and low-loss fusion splices have solved many backreflection problems. However, users of many deployed analog and multichannel systems may not know the backreflection quality of the connectors in the fiber plant, which can lead to unpredictable results. In the best case, performance may live up to expectation, or it may not. Figure 15.25 (next page) shows how the CNR of a CATV system can degrade as a variable optical reflecting element is added in the fiber path. Almost no degradation occurs at backreflections of -50 dB or lower. Above -45 dB backreflections, the CNR drops off quickly.

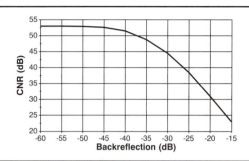

Figure 15.25 – Effects of Backreflection on CNR

Laser Clipping

The amount of light reaching the receiver dominates the achievable CNR. In the case of a multichannel CATV VSB/AM fiber optic link, 80 channels or more share the total light output. A common modulation depth for such a link is 3.5% per channel. That parameter gives the impression that the modulation of the laser will exceed 100% (80 times 3.5% yields 280%), which would result in extreme levels of distortion. In real life, assuming 80 independent channels, the RMS modulation equals the square root of 80 times 3.5% or 31.3%. Even so, the amplitude and phase of the RF carriers will occasionally line up to drive the laser below the threshold current, causing laser clipping, which will affect CNR, CSO, and CTB. Figure 15.26 shows the effect of laser clipping on the CSO performance. As the optical modulation depth increases, the CSO degrades rapidly.

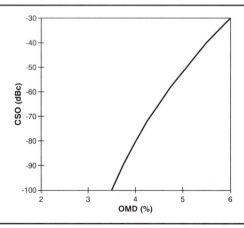

Figure 15.26 – Distortion Due to Laser Clipping versus OMD

DWDM

No survey of analog multichannel transmission systems would be complete without mentioning DWDM, which offers a way to multiply the capacity of a given fiber by 80 times or more. However, many challenges await aggressive DWDM applications of analog multichannel transmission systems. The SBS, RIN, and backreflection limitations mentioned earlier all apply, in addition to several other types of fiber nonlinearities, including stimulated Raman scattering (SRS), four wave mixing (FWM), self-phase modulation (SPM), and cross-phase modulation (XPM). These factors plague digital and analog systems alike. But because of the nature of analog systems, their effects will be seen more readily than in digital systems.

Understanding Specifications

The next section of this chapter examines a typical specification for a fiber optic CATV link. For clarity this section discusses the specifications one line at a time to see how to interpret various parameters and learn the important parameters for optimum performance of a typical link. The transmitter and receiver sections are separated into two parts.

Typical Transmitter Specifications

Table 15.1 – Typical CATV Tx Specifications

Transmitter Optical and Electrical Characteristics: @ 25 °C, SM Fiber				
	Minimum	**Typical**	**Maximum**	**Units**
Channel Loading			110	Channels
Bandwidth	40		860	MHz
Power Supply Voltage	85		264	V_{AC}
Power Supply Frequency	47		440	Hz
Power Dissipation		25		Watts
Operating Wavelength	1290	1310	1330	nm
Optical Output Power	+6		+13	dBm
Required Fiber Bandwidth	1,000			MHz
Input/Output Impedance		75		Ohms
Carrier-to-Noise Ratio (CNR)	See Figure 15.27			
Composite Second Order (CSO)		-64	-62	dB
Composite Triple Beat (CTB)		-69	-67	dB
Side Mode Suppression Ratio (SMSR)		30		dB
RF Input Signal Level (per ch.)	See Figure 15.28			
Backreflection Tolerance			-50	dB
Operating Temperature Range	0		+45	°C
Humidity	5		95	%

The table header indicates that the transmitter specifications are measured at +25°C over single-mode fiber. In the table itself, the first parameter lists the channel loading capability of the transmitter, 110 channels maximum. While not explicitly spelled out, this specification usually refers to 80 channels of VSB/AM and 30 digital channels at a 6 dB lower amplitude. The transmitter bandwidth ranges from 40 MHz minimum to 860 MHz maximum. The channels must fall between these frequency limits for proper operation. The transmitter requires a power supply voltage of 85 to 264 V_{AC} with a frequency range of 47 Hz to 440 Hz. With these power specifications, the transmitter should operate in virtually any country using the indigenous power grid. The transmitter typically dissipates 25 Watts of power. The operating wavelength, given nominally as 1310 nm, can range from 1290 nm to 1330 nm. While this range will have little impact of a systems analysis, the optical loss for most fibers will increase slightly at 1290 nm or 1330 nm versus the low attenuation point at 1310 nm. The optical output power ranges from +6 dBm to +13 dBm. The required fiber bandwidth is 1,000 MHz. The end-to-end fiber (between the transmitter and receiver) has to provide at least 1,000 MHz of bandwidth at the full range of operating wavelengths. The transmitter requires a typical input/output impedance of 75 Ohms.

Figure 15.27 determines the transmitter carrier-to-noise ratio (CNR), which depends on the number of transmitted channels, and especially the optical power (dBm) that reaches the input of the receiver. For instance, if the received power is -5 dBm at 110 channels, then the CNR will be 44 dB. At 10 channels and a received power of 0 dBm, the CNR will be 59 dB.

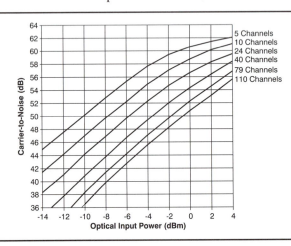

Figure 15.27 – Typical CNR versus Receiver Optical Input and Channel Loading
(Data based on the performance of Force, Inc. multichannel VSB/AM links.)

Composite second order (CSO) measures the linearity of the transmitter. It is listed as -64 dB typical and -62 dB maximum. Composite triple beat (CTB), another measure of transmitter linearity, is listed as -69 dB typical and -67 dB maximum. The side mode suppression ratio (SMSR), which measures the purity of the laser oscillation, is listed as 30 dB typical. Ideally, the laser would oscillate at a single pure wavelength. Realistically, all laser diodes oscillate at a number of wavelengths. The 30 dB SMSR parameter means that all other peaks will be at least 30 dB lower in amplitude than the primary peak.

Figure 15.28 determines the RF input signal level. The number of channels transmitted dictates the RF input signal level. Per the figure, a 40 channel transmitter requires an RF input signal level of +25 dBmV per channel.

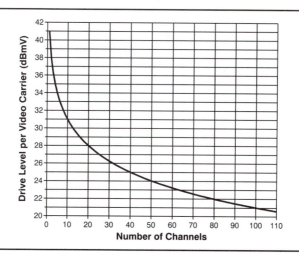

Figure 15.28 – Transmitter Level per Channel versus Number of Channels

Backreflection tolerance keeps the transmitter from suffering degraded performance. This transmitter can tolerate a maximum of -50 dB backreflection total. Any higher backreflection (e.g., -45 dB) will cause the performance of the transmitter to degrade and perhaps not meet the other published specifications. Finally, the operating temperature range is listed as 0°C to +45°C and the humidity range is 5% to 95%.

Typical Receiver Specifications

Table 15.2 – Typical CATV Rx Specifications

Receiver Optical and Electrical Characteristics: @ 25 °C, SM Fiber				
	Minimum	**Typical**	**Maximum**	**Units**
Bandwidth	40		860	MHz
CATV Channels			110	
Power Supply Voltage	+12		+16	V_{DC}
Power Dissipation		1.75		Watts
Optical Input Range	-4.5		+4.5	dBm
Input/Output Impedance		75		Ohms

Table 15.2 – Typical CATV Rx Specifications (Continued)

Receiver Optical and Electrical Characteristics: @ 25 °C, SM Fiber				
	Minimum	Typical	Maximum	Units
Carrier-to-Noise Ratio (CNR)	See Figure 15.27			
Composite Second Order (CSO)		-67	-65	dB
Composite Triple Beat (CTB)		-70	-68	dB
End-to-end Gain	See Figure 15.29			
Operating Temperature Range	-20		+70	°C
Humidity	5		95	%

Table 15.2 begins with the channel loading capability of the receiver, 110 channels maximum. As with the transmitter, this specification usually indicates 80 channels of VSB/AM and 30 digital channels at 6 dB lower amplitude. The receiver bandwidth ranges from 40 MHz minimum to 860 MHz maximum. The channels must fall between these frequency limits for proper operation. The power supply voltage is +12 to +16 V_{DC}, and the receiver typically dissipates 1.75 Watts of power. The optical input power ranges from -4.5 dBm to +4.5 dBm. The receiver requires a typical input/output impedance of 75 Ohms. Figure 15.27 also determines the receiver CNR. The CNR depends on the number of received channels and the optical power (dBm) that reaches the receiver input. For instance, if the received power is +3 dBm at 110 channels, then the CNR will be 54 dB. If the received power is +4 dBm and 10 channels are being received, then the CNR will be 60 dB. The next specification, CSO, is -67 dB typical and -65 dB maximum. Composite triple beat (CTB), is listed as -70 dB typical and -68 dB maximum. The amount of light reaching the receiver determines the end-to-end gain, and designers can calculate this using Figure 15.29.

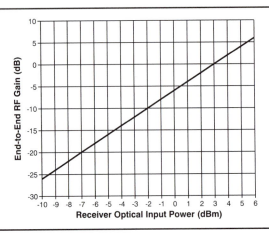

Figure 15.29 – End-to-end Link Gain

A typical CATV link will have unity gain (0 dB) at a received optical power of +3 dBm (2 milliwatts). The RF gain changes by 2 dB for every 1 dB change in received optical power. This curve will shift up and down by 3 or 4 dB due to variations in the lasers and amplifiers; however, the slope will always be 2. Finally, the operating temperature range is listed as 0°C to +45°C and the humidity range is 5% to 95%.

CATV System Design Considerations

Several procedures dictate the needs of a fiber optic CATV system.

1) The system must use single-mode fiber throughout.
2) The system must use angles physical contact (APC)connectors or high-quality fusion splices to minimize backreflections.
3) The designer should determine the optical loss of each fiber segment at the operating wavelength. Most single-mode fiber has 0.5 dB/km loss in the 1310 nm region and 0.25 dB/km in the 1550 nm region. These figures, however, do not take into account connector losses, splices losses or microbend losses in the installed fiber. Guessing can lead to an under-specified system, so measure each fiber segment's optical loss.
4) Many fiber optic CATV transmitters require relatively low RF input levels compared to the RF levels found in the copper side of CATV distribution systems, where the RF levels can run to +50 dBmV or more. The system must allow for proper attenuation at the transmitter input to correspond to the recommended RF input levels.

Before starting the design of a fiber optic CATV system, the designer should map the overall system configuration, including all transmit and receive sites and measure fiber losses in the system at the operating wavelength. In addition, the designer must consider the system performance goals, specifically CNR and channel loading.

The simplest approach to designing a fiber optic CATV system starts at the end, i.e., the receiver inputs, and moves towards the beginning. Carrier-to-noise ratio (CNR) represents the key performance parameter for video signals. Other important parameters include composite second order (CSO) and composite triple beat (CTB), but the nature of the transmitter defines these. By specifying a CSO and CTB with performance levels much higher than the typical system requirements, the designer can ignore these parameters in all conventional configurations.

To emphasize the importance of CNR and channel loading, we revisit the illustration seen earlier in the section on specifications. Figure 15.30 illustrates the achievable CNR for several channel loadings over a wide range of receiver powers in a typical CATV fiber optic link.

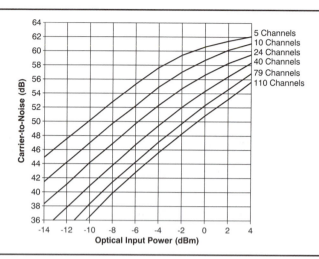

Figure 15.30 – Typical CNR versus Receiver Optical Input and Channel Loading

The figure shows six curves for channel loadings of 5 channels, 10 channels, 24 channels, 40 channels, 79 channels, and 110 channels. To determine performance for channel loading outside the values, use the curve closest to the channel count (e.g., use the 79 channel curve to evaluate the performance of an 80 channel system), or pick a midpoint between two existing curves. In other words, evaluate the performance of a seven channel system using the data midway between the five and ten channel curves.

To clarify and expand on this approach, the following scenarios show the detailed methodology and calculations for the parameters needed to design a typical CATV transmission system. However, before we delve into these detailed scenarios, we require two essential equations that allow us to easily change units from optical dBm to optical milliwatts.

Equation for Converting dBm to Milliwatts

P_1 = the power in dBm and P_2 = the power in milliwatts:

Eq. 15.5 $$P_2 = +10^{(P_1/10)}$$

Equation for Converting Milliwatts to dBm

Again, P_1 = the power in dBm and P_2 = the power in milliwatts:

Eq. 15.6 $$P_1 = +10 \cdot Log_{10}(P_2)$$

Now we have the information we need to run through the following scenarios. Configuration #1 shows a high split (fanout) configuration, illustrated in Figure 15.31.

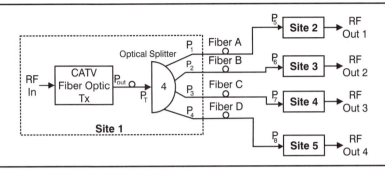

Figure 15.31 – Configuration 1: High-split (Fanout)

Site # 1 contains a CATV transmitter along with a 1 x 4 optical splitter. This optical splitter must exhibit very low backreflection. Individual fibers, labeled A through D, run to sites 2 through 5. In performing this analysis we will compute the transmitter's minimum optical output power and determine the required individual split ratios for the 1 x 4 optical splitter in order to deliver the correct amount of optical power to the receivers.

Table 15.3 – Configuration 1, Scenario 1

User Data	
Channel Load = 110 Channels	Usually a mix of 80 VSB/AM channels and 30 QAM channels. Under 110 channels, performance improves and vice versa.
Fiber A Loss = L_A = 4 dB	Total fiber loss, including splices and connectors, from Site #1 to Site #2 but excluding the losses of the 1 x 4 optical splitter.
Fiber B Loss = L_B = 6 dB	Total fiber loss, including splices and connectors, from Site #1 to Site #3 but excluding the losses of the 1 x 4 optical splitter.
Fiber C Loss = L_C = 3 dB	Total fiber loss, including splices and connectors, from Site #1 to Site #4 but excluding the losses of the 1 x 4 optical splitter.
Fiber D Loss = L_D = 5 dB	Total fiber loss, including splices and connectors from Site #1 to Site #5 but excluding the losses of the 1 x 4 optical splitter.
Site # 2 – Desired CNR = CNR_2 = 48 dB Site # 3 – Desired CNR = CNR_3 = 49 dB Site # 4 – Desired CNR = CNR_4 = 50 dB Site # 5 – Desired CNR = CNR_5 = 51 dB	Usually, a user will have a minimum CNR requirement that applies to all sites. In this case, for instance, the output of the Site #5 receiver may be split a much higher number times than Site #2, so it needs a higher CNR.

Table 15.3 – Configuration 1, Scenario 1 (Continued)

Computations

Step 1 – Look up the required receiver input optical powers (P_5 - P_8) to achieve the desired CNRs. (Refer to Figure 15.30, 110 ch. curve.) Look at CNR_2 - CNR_5.

For CNR_2 = 48 dB, 110 channels, required receiver power P_5 = -2 dBm

For CNR_3 = 49 dB, 110 channels, required receiver power P_6 = -1 dBm

For CNR_4 = 50 dB, 110 channels, required receiver power P7 = -0.5 dBm; round up to P_7 = 0.0 dBm

For CNR_5 = 51 dB, 110 channels, required receiver power P_8 = +0.5 dBm; round up to P_8 = +1.0 dBm

Step 2 – Compute the power at the output of the optical splitter (P_1 - P_4) based on the receiver input optical powers (P_5 - P_8) and the fiber losses (L_A - L_D).

$P_1 = P_5 + L_A$ = -2 dBm + 4 dB = +2 dBm   Add fiber loss L_A to receiver input power P_5

$P_2 = P_6 + L_B$ = -1 dBm + 6 dB = +5 dBm   Add fiber loss L_B to receiver input power P_6

$P_3 = P_7 + L_C$ = 0 dBm + 3 dB = +3 dBm   Add fiber loss L_C to receiver input power P_7

$P_4 = P_8 + L_D$ = +1 dBm + 5 dB = +6 dBm   Add fiber loss L_D to receiver input power P_8

Step 3 – Convert the powers at the output of the optical splitter (P_1 - P_4) to mW using equation 15.5.

$P_1 = +10^{(dBm/10)} = +10^{(+2/10)}$ = 1.58 mW

$P_2 = +10^{(dBm/10)} = +10^{(+5/10)}$ = 3.16 mW

$P_3 = +10^{(dBm/10)} = +10^{(+3/10)}$ = 2.00 mW

$P_4 = +10^{(dBm/10)} = +10^{(+6/10)}$ = 3.98 mW

Step 4 – Compute the total power output by all four legs (P_1 - P_4) of the optical splitter. Call that total P_{Sum}.

$P_{Sum} = (P_1+P_2+P_3+P_4) = (1.58+3.16+2.00+3.98) = 10.72$ mW

Step 5 – Increase P_{Sum} by 20% to account for the excess loss of the fiber optic splitter. Call that value P_T. P_T is the required input optical power to the optical splitter. It also equals the transmitter optical output power.

$P_T = 1.2 \cdot (P_{Sum}) = 12.9$ mW

Step 6 – Convert P_T to dBm.

$P_T = +10 \cdot Log_{10} (12.9) = +11.1$ dBm   Minimum required transmitter output = +11.1 dBm. Higher optical output from the transmitter will improve performance.

Step 7 – Now calculate the optical splitter ratios for each output leg.

$P_{LEG} = 100 \cdot (P_{LEG}/P_{SUM})$ General formula

P_1 Leg Percentage = $100 \cdot (1.58/10.72) = 15\%$ Divide optical splitter output # 1 by the total output

P_2 Leg Percentage = $100 \cdot (3.16/10.72) = 29\%$ Divide optical splitter output # 2 by the total output

Table 15.3 – Configuration 1, Scenario 1 (Continued)

P_3 Leg Percentage = $100 \cdot (2.00/10.72) = 19\%$	Divide optical splitter output # 3 by the total output
P_4 Leg Percentage = $100 \cdot (3.98/10.72) = 37\%$	Divide optical splitter output # 4 by the total output

Step 8 – Verify that the optical splitter ratios total 100%. In this case they do.

Table 15.4 – Configuration 1, Scenario 2

User Data

Channel Load = 40 Channels	Usually 40 VSB/AM channels. Under 40 channels improves performance and vice versa.
Fiber A Loss = L_A = 8 dB	Total fiber loss, including splices and connectors, from Site #1 to Site #2 but excluding the losses of the 1 x 4 optical splitter.
Fiber B Loss = L_B = 2 dB	Total fiber loss, including splices and connectors, from Site #1 to Site #3 but excluding the losses of the 1 x 4 optical splitter.
Fiber C Loss = L_C = 4 dB	Total fiber loss, including splices and connectors, from Site #1 to Site #4 but excluding the losses of the 1 x 4 optical splitter.
Fiber D Loss = L_D = 3 dB	Total fiber loss, including splices and connectors, from Site #1 to Site #5 but excluding the losses of the 1 x 4 optical splitter.
Site #2 – Desired CNR = CNR_2 = 50 dB	Usually, a user will have a minimum CNR requirement that applies to all sites. In this case, for instance, the output of the Site #2 receiver may be split a much higher number times than Site #5, so it needs a higher CNR.
Site #3 – Desired CNR = CNR_3 = 50 dB	
Site #4 – Desired CNR = CNR_4 = 49 dB	
Site #5 – Desired CNR = CNR_5 = 48 dB	

Computations

Step 1 – Look up the required receiver input optical powers (P_5 - P_8) for the desired CNRs. (Refer to Figure 15.30, 40 ch. curve.) Look at CNR_2 - CNR_5.

For CNR_2 = 50 dB, 40 channels, required receiver power P_5 = -3.5 dBm; round up to P_5 = -3.0 dBm

For CNR_3 = 50 dB, 40 channels, required receiver power P_6 = -3.5 dBm; round up to P_6 = -3.0 dBm

For CNR_4 = 49 dB, 40 channels required receiver power P_7 = -4.5 dBm; round up to P_7 -4.0 dBm

For CNR_5 = 48 dB, 40 channels, required receiver power P_8 = -5.0 dBm

Step 2 – Compute the power at the output of the optical splitter (P_1 - P_4) based on the receiver input optical powers (P_5 - P_8) and the fiber losses (L_A - L_D).

$P_1 = P_5 + L_A$ = -3.0 dBm + 8 dB = +5 dBm   Add fiber loss L_A to receiver input power P_5

Table 15.4 – Configuration 1, Scenario 2 (Continued)

$P_2 = P_6 + L_B = -3.0$ dBm + 2 dB = -1 dBm	Add fiber loss L_B to receiver input power P_6
$P_3 = P_7 + L_C = -4.0$ dBm + 4 dB = 0 dBm	Add fiber loss L_C to receiver input power P_7
$P_4 = P_8 + L_D = -5.0$ dBm + 3 dB = -2 dBm	Add fiber loss L_D to receiver input power P_8

Step 3 – Convert the powers at the output of the optical splitter (P_1 - P_4) to mW using equation 15.5.

$P_1 = +10^{(dBm/10)} = +10^{(+5/10)} = 3.16$ mW

$P_2 = +10^{(dBm/10)} = +10^{(-1/10)} = 0.79$ mW

$P_3 = +10^{(dBm/10)} = +10^{(0/10)} = 1.00$ mW

$P_4 = +10^{(dBm/10)} = +10^{(-2/10)} = 0.63$ mW

Step 4 - Compute the total power output by all four legs (P_1 - P_4) of the optical splitter. Call that total P_{Sum}.

$P_{Sum} = (P_1 + P_2 + P_3 + P_4) = (3.16 + 0.79 + 1.00 + 0.63) = 5.58$ mW

Step 5 – Now increase P_{SUM} by 20% to account for the excess loss of the fiber optic splitter. Call that value P_T. P_T is the required input optical power to the optical splitter. It also equals the transmitter optical output power.

$P_T = 1.2 \bullet (P_{Sum}) = 1.2 \bullet 5.58 = 6.70$ mW

Step 6 – Convert P_T to dBm.

$P_T = +10 \bullet Log_{10} (6.70) = +8.3$ dBm   Round P_T down to +8 dBm. Minimum transmitter optical output = +8.0 dBm

Step 7 – Now calculate the optical splitter ratios for each output leg.

$P_{Leg} = 100 \bullet (P_{Leg}/P_{Sum})$ General formula

P_1 Leg Percentage = $100 \bullet (3.16/5.58) = 57\%$ Divide optical splitter output # 1 by the total output

P_2 Leg Percentage = $100 \bullet (0.79/5.58) = 14\%$ Divide optical splitter output # 2 by the total output

P_3 Leg Percentage = $100 \bullet (1.00/5.58) = 18\%$ Divide optical splitter output # 3 by the total output

P_4 Leg Percentage = $100 \bullet (0.63/5.58) = 11\%$ Divide optical splitter output # 4 by the total output

Step 8 – Verify that the optical splitter ratios total 100%. In this case they do.

The second configuration, a linear bus, also consists of a single broadcast site and four receive sites as illustrated in Figure 15.32. Site #1 has a transmitter only. Fiber A runs to site #2 where fiber optic splitter #1 splits the light into two fibers. Most of the light gets routed to Fiber B, which travels on to site #3. The other fiber from the fiber optic splitter runs to the local CATV receiver. In order to simplify the presentation, we will simultaneously present optical powers in dBm and mW.

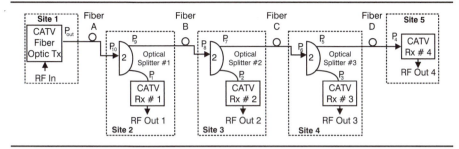

Figure 15.32 – Configuration 2: Linear Bus

Table 15.5 – Configuration 2, Scenario 1

User Data

Channel Load = 79 channels	Usually 79 VSB/AM channels. Under 79 ch. performance will improve and vice versa.
Fiber A Loss = L_A = 2 dB	Total fiber loss, including splices and connectors, from Site #1 to Site #2 but the losses of the 1 x 2 optical splitter.
Fiber B Loss = L_B = 3 dB	Total fiber loss, including splices and connectors, from Site #1 to Site #3 but excluding the losses of the 1 x 2 optical splitter.
Fiber C Loss = L_C = 1 dB	Total fiber loss, including splices and connectors, from Site #1 to Site #4 but excluding the losses of the 1 x 2 optical splitter.
Fiber D Loss = L_D = 2 dB	Total fiber loss, including splices and connectors, from Site #1 to Site #5 but excluding the losses of the 1 x 2 optical splitter.
Site #2 – Desired CNR = CNR_2 = 49 dB Site #3 – Desired CNR = CNR_3 = 48 dB Site #4 – Desired CNR = CNR_4 = 49 dB Site #5 – Desired CNR = CNR_5 = 46 dB	Usually, a user will have a minimum CNR requirement that applies to all sites. In this case, for instance, the output of the Site #4 receiver may be split a much higher number times than Site #5, so it needs a higher CNR.

Computations

Step 1 – Look up the required receiver input optical powers (P_1 - P_4) for the desired CNRs. (Refer to Figure 15.30, 79 channel curve.) Look at CNR_2 - CNR_5.

For CNR_2 = 49 dB, 79 channels, required receiver power P_1 = -2.5 dBm; round up to P_1 = -2.0 dBm

For CNR_2 = 48 dB, 79 channels, required receiver power P_2 = -3.2 dBm; round up to P_2 = -3.0 dBm

Table 15.5 – Configuration 2, Scenario 1 (Continued)

For CNR_2 = 49 dB, 79 channels, required receiver power P_3 = -2.5 dBm; round up to P_3 = -2.0 dBm

For CNR_2 = 46 dB, 79 channels, required receiver power P_4 = -4.8 dBm; round down to P_4 = -5.0 dBm

Step 2 – Convert the receiver input optical powers (P_1 - P_4) to milliwatts.

Convert P_1 to mW = $+10^{(-3/10)}$ = 0.50 mW

Convert P_2 to mW = $+10^{(-2/10)}$ = 0.63 mW

Convert P_3 to mW = $+10^{(-2/10)}$ = 0.63 mW

Convert P_4 to mW = $+10^{(-5/10)}$ = 0.32 mW

Step 3 – Compute the optical power from Site 4 (P_5) by adding the Site 4 receiver optical input power to the optical loss of fiber D.

$P_5 = P_4 + L_D$ = -5 dBm + 2 dB = -3 dBm   Convert P_5 to mW = $+10^{(-3/10)}$ = 0.50 mW

Step 4 – Compute P_6, increase by 20% to include coupler excess loss.

$P_6 = 1.2 \bullet (P_5 + P_3) = 1.2 \bullet (0.50 + 0.63) =$ Convert P_6 to dBm = $+10 \bullet Log_{10}(1.36)$ = 1.36 mW   +1.34 dBm

Step 5 – Compute P_7 by adding the power at Site 4 (P_6) to the loss of fiber C (L_C).

$P_7 = P_6 + L_C$

P_7 = +1.34 dBm + 1 dB = +2.34 dBm   Convert P_7 to mW = $+10^{(+2.34/10)}$ = 1.71 mW

Step 6 – Compute P_8, increase by 20% to include coupler excess loss.

$P_8 = 1.2 \bullet (P_7 + P_2) = 1.2 \bullet (1.71 + 0.63) =$ Convert P_8 to dBm = $+10 \bullet Log_{10}(2.81)$ = 2.81 mW   +4.49 dBm

Step 7 – Compute P_9 by adding the power at Site 3 (P_8) to the loss of fiber B (L_B).

$P_9 = P_8 + L_B$

P_9 = +4.49 dBm + 3 dB = +7.49 dBm   Convert P_9 to mW = $+10^{(+7.49/10)}$ = 5.61 mW

Step 8 – Compute P_{10}, increase by 20% to include coupler excess loss.

$P_{10} = 1.2 \bullet (P_9 + P_1) = 1.2 \bullet (5.61 + 0.63) =$ Convert P_{10} to dBm = $+10 \bullet Log_{10}(7.49)$ = 7.49 mW   +8.74 dBm

Step 9 – Compute P_{11} by adding the power at Site 2 (P_{10}) to the loss of fiber A (L_A).

$P_{11} = P_{10} + L_A$

P_{11} = +8.74 dBm + 2 dB = +10.74 dBm   Convert P_{11} to mW = $+10^{(+10.74/10)}$ = 11.9 mW

Step 10 – Choose a transmitter optical output power. Round P_{11} (dBm) up to +11 dBm.

Step 11 – Compute the split ratios for the three fiber optic splitters.

Table 15.5 – Configuration 2, Scenario 1 (Continued)

Coupler #3

Leg 1 (to site 5) = $100 \cdot P_5/(P_3 + P_5)$ = $100 \cdot 0.50/(0.63+0.50)$ = 44%

Leg 2 (to Rx #3) = 100% - 44% = 56%

Coupler #2

Leg 1 (to site 4) = $100 \cdot P_7/(P_2 + P_7)$ = $100 \cdot 1.71/(0.63 + 1.71)$ = 73%

Leg 2 (to Rx #2) = 100% - 73% = 27%

Coupler #3

Leg 1 (to site 3) = $100 \cdot P_9/(P_1 + P_9)$ = $100 \cdot 5.61/(0.63 + 5.61)$ = 90%

Leg 2 (to Rx #1) = 100% - 90% = 10%

High linearity CATV systems represent the state-of-the art for fiber optic video transmission at this time. However, they require a number of advanced optical components to facilitate long distances, high channel counts, and high bandwidth signals. The next chapter will examine these components in detail.

Chapter Summary

- The output of a linear system is directly proportional to the input; however, most real systems will always exhibit a degree of nonlinearity.

- Fourier synthesis, using Fourier's theorem, describes how distortion develops in a high linearity CATV system.

- Distortions to linear signals in the time domain can be grouped into two categories: asymmetrical (even-ordered) distortions and symmetrical (odd-ordered) distortions.

- High linearity CATV lasers usually require a predistortion circuit in the laser driver to maximize performance.

- External modulators prevent wavelength chirp caused by laser turn-off and turn-on because they allow the laser to run continuously.

- Lithium niobate, a popular material for external modulators, exhibits low optical loss and has a high electro-optic coefficient.

- PIN diode detectors exhibit higher linearity, compared to APDs, making them ideal for CATV transmission systems.

- Fiber optic CATV transmission systems may be designed in a high split configuration or a fanout configuration.

- In a fanout configuration, a single transmit site broadcasts to a large number of receive sites.

- In the high split or linear bus configuration, a single transmit site feeds one fiber, and a portion of the signal is tapped off via a splitter, allowing the majority of the optical signal to continue down the network.

- Before 1980, most CATV systems were copper coax based and required RF amplifiers spaced every 1,000-2,000 feet; however, in the early 1980s, the CATV industry began using direct modulated 1310 nm VSB/AM links for supertrunks, reducing the number of RF amplifiers.
- In the early 1990s, the CATV industry used hybrid fiber/coax CATV architectures that used digital multichannel links transporting very high quality digital signals to replace separate headend locations.
- In the mid-1990s, the paradigm changed when EDFAs and externally modulated 1550 nm lasers were developed.
- The basic requirements of a CATV system are: use single-mode fiber, use angled physical contact (APC) connectors, know the optical loss of each fiber segment, and properly attenuate the RF input to the transmitter.
- Carrier-to-noise ratio changes according to the received optical input as well as the number of CATV channels being transmitted.

Chapter 16

Advanced Optical Components

Many fiber optic applications, such as long-haul DWDM systems, require amplification of the optical signal. In the past, this entailed using expensive electronic repeaters at intermediate points every 100 km. Today's modern long-haul DWDM systems use several advanced optical components to replace multiple repeaters with a single optical device. These optical devices, once only laboratory curiosities, now see widespread use in field deployments.

Erbium-doped Fiber Amplifiers

Researchers developed erbium-doped fiber amplifiers (EDFAs) to replace numerous electronic repeaters with fewer optical repeaters, overall reducing system cost and complexity. EDFAs, such as the one pictured in Figure 16.1, also allow simple system upgrades by adding additional sources to different wavelengths and combining them onto a single fiber using a DWDM multiplexer.

Figure 16.1 – Typical Packaged EDFA
(Photo courtesy of Force, Inc.)

The fiber used in an EDFA is doped with erbium, a rare earth element that has the appropriate energy levels in its atomic structure to amplify light at 1550 nm. A 980 nm or 1480 nm "pump" laser injects energy into the erbium-doped fiber. When a weak signal at 1550 nm enters the fiber, the light stimulates the erbium atoms to release their stored energy as additional 1550 nm light. This process continues as the signal passes down the fiber, growing stronger and stronger until it reaches the erbium-doped region.

Figure 16.2 shows a two-stage EDFA with mid-stage access, an important element of very high performance fiber optic systems. In this case, two simple single-stage EDFAs are packaged together. The user receives the output of the first stage EDFA and the input of the second stage EDFA. These systems often require the periodic use of additional elements, such as dispersion-compensating fiber (DCF), in order to reduce the overall dispersion. A high insertion loss of 10 dB or more makes DCF problematic. Placing the DCF at the mid-stage access point of the two-stage EDFA reduces harmful effects on the system. The user still realizes significant gain through the EDFA, even with the addition of the high optical loss piece of DCF.

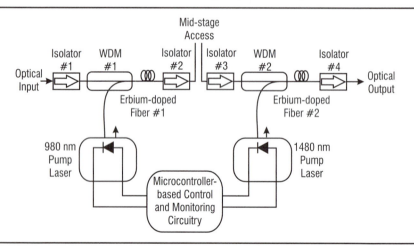

Figure 16.2 – Two-stage EDFA with Mid-stage Access

In Figure 16.2, the optical input first passes through optical isolator #1, which only allows light to pass from left to right. Next the light passes through WDM #1. WDM #1 provides a means of injecting the 980 nm pump wavelength into the first length of erbium-doped fiber. WDM #1 also permits coupling the optical input signal into the erbium-doped fiber with minimal optical loss.

The 980 nm energy pumps the erbium atoms into a slowly decaying, excited state. When light in the 1550 nm band travels through the erbium-doped fiber, which is usually tens of meters long, it causes the stimulated emission of radiation, much like a laser. In this way, the 1550 nm optical input signal gains strength. The output of the erbium-doped fiber then goes through optical isolator #2, which becomes available to the user. Typically, the mid-stage access point connects to some sort of dispersion compensating device. The light then travels through isolator #3 and the WDM #2. WDM #2 couples 1480 nm energy from a second pump laser into the other end of a second length of erbium-doped fiber, increasing gain and output power. Finally the light travels through isolator #4.

EDFAs avoid most active components because photons amplify the signal. The EDFA provides a high output power, requiring fewer amplifiers in a given system design. The most basic EDFA design amplifies light over a fairly narrow, 12 nm, band. The addition of gain equalization filters can increase the band to more than 25 nm. Other exotic doped fibers increase the amplification band to 40 nm or more. Furthermore, data rate independence in EDFAs means a system upgrade requires changing only the launch and receive terminals.

The EDFA's reliable performance makes it useful in long-haul, high data rate fiber optic communications systems and CATV delivery systems. In CATV applications, EDFAs boost the signal before and after an optical splitter to amplify the split signal for transmission over several fibers. In general, four major applications exist for optical amplifiers: power amplifier/booster, in-line amplifier, preamplifier or loss compensation for optical networks.

Power Amplifier/Booster

Power amplifiers (also called booster amplifiers) are placed directly after the optical transmitter. The EDFA must generate the maximum possible output level in relation to the large signal input. Small signal response is not as important because the direct transmitter output is usually -10 dBm or higher. The large SNR of the incoming signals has less impact than the effects of the noise added by the amplifier.

In-line Amplifier

The in-line amplifier or in-line repeater, takes a small input signal and boosts it for retransmission down the fiber. Controlling the small signal performance and noise will provide better system results. Noise added by amplifiers in series will limit the system length.

Preamplifier

Today's digital applications demand receiver sensitivities of -40 dBm or -45 dBm compared to -30 dBm in past requirements. An optical amplifier placed prior to the receiver input achieves this performance. Boosting the signal at this point presents a much larger signal into the receiver, thus easing the demands of the receiver design. For this application, the noise added by the EDFA is critical. The amplifier must add a minimum of noise to maximize the received SNR. Figure 16.3 illustrates these first three applications.

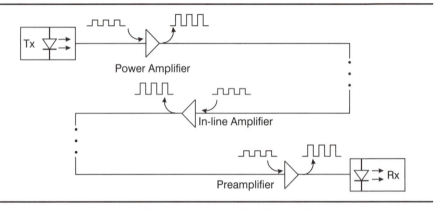

Figure 16.3 – Three Applications for an EDFA

Loss Compensation in Optical Networks

Figure 16.4 illustrates the insertion of an EDFA before an 1 x 8 optical splitter. The nominal optical insertion loss of 10 dB makes an optical output of +10 dBm at the transmitter, only 0 dBm without the EDFA. In digital applications, this output power suffices; however, in analog CATV applications, this output represents the minimum acceptable received power. Inserting an EDFA before the optical splitter, increases the power to perhaps +19 dBm, allowing each of the eight output legs to provide +9 dBm, nearly equal the original transmitter power.

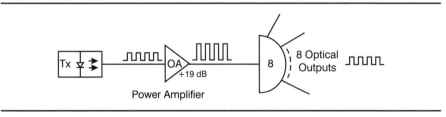

Figure 16.4 – Loss Compensation in Optical Networks

Raman Amplifiers

EDFAs and conventional lasers, achieve gain by pumping atoms into a high energy state. This allows the atoms to release their energy when a photon of a suitable wavelength passes nearby. Raman optical amplifiers utilize stimulated Raman scattering (SRS) to create optical gain. Because SRS robs energy from shorter wavelengths and feeds it to longer wavelengths, high channel count DWDM systems initially avoided this technique.

A Raman optical amplifier consists of little more than a high-power pump laser, usually called a Raman laser, and a WDM or directional coupler. The optical amplification occurs in the transmission fiber itself, distributed along the transmission path. With amplification up to 10 dB, Raman optical amplifiers provide a wide gain bandwidth (up to 100 nm), allowing them to operate using any installed optical fiber (single-mode optical fiber, TrueWave, etc.). By boosting the optical signal in transit, Raman amplifiers reduce the effective span loss and improve noise performance.

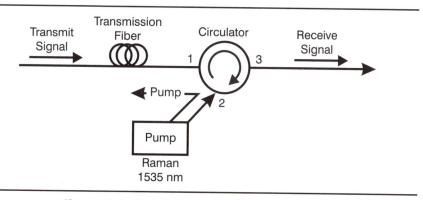

Figure 16.5 – Typical Raman Amplifier Configuration

Raman amplifiers, combined with EDFAs, create a wide gain-flattened optical bandwidth. Figure 16.5 shows the topology of a typical Raman optical amplifier. The pump laser and circulator comprise the two key elements of the Raman optical amplifier. The pump laser, in this case, has a wavelength of 1535 nm. The circulator provides a convenient means of injecting light backwards into the transmission path with minimal optical loss.

Figure 16.6 shows the optical spectrum of a forward-pumped Raman optical amplifier. The signal gets injected by the 1535 nm pump laser at the transmit end rather than the receive end. Generally, the amplitude of the pump laser exceeds that of the data signals.

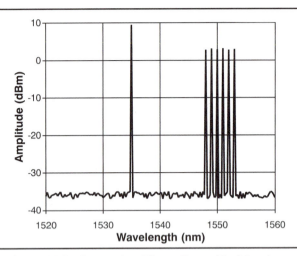

Figure 16.6 – Raman Amplifier — Transmitted Spectrum

Figure 16.7 shows the received signal after the same length of fiber used in the SRS example. With a significant decrease in the amplitude of the pump laser, the amplitude of the six data signals has increased, giving all six signals roughly equal amplitudes. In this case, the SRS effect robbed a great deal of energy from the 1535 nm pump laser signal and redistributed that energy to the six data signals.

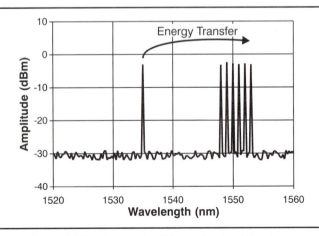

Figure 16.7 – Raman Amplifier — Received Spectrum

Dense Wavelength-division Multiplexing (DWDM)

Dense wavelength-division multiplexing involves sending a large number of closely spaced optical signals over a single fiber. Standards developed by the ITU (International Telecommunications Union) define the exact optical wavelengths used for DWDM applications. The center of the DWDM band occurs at 193.1 THz with standard channel spacings of 200 GHz and 100 GHz. The 100 GHz standard spacing allows transmission of 45 channels on one fiber. A 45 channel system spaced at 100 GHz would cover an optical span of 35 nm and require a costly wide bandwidth, gain-flattened EDFA.

Packing more than the 45 channels at 100 GHz spacing required system designers to use very closely spaced optical channels. The channel spacing, in GHz, relates to the optical wavelength as follows: A spacing of 200 GHz corresponds to about 1.6 nm, 100 GHz corresponds to about 0.8 nm, and 50 GHz corresponds to about 0.4 nm channel spacing. Most commonly 50 GHz follows 100 GHz, although attempts at 75 GHz and 37.5 GHz show up in literature. A channel spacing of 50 GHz (0.4 nm) allows 45 channels to occupy only 17.5 nm of optical bandwidth, making 50 GHz the next logical step below 100 GHz and greatly reducing the number of required optical amplifiers in the system. Further increases in channels per fiber would likely lead to the use of 25 GHz spacing. Figure 16.8 illustrates the transmission spectra of 0.4 nm spacing DWDM.

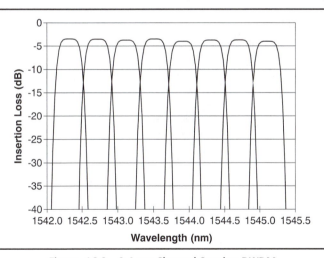

Figure 16.8 – 0.4 nm Channel Spacing DWDM

Designing the optical demultiplexer to separate the signals at the receive end defines the greatest challenge in closely spaced optical channels. Because of subtle color differences in each of the optical channels, high performance DWDM optical demultiplexers must have three characteristics. First, they must be very stable over time and temperature. Second, they must have a relatively flat passband or region of frequencies. Third, they must reject adjacent optical channels to avoid crosstalk.

Red and Blue Bands

The ITU approved DWDM band extends from 1528.77 nm to 1563.86 nm, and divides into the red band and the blue band. The red band encompasses the longer wavelengths of 1546.12 nm and higher. The blue band wavelengths fall below 1546.12 nm. The useful gain region of the lowest cost EDFAs corresponds to the red band wavelengths; therefore, if a system only requires a limited number of DWDM wavelengths, use of the red band wavelengths yields the lowest overall system cost.

Coarse Wavelength-division Multiplexing (CWDM)

In response to the ever-growing fiber network demand, the fiber optic industry developed an intermediate technology called CWDM (coarse wavelength-division multiplexing). With a capacity greater than WDM and smaller than DWDM, CWDM allows the user to stack eight or fewer channels in the 1550 nm region of the fiber called the C-Band. Figure 16.9 shows a typical packaged CWDM 3RU (three rack units, equal to 5.75" in height) rack-mount module.

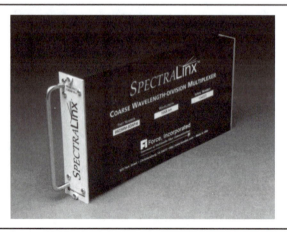

Figure 16.9 – Typical Packaged CWDM
(Photo courtesy of Force, Inc.)

In order to dramatically reduce cost, CWDMs use uncooled lasers with a relaxed tolerance of ± 3 nm. Whereas a DWDM system has channels spaced as close as 0.4 nm, CWDM uses a spacing of 20 nm. The wide spacing accommodates the uncooled laser wavelength drift, about ± 0.06 nm/ °C, that occurs as the ambient temperature varies. Typical CWDM transmission wavelengths include: 1470 nm, 1490 nm, 1510 nm, 1530 nm, 1550 nm, 1570 nm, 1590 nm, and 1610 nm.

Figure 16.10 shows the typical passband characteristics of an eight channel CWDM multiplexer. Insertion loss for an eight channel device averages about 2 dB per end. The passband is about 13 nm wide at the -0.5 dB loss point. CWDM demultiplexers typically have higher insertion loss and significantly better isolation loss compared to DWDM multiplexers. When used in a unidirectional application, the multiplexer combines various transmitter outputs, so isolation does not matter. In bidirectional applications, any input on either end of the fiber can be an input or an output, requiring the higher isolation of demultiplexers to guarantee that the system will work without interference between channels.

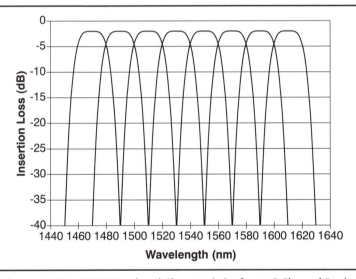

Figure 16.10 – CWDM Passband Characteristics for an 8 Channel Device

All of these components contribute greatly to long-haul telecommunications network. Without the advantages of EDFAs and wavelength-division multiplexers, the end-to-end systems discussed in the next chapter would not be possible.

Chapter Summary

- The development of erbium-doped fiber amplifiers allowed DWDM long-haul transmission systems to develop by eliminating the need for numerous, costly repeaters.
- To create an EDFA, optical fiber is doped with erbium, a rare earth element that amplifies light at 1550 nm.

- Major applications for optical fiber amplifiers include: power amplifier/booster, in-line amplifier, and preamplifier.
- Power amplifiers, or booster amplifiers, are placed directly after the optical transmitter to provide the maximum possible output level.
- The in-line amplifier or in-line repeater, takes a small input signal and boosts it for retransmission down the fiber.
- Preamplifiers are placed prior to the receiver to boost the incoming signal.
- In loss compensation for optical networks, the EDFA is inserted before an 8 x 1 optical splitter to increase signal power before splitting the signal, allowing each of the eight output legs to provide an optical output nearly equal to the original transmitter power.
- Raman optical amplifiers use stimulated Raman scattering (SRS) to create optical gain.
- Dense wavelength-division multiplexing involves sending a large number of closely spaced optical signals over a single fiber.
- At the transmit end of a DWDM system, optical wavelengths are closely spaced to pack more channels onto one fiber.
- Because of subtle color differences in each of the optical channels, high performance DWDM optical demultiplexers must be very stable over time and temperature, must have a relatively flat passband or region of frequencies, and must reject adjacent optical channels so that they do not interfere.
- The ITU approved DWDM band divides into the red band, with wavelengths of 1546.12 nm and higher, and the blue band, whose wavelengths fall below 1546.12 nm.
- With a capacity greater than WDM and smaller than DWDM, CWDM allows eight or less channels to be stacked in the 1550 nm region of the fiber.
- CWDMs reduce system cost because the wider channel spacing allows the use of less expensive, uncooled lasers.

Chapter 17

End-to-End Systems

Today's end-to-end systems must make use of a number of recent and advanced techniques in order to comply with the demands of today's video services to consumers. To meet transmission demands, end-to-end systems must utilize every available Hertz of bandwidth in the electromagnetic spectrum.

Advanced Digital Modulation Techniques

Digital data is usually thought of as strings of ones and zeros. Relating this to analog video signals, this could be appropriately called baseband digital data. A variety of complex modulation schemes can encode digital data signals for transport. These modulation schemes serve to pack more data per Hz of the spectrum. Spectral efficiency measures the number of bits packed into each Hz of bandwidth. The FCC's mandate to adopt HDTV standards can only occur by using high spectral efficiency modulation schemes such as 256 QAM, which can achieve up to 8 bits/second/Hz. Older modulation schemes such as NRZ (non-return-to-zero) only achieve a spectral efficiency of 0.5 bit/second/Hz. However, higher spectral efficiency achieved by techniques such as 256 QAM do not equate to digital compression techniques, because unlike digital compression, no data gets thrown away or lost in 256 QAM (assuming that no errors occur in the transmission channel).

Advanced digital modulation techniques take advantage of amplitude and phase modulation. Simple modulation techniques such as NRZ only take advantage of amplitude modulation. Figure 17.1 shows a diagram of how this works. The circle, known as an "IQ" diagram, represents modulation vectors of constant amplitude and varying phase. The vertical axis, labeled Q, is the quadrature component (the carrier shifted by 90°). The horizontal axis, labeled I, is the in-phase component (in phase with the carrier).

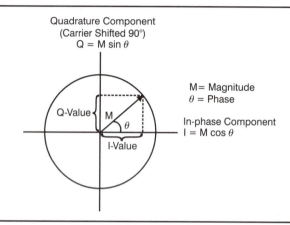

Figure 17.1 – Complex Amplitude and Phase Modulation

Binary phase-shift keying (BPSK), a relatively simple digital modulation scheme, takes advantage of phase modulation. Figure 17.2 shows how BPSK works. The top line represents the input digital data. This data generates two modulation waveforms: a "carrier" sine wave that is synchronized with the transitions in the input data, and a "carrier+π" sine wave that is shifted 180° from the first sine wave. Gating the first sine wave to the output when the input digital data is a one and the second waveform to the output when the digital input data is a zero forms the modulated output know as the BPSK waveform. The BPSK waveform changes phase whenever there is a transition in the digital input data. The right hand side of the figure shows the IQ diagram for this modulation scheme.

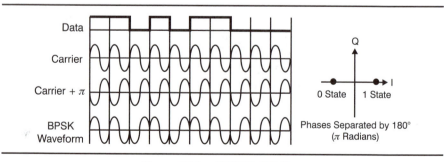

Figure 17.2 – BPSK Modulation

Figure 17.3 shows how a real transmitter generates the carrier, carrier+π, and BPSK waveform signals.

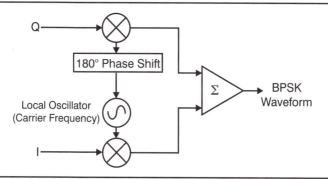

Figure 17.3 – Generation of Carrier, Carrier+π Signals, and a BPSK Waveform

Figure 17.4 shows a more advanced digital modulation technique, 16 QAM, that uses both amplitude and phase modulation. This scenario defines 16 specific amplitudes and phases. The digital input data stream is divided into groups of four bits, which determines one of the 16 IQ states shown in Figure 17.4. Each of these IQ states, called a symbol, carries four bits of digital data, giving 16 QAM a high spectral efficiency.

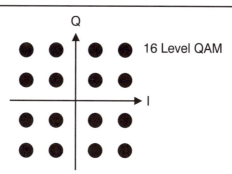

Figure 17.4 – 16 QAM Modulation

Bit Error Rate (BER)

Analog video formats usually express the signal quality in terms of SNR for baseband signals or CNR for RF-based measurements. Bit error rate (BER) describes the quality of a digital video signal. The BER determines the number of corrupt bits per second in a digital transmission. When a bit error occurs in a digital video system, a wide range of results may occur depending on the importance of the bit and how the coding scheme deals with errors. In many cases, the error may be invisible to any but the most skilled viewer. At the other end of the spectrum, a bit error may destroy an entire frame, causing a major disturbance to the picture.

For a given modulation format, the transmission bandwidth increases proportionally. If a 100 kb/s data stream requires 50 kHz of bandwidth, then a 200 kb/s data stream requires 100 kHz of bandwidth. Thus as the data rate increases, the amount of noise increases proportionally. The noise has the same amplitude at all frequencies, known as white noise.

Several important factors must be considered when evaluating a digital modulation scheme, including spectral efficiency, the minimum carrier-to-noise ratio required to achieve a given BER, and the robustness of the modulation format. A highly robust modulation format will degrade gracefully in the face of a declining carrier-to-noise ratio, whereas a less robust format will degrade drastically as the carrier-to-noise ratio declines. As is the case with most engineering decisions, you do not get something for nothing.

In order to compare the performance of various modulation formats used to transmit a wide range of different data rates, a means of normalizing the carrier-to-noise ratio is required. The commonly accepted measure is the energy per bit (E_b) divided by noise power per Hertz (N_o). This measure removes data rate and bandwidth from the expression, which allows one to evaluate the underlying modulation format regardless of the format's data rate or bandwidth. The carrier-to-noise ratio relates to E_b/N_o as follows:

Eq. 17.1

$$\frac{C}{N} = \frac{E_b}{N_o} + 10 \cdot Log_{10}(\text{bit rate in b/s}) - 10 \cdot Log_{10} (\text{noise bandwidth in Hz}) \text{ (dB)}$$

Conversely, E_b/N_o can be derived from the CNR as follows:

Eq. 17.2

$$\frac{E_b}{N_o} = \frac{C}{N} - 10 \cdot Log_{10}(\text{bit rate in b/s}) + 10 \cdot Log_{10} (\text{noise bandwidth in Hz}) \text{ (dB)}$$

Spectral Efficiency

Shannon's Mathematical Theory of Communication, devised by mathematician and electrical engineer, Claude Shannon, in 1948, is often cited as one of the foundations of modern electronic communications. Shannon's theory sets limits for how much energy a given spectral efficiency (and thus carrier-to-noise ratio) requires.

Shannon's formula for the capacity of a band-limited channel with additive white Gaussian noise (AWGN) is as follows:

Eq. 17.3
$$C = W \cdot Log_2\left(1 + \frac{P}{N}\right)$$

Where:

C   = Capacity or maximum average rate at which information can be transmitted over the channel in Hz

W   = Bandwidth

P/N = The ratio of signal power divided by noise power passed by the receiver front-end filtering (a dimensionless quantity)

Shannon's equation is more useful if we rearrange it in terms of E_b/N_0. The following equations derive the spectral efficiency form of Shannon's capacity. In order to get the capacity equation that involves spectral efficiency in terms of E_b/N_0, the $N = W \cdot N_0$ must be substituted into equation 17.3. After manipulating the equation, we get:

Eq. 17.4
$$\frac{P}{N_0} = W\left[2^{C/W} - 1\right]$$

Dividing both sides of Equation 17.4 by C gives:

Eq. 17.5
$$\frac{P}{N_0 C} = \frac{W}{C}\left[2^{C/W} - 1\right]$$

When operating at capacity, the average energy per information bits equals the average signal power divided by the average information rate in bits per second, yielding:

Eq. 17.6
$$E_b = P/C$$

By substituting Equation 17.5 into Equation 17.6, one gets a useful formula that relates the achievable spectral efficiency C/W to the E_b/N_0 SNR as follows:

Eq. 17.7
$$\frac{E_b}{N_0} = \frac{W}{C}\left[2^{C/W} - 1\right] \quad \text{(dimensionless)}$$

To find the minimum E_b/N_o required to achieve a spectral efficiency of 8 b/s/Hz, we can substitute in Equation 17.7 and find that the minimum $E_b/N_o = 31.9 = 15.0$ dB. Figure 17.5 illustrates the minimum theoretical E_b/N_o versus spectral efficiency.

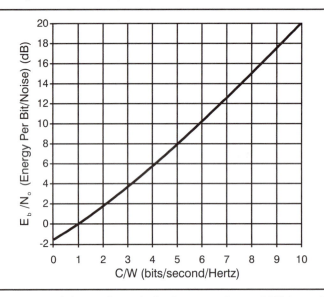

Figure 17.5 – Minimum Theoretical E_b/N_o versus Spectral Efficiency (C/W)

While Shannon's equation tells us the minimum theoretical E_b/N_o, it does not indicate the optimum digital modulation format to achieve a given spectral efficiency, nor does it tell us how close a given implementation may get to the minimum theoretical E_b/N_o. Table 17.1 shows the maximum achievable spectral efficiency for a variety of popular digital modulation formats. All but the last format, 1,024 QAM, represent formats currently in use in communications systems.

Table 17.1 – Spectral Efficiency

Modulation Format	Max. Spectral Efficiency (bits/second/Hz)
MSK	1
BPSK	1
QPSK	2
8 PSK	3
16 QAM	4
32 QAM	5
64 QAM	6
256 QAM	8
1,024 QAM	10

Figure 17.6 shows the achievable BER using a range of digital modulation formats. QPSK offers lower spectral efficiency, but requires about 12 dB less E_b/N_o than the higher spectral efficiency 256 QAM technique.

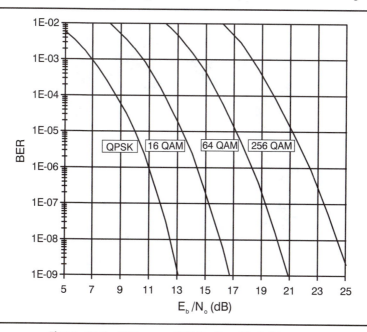

Figure 17.6 – BER versus SNR for Four Digital Formats

Modal Noise

Modal noise represents one major, widely misunderstood, pitfall in fiber optics. We learned earlier that multimode fibers, as their name implies, propagate hundreds of individual modes in their large core (compared to the wavelength of light). When used with very low coherence light sources, such as LEDs, multimode fibers exhibit no problems with modal noise. As the coherence of the light source increases, constructive and destructive interference patterns will appear within the core of the multimode fiber, resulting in speckle. Speckle occurs in helium-neon lasers; by shining the laser on a distant wall and examining the wall, one can see that the projected light appears to crawl with light and dark regions. This speckle occurs as the laser light pattern drifts slightly with time causing the interference pattern to change.

The interference pattern (speckle) within the core of the multimode fiber only becomes an issue at points in the fiber that have splices or optical connectors in the signal path. Usually some of the light will be lost, a phenomenon called modal filtering, as some of the modes escape at the splice or optical connector. Figure 17.7 shows the light at the end of a multimode fiber that is illuminated with a low coherence LED source. As we might expect, the light is uniform across the entire core.

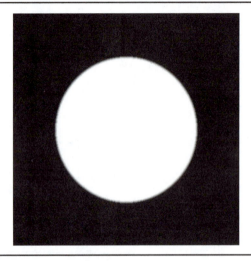

Figure 17.7 – Uniform Light Across a Multimode Fiber

Figure 17.8 (next page) shows the speckle pattern at the end of a multimode fiber illuminated with a high coherence laser source. The light and dark regions caused by constructive and destructive interference can be seen. The gray circle shows the misalignment of the mating optical connector. Because, as with the helium-neon laser, the speckle pattern constantly changes with time, a portion of the light at the left side of the picture will not couple into the output optical connector.

Modal filtering can generate amplitude noise at the connector interface. Each optical connector in the fiber path will aggravate this condition, quickly generating ever larger amounts of noise. This fact makes analog transmission techniques over multimode fiber with lasers nearly impossible. The problem of modal filtering and modal noise can even be observed by placing an optical power meter at the end of the multimode fiber run. As the speckle pattern changes and different modes are filtered out at the connectors and splices, the optical power at the end of the fiber will be seen to rise and fall over time. Table 17.2 summarizes the common light emitters used in fiber optics along with their coherence.

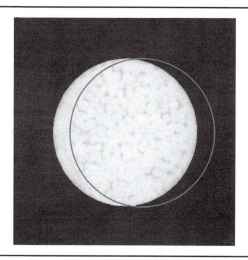

Figure 17.8 – Speckle Pattern in a Multimode Fiber Showing Improper Alignment of the Optical Connector

Table 17.2 – Coherence of Common Fiber Optic Light Sources

Light Emitter Type	Coherence	Modal Noise Problem
LED	Very Low	None
Multimode VCSEL	Moderate	Moderate
FP Laser	Moderate to High	Moderate to Severe
Single-mode VCSEL	High	Severe
DFB Laser	Very High	Extremely Severe

As data rates push towards 10 Gb/s over short lengths of multimode fiber, modal noise will become a big problem to contend with, even on digital systems. However, the push for ever higher performance over multimode fiber has led to the rediscovery of 50/125 μm multimode fiber and the development of special multimode fibers that have less modal dispersion than conventional multimode fibers.

The ongoing development of long-haul communications technology will yield ever more sophisticated end-to-end systems. Already, next generation technologies find their way into today's white papers and technology magazine. The final chapter will investigate the future of fiber optic video transmission.

Chapter Summary

- A variety of complex modulation schemes can encode digital data in order to pack the maximum amount of data per bandwidth Hz.
- Spectral efficiency measures how many data bits can be packed into one Hz of bandwidth.
- High spectral efficiency modulation schemes differ from digital compression in that no information is thrown out or lost.
- Binary phase-shift keying (BPSK) offers one technique for moderate spectral efficiency modulation.
- Digital video signal quality is specified in terms of the bit error rate (BER), which measures the number of corrupted data transmission bits per unit time.
- The E_b/N_o measurement is used to compare the performance of various modulation formats without relating to data rate or bandwidth.
- Shannon's Mathematical Theory of Communication is a fundamental concept of electronic communications that sets limits for how much energy a given spectral efficiency requires.
- Modal noise occurs when multimode fiber links use high coherence light sources, such as laser diodes.
- Modal filtering, the loss of light in a multimode fiber, occurs at the optical connectors and splices within a transmission path.
- Modal filtering can generate amplitude noise at each connector; as the signal passes through more connectors and splices, the noise value increases until the signal is completely disrupted.
- LEDs offer no issues with modal noise while DFB lasers can create a severe modal noise problem.

Chapter 18

The Future of Fiber Optic Video Transmission

After exploring current fiber optic video transmission schemes, let us take some guesses as to the future of this technology. Clearly the trend toward digital is evident, but analog still has many uses. While digital video has made some tremendous inroads in the consumer market, it often still costs more compared to analog solutions. Digital video at the consumer level also suffers from a number of annoying video artifacts. However, mass acceptance of DVDs and satellite TV proves that the general consumer tolerates MPEG image artifacts and considers these less annoying than noise in an analog picture. The force that will tip the balance to digital in the future is the fact that digital quality should continue to evolve, while analog video techniques have reached a performance plateau.

Moore's Law and Video Compression

The powerful technology of video compression dramatically reduces the required bandwidth per video channel. Early in this book we learned that a single digitized video channel can generate serial data rates from 270 Mb/s for standard NTSC to 1,485 Mb/s for HDTV. If not for video compression, a digitized NTSC video signal would require greater than 20 times more transmission bandwidth compared to standard 6 MHz wide CATV VSB/AM channel. Compression uses algorithms to remove redundant picture information and finds more efficient ways to encode the picture's elements.

The quality of digital video closely ties to the power of computer chips. The success and prevalence of video compression technology relates directly to Moore's Law and the power of computers. As computers, and associated

ICs, become larger and faster, they can perform more calculations on each video frame. This increased computing power allows the implementation of even more elaborate algorithms. As the sophistication of compression algorithms improves, the compression ratio increases, which decreases the serial data rate while maintaining the same image quality. Today, MPEG-2 dominates as the video compression algorithm in use. Some systems still use the older MPEG-1, although it offers decidedly inferior results compared to MPEG-2.

The DVD (acronym for digital versatile disk) has the capability to produce high-quality video and better-than-CD-quality audio. Configured as a 5" optical disk, DVDs can store from 4.7 gigabytes of information, for a single-sided, single layer disk, and up to 17 gigabytes for a dual-sided, dual layer disk. This can accommodate up to nine hours of video material. A typical DVD produces a serial data rate ranging from 3.5 to 5 Mb/s.

The DVD outperforms consumer videotapes in many ways. DVDs have no tape to wear out or scratch, and they completely eliminate the need to rewind. On the other hand, a DVD may exhibit compression artifacts not seen on videotapes. A trained observer can see some artifacts at the average DVD serial data rate of 3.5 to 5 Mb/s. Video from DVD sometimes contains visible artifacts such as color banding, blurriness, blockiness, fuzzy dots, shimmering, and missing details.

The Push for DTV

Digital television, the latest broadcast technology, will bring television to a whole new level of sound and picture quality. While individual broadcasters must determine which services they will make available with DTV, the technology itself enables television with movie-quality picture and CD-quality sound, as well as a variety of other enhancements. DTV rapidly delivers large amounts of information services, and its implementation will free up portions of the valuable broadcast spectrum, making it available for other information and communications services.

As of this writing, U.S. broadcasters are involved in a large, legislated, rollout of digital video for the masses. Since the passing of the Telecommunications Act of 1996, TV stations have been converting to digital facilities. The changeover represents an enormous and expensive undertaking, and many public TV stations, as well as commercial ones, will most likely miss the FCC's deadline to start simulcasting in digital in 2002 (commercial) and 2003 (public). A significant percentage of TV stations have requested and been granted extensions on the original May 1, 2002 deadline for commercial stations. Many factors created these delays, including high cost with no clear way to recover the investment, as well as slow sales of digital TV sets, most likely a result of their high cost at this time.

DTV presents broadcasters with many new options for offering service to the public. With digital television, broadcasters can transmit data and present television programs in new ways. Offerings might include an entire edition of a newspaper, sports information, computer software, telephone directories, or stock market updates. Not only will broadcasters be able to broadcast at least one high definition TV program, they could also simultaneously transmit several standard definition TV programs (perhaps eight or more using 256 QAM). Stations could broadcast in multiple languages with picture and information inserts, and in some cases viewers will have the opportunity to select camera angles.

The move to DTV will also free up parts of the broadcast spectrum for public safety as well as other valuable business uses. DTV technology transmits more efficiently than analog TV technology, allowing the same number of stations to broadcast fewer channels or use less of the broadcast spectrum, which has become a scarce and valuable commodity. Other communication types will use the newly available spectrum. Parts of the broadcast spectrum, no longer needed by broadcasters, will revert to the government for a variety of uses, including specific allocations to meet the vital communications needs of public safety, police and fire departments.

To smooth the transition to DTV service, the FCC granted each existing broadcaster an additional 6 MHz channel to use for digital transmissions. Each broadcaster will also retain its existing channel to continue broadcasting its current analog technology signal during the transition period. At the end of the transition period — which is now scheduled for the year 2006 — the FCC will require broadcasters to surrender one of the two channels.

The Frequency Allocation Chart

Figure 18.1 (next page) represents an attempt to simplify the overwhelmingly cluttered U.S. Frequency Allocation chart (which can be accessed in its entirety at http://www.ntia.doc.gov/osmhome/allochrt.pdf). At a glance, the advantages of moving to DTV become clear.

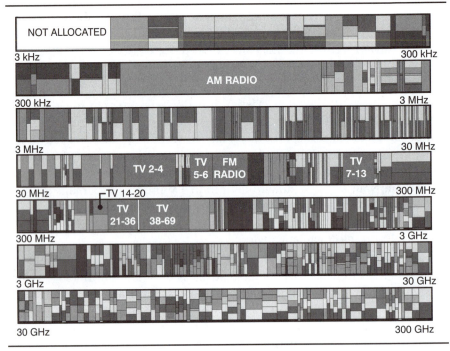

Figure 18.1 – Simplified U.S. Frequency Allocation Chart

In Figure 18.1, each block of gray represents a specific frequency assignment for each type of free-space transmission. This includes aeronautical, mobile, satellite (broadcast, meteorological, or mobile phone satellites), AM and FM radio, amateur radio, space research, and radio astronomy, just to name a few of the 30 different radio services.

Television Channel Frequency Allocations

Table 18.1 lists the current frequency allocations for TV channels 2-69 as designated in the U.S. by the FCC. As mentioned above, upon completion of the full transition to HDTV standards, the FCC will reallocate portions of the UHF, specifically channels 14 through 69 (shaded in the table) for other types of radio services. In fact, channels 70 through 83, formerly assigned as NTSC TV channels in the frequency range between 806 MHz and 890 MHz, have already been reallocated for land mobile communications.

Table 18.1 – Frequency Allocations for U.S. TV Channels 2 through 69

Channel	Frequency Band (MHz)	Channel	Frequency Band (MHz)	Channel	Frequency Band (MHz)
2	54–60	25	536–542	48	674–680
3	60–66	26	542–548	49	680–686
4	66–72	27	548–554	50	686–692
5	76–82	28	554–560	51	692–698
6	82–88	29	560–566	52	698–704
7	174–180	30	566–572	53	704–710
8	180–186	31	572–578	54	710–716
9	186–192	32	578–584	55	716–722
10	192–198	33	584–590	56	722–728
11	198–204	34	590–596	57	728–734
12	204–210	35	596–602	58	734–740
13	210–216	36	602–608	59	740–746
14	470–476	37	608–614	60	746–752
15	476–482	38	614–620	61	752–758
16	482–488	39	620–626	62	758–764
17	488–494	40	626–632	63	764–770
18	494–500	41	632–638	64	770–776
19	500–506	42	638–644	65	776–782
20	506–512	43	644–650	66	782–788
21	512–518	44	650–656	67	788–794
22	518–524	45	656–662	68	794–800
23	524–530	46	662–668	69	800–806
24	530–536	47	668–674		

Video Transmission Over Fiber Optic Legacy Systems

Today's video and audio transmission systems use every imaginable type of legacy transmission equipment, ranging from IP, ISDN, ATM, SONET, and many more. The video quality ranges from barely acceptable for some of the slower data rates, teleconferencing types of applications to excellent over the higher bandwidth platforms.

As discussed earlier in the book, the challenge is to deliver a high enough data rate, and thus quality, while not overloading the data network and providing guaranteed quality of service (QoS) so that the video is displayed in a continuous and natural manner. Improving data compression techniques will continue to ease these concerns, opening the door to more widespread use of legacy transmission systems.

Video on Demand (VOD)

Video on demand, alledgedly one of video's "killer apps," would allow the viewer to choose which movie or program he or she wants to see when he or she wants to see it. To be practical, the video transmission system would have to carry a very large amount of information to serve even a modest size neighborhood. Supposedly, VOD would displace trips to the video rental store, allowing viewers to acquire the desired entertainment from home. Figure 18.2 illustrates one configuration for a VOD network.

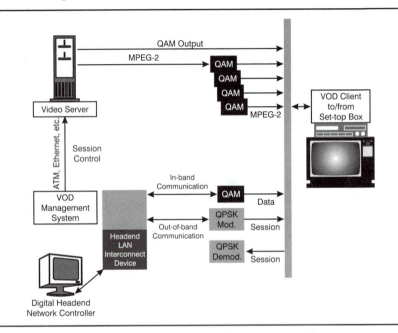

Figure 18.2 – Architecture for a VOD Network

As good as it sounds though, VOD faces several significant technical, economic, and social hurdles. The key technical challenge is designing an affordable video transmission system with the required capacity — fiber optic systems would be the obvious choice from a pure technology point of view. At present, the cost of such a system is still high. As with most industries, one hurdle drives another hurdle, in this case, the economics of widespread implementation.

The inability to identify a billing model that provides sufficient income to justify the staggering capital cost of installing the system represents another hurdle. The last, often overlooked, factor is the social impact of such a system. People are gregarious by nature — they like to be with other people. For example, in the late 1970s when VHS and Betamax VCRs hit the market, the press promptly predicted the demise of the movie theatre. However, movie ticket revenues have grown nearly every year and are now larger than at any time in history. Movies are more fun to see with other people. VOD, by increasing social isolation, could face social backlash.

Passive Optical Networks (PONs)

Actually, the technology to create a VOD network exists today — up to the last mile. High speed fiber optic networks, already installed in central offices, headends, and telcos can handle high bandwidth transmission as far as the curb outside the subscriber's home. Currently, high speed access to the home comes in the form of a digital subscriber line (DSL) or cable-modem access, which cannot keep up with the multimegabit data rates of the future. Another option, fixed wireless, lacks high performance and long distance capabilities. In addition, one must address the high cost to connect an individual fiber line to each home.

Passive optical networks currently in development would offer broad-band access with potentially unlimited bandwidth capability that allows easy upgrades in both the number of users as well as the bandwidth — a future proof solution. The Full Service Access Network (FSAN) Initiative oversees this development, and they are currently working with a number of telecommunications companies and equipment vendors to collaborate on a solution. Figure 18.3 illustrates the basic configuration of a passive optical network in a fiber-to-the-home (FTTH) application.

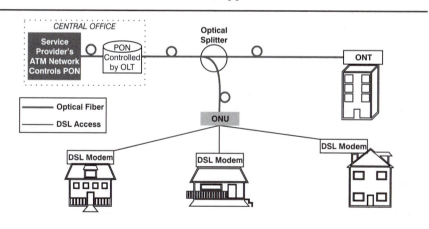

Figure 18.3 – Passive Optical Network in FTTH Application

A passive optical network incorporates an optical line terminal (OLT), optical network units (ONU) or optical network terminations (ONT), opti-cal splitters, and optical cable. It uses a number of access protocols, includ-ing time-division multiplexing, ATM, and, increasingly, gigabit Ethernet, to deliver signals to the subscribers. In an ATM-based PON (APON), the customer establishes a virtual circuit with another office or ISP premise.

Optical access networks (OANs) represent another application for PONs. This emerging technology provides an alternative to SONET, an expensive networking system, for the interconnection of office buildings with high speed transmission lines. An OAN uses an optical access switch (OAS) in the central office and an intelligent optical terminal (IOT) at the customer premises, which connects to the passive optical network. Inexpensive optical splitters join the end user with the expensive equipment in the central office. The optical access switch uses a standard interface that allows it to easily integrate into a wide area network, and the intelligent optical terminal is an inexpensive interface at the end user location that supports the transmission of broadband voice and data signals at bandwidths that range from 1 Mb/s to 100 Mb/s per dedicated wavelength.

Merging Television and Computer Video Standards

The latest "hot debate" in the press revolves around potentially merging broadcast video and computer video standards. Web TV and computers equipped to play movie DVDs illustrate why the industry is considering this convergence. Perhaps the press seeks to create the next "battle of the titans" since yesterday's headlines about the looming battle between telcos and CATV service providers, to offer services that include phone, voice, Internet and broadband video, have apparently fizzled. It seems unlikely at this point that either telcos or the CATV service providers can offer that level of service. More likely, both the telcos and CATV service providers will continue to dominate in their conventional roles. The networks, functions and service reliability requirements differ too widely to fit the culture of either one of the potential suppliers.

As mentioned, TV's migration from analog to digital technology will allow TVs to receive data in addition to video. A variety of applications are possible. Broadcasts could carry additional information as a background stream or offer the synchronized broadcast of Web content and television. Some applications might involve clicking on hypertext links using the TV's remote control to provide for two-way interaction with Web and television content. For example, Web text might accompany programs, allowing the viewer of a talk show to click on the names of guests to access information about them: a politician's biography, an author's bibliography, facts about a popular movie star, etc. Additionally, text could appear in part of the screen to give commentary on a program or to advertise products associated with the program, such as a toy based on a child's cartoon show or a book written by the author on that talk show. These applications assume two-way interaction with a television, a natural progression of today's technology, but one that has not become affordable at this time. The technology exists today to implement such systems. The ultimate success of many of these applications, however, depends on the creation of a business model that will assure the required revenue stream.

Standards

Mass acceptance of any new technology requires the creation of standards. However, these days, the sheer number of competing standards has become a problem. In addition to a large number of standards in force, an equally large number of new standards are under development. This plethora of standards makes it increasingly difficult for any one standard or technology to dominate and capture a large piece of market share.

Today, so many digital standards and formats exist that it can be a challenge to convert from one format to another. Proponents of digital transmission touted it as having the ability to easily process and transport differing video signal formats. However, the consumer is often left holding pieces of equipment that, while having digital outputs and inputs, cannot talk to each other in a digital format. Too often the consumer must interconnect the equipment using analog video signals because it is the only universal exchange format. This negates much or all of the advantage of the equipment's digital capability. These problems will be sorted out, but probably not fully before 2006.

Regardless of how the future actually turns out, no doubt it will be an interesting one. Fiber optic video transmission has the ability to remove the barrier, "the last mile" of public networks. Fiber provides the bandwidth needed to accomplish affordable real-time Internet access, which will allow customers to enjoy broadband services, e-commerce, private networks, video on demand, and all of the applications yet to come.

Chapter Summary

- The move to digital has begun, and while analog is still in use, digital transmission quality will continue to improve while analog technology has reached its performance plateau.
- Video compression dramatically reduces the required bandwidth per video channel.
- The success and prevalence of video compression relates to Moore's Law and the power of computers, stating that as computers evolve to use more elaborate compression algorithms, the compression rates will improve while maintaining high image quality.

- U.S. broadcasters are currently involved in a large, FCC legislated conversion to digital television transmission.
- Due to the scope and cost of a transition to DTV, many TV stations will not meet the FCC's deadlines to simulcast digital and analog transmissions by 2002 for commercial stations and 2003 for public television stations.
- DTV will allow broadcasters to greatly expand the services they can offer to the general consumer and will free up parts of the broadcast spectrum for public safety transmission and other radio transmission services.
- In order to assure a smooth transition, the FCC granted existing broadcasters an additional 6 MHz channel to use for the simulcast of digital signals; however, at the completion of the transition, the broadcast stations will be required to surrender one of these two channels.
- The U.S. frequency allocation chart assigns specific transmission frequencies to all broadcasters that have an FCC license to broadcast.
- Today, video and audio transmission occurs on every imaginable legacy transmission system including IP, ISDN, ATV, and SONET, to name only a few.
- Improved data compression techniques will allow broadcasters to deliver the highest possible quality of service (QoS) and allow a more widespread use of video legacy systems.
- Video on demand (VOD) would allow viewers to choose their own television viewing content.
- Passive optical networks have the potential to help make VOD a feasible technology by providing a means of fiber sharing between multiple subscribers rather than having to install a fiber line in every home.
- Optical access networks incorporate PONs to provide a cost-effective means for business to gain access to broadband voice and video services.
- The merging of television and computer video standards will allow TVs to receive data as well as video and audio, allowing additional content to be sent with the broadcast.
- The sheer number of existing video standards has become an issue that hinders the acceptance of new video technology.

Appendix A

Glossary of Terms

Numbers

1U Abbreviation for "One Unit (U)". U = 1.75 inches. Used to specify the height of units designated for rack-mounting in a standard EIA 19" wide equipment rack.

4:1:1 The set of sampling frequencies used to digitize the luminance and color difference components (Y, R-Y, B-Y) of a video signal. The four represents 13.5 MHz, the sampling frequency of Y, and the ones each 3.75 MHz for R-Y and B-Y.

4:2:0 A sampling system used to digitize the luminance and color difference components (Y, R-Y, B-Y) of a video signal. The four represents the 13.5 MHz sampling frequency of Y, while the R-Y and B-Y are sampled at 6.75 MHz — effectively between every other line only (one line is sampled at 4:0:0, luminance only, and the next at 4:2:2).

4:2:2 A commonly used term for a component digital video format. It is generally used as shorthand for ITU-R 601. 4:2:2 is the standard for digital studio equipment.

4B5B Encoding A signal modulation scheme used in FDDI that encodes groups of four bits and transmits them in five bits in order to guarantee that no more than three consecutive zeros ever occur.

$4f_{sc}$ Abbreviation for four times the frequency of SC (subcarrier). The sampling rate of a D2 digital video signal with respect to the subcarrier frequency of a video signal. The $4f_{sc}$ frequency is 14.3 MHz in NTSC and 17.7 MHz in PAL.

8B10B Encoding A signal modulation scheme in which eight bits are encoded in a 10-bit word to ensure that too many consecutive zeros do not occur; used in ESCON and fibre channel.

802.3 Network A CSMA/CD bus-based network; commonly called Ethernet.

802.5 Network A token-passing ring network operating at 4 Mb/s or 16 Mb/s.

A

Absorption That portion of optical attenuation in optical fiber resulting from the conversion of optical power to heat, caused by impurities in the fiber such as hydroxyl (OH⁻) ions.

AC Abbreviation for alternating current. An electric current that reverses its direction at regularly recurring intervals.

Acceptance Angle The half-angle of the cone within which incident light is totally internally reflected by the fiber core. It is equal to $\sin^{-1}(NA)$.

Active Device A device that requires a source of energy for its operation and has an output that is a function of present and past input signals. Examples include controlled power supplies, transistors, LEDs, amplifiers, and transmitters.

ACTS Abbreviation for advanced communications technologies and services. A program for developing long-haul telecommunications networks.

A/D or ADC Abbreviation for analog-to-digital converter. A device used to convert analog signals to digital signals.

Add-Drop Multiplexer (ADM) A device which adds or drops signals from a communications network.

ADSL Abbreviation for asymmetric digital subscriber line. See DSL.

Aerial Plant Transmission cable suspended in the air on telephone or utility poles.

AES/EBU A digital audio standard established jointly by the AES (Audio Engineering Society) and EBU (European Broadcasting Union) organizations. The sampling frequencies for this standard vary depending on the format being used; the sampling frequency for D1 and D2 audio tracks is 48 kHz.

AGC Automatic gain control. A process or means by which gain is automatically adjusted in a specified manner as a function of input level or another specified parameter.

Aliasing The production of artifacts as a result of sampling at intervals too great to permit faithful replication of the original signal. The effects of aliasing in the replicated signal may be avoided by filtering the original signal to remove frequency components that are higher than those desired in the replicated signal.

AM (Amplitude Modulation) A transmission technique in which the amplitude of the carrier varies in accordance with the signal.

Amplified Spontaneous Emission (ASE) A background noise mechanism common to all types of erbium-doped fiber amplifiers (EDFAs). It contributes to the noise figure of the EDFA which causes loss of signal-to-noise ratio (SNR).

Amplifier A device that boosts the strength of an electronic signal. In a fiber optic cable system, amplifiers spaced at regular intervals throughout the system maintain signal fidelity.

Analog A continuously variable signal. A mercury thermometer, which gives a variable range of temperature readings, is an example of an analog instrument. Antonym of digital.

Angular Misalignment Loss at a connector due to misalignment of fiber end face angles.

ANSI Abbreviation for American National Standards Institute. The U.S. standards organization that establishes procedures for the development and coordination of voluntary American National Standards.

APC Abbreviation for angled physical contact. A fiber end face that is polished at a 5°-15° angle for the minimum possible backreflection. Sometimes referred to as angle polished connector.

APL Abbreviation for average picture level. The average signal level (with respect to blanking) during active picture time, expressed as a percentage of the difference between the blanking and reference white levels. A video quality parameter.

AR Coating Antireflection coating. A thin, dielectric or metallic film applied to an optical surface to reduce its reflectance and thereby increase its transmittance.

Armor A protective layer, usually metal, wrapped around a cable.

Artifact In facsimile or television, a defect or distortion of the image, not present in the original transmitted signal, introduced along the sequence from origination and image capture to final display.

ASE See amplified spontaneous emission.

Aspect Ratio The ratio of television picture width to height. In NTSC and PAL video, the present standard is 4:3. In widescreen video, it is typically 16:9; however, a transitional ratio is 14:9.

ASTM Abbreviation for American Society for Testing and Materials. Organization founded to provide a global forum for the development and publication of voluntary consensus standards for materials, products, systems, and services.

Asynchronous Data that is transmitted without an associated clock signal.

Asynchronous Transfer Mode (ATM) A transmission standard widely used by the telecom industry. A digital transmission switching format with cells containing 5 bytes of header information followed by 48 data bytes. Part of the B-ISDN standard.

ATSC Abbreviation for Advanced Television Systems Committee. Formed to establish technical standards for advanced television systems, including digital high definition television (HDTV).

Attenuation The decrease in signal strength along a fiber optic waveguide caused by absorption and scattering. Attenuation is usually expressed in dB/km.

Attenuation Constant For a particular propagation mode in an optical fiber, the real part of the axial propagation constant.

Attenuation-limited Operation The condition in a fiber optic link when operation is limited by the power of the received signal (rather than by bandwidth or distortion).

Attenuator In optical or electrical systems, a usually passive device or network for reducing the amplitude of a signal without distorting the waveform.

Avalanche Photodiode (APD) A photodiode that exhibits internal amplification of photocurrent through avalanche multiplication of carriers in the junction region.

Average Power The average level of power in a signal that varies with time.

AWG (Arrayed Waveguide Grating) A device, built with silicon planar lightwave circuits, that allows multiple wavelengths to be combined and separated in DWDM systems.

Axial Propagation Constant For an optical fiber, the propagation constant evaluated along the axis of a fiber in the direction of transmission.

Axis The center of an optical fiber.

B

B See bel.

Back Channel A means of communication from users to content providers. A simple type of back channel is an Internet connection using a modem. At the same time that content providers are transmitting interactive television (analog or digital) to users, users can connect through a back channel to a Web site, for example.

Backreflection (BR) In cases where light is launched into an optical fiber, backreflection refers to the light that is returned to the launch point.

Backscattering The return of a portion of scattered light to the input end of a fiber; the scattering of light in the direction opposite to its original propagation.

Bandgap Energy The energy gap in semiconductors and insulators. The forbidden energy level separating the valence band and the conduction band in a semiconductor or insulator. Expressed in electron Volts (eV).

Bandwidth (BW) The range of frequencies within which a fiber optic waveguide or terminal device can transmit data or information.

Bandwidth-limited Operation The condition in a fiber optic link when bandwidth, rather than received optical power, limits performance. This condition happens when the signal becomes distorted, principally by dispersion, beyond specified limits.

Baseband A method of communication in which a signal is transmitted at its original frequency without being impressed on a carrier.

Base Earth Station An Earth station in the fixed-satellite service or, in some cases, in the land mobile-satellite service, located at a specified fixed point or within a specified area on land to provide a feeder link for the land mobile-satellite service.

Baud A unit of signaling speed equal to the number of signal symbols per second, which may or may not be equal to the data rate in bits per second.

BB-I Abbreviation for broadband interactive services. The delivery of all types of interactive video, data, and voice services over a broadband communications network.

Beamsplitter An optical device, such as a partially reflecting mirror, that splits a beam of light into two or more beams. Used in fiber optics for directional couplers.

Bel (B) The logarithm to the base 10 of a power ratio, expressed as $B = \log_{10}(P_1/P_2)$, where P_1 and P_2 are distinct powers. The decibel, equal to one-tenth Bel, is a more commonly used unit.

Bending Loss Attenuation caused by high-order modes radiating to the outside of a fiber optic waveguide as a result of a bend in the fiber. *See also* macrobending, microbending.

BER (Bit Error Rate) The fraction of bits transmitted that are received incorrectly.

BERT Abbreviation for bit error rate tester, a testing device that compares a received data pattern with a known transmitted pattern to determine the quality of the transmission.

BIDI Abbreviation for bidirectional transceiver, a device that sends information in one direction and receives information from the opposite direction.

Bidirectional Operating in both directions.

Binary Base two numbers with only two possible values, 0 or 1. Primarily used by communications and computer systems.

Birefringent Having a refractive index that differs with respect to different polarizations of light.

Bit The smallest unit of information carried by a electrical or optical pulse, the basis for digital communications. Also refers to the pulse carrying the information.

Bit Depth The number of levels that a pixel might have, such as 256 with an 8-bit depth or 1,024 with a 10-bit depth.

Bit Period (T) The amount of time required to transmit a logical one or a logical zero.

Blanking The period of time in which no video image is displayed. In graphic displays, the suppression of the display of one or more display elements or display segments.

Blanking Interval In raster-scanned television technology, the period between the end of one horizontal scanning line and the beginning of the next (the horizontal blanking interval), or the end of one field and the beginning of the next (the vertical blanking interval), during which the display of picture information is suppressed.

Block 1) A group of bits or digits that is transmitted as a unit and that may be encoded for error-control purposes. 2) A string of records, words, or characters, that for technical or logical purposes are treated as a unit.

BNC Popular coax bayonet style connector. Often used for baseband video.

Bragg Grating A technique for building optical filtering functions directly into a piece of optical fiber based on interferometric techniques. Exposure to deep UV light through a grating makes the fiber photosensitive, forming regions of higher and lower refractive indices in the fiber core.

Brightness An attribute of visual perception in which a source appears to emit a given amount of light.

Broadband A method of communication where the transmitted signal is impressed on a high-frequency carrier.

Buffer 1) A protective coating applied directly to the coating of an optical fiber. 2) A computer routine or memory storage area used to compensate for a difference in rate of flow of data, or time of occurrence of events, when transferring data from one device to another.

Bus A group of conductors that together constitute a major signal path. A signal path to which a number of inputs may be connected to feed to one or more outputs.

Bus Address A code number sent out to activate a particular device on a shared communications bus.

Bus Topology A network topology in which all nodes, i.e., stations, are connected together by a single bus.

Butt Splice Two fibers joined without optical connectors and arranged end-to-end by means of a coupling. Fusion splicing is an example.

Bypass The ability of a station to isolate itself optically from a network while maintaining the continuity of the cable plant.

Byte A unit of eight bits.

C

c Abbreviation for the speed of light. 299,792.5 km per second in a vacuum.

C Abbreviation for Celsius. Measure of temperature where pure water freezes at 0° and boils at 100°.

Cable One or more optical fibers enclosed, with strength members, in a protective covering.

Cable Assembly A cable that is connector-terminated and ready for installation.

Cable Plant All of the optical elements, including fiber connectors, splices, etc., between a transmitter and a receiver.

Cable Television A communications system that distributes broadcast signals, non-broadcast signals, multiple satellite signals, original programming, and other signals by means of a coaxial cable and/or optical fiber. Originally CATV stood for community antenna television.

Carrier-to-Noise Ratio (CNR) The ratio, in decibels, of the level of the carrier to that of the noise in a receiver's IF bandwidth before any nonlinear process such as amplitude limiting and detection takes place.

Carson Bandwidth Rule A rule defining the approximate bandwidth requirements of communications system components for a carrier signal that is frequency modulated by a continuous or broad spectrum of frequencies rather than a single frequency.

CATV See cable television.

C-Band The wavelength range between 1530 nm and 1562 nm used in some CWDM and DWDM applications.

CCTV Abbreviation for closed-circuit television. An arrangement in which programs are directly transmitted to specific users and not broadcast to the general public.

CD Abbreviation for compact disk. Often used to describe high-quality audio, CD-quality audio, or short-wavelength lasers.

CDMA Abbreviation for code-division multiple access. A coding scheme in which multiple channels are independently coded for transmission over a single wideband channel using an individual modulation scheme for each channel.

Center Wavelength In a laser, the nominal value central operating wavelength defined by a peak mode measurement where the effective optical power resides. In an LED, the average of the two wavelengths measured at the half amplitude points of the power spectrum.

Central Office (CO) A common carrier switching office in which users' lines terminate. The nerve center of a communications system.

CGA Abbreviation for color graphics adapter. A low-resolution standard for computer monitors.

Channel A communications path or the signal sent over that path. By multiplexing several channels, many voice channels can be transmitted over an optical channel.

Channel Capacity Maximum number of channels that a cable system can carry simultaneously.

Channel Coding Data encoding and error correction techniques used to protect the integrity of data. Typically used in channels with high bit error rates such as terrestrial and satellite broadcast and videotape recording.

Checksum A simple check value of a block of data, calculated by adding all the bytes in a block. Most applications require a more sophisticated system such as cyclic redundant check (CRC).

Chirp In laser diodes, the shift of a laser's central wavelength during single pulse durations due to laser instability.

Chromatic Dispersion Reduced optical signal strength caused by different wavelengths of light traveling at different speeds down the optical fiber. Chromatic dispersion occurs because the speed at which an optical pulse travels depends on its wavelength, a property inherent to all optical fiber. May be caused by material dispersion, waveguide dispersion, and profile dispersion.

Chrominance The color component of a video signal that includes information about hue and saturation.

Circulator A passive three-port device that couples light from Port 1 to 2 and Port 2 to 3 and have high isolation in other directions.

Cladding Material that surrounds the core of an optical fiber. Its lower index of refraction, compared to that of the core, confines the light in the core by total internal reflection.

Cladding Mode 1) A mode confined to the cladding. 2) A light ray that propagates in the cladding.

Clock 1) A reference source of timing information. 2) A device providing signals used in a transmission system to control the timing of certain functions such as the duration of signal elements or the sampling rate. 3) A device that generates periodic, accurately spaced signals used for such purposes as timing, regulation of the operations of a processor, or generation of interrupts.

Clock Frequency The master frequency of periodic pulses used to synchronize the operation of equipment.

Clock Jitter Undesirable random changes in clock phase.

Clock Recovery The reconstruction of timing information from digital data.

Clock Skew A fixed deviation from proper clock phase that commonly appears in D1 digital video equipment. Also called clock phase deviation.

cm Abbreviation for centimeter. Approximately 0.4 inches.

CMTS Abbreviation for cable modem termination system. A computerized device that converts cable modem data into data packets for the Internet. The CMTS provides several functions, including routing to contain local data within the cable system, filtering to protect cable operators from unwanted hacking, and traffic shaping to deliver the quality of service specified by a subscriber.

Coarse Wavelength-division Multiplexing (CWDM) A technique that allows eight or fewer channels to be stacked in the 1550 nm region of optical fiber, the C-Band.

Coating The material surrounding the cladding of a fiber. Generally a soft plastic material that protects the fiber from damage. Synonymous with buffer.

Codec Acronym for coder/decoder. A device that converts analog video and audio signals into a digital format for transmission over telecommunications facilities and also converts received digital signals back into analog format.

Coding Representing each video signal level as a number, usually in binary form.

Coherent Communications A communication system where the output of a local laser oscillator mixes optically with a received signal, and the difference frequency is detected and amplified.

Color Burst In analog color television technology, a signal consisting of several cycles of unmodulated color subcarrier, superimposed at a specified location within the composite signal. The color burst enables the color-decoding circuits in the receiver, and serves as an amplitude, frequency, and phase reference to which the local color (subcarrier frequency) oscillator in the receiver is phase-locked to ensure color fidelity and stability in the displayed picture.

Color Subcarrier The signal which carries color information in a TV signal (e.g., 3.58 MHz in NTSC).

Composite Second Order (CSO) An important distortion measure of analog CATV systems caused by second-order distortion in the transmission system.

Composite Sync A signal consisting of horizontal sync pulses, vertical sync pulses, and equalizing pulses only, with a no-signal reference level.

Composite Triple Beat (CTB) An important distortion measure of analog CATV systems caused by third-order distortion in the transmission system.

Composite Video A signal which consists of the luminance (black and white), chrominance (color), blanking pulses, sync pulses, and color burst.

Compression A process in which the dynamic range or data rate of a signal is reduced by controlling it as a function of the inverse relationship of its instantaneous value relative to a specified reference level. Used to improve signal-to-noise ratios, prevent overloading succeeding elements of a system, or match the dynamic ranges of two devices.

Concatenation 1) The process of connecting pieces of fiber together. 2) In video transmission, linking together systems.

Concentrator A device that aggregates a number of inputs into a single transmission line.

Concentricity The measurement of how well-centered the core is within the cladding of an optical fiber.

Connector A mechanical or optical device that provides a demountable connection between two fibers or a fiber and a source or detector.

Connector Receptacle The fixed or stationary half of a connection that is mounted on a panel/bulkhead. Receptacles mate with plugs.

Connector Variation The maximum value in dB of the difference in insertion loss between mating optical connectors (e.g., with remating, temperature cycling, etc.). Also called optical connector variation.

Converter A device attached between the television set and the cable system that decodes channels and makes them available to the TV set.

Core The light-conducting central portion of an optical fiber, composed of material with a higher index of refraction than the cladding. The portion of the fiber that transmits light.

Counter-rotating An arrangement whereby two signal paths, one in each direction, exist in a ring topology.

Coupler An optical device that combines or splits power from optical fibers.

Coupling Ratio/Loss (C_R,C_L) The ratio/loss of optical power from one output port to the total output power, expressed as a percent. For a 1 x 2 WDM or coupler with output powers O_1, O_2, and O_i representing both output powers:

$$C_R (\%) = \left(\frac{O_i}{O_1 + O_2}\right) \times 100\%$$

$$C_R (\%) = -10 \cdot Log_{10}\left(\frac{O_i}{O_1 + O_2}\right)$$

CRC Abbreviation for cyclic redundant check. Used in data transfer to check for corrupted data. It performs the same function as a checksum but offers a more reliable check of the transmission data.

Critical Angle In geometric optics, at a refractive boundary, the smallest angle of incidence at which total internal reflection occurs.

Cross-connect Connections between terminal blocks on the two sides of a distribution frame, or between terminals on a terminal block (also called straps). Also called cross-connection or jumper.

Cross-gain Modulation (XGM) A technique used in wavelength converters where gain saturation effects in an active optical device, such as a semiconductor optical amplifier (SOA), allow the conversion of the optical wavelength. Better at shorter wavelengths (e.g., 780 nm or 850 nm).

Cross-phase Modulation (XPM) A fiber nonlinearity caused by the index of refraction of glass. The index of refraction varies with optical power level causing different optical signals to interact.

Crosstalk (XT) 1) Undesired coupling from one circuit, part of a circuit, or channel to another. 2) Any phenomenon by which a signal transmitted on one circuit or channel of a transmission system creates an undesired effect in another circuit or channel.

CRT Abbreviation for cathode ray tube.

Customer Premises Equipment (CPE) Terminal and associated equipment and inside wiring located at a subscriber's premises and connected with a carrier's communication channel(s) at the demarcation point ("demarc"), a point established in a building or complex to separate customer equipment from telephone company equipment. CPE does not include over-voltage protection equipment and pay telephones.

Cutoff Wavelength In single-mode fiber, the wavelength below which the fiber ceases to be single-mode.

CW Abbreviation for continuous wave. Usually refers to the constant optical output from an optical source when it is biased (i.e., turned on) but not modulated with a signal.

CWDM See coarse wavelength-division multiplexing.

D

D1 A format for component digital video tape recording working to the ITU-R 601, 4:2:2 standard using 8-bit sampling.

D2 The VTR standard for digital composite (coded) NTSC or PAL signals that uses data conforming to SMPTE 244M.

D3 A composite digital video recording format that uses data conforming to SMPTE 244M.

D5 An uncompressed tape format for component digital video which has provisions for HDTV recording by use of 4:1 compression.

D/A or DAC Abbreviation for digital-to-analog converter. A device used to convert digital signals to analog signals.

Dark Current The induced current that exists in a reversed biased photodiode in the absence of incident optical power. It is better understood to result from the shunt resistance of the photodiode. A bias voltage across the diode (and the shunt resistance) causes current to flow in the absence of light.

Data Dependent Jitter (DDJ) Jitter related to the transmitted symbol sequence caused by the limited bandwidth characteristics, non ideal individual pulse responses, and imperfections in the optical channel components. Also called data dependent distortion.

Data Rate The number of bits of information in a transmission system, expressed in bits per second (b/s or bps), and which may or may not be equal to the signal or baud rate.

dB See decibel.

dBμ Decibels relative to microwatt.

dBc Decibel relative to a carrier level.

dBm Decibels relative to milliwatt.

DBS Abbreviation for digital broadcast system. An alternative to cable and analog satellite reception that uses a fixed 18-inch dish focused on one or more geostationary satellites. DBS units receive multiple channels of multiplexed video and audio signals as well as programming information, and related data. Also known as digital satellite system.

DC Abbreviation for direct current. An electric current flowing in one direction only and substantially constant in value.

DCD See duty cycle distortion jitter.

DCF See dispersion-compensating fiber.

DCM See dispersion-compensating module.

DCT See discrete-cosine transform.

DDJ See data dependent jitter.

Decibel (dB) A unit of measurement indicating relative optical power on a logarithmic scale. Often expressed in reference to a fixed value, such as dBm (1 milliwatt) or dBμ (1 microwatt).

$$dB = 10 \bullet Log_{10}\left(\frac{P_1}{P_2}\right)$$

Delay 1) The amount of time by which an event is retarded. 2) The time between the instant at which a given event occurs and the instant at which a related aspect of that event occurs.

Demultiplexer A module that separates two or more previously combined signals by compatible multiplexing equipment.

Dense Wavelength-Division Multiplexing (DWDM) This refers to the transmission of numerous closely spaced wavelengths in the 1550 nm region. Wavelength spacings are usually 100 GHz or 200 GHz which corresponds to 0.8 nm or 1.6 nm. DWDM bands include the C-Band, the S-Band, and the L-Band.

Detector An opto-electronic transducer used in fiber optics to convert optical power to electrical current. Usually referred to as a photodiode.

DFB See distributed feedback laser.

DG See differential gain.

Diameter-mismatch Loss The loss of power at a joint, when coupling light from a source to a fiber, from fiber to fiber, or from fiber to detector, that occurs when the transmitting fiber has a diameter greater than the diameter of the receiving fiber.

Dichroic Filter An optical filter that transmits light according to wavelength. Dichroic filters reflect light that they do not transmit.

Dielectric Any substance in which an electric field may be maintained with zero or near-zero power dissipation. This term usually refers to nonmetallic materials.

Differential Gain (DG) A type of distortion in a video signal that causes the brightness information to be distorted.

Differential Phase (DP) A type of distortion in a video signal that causes the color information to be distorted.

Differential Pulse-code Modulation (DPCM) Pulse-code modulation in which an analog signal is sampled and the difference between the actual value of each sample and its predicted value, derived from the previous sample or samples, is quantized and converted, by encoding, to a digital signal.

Diffraction Grating An array of fine, parallel, equally spaced reflecting or transmitting lines that mutually enhance the effects of diffraction to concentrate the diffracted light in a few directions determined by the spacing of the lines and by the wavelength of the light.

Digital A signal that consists of discrete states. A binary signal has only two states, 0 and 1. Antonym of analog.

Digital Compression A technique for converting a digital video signal to a lower data rate by eliminating redundant information.

Digital Word The number of bits treated as a single entity by the system.

Diode An electronic device that allows current to flow in only one direction. Semiconductor diodes used in fiber optics contain a junction between regions of different doping. They include light emitters (LEDs and laser diodes) and detectors (photodiodes).

Diode Laser See injection laser diode.

Diplexer A device that combines two or more types of signals into a single output.

Directional Coupler A coupling device for separately sampling either the forward (incident) or the backward (reflected) wave in a transmission line through a known coupling loss.

Directivity See near-end crosstalk.

Discrete-cosine Transform A widely used method of data compression of digital video pictures that resolves blocks of the picture (usually 8 x 8 pixels) into frequencies, amplitudes, and colors. JPEG and DV depend on DCT.

Dispersion The temporal spreading of a light signal in an optical waveguide caused by light signals traveling at different speeds through a fiber either due to modal or chromatic effects.

Dispersion-compensating Fiber (DCF) A fiber that has the opposite dispersion of the fiber being used in a transmission system, used to nullify the dispersion caused by that fiber.

Dispersion-compensating Module (DCM) A module with the opposite dispersion of the fiber being used in a transmission system. It nullifies the dispersion caused by that fiber. Module configurations include a spool of a special fiber or a grating based module.

Dispersion-shifted Fiber (DSF) A type of single-mode fiber designed to have zero dispersion near 1550 nm. This fiber type works very poorly for DWDM applications because of high fiber nonlinearity at the zero-dispersion point.

Dispersion Management A technique used in the system design of a fiber optic transmission to be able to cope with the dispersion introduced by the optical fiber.

Dispersion Penalty The loss of sensitivity in a receiver caused by dispersion in an optical fiber. Expressed in dB.

Distortion Nonlinearities in a device or transmission path that generate harmonics and beat products.

Distributed Feedback Laser (DFB) An injection laser diode which has a Bragg reflection grating in the active region in order to suppress multiple longitudinal modes and enhance a single longitudinal mode.

Distribution System Part of a cable system consisting of trunk and feeder cables used to carry signal from headend to customer terminals.

Dopant An impurity added to an optical medium to change its optical properties. EDFAs use erbium as a dopant for optical fiber.

Dope Thick liquid or paste used to prepare a surface or a varnish-like substance used for waterproofing or strengthening a material.

Double-Window Fiber An optical fiber optimized for use in two wavelengths. In multimode fibers, the fiber is optimized for 850 nm and 1310 nm operation. In single-mode fibers, the fiber is optimized for 1310 nm and 1550 nm operation.

DP See differential phase.

DPCM See differential pulse-code modulation.

DS1 A telephone company format for transmitting information digitally. DS1 has a capacity of 24 voice circuits at a transmission speed of 1.544 megabits per second.

DS3 A terrestrial and satellite format for transmitting information digitally. DS3 has a capacity of 672 voice circuits at a transmission speed of 44.736 Mbps (commonly referred to as 45 Mbps).

DSF See dispersion-shifted fiber.

DSL Abbreviation for digital subscriber line. In an integrated services digital network (ISDN), equipment that provides full-duplex service on a single twisted metallic pair at a rate sufficient to support ISDN basic access and additional framing, timing recovery, and operational functions. *See also* integrated services digital network.

DSR Abbreviation for data signaling rate. The aggregate rate at which data pass a point in the transmission path of a data transmission system, expressed in bits per second (bps or b/s).

DST Abbreviation for dispersion supported transmission. In electrical TDM systems, a transmission system that allows data rates up to 40 Gb/s by incorporating devices such as SOAs.

DSx A transmission rate in the North American digital telephone hierarchy. Also called T-carrier.

Dual Attachment Concentrator A concentrator that offers two attachments to the FDDI network, which accommodate a dual (counter-rotating) ring.

Dual Attachment Station A station that offers two attachments to the FDDI network, which accommodate a dual (counter-rotating) ring.

Dual Ring (FDDI Dual Ring) A pair of counter-rotating logical rings.

Duplex Cable A two-fiber cable suitable for duplex transmission.

Duplex Transmission Transmission in both directions, either one direction at a time (half-duplex) or both directions simultaneously (full-duplex).

Duty Cycle In a digital transmission, the fraction of time a signal is at the high level.

Duty Cycle Distortion Jitter (DCD) Distortion usually caused by propagation delay differences between low-to-high and high-to-low transitions. DCD is manifested as a pulse width distortion of the nominal baud time.

DVD Abbreviation for digital versatile disk. A high density development of the compact disk that stores seven times more than a CD of the same size.

DWDM See dense wavelength-division multiplexing.

Dynamic Range 1) In a system or device, the ratio of a specified maximum level of a parameter to the minimum detectable value of that parameter, usually expressed in dB. 2) In a transmission system, the ratio of the maximum signal power that the system can tolerate without distortion of the signal, to the noise level of the system. Also expressed in dB. 3) In digital systems or devices, the ratio of maximum and minimum signal levels required to maintain a specified bit error ratio.

E

EBU Abbreviation for European Broadcasting Union, an independent, nongovernmental, noncommercial body which promotes cooperation in international radio and television broadcasting. The EBU acts as a broker through which broadcasters worldwide can exchange radio and television services, and has its administrative headquarters in Geneva, Switzerland.

ECL Emitter-coupled logic. A high-speed logic family capable of GHz rates.

EDFA See erbium-doped fiber amplifier.

Edge-emitting Diode An LED that emits light from its edge, producing more directional output than surface-emitting LEDs, which emit light from the top.

Effective Area The area of a single-mode fiber that carries the light.

EGA Abbreviation for enhanced graphics adapter. A medium-resolution color standard for computer monitors.

EIA Abbreviation for Electronic Industries Alliance. An organization of electronic and high tech associations and companies who develop voluntary standards for the industry.

Electromagnetic Interference (EMI) 1) Any electromagnetic disturbance that interrupts, obstructs, or otherwise degrades or limits the effective performance of electronics/electrical equipment. It can be induced intentionally, as in some forms of electronic warfare, or unintentionally, as a result of spurious emissions and responses, intermodulation products, and the like. 2) An engineering term used to designate interference in a piece of electronic equipment caused by another piece of electronic or other equipment.

Electromagnetic Pulse (EMP) A burst of electromagnetic radiation that creates electric and magnetic fields that may couple with electrical/electronic systems to produce disruptive or damaging current and voltage surges.

Electromagnetic Radiation (EMR) Radiation made up of oscillating electric and magnetic fields and propagated with the speed of light. Includes gamma radiation, X-rays, ultraviolet, visible and infrared radiation, radar, and radio waves.

Electromagnetic Spectrum The range of frequencies of electromagnetic radiation from zero to infinity.

Electromagnetic Wave (EMW) A wave produced by the interaction of time-varying electric and magnetic fields.

Electro-optic Effect Any one of a number of phenomena that occur when an electromagnetic wave in the optical spectrum interacts with an electric field, or with matter under the influence of an electric field.

ELED See edge-emitting diode.

Ellipticity Describes a fiber's core or cladding as elliptical rather than circular.

EM Abbreviation for electromagnetic.

EMD See equilibrium mode distribution.

EMI See electromagnetic interference.

E/O Abbreviation for electrical-to-optical converter. A device that converts electrical signals to optical signals.

Equilibrium Mode Distribution (EMD) The steady modal state of a multimode fiber in which the relative power distribution among modes is independent of fiber length.

Erbium-doped Fiber Amplifier (EDFA) Optical fibers doped with the rare earth element erbium, which can amplify light in the 1550 nm region when pumped by an external light source.

Error Correction In digital transmission systems, a scheme that adds overhead to the data to permit a certain level of errors to be detected and corrected.

Error Detection Checking for errors in data transmission. A calculation based on the data being sent; the results of the calculation are sent along with the data. The receiver then performs the same calculation and compares its results with those sent. If the receiver detects an error, it can be corrected, or it can simply be reported.

Ethernet A standard protocol (IEEE 802.3) for a 10-Mb/s baseband local area network (LAN) bus using carrier-sense multiple access with collision detection (CSMA/CD) as the access method, implemented at the physical layer in the International Standards Organization's open systems interconnection (OSI). Ethernet is a standard for using various transmission media, such as coaxial cables, unshielded twisted pairs, and optical fibers.

Evanescent Wave Light guided in the inner part of an optical fiber's cladding rather than in the core.

Excess Loss In a fiber optic coupler, the optical loss from that portion of light that does not emerge from the nominal operation ports of the device.

External Modulation Modulation of a light source by an external device that acts like an electronic shutter.

Extinction Ratio The ratio of the high, or ON optical power level (P_H) to the low, or OFF optical power level (P_L).

$$\text{Extinction Ratio (\%)} = \left(\frac{P_L}{P_H}\right) \times 100$$

Extrinsic Loss In a fiber interconnection, that portion of loss not intrinsic to the fiber but related to imperfect joining of a connector or splice.

Eye Pattern A diagram used to determine the proper function of a digital system which is crated by looking at the data while triggering on the clock signal. The "openness" of the eye relates to the BER that can be achieved. Also called eye diagram.

F

F Abbreviation for Fahrenheit. Measure of temperature where pure water freezes at 32° and boils at 212°.

Fall Time Also called turn-off time. The time required for the trailing edge of a pulse to fall from 90% to 10% of its amplitude, or the time required for a component to produce such a result. Typically measured between the 90% and 10% points or alternately the 80% and 20% points.

Faraday Effect A phenomenon that causes some materials to rotate the polarization of light in the presence of a magnetic field parallel to the direction of propagation. Also called magneto-optic effect.

Far-end Crosstalk See wavelength isolation.

FBG Abbreviation for fiber Bragg gratings. See Bragg grating.

FC A threaded optical connector that originated in Japan. Good for single-mode or multimode fiber and applications requiring low backreflection.

FCC Abbreviation for Federal Communications Commission. The U.S. Government board of five presidential appointees that has the authority to regulate all non-Federal Government interstate telecommunications as well as all international communications that originate or terminate in the United States.

FC/PC See FC. A special curved polish on the connector for very low backreflection.

FCS Abbreviation for frame check sequence. An error-detection scheme that uses parity bits generated by encoding of digital signals, appends those parity bits to the digital signal, and uses decoding algorithms that detect errors in the received digital signal.

FDA Abbreviation for Food and Drug Administration. Organization responsible for laser safety warnings.

FDDI Abbreviation for fiber distributed data interface. Standards for a 100 Mbps local area network, based upon fiber optic or wired media configured as dual counter-rotating token rings. This configuration provides a high level of fault tolerance by creating multiple connection paths between nodes allowing connections to be re-established even if a ring is broken.

FDM See frequency-division multiplexing.

FEC See forward error correcting.

Ferrule A rigid tube that confines or holds a fiber as part of a connector assembly.

Fiber Fuse A mechanism whereby the core of a single-mode fiber can be destroyed at high optical power levels.

Fiber Grating An optical fiber in which the refractive index of the core varies periodically along its length, scattering light in a way similar to a diffraction grating, and transmitting or reflecting certain wavelengths selectively.

Fiber Optic Attenuator A component installed in a fiber optic transmission system that reduces the optical signal strength. It is often used to limit the optical power received by the photodetector to within the limits of the optical receiver.

Fiber Optic Cable A cable containing one or more optical fibers.

Fiber Optic Communication System The transfer of modulated or unmodulated optical energy through optical fiber media which terminates in the same or different media.

Fiber Optic Link A transmitter, receiver, and cable assembly that can transmit information between two points.

Fiber Optic Span An optical fiber/cable terminated at both ends which may include devices that add, subtract, or attenuate optical signals.

Fiber Optic Subsystem A part of a system acting as a functional entity with defined bounds and interfaces. It contains solid state and/or other components and is specified as a subsystem for the purpose of trade and commerce.

Fiber-to-the-Curb (FTTC) Fiber optic service from the central office to the end customer's exterior cable box. Connections from exterior box to television set use copper cable connections.

Fiber-to-the-Home (FTTH) Fiber optic service to a node located inside an individual home.

Fiber-to-the-Loop (FTTL) Fiber optic service to a node that is located in a neighborhood.

Fibre Channel (also Fiber Channel) A high speed data link planned to run up to 2 Gb/s on a fiber optic cable. The standard supports data transmission and framing protocols for the most popular channel and network standards including SCSI, HIPPI, Ethernet, Internet Protocol, and ATM.

Field 1) In interlaced scan systems, the information for one picture is divided up into two fields. Each field contains one-half of the lines required to produce the entire picture. Adjacent lines in the picture are in alternate fields. 2) Half of the horizontal lines (262.5 in NTSC and 312.5 in PAL) needed to create a complete picture. 3) One complete vertical scan of an image. In a progressive scanning system, all of the scanning lines comprising a frame also comprise a field.

Field Period The reciprocal of twice the frame rate.

Field Rate Number of fields per second.

Filter A device which transmits only part of the incident energy and may thereby change the spectral distribution of energy.

Flicker In video, any of several visual artifacts similar to (i.e., manifested as) a stroboscopic effect (jerkiness), sometimes caused by or related to vertical synchronization characteristics or video field display rates.

Fluoride Glasses Materials that have the amorphous structure of glass but are made of fluoride compounds (e.g., zirconium fluoride) rather than oxide compounds (e.g., silica). Suitable for very long wavelength transmission.

FM (Frequency Modulation) A method of transmission in which the carrier frequency varies in accordance with the signal.

Forward Error Correcting (FEC) A communication technique used to compensate for a noisy transmission channel. Extra information is sent along with the primary data payload to correct for errors that occur in transmission.

Four Wave Mixing (FWM) A nonlinearity common in DWDM systems where multiple wavelengths mix together to form new wavelengths. Most prevalent near the zero-dispersion point and at close wavelength spacings.

FP Abbreviation for Fabry-Perot. Generally refers to any device such as a type of laser that uses mirrors in an internal cavity to produce multiple reflections.

Frame 1) In data transmission, the sequence of contiguous bits delimited by, and including, beginning and ending flag sequences. 2) In the multiplex structure of pulse-code modulation (PCM) systems, a set of consecutive time slots in which the position of each digit can be identified by reference to a frame-alignment signal. 3) In a time-division multiplexing (TDM) system, a repetitive group of signals resulting from a single sampling of all channels, including any required system information, such as additional synchronizing signals. 4) In video display, the set of all picture elements that represent one complete image. In NTSC and other television standards used throughout the world, a frame consists of two interlaced fields, each of which has half the number of scanning lines, and consequently, half the number of pixels, of one frame.

Frame Rate The number of frames transmitted or received per unit time. Usually expressed in frames per second (fps or f/s). Also known as frame frequency.

Frequency-division Multiplexing (FDM) A method of deriving two or more simultaneous, continuous channels from a transmission medium by assigning separate portions of the available frequency spectrum to each of the individual channels.

Frequency-shift Keying (FSK) Frequency modulation in which the modulating signal shifts the output frequency between predetermined values. Also called frequency-shift modulation, frequency-shift signaling.

Fresnel Reflection Loss Reflection losses at the ends of fibers caused by differences in the refractive index between glass and air. The maximum reflection caused by a perpendicular air-glass interface is about 4% or about -14 dB.

FSAN Abbreviation for full service access network. A forum for the world's largest telecommunications services providers and equipment suppliers to work define broadband access networks based primarily on the ATM passive optical network structure.

FSK See frequency-shift keying.

FTTC See fiber-to-the-curb.

FTTH See fiber-to-the-home.

FTTL See fiber-to-the-loop.

Full-duplex Transmission Simultaneous bidirectional transfer of data.

Fused Coupler A method of making a multimode or single-mode coupler by wrapping fibers together, heating them, and pulling them to form a central unified mass so that light on any input fiber is coupled to all output fibers.

Fused Fiber A bundle of fibers fused together so that they maintain a fixed alignment with respect to each other in a rigid rod.

Fusion Splicer An instrument that permanently bonds two fibers together by heating and fusing them.

FWHM Abbreviation for full width half maximum. Used to describe the width of a spectral emission at the 50% amplitude points. Also known as FWHP (full width half power).

FWM See four wave mixing.

G

G Abbreviation for giga. One billion or 10^9.

GaAlAs Abbreviation for gallium aluminum arsenide. A semiconductor material used to make short wavelength light emitters.

GaAs Abbreviation for gallium arsenide. A semiconductor material used to make light emitters.

Gain The ratio of output current, voltage, or power to input current, voltage, or power, respectively. Usually expressed in dB.

GaInAsP Abbreviation for gallium indium arsenide phosphide. A semiconductor material used to make long wavelength light emitters.

Gamma A factor that determines the relationship between the drive signals and the light produced by a cathode ray tube. The transfer curve is generally the drive signal raised to the gamma power.

Gap Loss Loss resulting from the end separation of two axially aligned fibers.

Gaussian Beam A beam pattern used to approximate the distribution of energy in a fiber core. It can also be used to describe emission patterns from surface-emitting LEDs. Most people would recognize it as the bell curve. The equation that defines a Gaussian beam is:

$$E(x) = E(0)e^{-x^2/W_0^2}$$

GBaud One billion symbols of data per second or 10^9 bits. Equivalent to 1 Gb/s for binary signaling.

Gb/s Gigabits per second. *See also* GBaud.

Ge Abbreviation for germanium. An element used to make detectors. Good for most wavelengths (e.g., 800-1600 nm).

Genlock A process of sync generator locking. This is usually performed by introducing a composite video signal from a master source to the subject sync generator. The generator to be locked has circuits to isolate the subcarrier, vertical drive, and horizontal drive. The subject generator locks to the master subcarrier, horizontal, and vertical drives, resulting in both sync generators running at the same frequency and phase.

GHz Abbreviation for gigahertz. One billion Hertz (cycles per second) or 10^9 Hertz.

Graded-index Fiber Optical fiber in which the refractive index of the core is in the form of a parabolic curve, decreasing toward the cladding.

GRIN Gradient index. Generally refers to the SELFOC lens often used in fiber optics.

Ground Loop Noise Noise that results when equipment is grounded at points having different potentials, thereby creating an unintended current path. The dielectric properties of optical fiber provide electrical isolation that eliminates ground loops.

Group Index Also called group refractive index. In fiber optics, for a given mode propagating in a medium of refractive index (n), the group index (N), is the velocity of light in a vacuum (c), divided by the group velocity of the mode.

Group Velocity 1) The velocity of propagation of an envelope produced when an electromagnetic wave is modulated by, or mixed with, other waves of different frequencies. 2) For a particular mode, the reciprocal of the rate of change of the phase constant with respect to angular frequency. 3) The velocity of the modulated optical power.

H

Half-duplex Transmission A bidirectional link that is limited to one-way transfer of data, i.e., data cannot be sent both ways at the same time.

Hard-clad Silica Fiber An optical fiber having a silica core and a hard polymeric plastic cladding intimately bonded to the core.

HBT Abbreviation for heterojunction bipolar transistors. A very high performance transistor structure built using more than one semiconductor material.

HDSL Abbreviation for high data-rate digital subscriber line. A DSL operating at a high data rate compared to the data rates specified for ISDN. *See also* DSL.

HDTV Abbreviation for high-definition television. Television that has approximately twice the horizontal and twice the vertical emitted resolution specified by the NTSC standard.

Headend 1) A central control device required within some local area network (LAN and metropolitan area network (MAN) systems to provide such centralized functions as remodulation, retiming, message accountability, contention control, diagnostic control, and access to a gateway. 2) A central control center within CATV systems to provide such centralized functions as remodulation and origination of signals. *See also* LAN.

Hertz One cycle per second.

HFC See hybrid fiber/coax.

HP Abbreviation for homes passed. Homes that could easily and inexpensively be connected to a cable network because the feeder cable is nearby.

Hue 1) Property of light by which the color of an object is classified as red, green, blue, or yellow in reference to the spectrum. 2) A gradation or variety of a color.

Hybrid Fiber/Coax (HFC) A cable construction that incorporates both fiber optic transmission components and copper coax transmission components.

Hydrogen Losses Increases in fiber attenuation that occur when hydrogen diffuses into the glass matrix and absorbs light.

Hz See Hertz.

I

IC See integrated circuit.

Iconoscope A camera tube in which a high-velocity electron beam scans a photo-emissive mosaic which has electrical storage capability.

IDP See integrated detector/preamplifier.

IEEE Abbreviation for Institute of Electrical and Electronic Engineers. A technical professional association that contributes to voluntary standards in technical areas ranging from computer engineering, biomedical technology and telecommunications, to electric power, aerospace and consumer electronics, among others.

IIN See interferometric intensity noise.

IM See intensity modulation.

Index of Refraction Also refractive index. The ratio of the velocity of light in free space to the velocity of light in a fiber material. Symbolized by n. Always greater than or equal to one.

Infrared (IR) The region of the electromagnetic spectrum bounded by the long-wavelength extreme of the visible spectrum (about 0.7 μm) and the shortest microwaves (about 0.1 μm). *See also* light.

Infrared Fiber Colloquially, optical fibers with best transmission at wavelengths of 2 μm or longer, made of materials other than silica glass. *See also* fluoride glasses.

InGaAs Indium gallium arsenide. A semiconductor material used to make high-performance long-wavelength detectors.

InGaAsP Indium gallium arsenide phosphide. A semiconductor material used to make long-wavelength light emitters.

Injection Laser Diode (ILD) A laser employing a forward-biased semiconductor junction as the active medium. Stimulated emission of coherent light occurs at a p-n junction where electrons and holes are driven into the junction.

In-line Amplifier An EDFA or other type of all-optical amplifier placed in the transmission line to amplify the attenuated signal before being sent onto the next, distant site.

InP Indium phosphide. A semiconductor material used to make optical amplifiers and HBTs.

Insertion Loss The loss of power that results from inserting a component, such as a connector, splice, coupler, or WDM, into a previously continuous path.

Integrated Circuit (IC) An electronic circuit that consists of many individual circuit elements, such as transistors, diodes, resistors, capacitors, inductors, and other active and passive semiconductor devices, formed on a single chip of semiconducting material and mounted on a single piece of substrate material.

Integrated Detector/Preamplifier (IDP) A detector package containing a PIN photodiode and transimpedance amplifier.

Integrated Services Digital Network (ISDN) An integrated digital network in which the same time-division switches and digital transmission paths are used to establish connections for services such as telephone, data, electronic mail, and facsimile. How a connection is accomplished is often specified as a switched connection, nonswitched connection, exchange connection, ISDN connection, etc.

Intensity The square of the electric field strength of an electromagnetic wave. Intensity is proportional to irradiance and may get used in place of the term "irradiance" when only relative values are important.

Intensity Modulation (IM) In optical communications, a form of modulation in which the optical power output of a source varies in accordance with some characteristic of the modulating signal.

Interchannel Isolation The ability to prevent undesired optical energy from appearing in one signal path as a result of coupling from another signal path. Also called crosstalk.

Interferometer An instrument that uses the principle of interference of electromagnetic waves for purposes of measurement. Used to measure a variety of physical variables, such as displacement (distance), temperature, pressure, and strain.

Interferometric Intensity Noise (IIN) Noise generated in optical fiber caused by the distributed backreflection that all fiber generates, mainly due to Rayleigh scattering. OTDRs make use of this scattering power to deduce the fiber loss over distance.

Interferometric Sensors Fiber optic sensors that rely on interferometric detection.

Interframe Time Fill In digital data transmission, a sequence of bits transmitted between consecutive frames not including any bits stuffed within a frame.

Interlaced Short for interlaced scanning. Also called line interlace. A system of video scanning whereby the odd- and even-numbered lines of a picture are transmitted consecutively as two separate interleaved fields. Interlace is a form of compression.

International Telecommunications Union (ITU) A civil international organization, headquartered in Geneva, Switzerland, established to promote standardized telecommunications on a worldwide basis. The ITU-R and ITU-T are committees under the ITU which is recognized by the United Nations as the specialized agency for telecommunications.

Intraframe Coding Video coding within a frame of a video signal.

Intrinsic Losses Splice losses arising from differences in the two fibers being spliced.

IP Abbreviation for Internet protocol. A standard protocol designed for use in interconnected systems of packet-switched computer communication networks.

IR See infrared.

IRE Unit An arbitrary unit created by the Institute of Radio Engineers to describe the amplitude characteristic of a video signal, where pure white is defined as 100 IRE and the blanking level is 0 IRE.

Irradiance Power per unit area. *See also* intensity.

ISA Abbreviation for Instrumentation, Systems, and Automation Society. A standards writing organization, developing consensus standards for factory automation, power plants, computer technology, telemetry, and communications.

ISDN See integrated services digital network.

ISO Abbreviation for International Standards Organization. An international organization responsible for the development and publication of international standards in various technical fields, after developing a suitable consensus.

Isolator A device that prevents backreflected light from re-entering an amplifier or other optical component.

Isolation See near-end crosstalk.

ITU See International Telecommunications Union.

J

Jacket The outer, protective covering of a fiber optic or other type of cable.

Jitter Small and rapid variations in the timing of a waveform due to noise, changes in component characteristics, supply voltages, imperfect synchronizing circuits, etc. *See also* data dependant jitter, duty cycle distortion jitter, random jitter.

JPEG Acronym for Joint Photographers Expert Group. International standard for compressing still photography.

Jumper A short fiber optic cable with connectors on both ends.

K

k Abbreviation for kilo. One thousand or 10^3.

K Abbreviation for Kelvin. Measure of temperature where pure water freezes at 273° and boils at 373°.

kBaud One thousand symbols of data per second. Equivalent to 1 kb/s for binary signaling.

kb/s Kilobits per second. *See also* kBaud.

Kevlar® A very strong, very light, synthetic compound developed by DuPont which is used to strengthen optical cables.

Keyframe A set of parameters defining a point in a transition, such as a digital video effect. A keyframe may define a picture size, position, and rotation. Any digital effect must have a minimum of two keyframes, start and finish, although more complex moves will use as many as 100. Increasingly, more parameters are becoming "keyframeable," meaning they can be programmed to transition between two, or more, states. Examples are color correction to make a steady change of color, and keyer settings, perhaps to make an object slowly appear or disappear.

Keying Generating signals by the interruption or modulation of a steady signal or carrier.

K-factor 1) In tropospheric radio propagation, the ratio of the effective Earth radius to the actual Earth radius. 2) In ionospheric radio propagation, a correction factor that is applied in calculations related to curved layers, and is a function of distance and the real height of ionospheric reflection.

kg Abbreviation for kilogram. Approximately 2.2 pounds.

kHz Abbreviation for kilohertz. One thousand cycles per second.

km Abbreviation for kilometer. 1 km = 3,280 feet or 0.62 miles.

L

Lambertian Emitter An emitter that radiates according to Lambert's cosine law. This law states that the radiance of certain idealized surfaces depends upon the angle at which the surface is viewed. The radiant intensity of such a surface is maximum normal to the surface and decreases in proportion to the cosine of the angle from the normal. Given by:

$$N = N_0 \cos(A)$$

Where:

N = The radiant intensity.

N_0 = The radiance normal (perpendicular) to an emitting surface.

A = The angle between the viewing direction and the normal to the surface.

LAN (Local Area Network) A communication link between two or more points within a small geographic area, such as between buildings.

Large Core Fiber Usually, a fiber with a core of 200 μm or more.

Large Effective Area Fiber (LEAF) An optical fiber, developed by Corning, designed to have a large area in the core, which carries the light.

Laser Acronym for Light Amplification by Stimulated Emission of Radiation. A light source that produces, through stimulated emission, coherent, near monochromatic light. Lasers in fiber optics are usually solid-state semiconductor types.

Laser Diode (LD) A semiconductor that emits coherent light when forward biased.

Lateral Displacement Loss The loss of power that results from lateral displacement of optimum alignment between two fibers or between a fiber and an active device.

Launch Fiber An optical fiber used to couple and condition light from an optical source into an optical fiber. Often the launch fiber is used to create an equilibrium mode distribution in multimode fiber. Also called launching fiber.

L-Band The wavelength range between 1570 nm and 1610 nm used in some CWDM and DWDM applications.

LD See laser diode.

LEAF See large effective area fiber.

Least Significant Bit In a binary code, the bit or bit position assigned to the smallest quantity or increment that can be represented by the code.

LEC See local exchange carrier.

LED See light-emitting diode.

LEX Abbreviation for local exchange. Synonym for central office.

LH Abbreviation for long-haul. A classification of video performance under RS-250C. Lower performance than medium-haul or short-haul.

L-I Curve The plot of optical output (L) as a function of current (I) which characterizes an electrical to optical converter.

Light In a strict sense, the region of the electromagnetic spectrum that can be perceived by human vision, designated the visible spectrum and nominally covering the wavelength range of 0.4 μm to 0.7 μm. In the laser and optical communication fields, custom and practice have extended usage of the term to include the much broader portion of the electromagnetic spectrum that can be handled by the basic optical techniques used for the visible spectrum. This region has not been clearly defined, but, as employed by most workers in the field, may be considered to extend from the near-ultraviolet region of approximately 0.3 μm, through the visible region, and into the mid-infrared region to 30 μm.

Light-emitting Diode (LED) A semiconductor that emits incoherent light when forward biased.

Lightguide See optical fiber.

Light Wave The path of a point on a wavefront. The direction of the light wave is generally normal to the wavefront.

Linear Device A device for which the output is, within a given dynamic range, linearly proportional to the input.

Linearity The basic measurement of how well analog-to-digital and digital-to-analog conversions are performed. To test for linearity, a mathematically perfect diagonal line is converted and then compared to a copy of itself. The difference between the two lines is calculated to show linearity of the system and is given as a percentage or range of least significant bits.

Local Exchange Carrier (LEC) A local telephone company, i.e., a communications common carrier that provides ordinary local voice-grade telecommunications service under regulation within a specified service area.

Local Loop See loop.

Long-haul Telecommunications Long-distance telecommunications links such as cross-country or transoceanic.

Longitudinal Mode An optical waveguide mode with boundary condition determined along the length of the optical cavity.

Loop 1) A communication channel from a switching center or an individual message distribution point to the user terminal. 2) In telephone systems, a pair of wires from a central office to a subscriber's telephone. 3) A closed path under measurement in a resistance test. 4) A type of antenna used extensively in direction-finding equipment and in UHF reception.

Loose-tube A type of fiber optic cable construction where the fiber is contained within a loose tube in the cable jacket.

Loss The amount of a signal's power, expressed in dB, that is lost in connectors, splices, or fiber defects.

Loss Budget An accounting of overall attenuation in a system.

Luminance The component of a video signal that includes information about its brightness.

M

m Abbreviation for meter. 39.37 inches.

M Abbreviation for mega. One million or 10^6.

mA Abbreviation for milliamp. One thousandth of an Amp or 10^{-3} Amps.

MAC 1) Abbreviation for multiplexed analog components. A video standard developed by the European Community. An enhanced version, HD-MAC delivers 1250 lines at 50 frames per second, HDTV quality. 2) See medium access control.

Macrobending In a fiber, all macroscopic deviations of the fiber's axis from a straight line.

MAN (Metropolitan Area Network) A network covering an area larger than a local area network. A wide area network that covers a metropolitan area. Usually, an interconnection of two or more local area networks.

MAP Abbreviation for manufacturing automation protocol. Computer programs that run manufacturing automation systems.

Margin Allowance for attenuation in addition to that explicitly accounted for in system design.

Mass Splicing Simultaneous splicing of many fibers in a cable.

Material Dispersion Dispersion resulting from the different velocities of each wavelength in a material.

Maxwell's Equations A set of partial differential equations that describe and predict the behavior of electromagnetic waves in free space, in dielectrics, and at conductor-dielectric boundaries.

MBaud One million symbols of information per second. Equivalent to 1 Mb/s for binary signaling.

Mb/s Megabits per second. *See also* MBaud.

Mean Launched Power The average power for a continuous valid symbol sequence coupled into a fiber.

Mechanical Splice An optical fiber splice accomplished by fixtures or materials, rather than by fusion splicing.

Medium Access Control (MAC) 1) A service feature or technique used to permit or deny use of the components of a communication system. 2) A technique used to define or restrict the rights of individuals or application programs to obtain data from, or place data onto, a storage device, or the definition derived from that technique.

Mezzanine Compression Contribution level quality encoded high-definition television signals. Typically split into two levels: high level at 140 Mb/s and low level at 39 Mb/s. For high definition within the studio, 270 Mb/s is being considered.

MFD See mode field diameter.

MH Abbreviation for medium-haul. A classification of video performance under RS-250C. Higher performance than long-haul and lower performance than short-haul.

MHz Abbreviation for megahertz. One million Hertz (cycles per second).

Microbending Mechanical stress on a fiber may introduce local discontinuities that result in light leaking from the core to the cladding by a process called mode coupling, which causes additional loss.

Micrometer One millionth of a meter or 10^{-6} meters. Abbreviated μm.

Microsecond One millionth of a second or 10^{-6} seconds. Abbreviated μs.

Microwatt One millionth of a Watt or 10^{-6} Watts. Abbreviated μW.

Microwave Dish A parabolic shaped antenna used for high-frequency RF signals.

Microwave Transmission Communication systems using very high-frequency RF to carry the signal information.

MIL-SPEC Abbreviation for military specification. Performance specifications issued by the Department of Defense that must be met in order to pass a MIL-STD.

MIL-STD Abbreviation for military standard. Standards issued by the Department of Defense.

Minimum Bend Radius The smallest radius an optical fiber or fiber cable can bend before increased attenuation or breakage occurs.

Misalignment Loss The loss of power resulting from angular misalignment, lateral displacement, and end separation.

MLM See multilongitudinal mode laser.

mm Abbreviation for millimeter. One thousandth of a meter or 10^{-3} meters.

MM See multimode fiber.

Modal Dispersion See multimode dispersion.

Modal Noise Noise that occurs whenever the optical power propagates through mode-selective devices. It is usually only a factor with laser light sources and multi-mode fiber.

Mode A single electromagnetic wave traveling in a fiber.

Mode Coupling The transfer of energy between modes. In a fiber, mode coupling occurs until equilibrium mode distribution (EMD) is reached.

Mode Evolution The dynamic process a multilongitudinal laser undergoes whereby the changing distribution of power among the modes creates a continuously changing envelope of the laser's spectrum.

Mode Field Diameter (MFD) A measure of distribution of optical power intensity across the end face of a single-mode fiber.

Mode Filter A device that removes higher-order modes to simulate equilibrium mode distribution.

Modem Acronym for modulator/demodulator. 1) In general, a device that both modulates and demodulates signals. 2) In computer communications, a device used for converting digital signals into, and recovering them from, quasi-analog signals suitable for transmission over analog communications channels such as telephone lines.

Mode Partition Noise Noise generated in multimode lasers (e.g., Fabry-Perot type) which is caused by the rapid distribution of energy among the various modes.

Mode Scrambler A device that mixes modes to uniform power distribution.

Mode Stripper A device that removes cladding modes.

Modulation The process by which the characteristic of one wave (the carrier) is modified by another wave (the signal). Examples include amplitude modulation (AM), frequency modulation (FM), pulse-coded modulation (PCM), and digital modulation.

Modulation Index In an intensity-based system, the modulation index measures how much the modulation signal affects the light output. It is defined as follows:

$$m = \frac{\text{highlevel-lowlevel}}{\text{highlevel+lowlevel}}$$

Monitor 1) a CRT that receives its signal directly from a VCR, camera, or separate TV tuner for high-quality picture reproduction. 2) A device used for the real-time temporary display of computer output data. 3) Software or hardware that is used to scrutinize and to display, record, supervise, control, or verify the operations of a system.

Monochrome Black and white TV signal.

Moore's Law A prediction for the rate of development of modern electronics. It states that the density of information storable in silicon roughly doubles every year. Or, the performance of silicon will double every eighteen months, with proportional decreases in cost. For more than two decades this prediction has held true. Named after Gordon E. Moore, physicist, cofounder and chairman emeritus of Intel Corporation.

Most Significant Bit In a binary code, the bit or bit position that is assigned to, or represents, the largest quantity or increment that the code can represent.

MPEG Acronym for Motion Picture Experts Group. An international standard for compressing video that provides high compression ratios. The standard has two recommendations: MPEG-1 compresses lower-resolution images for videoconferencing and lower-quality desktop video applications and transmits at around 1.5 Mb/s. MPEG-2 primarily delivers compressed television for home entertainment at CCIR resolution when bit rates exceed 5.0 Mb/s, as in hard disk-based applications.

MQW See multi-quantum well laser.

ms Abbreviation for milliseconds. One thousandth of a second or 10^{-3} seconds.

MSO Abbreviation for Multiple Service Operator. A telecommunication company that offers more than one service, e.g., telephone service, Internet access, satellite service, etc. Also called multiple system operator.

Multilongitudinal Mode Laser (MLM) An injection laser diode which has a number of longitudinal modes.

Multimode Dispersion Dispersion resulting from the different transit lengths of different propagating modes in a multimode optical fiber. Also called modal dispersion.

Multimode Fiber (MM) An optical fiber that has a core large enough to propagate more than one mode of light. The typical diameter is 62.5 micrometers.

Multimode Laser Diode (MMLD) See multilongitudinal mode laser.

Multiple Reflection Noise (MRN) The fiber optic receiver noise resulting from the interference of delayed signals from two or more reflection points in a fiber optic span. Also known as multipath interference.

Multiplexer A device that combines two or more signals into a single output.

Multiplexing The process by which two or more signals are transmitted over a single communications channel. Examples include time-division multiplexing and wavelength-division multiplexing.

Multi-quantum Well Laser (MQW) A laser structure with a very thin (about 10 nm thick) layer of bulk semiconductor material sandwiched between the two barrier regions of a higher bandgap material. This restricts the motion of the electrons and holes, forcing energies for motion to be quantized and only occur at discrete energies.

MUSE Abbreviation for multiple sub-Nyquist encoder. A high-definition standard developed in Europe that delivers 1,125 lines at 60 frames per second.

mV Abbreviation for millivolt. One thousandth of a Volt or 10^{-3} Volts.

mW Abbreviation for milliwatt. One thousandth of a Watt or 10^{-3} Watts.

MZ Abbreviation for Mach-Zehnder, a structure used in fiber Bragg gratings and interferometers. Named for the two men who developed the underlying principles of the structure.

N

n Abbreviation for nano. One billionth or 10^{-9}.

N Abbreviation for Newtons. Measure of force generally used to specify fiber optic cable strength.

nA Abbreviation for nanoamp. One billionth of an Amp or 10^{-9} Amps.

NA See numerical aperture.

NAB Abbreviation for the National Association of Broadcasters. A trade association that promotes and protects the interests of radio and television broadcasters before Congress, federal agencies, and the Courts.

NA Mismatch Loss The loss of power at a joint that occurs when the transmitting half has a numerical aperture greater than the NA of the receiving half. The loss occurs when coupling light from a source to fiber, from fiber to fiber, or from fiber to detector.

National Electric Code (NEC) A standard governing the use of electrical wire, cable, and fixtures installed in buildings; developed by the NEC Committee of the American National Standards Institute (ANSI), sponsored by the National Fire Protection Association (NFPA), identified by the description ANSI/NFPA 70-1990.

NCTA (National Cable Television Association) The major trade association for the cable television industry.

NDSF See non dispersion-shifted fiber.

Near-end Crosstalk (NEXT, RN) The optical power reflected from one or more input ports, back to another input port. Also known as isolation directivity.

Near Infrared The part of the infrared near the visible spectrum, typically 700 nm to 1500 nm or 2000 nm; it is not rigidly defined.

NEMA Abbreviation for National Electrical Manufacturers Association. Organization responsible for the standardization of electrical equipment, enabling consumers to select from a range of safe, effective, and compatible electrical products.

NEP See noise equivalent power.

Network 1) An interconnection of three or more communicating entities and (usually) one or more nodes. 2) A combination of passive or active electronic components that serves a given purpose.

Network Topology The specific physical, i.e., real, logical, or virtual, arrangement of the elements of a network. Common network topologies include a bus (or linear) topology, a ring topology, and a hybrid topology, which can be a combination of any two or more network topologies.

NF See noise figure.

nm Abbreviation for nanometer. One billionth of a meter or 10^{-9} meters.

Noise Equivalent Power (NEP) The noise of optical receivers, or of an entire transmission system, is often expressed in terms of noise equivalent optical power.

Noise Figure (NF) The ratio of the output signal-to-noise ratio to the input signal-to-noise ratio for a given element in a transmission system. Used for optical and electrical components.

Non Dispersion-shifted Fiber (NDSF) The most popular type of single-mode fiber deployed. It is designed to have zero dispersion near 1310 nm.

Nonlinearity The deviation from linearity in an electronic circuit, an electro-optic device or a fiber that generates undesired components in a signal.

Non-zero Dispersion-shifted Fiber (NZ-DSF) A dispersion-shifted SM fiber that has the zero-dispersion point near the 1550 nm window, outside the window actually used to transmit signals. This strategy maximizes bandwidth while minimizing fiber nonlinearities.

NRZ Abbreviation for non-return-to-zero. A common means of encoding data that has two states termed "zero" and "one" and no neutral or rest position.

ns Abbreviation for nanosecond. One billionth of a second or 10^{-9} seconds.

NTSC 1) National Television Systems Committee. The organization which formulated the NTSC system. 2) Standard used in the U.S. that delivers 525 lines at 60 frames per second.

Numerical Aperture (NA) The light-gathering ability of a fiber; the maximum angle to the fiber axis at which light will be accepted and propagated through the fiber. The measure of the light-acceptance angle of an optical fiber. NA = sin α, where α is the acceptance angle. NA is also used to describe the angular spread of light from a central axis, as in exiting a fiber, emitting from a source, or entering a detector.

$$NA = \sin\alpha = \sqrt{n_1^2 - n_2^2}$$

Where:

$\quad\alpha$ = Full acceptance angle.
$\quad n_1$ = Core refractive index.
$\quad n_2$ = Cladding refractive index.

nW Abbreviation for nanowatt. One billionth of a Watt or 10^{-9} Watts.

Nyquist Frequency The lowest sampling frequency that can be used for analog-to-digital conversion of a signal without resulting in significant aliasing. Normally, this frequency is twice the rate of the highest frequency contained in the signal being sampled. Also called Nyquist rate.

NZ-DSF See non-zero dispersion-shifted fiber.

O

OADM See optical add/drop multiplexer.

OAM Abbreviation for operation, administration, and maintenance. Refers to telecommunications networks.

OAN Abbreviation for optical access network. A network technology, based on passive optical networks (PONs), that includes an optical switch at the central office, an intelligent optical terminal at the customer's premises, and a passive optical network between the two, allowing services providers to deliver fiber-to-the-home while eliminating the expensive electronics located outside the central office.

OCH See optical channel.

OC-x Abbreviation for optical carrier. A carrier rate specified in the SONET standard.

ODN Abbreviation for optical distribution network. Term for optical networks being developed for interactive video, audio, and data distribution.

O/E Abbreviation for optical-to-electrical converter. A device used to convert optical signals to electrical signals. Also OEC.

OEIC Abbreviation for opto-electronic integrated circuit. An integrated circuit that includes both optical and electrical elements.

OLT Abbreviation for optical line terminal. Optical network elements that either generates its own optical signals or receives signals from other OLTs and rebroadcasts them.

OLTS Optical loss test set. A device used to measure optical loss.

OMD Abbreviation for optical modulation depth. *See also* modulation index.

OMS Abbreviation for optical multiplex section. A section of a DWDM system that incorporates an optical add/drop multiplexer.

ONI Abbreviation for optical network interface. A device used in an optical distribution network to connect two parts of that network.

ONT Abbreviation for optical network termination. Optical network element that terminates a line signal in installations where the fiber extends into the customer premises.

ONU Abbreviation for optical network unit. Optical network element that terminates a line signal in installations where the fiber terminates outside the customer's home.

OOI Abbreviation for open optical interface. A point at which an optical signal is passed from one equipment medium to another without conversion to an electrical signal.

Open Systems Interconnection (OSI) Pertaining to the logical structure for communications networks standardized by the International Organization for Standardization (ISO).

Optical Add/Drop Multiplexer A device which adds or drops individual wavelengths from a DWDM system.

Optical Amplifier A device that amplifies an input optical signal without converting it into electrical form. The best developed are optical fibers doped with the rare earth element, erbium.

Optical Bandpass The range of optical wavelengths that can be transmitted through a component.

Optical Channel (OCH) An optical wavelength band for WDM optical communications.

Optical Channel Spacing The wavelength separation between adjacent WDM channels.

Optical Channel Width The optical wavelength range of a channel.

Optical Continuous Wave Reflectometer (OCWR) An instrument used to characterize a fiber optic link wherein an unmodulated signal is transmitted through the link, and the resulting light scattered and reflected back to the input is measured. Useful in estimating component reflectance and link optical return loss.

Optical Directional Coupler (ODC) A component used to combine and separate optical power.

Optical Fall Time The time interval for the falling edge of an optical pulse to transition from 90% to 10% of the pulse amplitude. Alternatively, values of 80% and 20% may be used.

Optical Fiber A glass or plastic fiber that has the ability to guide light along its axis.

Optical Isolator A component used to block out reflected and unwanted light. Also called an isolator.

Optical Link Loss Budget The range of optical loss over which a fiber optic link will operate and meet all specifications. The loss is relative to the transmitter output power.

Optical Loss Test Set (OLTS) A source and power meter combined to measure attenuation.

Optical Modulation Depth (OMD) See modulation index.

Optical Path Power Penalty The additional loss budget required to account for degradations due to reflections, and the combined effects of dispersion resulting from intersymbol interference, mode-partition noise, and laser chirp.

Optical Power Meter An instrument that measures the amount of optical power present at the end of a fiber or cable.

Optical Pump Laser A shorter wavelength laser used to pump a length of fiber with energy to provide amplification at one or more longer wavelengths. *See also* EDFA.

Optical Return Loss (ORL) The ratio (expressed in units of dB) of optical power reflected by a component or an assembly to the optical power incident on a component port when that component or assembly is introduced into a link or system.

Optical Rise Time The time interval for the rising edge of an optical pulse to transition from 10% to 90% of the pulse amplitude. Alternatively, values of 20% and 80% may be used.

Optical Signal-to-Noise Ratio (OSNR) The optical equivalent of SNR.

Optical Spectrum Analyzer (OSA) A device that allows the details of a region of an optical spectrum to be resolved. Commonly used to diagnose DWDM systems.

Optical Time-division Multiplexing (OTDM) See time-division multiplexing.

Optical Time Domain Reflectometer (OTDR) An instrument, which operates using Rayleigh scattering, that locates faults in optical fibers or infers attenuation by backscattered light measurements.

Optical Waveguide See optical fiber.

OSA See optical spectrum analyzer.

OSI See open systems interconnection.

OSNR See optical signal-to-noise ratio.

OSP See outside plant.

OTDM See optical time-division multiplexing.

OTDR See optical time domain reflectometer.

Outside Plant (OSP) 1) In telephony, all cables, conduits, ducts, poles, towers, repeaters, repeater huts, and other equipment located between a demarcation point in a switching facility and a demarcation point in another switching facility or customer premises. 2) In Department of Defense communications, the portion of intrabase communications equipment between the main distribution frame (MDF) and a user end instrument or the terminal connection for a user instrument.

Oversampling Sampling data at a higher rate than normal to obtain more accurate results or to make it easier to sample.

OXC Abbreviation for optical cross-connect. *See also* cross-connect.

P

p Abbreviation for pico. One trillionth or 10^{-12}.

pA Abbreviation for picoamp. One trillionth of an Amp or 10^{-12} Amps.

PABX Abbreviation for private automatic branch exchange. *See also* PBX.

Packet In data communications, a sequence of binary digits, including data and control signals, that is transmitted and switched as a composite whole. The packet contains data, control signals, and possibly error control information, arranged in a specific format.

Packet Switching The process of routing and transferring data by means of addressed packets so that a channel is occupied during the transmission of the packet only, and upon completion of the transmission the channel is made available for the transfer of other traffic.

PAL Abbreviation for phase alternation by line. A composite color standard used in many parts of the world for TV broadcast. The phase alternation makes the signal relatively immune to certain distortions (compared to NTSC). Delivers 625 lines at 50 frames per second. PAL-plus is an enhanced-definition version.

Parity A term used in binary communication systems to indicate whether the number of 1's in a transmission is even or odd. If the number of 1's is an even number, then parity is said to be even, if the number of 1's is odd, the parity is said to be odd.

Passband The usable region of frequency in electronics or wavelength in optics.

Passive Branching Device A device that divides an optical input into two or more optical outputs.

Passive Device Any device that does not require a source of energy for its operation. Examples include electrical resistors or capacitors, diodes, optical fiber, cable, wires, glass lenses, and filters.

Pathological Test Code A special test pattern used with DTV and HDTV signals to create the longest strings of zeros and ones over the serial link. This requires the serial transport link to handle much lower frequency components than is typical in a normal data link.

PBX Abbreviation for private branch exchange. A subscriber-owned telecommunications exchange that usually includes access to public switched networks.

PC Physical contact. Refers to an optical connector that allows the fiber ends to physically touch. Used to minimize backreflection and insertion loss.

PCM See pulse-code modulation.

PCS Fiber See plastic clad silica.

PD See photodiode.

Peak Power Output The output power averaged over that cycle of an electromagnetic wave having the maximum peak value that can occur under any combination of signals transmitted.

Peak Wavelength In optical emitters, the spectral line having the greatest output power. Also called peak emission wavelength.

PFM Pulse-frequency modulation. Also referred to as square wave FM.

Phase Constant The imaginary part of the axial propagation constant for a particular mode, usually expressed in radians per unit length. *See also* attenuation.

Phase Noise Rapid, short-term, random fluctuations in the phase of a wave caused by time-domain instabilities in an oscillator.

Phase-shift Keying (PSK) 1) In digital transmission, angle modulation in which the phase of the carrier is discretely varied in relation either to a reference phase or to the phase of the immediately preceding signal element, in accordance with data being transmitted. 2) In a communications system, representing characters, such as bits or quaternary digits, by a shift in the phase of an electromagnetic carrier wave with respect to a reference, by an amount corresponding to the symbol being encoded. Also called biphase modulation, phase-shift signaling.

Photoconductive Losing an electrical charge on exposure to light.

Photodetector An optoelectronic transducer such as a PIN photodiode or avalanche photodiode.

Photodiode (PD) A semiconductor device that converts light to electrical current.

Photon A quantum of electromagnetic energy. A particle of light.

Photonic A term coined for devices that work using photons, analogous to "electronic" for devices working with electrons.

Photovoltaic Providing an electric current under the influence of light or similar radiation.

PIN Photodiode Acronym for positive-intrinsic-negative photodiode. A photodiode with a large, neutrally doped intrinsic region sandwiched between p-doped and n-doped semiconducting regions. A PIN diode exhibits an increase in its electrical conductivity as a function of the intensity, wavelength, and modulation rate of the incident radiation.

Pixel In a raster-scanned imaging system, the smallest discrete scanning line sample that can contain gray scale information.

Planar Waveguide A dielectric waveguide fabricated in a flat material such as thin film, that may be used in optical circuits.

Plastic Clad Silica (PCS) Also called hard clad silica (HCS). An optical fiber with a glass core and plastic or polymer cladding instead of glass.

Plastic Fiber An optical fiber having a plastic core and plastic cladding.

PLC Abbreviation for planar light wave circuit. A device which incorporates a planar waveguide.

Plenum The air handling space between walls, under structural floors, and above drop ceilings, which can be used to route intrabuilding cabling.

Plenum Cable A cable whose flammability and smoke characteristics allow it to be routed in a plenum area without being enclosed in a conduit.

PLUGE (Picture Line-Up Generation Equipment) Used for aligning monitors and other video devices. In some versions of color bars, PLUGE is the black set at the bottom of the red bar that contains bars that are blacker than black, black, and whiter than black. Used to adjust monitor brightness by watching the PLUGE so that the whiter than black bar is just visible and both the black and blacker than black bars are no longer distinct.

PMD See polarization mode dispersion.

Point-to-multipoint Transmission Transmission from a single point of origin to multiple destinations; the arrival of the data at all the destinations is expected to occur at the same time or nominally the same time.

Point-to-point Transmission Transmission from a single point of origin to a single destination.

Polarization The direction of the electric field in the lightwave.

Polarization-maintaining Fiber Fiber that maintains the polarization of light that enters it.

Polarization Mode Dispersion (PMD) An inherent property of all optical media caused by the difference in the propagation velocities of light in the orthogonal principal polarization states of the transmission medium. The net effect is that if an optical pulse contains both polarization components, then the different polarization components will travel at different speeds and arrive at different times, smearing the received optical signal.

PON Abbreviation for passive optical network. A broadband fiber optic access network that uses a means of sharing fiber to the home without running individual fiber optic lines from an exchange point, telco CO, or a CATV headend and the subscriber's home.

Port Hardware entity at each end of the link.

POTS Abbreviation for plain old telephone service. A call that requires nothing more than basic call handling without additional features.

p-p Abbreviation for peak-to-peak, the algebraic difference between extreme values of a varying quantity.

PPM Abbreviation for pulse-position modulation. A method of encoding data.

Profile Dispersion Dispersion attributed to the variation of refractive index contrast with wavelength.

Progressive Abbreviation for progressive scanning. A system of video scanning whereby lines of a picture are transmitted consecutively, such as computer monitor images.

ps Abbreviation for picosecond. One trillionth of a second or 10^{-12} seconds.

PSK See phase-shift keying.

PSTN Abbreviation for public switched telephone network. A domestic telecommunications network usually accessed by telephones, key telephone systems, private branch exchange trunks, and data arrangements.

Pulse A current or voltage which changes abruptly from one value to another and back to the original value in a finite length of time. Used to describe one particular variation in a series of wave motions.

Pulse-code Modulation (PCM) A technique in which an analog signal, such as a voice, is converted into a digital signal by sampling the signal's amplitude and expressing the different amplitudes as a binary number. The sampling rate must be at least twice the highest frequency in the signal.

Pulse Dispersion The dispersion of an optical signal as it propagates through an optical fiber. Also called pulse spreading.

Pulse-to-Bar Ratio A K-factor (distortion) measurement using a T pulse and bar video test signal. *See also* T-pulse to bar.

Pump Laser A power source for signal amplification, typically a 980 nm or 1480 nm laser, used in EDFA applications.

pW Abbreviation for picowatt. One trillionth of a Watt or 10^{-12} Watts.

Q

QAM See quadrature amplitude modulation.

QDST Abbreviation for quaternary dispersion supported transmission. See DST.

QoS See quality of service.

QPSK See quadrature phase-shift keying.

Quadrature Amplitude Modulation (QAM) A coding technique that uses many discrete digital levels to transmit data with minimum bandwidth. 256 QAM uses 256 discrete levels to transmit digitized video.

Quadrature Phase-shift Keying (QPSK) Phase-shift keying that uses four different phase angles out of phase by 90°. Also called quadriphase or quaternary phase-shift keying.

Quality of Service (QoS) 1) The performance specification of a communications channel or system which may be quantitatively indicated by channel or system performance parameters, such as signal-to-noise ratio, bit error rate, message throughput rate, and call blocking probability. 2) A subjective rating of telephone communications quality in which listeners judge transmissions by qualifiers, such as excellent, good, fair, poor, or unsatisfactory.

Quantization The process of converting the voltage level of a signal into digital data before or after the signal has been sampled.

Quantizing Error Inaccuracies in the digital representation of an analog signal. These errors occur because of limitations in the resolution of the digitizing process.

Quantizing Noise Noise which results from the quantization process. In serial digital video, a granular type of noise that occurs only in the presence of a signal.

Quantum Efficiency In a photodiode, the ratio of primary carriers (electron-hole pairs) created to incident photons. A quantum efficiency of 70% means seven out of ten incident photons create a carrier.

Quaternary Signal A digital signal having four significant conditions.

R

Radiation-hardened Fiber An optical fiber made with core and cladding materials that are designed to recover their intrinsic value of attenuation coefficient, within an acceptable time period, after exposure to a radiation pulse.

Raman Amplifier An optical amplifier based on the Raman scattering, the generation of many different wavelengths of light from a nominally single-wavelength source by means of lasing action or by the beating together of two frequencies. The optical signal can be amplified by collecting the Raman scattered light.

Random Jitter (RJ) Random jitter is due to thermal noise and may be modeled as a Gaussian process. The peak-to-peak value of RJ is of a probabilistic nature, and thus any specific value requires an associated probability.

Raster A predetermined pattern of scanning lines within a display space.

Raster Scan Scan in which the motion of the scanning spot follows a raster.

Rayleigh Scattering The scattering of light that results from small inhomogeneities of material density or composition.

Rays Lines that represent the path taken by light.

Receiver A terminal device that includes a detector and signal processing electronics. In fiber optics it functions as an optical-to-electrical converter.

Receiver Overload The maximum acceptable value of average received power for an acceptable BER or performance.

Receiver Sensitivity The minimum acceptable value of received power needed to achieve an acceptable BER or performance. It takes into account power penalties caused by use of a transmitter with worst-case values of extinction ratio, jitter, pulse rise and fall times, optical return loss, receiver connector degradations, and measurement tolerances. The receiver sensitivity does not include power penalties associated with dispersion, jitter, or reflections from the optical path; these effects are specified separately in the allocation of maximum optical path penalty. Sensitivity usually takes into account worst-case operating and end-of-life (EOL) conditions.

Reclocking The process of clocking the data with a regenerated clock.

Recombination Combination of an electron and a hole in a semiconductor that releases energy leading to light emission.

Refraction The changing of direction of a wavefront when passing through a boundary between two dissimilar media, or in a graded-index medium where refractive index is a continuous function of position.

Refractive Index See index of refraction.

Refractive Index Profile The description of the value of the refractive index as a function of distance from the optical axis along an optical fiber diameter. Also called refractive index gradient.

Regenerative Repeater A repeater, designed for digital transmission, in which digital signals are amplified, reshaped, retimed, and retransmitted.

Regenerator See regenerative repeater.

Repeater A receiver and transmitter set designed to regenerate attenuated signals. Used to extend operating range.

Residual Loss The optical loss of an optical attenuator at its minimum setting.

Resolution The sharpness or "crispness" of the picture. Resolution can be measured numerically by establishing the number of scanning lines used to create each frame of video.

Responsivity The ratio of a photodetector's electrical output to its optical input in Amperes/Watt (A/W).

Return Loss See optical return loss.

RF Abbreviation for radio frequency. Any frequency within the electromagnetic spectrum normally associated with radio wave propagation.

RFI Abbreviation for radio frequency interference. *See also* electromagnetic interference.

RGB Red, green, and blue. The basic parallel component set in which a signal is used for each primary color; or the related equipment or interconnect formats or standards.

Ribbon Cables Cables in which many parallel fibers are embedded in a plastic material, forming a flat ribbon-like structure.

RIN Abbreviation for relative intensity noise. Often used to quantify the noise characteristics of a laser.

Rise Time The time taken to make a transition from one state to another, usually measured between the 10% and 90% completion points of the transition. Alternatively the rise time may be specified at the 20% and 80% amplitudes. Shorter or faster rise times require more bandwidth in a transmission channel.

RJ See random jitter.

RMS Abbreviation for root mean square. Technique used to measure AC voltages.

RZ Abbreviation for return-to-zero. A common means of encoding data that has two information states called "zero" and "one" in which the signal returns to a rest state during a portion of the bit period.

S

s Abbreviation for second.

Sampling Rate The number of discrete sample measurements made in a given period of time. Often expressed in megahertz (MHz) for video.

SAN (Storage Area Network) Connects a group of computers to high-capacity storage devices.

Saturation 1) In a communications system, the condition in which a component of the system has reached its maximum traffic handling capacity. 2) The point at which the output of a linear device, such as a linear amplifier, deviates significantly from being a linear function of the input when the input signal is increased. 3) The degree of the chroma or purity of a color.

S-Band The wavelength range between 1485 nm and 1520 nm used in some CWDM and DWDM applications.

SBS See stimulated Brillouin scattering.

SC Subscription channel connector. A cost-effective push-pull type of optical connector that originated in Japan. Features high packing density, low loss, and low backreflection.

Scalable Coding The ability to encode a visual sequence so as to enable the decoding of the digital data stream at various spatial and/or temporal resolutions.

Scalable Video Refers to video compression that can handle a range of bandwidths, scaling smoothly over them.

Scanning 1) In telecommunications systems, periodic examination of traffic activity to determine whether further processing is required. 2) In television, facsimile, and picture transmission, the process of successively analyzing the colors and densities of the object according to a predetermined pattern.

Scattering The change of direction of light rays or photons after striking small particles. It may also be regarded as the diffusion of a light beam caused by the inhomogeneity of the transmitting material.

S-CDMA Abbreviation for synchronous code division multiple access. A synchronized version of CDMA.

SCM Abbreviation for subcarrier multiplexing. The process by which multiple subcarrier signals are combined into one signal.

Scrambling To transpose or invert digital data according to a prearranged scheme in order to break up the low-frequency patterns associated with serial digital signals.

SDTV Abbreviation for standard-definition television. *See also* NTSC.

SECAM Abbreviation for Système Electronique Couleur avec Memoire. A TV standard used in various parts of the world. Delivers 625 lines at 50 frames per second.

Selfoc Lens A trade name used by the Nippon Sheet Glass Company for a graded-index fiber lens; a segment of graded-index fiber made to serve as a lens.

Self-phase Modulation (SPM) A fiber nonlinearity caused by the nonlinear index of refraction of glass. The index of refraction varies with optical power level which causes distortion in the waveform.

Semiconductor Optical Amplifier (SOA) A laser diode without end mirrors (and with anti-reflection coating) coupled to both fiber ends. Light coming in either fiber is amplified by a single pass through the laser diode. An alternative to EDFAs.

Sensitivity See receiver sensitivity.

Serial One bit at a time, along a single transmission path.

Serial Digital Digital information that is transmitted in serial form. Often used informally to refer to serial digital television signals.

Serial Digital Interface (SDI) A 10-bit, scrambled, polarity independent interface, based on a 270 Mb/s data rate, with common scrambling for both component ITU-R 601, composite digital video, and four channels of (embedded) digital audio. Most new broadcast digital equipment includes SDI.

Serial Digital Transport Interface (SDTI) Another name for SMPTE 305M. Allows faster-than-real-time transfers between various servers and between acquisition tapes, disk-based editing systems and servers. Supports both 270 Mb/s and 360 Mb/s data rates.

SH Abbreviation for short-haul. A classification of video performance under RS-250C. Higher performance than long-haul or medium-haul.

Sheath An outer protective layer of a fiber optic cable.

Shot Noise Noise caused by current fluctuations arising from the discrete nature of electrons.

Si Abbreviation for silicon. An element used to make detectors. Good for short wavelengths only (e.g., < 1000 nm).

Sideband Frequencies distributed above and below the carrier that contain energy resulting from modulation. The frequencies above the carrier are called upper sidebands, and the frequencies below the carrier are called lower sidebands.

Signal-to-Noise Ratio (SNR) The ratio of the total signal to the total noise, which shows how much higher the signal level is than the level of the noise. A measure of signal quality.

Silica Glass Glass made mostly of silicon dioxide, SiO_2, used in conventional optical fibers.

Simplex Single element (e.g., a simplex connector is a single-fiber connector).

Simplex Cable A term sometimes used for a single-fiber cable.

Simplex Transmission Transmission in one direction only.

Single Attachment Concentrator A concentrator that offers one attachment to the FDDI network.

Single-line Laser See single-longitudinal mode laser.

Single-longitudinal Mode Laser (SLM) An injection laser diode which has a single dominant longitudinal mode. A single-mode laser with a side mode suppression ratio (SMSR) > 25 dB.

Single-mode (SM) Fiber A small-core optical fiber through which only one mode will propagate. The typical diameter is 8-9 microns.

Single-mode Laser Diode (SMLD) See single-longitudinal mode laser.

Single-mode Optical Loss Test Set (SMOLTS) A device, for use with single-mode fiber, that measures optical loss.

SI Units Abbreviation for Système Internationale (in English, International System) units, commonly known as the metric system.

SLED See surface-emitting diode.

SLM See single-longitudinal mode laser.

Slope Efficiency (SE) This is the mean value of the incremental change in optical power for an incremental change in forward current when the device is operating in the lasing region of the optical power output versus forward current curve. Also referred to as differential efficiency.

SMD Abbreviation for surface-mount device. See SMT.

SMF Abbreviation for single-mode fiber (also SM).

SMPTE Abbreviation for Society of Motion Picture and Television Engineers. Organization that publishes ANSI-approved standards, recommended practices, and engineering guidelines.

SMT Abbreviation for surface-mount technology. The practice and method of attaching leaded and nonleaded electrical components to the surface of a conductive pattern that does not utilize leads in feed-through holes.

S/N See signal-to-noise ratio.

Snell's Law A law of geometric optics that defines the amount of bending that takes place when a light ray strikes a refractive boundary, e.g., an air-glass interface, at a non-normal angle.

SNR See signal-to-noise ratio.

SOA See semiconductor optical amplifier.

Soliton Pulse An optical pulse having a shape, spectral content, and power level designed to take advantage of nonlinear effects in an optical fiber waveguide, for the purpose of essentially negating dispersion over long distances.

SONET Abbreviation for synchronous optical network transport system. An interface standard widely used by the telecom industry to move data. OC-3 is the lowest current rate (155.5 Mb/s) and OC-768 (39.808 Gb/s) is the highest being contemplated. Valid rates increase by a factor of four from the OC-3 rate up to OC-768.

Source In fiber optics, a transmitting LED or laser diode, or an instrument that injects test signals into fibers.

Span Engineering The process of designing a DWDM transmission span to achieve the required performance based on the fiber type, the transmission distance, amplifier spacing, noise, power, and the channel count.

Spectral Efficiency The number of data bits per second that a device can transmit in a one Hertz bandwidth range.

Spectral Width A measure of the extent of a spectrum. For a source, the width of wavelengths contained in the output at one half of the amplitude of peak power. Typical spectral widths are 50 to 160 nm for an LED and 0.1-5 nm for a laser diode.

Spectral Width, Full Width, Half Maximum (FWHM) The absolute difference between the wavelengths at which the spectral radiant intensity is 50% of the maximum power.

Splice A permanent connection of two optical fibers through fusion or mechanical means.

Splitting Ratio The ratio of power emerging from two output ports of a coupler.

SPM See self-phase modulation.

SRS See stimulated Raman scattering.

ST Straight tip connector. Popular fiber optic connector developed by AT&T.

Stabilized Light Source An LED or laser diode that emits light with a controlled and constant spectral width, central wavelength, and peak power with respect to time and temperature.

Star Coupler A coupler in which power at any input port is distributed to all output ports. Used in star network topologies.

STB Abbreviation for set-top box. An auxiliary device that usually sits on top of or adjacent to a television receiver used in direct analog or digital satellite transmission, CATV, and digital television to view the signals on an analog TV. Also called a set-top converter.

Step-index Fiber Fiber that has a uniform index of refraction throughout the core.

Stimulated Brillouin Scattering (SBS) The easiest fiber nonlinearity to trigger. When a powerful light wave travels through a fiber it interacts with acoustical vibration modes in the glass. This causes the formation of a scattering mechanism that reflects much of the light back to the source.

Stimulated Raman Scattering (SRS) A fiber nonlinearity similar to SBS but having a much higher threshold. This mechanism can also cause power to be robbed from shorter wavelength signals and provide gain to longer wavelength signals.

Strength Member The part of a fiber optic cable composed of aramid yarn, steel strands, or fiberglass filaments that increase the tensile strength of the cable.

Subscriber Loop Also called local loop. The link from the telephone company central office (CO) to the home or business (customer premises).

Super Trunk A cable that carries several video channels between facilities of a cable television company.

Surface-emitting Diode An LED that emits light from its flat surface rather than its side. Simple and inexpensive, with emission spread over a wide angle.

S-Video Abbreviation for Super-Video, a technology for transmitting video signals over a cable by dividing the video information into two separate signals: one for color (chrominance or C), and the other for brightness (luminance or Y). When sent to a television, which is designed to display separate luminance and chrominance signals, S-Video produces sharper images than composite video, which transmits video as a single signal over one wire. Synonym of Y/C video.

Synchronization Pulse 1) A signal derived from the composite or combination of the horizontal and vertical drives. 2) A pulse used to achieve or maintain synchronism, usually applied to analog signals. (The term "synchronization bit" is usually applied to digital data streams.) Commonly called the sync pulse.

Synchronous Data signals in a network or between networks that occur at the same clock rate.

T

T Abbreviation for tera. One trillion or 10^{12}.

T1 In telecommunications, the cable used to transport DS1 service.

Tap Loss In a fiber optic coupler, the ratio of power at the tap port to the power at the input port.

Tap Port In a coupler where the splitting ratio between output ports is not equal, the output port containing the lesser power.

TBC Abbreviation for timebase corrector, which takes a video signal from a video tape recorder (VTR) or VCR and locks it to an external sync signal. Used to correct the time distortion that results from the stretching of the video tape itself; the distortion of first lines of video usually reduces as the head proceeds further down the tape. All lines are affected, but the first 10% to 20% at the top of the picture are the worst and cause the effect known as flagging which can be seen on any video monitor with slow horizontal synchronization.

T-Carrier Generic designator for any of several digitally multiplexed telecommunications carrier systems.

TDM See time-division multiplexing.

TDMA See time-division multiple access.

TEC Abbreviation for thermoelectric cooler. A device used to dissipate heat in electronic assemblies.

Tee Coupler A three-port optical coupler.

Telecommunications Management Network (TMN) A network that interfaces with a telecommunications network at several points in order to receive information from, and to control the operation of, the telecommunications network.

Ternary A semiconductor compound made of three elements (e.g., GaAlAs).

Thermal Noise Noise resulting from thermally induced random fluctuation in current in the receiver's load resistance.

Throughput Loss In a fiber optic coupler, the ratio of power at the throughput port to the power at the input port.

Throughput Port In a coupler where the splitting ratio between output ports is not equal, the output port containing the greater power.

Tight-buffer A cable construction in which a material tightly surrounds a fiber, holding it rigidly in place.

Time-division Multiple Access (TDMA) A communications technique that uses a common channel (multipoint or broadcast) for communications among multiple users by allocating unique time slots to different users. Used extensively in satellite systems, local area networks, physical security systems, combat-net radio systems, and cellular telephone systems.

Time-division Multiplexing (TDM) A transmission technique whereby several low-speed channels are multiplexed into a high-speed channel for transmission. Each low-speed channel is allocated a specific position based on time.

TMN See telecommunications management network.

Total Internal Reflection The reflection that occurs when light strikes an interface at an angle of incidence (with respect to the normal) greater than the critical angle.

TP See twisted pair cable.

T-pulse A sine-squared pulse used as an indication of frequency and phase response.

T-pulse to Bar A specification term relating to frequency response of video equipment. A video signal containing equal amplitude T-pulse and bar portions is passed through the equipment and the relative amplitudes of the T-pulse and bar are measured at the output. A loss of response is indicated when one portion of the signal is lower in amplitude than the other.

Transceiver A device that performs, within one chassis, both transmitting and receiving functions.

Transducer A device for converting energy from one form to another, such as optical energy to electrical energy.

Transmitter A device that includes a source and driving electronics. In fiber optics, it functions as an electrical-to-optical converter.

Transponder The part of a satellite that receives and transmits a signal.

Tree A physical topology consisting of a hierarchy of master-slave connections between a concentrator and other FDDI nodes (including subordinate concentrators).

Trunk 1) In a communications network, a single transmission channel between two switching centers or nodes, or both. 2) A circuit between switchboards or other switching equipment, as distinguished from circuits which extend between central office switching equipment and information origination/termination equipment. Trunks may be used to interconnect switches, such as major, minor, public and private switches, to form networks.

TTL Abbreviation for transistor-transistor logic. A type of data format.

Twisted Pair (TP) Cable A cable made up of one or more separately insulated twisted-wire pairs, none of which is arranged with another to form quads.

U

UHF (Ultra High Frequency) In the electromagnetic spectrum, frequencies from 300 MHz to 3,000 MHz.

UL Abbreviation for Underwriter's Laboratory. An organization that tests product safety for a wide variety of products.

Unidirectional Operating in one direction only.

UV Abbreviation for ultraviolet. The portion of the electromagnetic spectrum in which the longest wavelength is just below the visible spectrum, extending from approximately 4 nm to approximately 400 nm.

V

V Abbreviation for Volt.

VAC Abbreviation for Volts, AC. Voltage using alternating current.

VCSEL See vertical cavity surface-emitting laser.

VDC Abbreviation for Volts, DC. Voltage using direct current.

VDSL Abbreviation for very high data rate digital subscriber line. A DSL operating at a data rate higher than those of HDSL. *See also* DSL.

Vector Quantization (VQ) A digital video compression technique based on Shannon's distortion-rate theory which states that the performance of data compression systems improves if blocks of data are coded, with larger coded data blocks giving better performance.

Vertical Cavity Surface-emitting Laser Lasers that emit light perpendicular to the plane of the wafer they are grown on. They have very small dimensions and very high efficiency compared to conventional lasers.

VHF (Very High Frequency) In the electromagnetic spectrum, frequencies from 30 MHz to 300 MHz.

Vestigial-sideband (VSB) Transmission A modified double-sideband transmission in which one sideband, the carrier, and only a portion of the other sideband are transmitted. *See also* sideband.

VGA Video graphics array. A high-resolution color standard for computer monitors.

Videoconferencing Conducting conferences via a video telecommunications system.

Video on Demand (VOD) A term used for interactive or customized video delivery service.

Videophone A telephone-like service with a picture as well as sound.

Virtual Circuit (VC) A communications arrangement in which data from a source user may be passed to a destination user over various real circuit configurations during a single period of communication, usually on a per call basis, although permanent connections can be established.

Visible Light Electromagnetic radiation visible to the human eye; wavelengths of 400-700 nm.

VOD See video on demand.

Voice Circuit A circuit capable of carrying one telephone conversation or its equivalent; the standard subunit in which telecommunication capacity is counted. The U.S. analog equivalent is 4 kHz. The digital equivalent is 64 kbit/s in North America and in Europe.

VPN Abbreviation for virtual private network. A protected information-system link utilizing tunneling, security controls, and end-point address translation giving the end user the impression that a dedicated line exists between nodes.

VSB See vestigial-sideband transmission.

W

W Abbreviation for Watt. A linear measurement of optical power, usually expressed in milliwatts, microwatts, and nanowatts.

WAN (Wide Area Network) A physical or logical network that provides capabilities for a number of independent devices to communicate with each other over a common transmission-interconnected topology in geographic areas larger than those served by local area networks.

Waveguide A material medium that confines and guides a propagating electromagnetic wave. In the microwave regime, a waveguide normally consists of a hollow metallic conductor, generally rectangular, elliptical, or circular in cross-section. This type of waveguide may, under certain conditions, contain a solid or gaseous dielectric material. In the optical regime, a waveguide used as a long transmission line consists of a solid dielectric filament (optical fiber), usually circular in cross-section. In integrated optical circuits an optical waveguide may consist of a thin dielectric film. In the RF regime, ionized layers of the stratosphere and the refractive surfaces of the troposphere may also serve as a waveguide.

Waveguide Coupler A coupler in which light is transferred between planar waveguides.

Waveguide Dispersion The part of chromatic dispersion arising from the different speeds light travels in the core and cladding of a single-mode fiber (i.e., from the fiber's waveguide structure).

Wavelength The distance between points of corresponding phase of two consecutive cycles of a wave. The wavelength, is related to the propagation velocity, and the frequency, by:

$$\text{Wavelength} = \frac{\text{Propagation Velocity}}{\text{Frequency}}$$

Wavelength Adapter A device which receives one wavelength and outputs a second wavelength, usually to take a standard signal and convert it to an ITU wavelength.

Wavelength-division Multiplexing (WDM) Sending several signals through one fiber with different wavelengths of light.

Wavelength Isolation A WDM's isolation of a light signal in the desired optical channel from the unwanted optical channels. Also called far-end crosstalk.

Wavelength Routing Switch (WRS) A switch, used in optical networks, that routes wavelengths as required to specific terminals in the network.

Wavelength Selective Coupler A device which couples the pump laser wavelength to the optical fiber while filtering out all other unwanted wavelengths. Used in erbium-doped fiber amplifiers.

Wavelength Stability The maximum deviation of the peak wavelength of an optical source from its average wavelength.

WDM See wavelength-division multiplexing.

Web TV The concept of providing Internet access (usually Web access and e-mail) in a format that can be viewed on a standard television set rather than on a computer. The service usually consists of a set-top box that is connected to the user's television, a keyboard, and a telephone line.

Wideband Possessing large bandwidth.

Widescreen Term given to picture displays that have a wider aspect ratio than normal. For example, TV's normal aspect ratio is 4:3 and widescreen is 16:9. Used by HDTV and normal definition systems.

WRS See wavelength routing switch.

X

XC See cross-connect.

XGM See cross-gain modulation.

XPM See cross-phase modulation.

X-Series Recommendations Sets of data telecommunications protocols and interfaces defined by ITU.

XT See crosstalk.

Y

Y Coupler A variation on the tee coupler in which input light is split between two channels (typically planar waveguide) that branch out like a Y from the input.

YUV A color model used chiefly for video signals in which colors are specified according to their luminance — the Y component — and their hue saturation — the U and V components.

Z

Zero-dispersion Slope In single-mode fiber, the rate of change of dispersion with respect to wavelength, at the fiber's zero-dispersion wavelength.

Zero-dispersion Wavelength (λ_0) In a single-mode optical fiber, the wavelength at which material dispersion and waveguide dispersion cancel one another. The wavelength of maximum bandwidth in the fiber. Also called zero-dispersion point.

Zipcord A two-fiber cable consisting of two single-fiber cables having conjoined jackets. A zipcord cable can be easily divided by slitting and pulling the conjoined jackets apart.

Appendix B

Bibliography

Abbott, John S. et al. "Analysis of Multimode Fiber Behavior with Laser Sources in the Development of the Gigabit Ethernet Fiber Optic Specification." N.p.: n.p., November 1998: 1-11.

AT&T Microelectronics. "Power Margin Analysis." *Technical Note*. November 1995: 1-12.

Bala, Krishna. "Tutorial: Multiwavelength Optical Networks." Annual Multiplexed Technology Conference. San Diego, CA: n.p., 16-20 July 2000.

Bartlett, Eugene R. *Cable Television Technology & Operations.* New York: McGraw-Hill, Inc., 1990.

Benson, K. Blair, ed. *Television Engineering Handbook*. New York: McGraw-Hill, Inc., 1986.

Blattenberger, Kirt. "Frequency Modulation." 1 July 2002 <http://www.rfcafe.com/references/electrical/frequency_modulation.html>.

Blondel, J.P. "Achievable Budget Improvement with Raman Amplification and Remotely Pumped Postamplification at Transmit Side of 622Mbits/s and 2.5 Gbit/s Repeaterless Systems." *IEEE Photonics Technology Letters* 7.1 (January 1995):108-110.

Blonder-Tongue Laboratories, Inc. *Broadband Reference Guide 2002: Everything You Need to Know but Shouldn't Have to Remember*. New Jersey: Blonder-Tongue Laboratories, 2001.

"broadcasting." *Encyclopedia Britannica*. <http://www.britannica.com/eb/article?query=broadcast&eu=108698&tocid=25182>.

Bullinger, Rex. "Complying with FCC Standards: How to Measure Carrier-to-Noise." *Communications Engineering & Design* November 1994: 68-71.

Carlisle, Robert. "Fiber Tutorial." 1 July 2002 <http://grouper.ieee.org/groups/802/3/efm/public/nov01/carlisle_1_1101.pdf>.

Ciciora, Walter S. *Cable Television in the United States: An Overview, 2nd ed.* Colorado: Cable Television Laboratories, Inc., 1995.

Ciciora, Walter S., James Farmer, and David Large. *Modern Cable Television Technology: Video, Voice, and Data Communications.* San Francisco, CA: Morgan Kaufmann Publishers, Inc., 1999.

Coenen, R.B., and M.K. Jackson. "Fundamental Performance Limits in Wideband FM Analog Transmission." Vancouver: University of British Columbia, n.d.: 1-2.

Coppinger, F., M.D. Selker, and D. Piehler. "The Effect of SPM, EPM, on the Second Order Distortion in Analog Link." Optical Fiber Communication Conference. Anaheim, CA: 17-22 May 2001: N. pag.

Davis, D.D. "Effects of Higher Power Levels on Optical Connectors, Splices, and Related Components." *2001 Technical Proceedings.* National Fiber Optic Engineers Conference. Baltimore, MD: 8-12 July 2001: 561-663.

Davis, D.D, D.J. DiGiovanni, and S.C. Mettler. "Experimental Data on the Fiber Fuse." in *Proc. Laser-Induced Damage in Optical Materials: 1995* (H.E. Bennett, A. H. Guenther, M.R. Kozlowski, B. E. Newman, and M.J. Soileau, eds.) Boulder, CO:SPIE, 1995, pp. 202-210.

---. "A Comparative Evaluation of Fiber Fuse Models." in *Proc. Laser-Induced Damage in Optical Materials: 1996* (H.E. Bennett, A. H. Guenther, M.R. Kozlowski, B. E. Newman, and M.J. Soileau, eds.) Boulder, CO:SPIE, 1996, pp. 596-606.

De Rosa, Michael, Joel Carberry, Venkata Bhagavutula, Karl Wagner, and Costas Saravanos. "High-power Performance of Single-mode Fiber-optic Connectors." *Journal of Lightwave Technology* 20.5 (May 2002): 879-885.

Dorf, Richard C., ed. *The Electrical Engineering Handbook, 2nd ed.* Boca Raton, FL: CRC Press, 1997.

Dye, Norman E. "AN1107: Understanding RF Data Sheet Parameters." Motorola Semiconductor, 1991: 1-17.

Federal Communications Commission (FCC). "U.S. Frequency Allocation Chart." 28 June 2002 <http://www.ntia.doc.gov/osmhome/allochrt.pdf>.

Feher, Kamilo. *Digital Communications: Microwave Applications.* Englewood Cliffs, NJ: Prentice-Hall Inc., 1981.

Fibush, David K. *A Guide to Digital Television Systems and Measurements.* Oregon: Tektronix, Inc., 1997.

---. "Video Testing in a DTV World." *SMPTE Journal* (2002): 1-8.

Force, Incorporated. *Applying Optical Amplifiers.* 1 July 2002 <http://www.forceinc.com/an.htm>.

---. *Care and Feeding of Analog CATV Fiber Optic Links.* 1 July 2002 <http://www.forceinc.com/an.htm>.

---. *Comlux® Series Digital Fiber Optic Transmission Systems.* 1 July 2002 <http://www.forceinc.com/an.htm>.

---. *Comlux® System Design: Recommended Specs & Considerations for Optical Fiber Plants.* 1 July 2002 <http://www.forceinc.com/at.htm>.

---. *Digital Fiber Optic Networks for Multichannel Video Transmission.* 1 July 2002 <http://www.forceinc.com/an.htm>.

---. *Digitized Video Transmission: Copper vs. Fiber.* 1 July 2002 <http://www.forceinc.com/an.htm>.

---. *Fiber Optic CATV Transport: A Step-by-Step Guide to System Design.* 1 July 2002 <http://www.forceinc.com/an.htm>.

---. *High Capacity Digitized Video Switch Fiber Optic Networks.* 1 July 2002 <http://www.forceinc.com/an.htm>.

---. *ITU Channels for Dense Wavelength-division Multiplexing (DWDM).* 1 July 2002 <http://www.forceinc.com/an.htm>

---. *Laser Backreflection – The Bane of Good Performance.* 1 July 2002 <http://www.forceinc.com/an.htm>.

---. *The Effects of Dispersion on High-speed Fiber Optic Data Transmission: Fiber Bandwidth Isn't Infinite.* 1 July 2002 <http:// www.forceinc.com/an.htm>.

---. *The Effects of Fiber Nonlinearities on High-speed Fiber Optic Data Transmission – A Brave New World of Complexity.* 1 July 2002 <http://ww.forceinc.com/an.htm>.

Frigo, Nicholas J., Mary R. Phillips, and George E. Bodeep. "Clipping Distortion in Lightwave CATV Systems: Models, Simulations, and Measurements." *Journal of Lightwave Technology* 2.1 (January 1993): 138-146.

Giaretta, G., et al. "High Bandwidth, Multimode Fiber Systems." Paper presented at the Conference for the Institute of Electrical and Electronics Engineers. Montreal, Canada: Lucent Technologies, 1999.

Gildor, George. "Into the Telecoms." *Harvard Business Review* March 1991: 150-161.

Goff, David R. "Analog Multichannel Transmission Systems." *Fiberoptic Product News* (June 2000): 75-77.

---. *Fiber Optic Reference Guide, 3rd ed.* Massachusetts: Focal Press, 2002.

---. "High-Speed Data Over Multimode Fiber." *Lightwave* June 1992: 38-40.

Grant, William. *Cable Television, 3rd ed.* Exton, PA: SCTE, Inc., 1988.

Greenfield, David. "Passive Optical Networks." *Network Magazine.* 17 July 2002 <http://www.networkmagazine.com/article/NMG20011203S0021>.

Grofinkel, V.B., and S. Luryi. "Fundamental Limits for Linearity of CATV Lasers." *Journal of Lightwave Technology* 13.2 (February 1995): 252-260.

Gwynne, Jeff. "Optical Access Networking Pays Off." Network World Fusion. 17 July 2002 <http://www.nwfusion.com/news/tech/1220tech.html>.

Hass, Zygmunt, and Mario Santoro. "Extending the Bandwidth x Distance Product for Multimode Fibers." *SPIE* Vol. 1577 (September 1991): 132-141.

Hass, Zygmunt, and Mario Santoro. "A Mode-Filtering Scheme for Improvement of the Bandwidth x Distance Product in Multimode Fiber Systems." ms. [accepted for publication in *Lightwave Technology*].

Henderson, Michael P. "Introduction to Optical Networks." California: Conexant Systems, Inc., 29 January 2001: 1-36.

"Hertz, Heinrich (Rudolph)." *Encyclopedia Britannica.* <http://www.britannica.com/eb/article?eu=41117&query=hertz>.

Hewlett-Packard Company. *Application Note 1298: Digital Modulation in Communication Systems - An Introduction*. California: Hewlett-Packard Company, 1997.

---. *Cable System Preparation Guide for Two-Way Data*. California: Hewlett-Packard Company, 1997.

---. *Cable Television System Measurements Handbook: NTSC Systems*. California: Hewlett-Packard Company, February 1994.

---. *Delivering Two-Way Services: A Return Path Primer*. California: Hewlett-Packard Company, n.d.

Hold, David F. ed. "Network Convergence." 1 July 2002 <http://www.broadbandpub.com/whitepaper.htm>.

Inglis, Andrew F. *Video Engineering*. New York: McGraw-Hill, Inc., 1993.

Kempster, Kurt A. "Frame Rate Effect on Human Spatial Perception in Video Intelligence." Thesis. Naval Postgraduate School. Monterey, California: September 2002.

Kenneally, John. "Testing with Noise in the New World of Cable: How to Verify Equipment Performance in the Real World." *Communications Engineering & Design* May 2001: 108-110.

King, Bevis. *Broadcasting System Details*. 8 May 2002 <http://www.ee.surrey.ac.uk/Contrib/WorldTV/broadcast.html>.

---. *TV Systems: A Comparison*. 8 May 2002 <http://www.ee.surrey.ac.uk/Contrib/WorldTV.compare.html>.

---. *Video Formats*. 8 May 2002 <http://www.ee.surrey.ac.uk/Contrib/WorldTV/video.html>.

Kuhn, Kelin J. "HDTV Television- An Introduction." 25 February 2002 <http://www.ee.washington.edu/conselec/CE/kuhn/hdtv/95x5.html>.

Liu, Dong X. "Passive Optical Network as the Ultimate Solution for Broadband Access." Conference proceedings from IC International March 2001. China: 296-303.

Lucent Technologies Bell Labs Innovations. "System Analysis, Component Selection, and Testing Consideration for 1310 nm Analog Fiber-Optic CATV Applications." *Application Note*. New Jersey: Lucent Technologies Microelectronics Group, June 1998.

Martinez, Daniel, and Greg Shreve. "Digital Routing Switchers." *Broadcast Engineering* August 1992: 48+.

Mears, James A. "Use Video Standards for Eye-Opening Data Transmission: Mega-bits at Many Meters." DesignCon 2002 Wireless and Broadband System Design Conference. Santa Clara, CA. N.p.: n.p. 28-31 January 2002: no pag.

Morgan, Bill. "How to Comply with FCC Regulation: Measuring Cable System Distortion." *Communications Engineering & Design* October 1994: 72-76.

Morgan, Bill. "Digital Troubleshooting is a Whole New Ball Game: Insights into Proper Return Path Alignment." *Communications Engineering & Design* October 1996: 42-53.

Motorola, Inc. "High-Definition Television Over Cable." San Diego, CA: Broadband Communications Sector, July 2001.

Movassaghi, M., M.K. Jackson, and V.M. Smith. "DFB Laser RIN Degradation in CATV Lightwave Transmission." Vancouver: University of British Columbia, n.d.: 1-2.

Murakami, Tokumichi et al. "Overview: The Present and Future of Digital TV Broadcasting." *Advance.* California: Mitsubishi Electric, December 1998: 3-7.

Nazarathy, Moshc, Josef Berger, Anthony J. Ley, Isreal M Levi, and Yishai Kagan. "Progress in Externally Modulated AM CATV Transmission Systems. *Journal of Lightwave Technology,* 11.1 (January 1993): 82-105.

Nebeling, Marcus. "CWDM: Lower Cost for More Capacity in the Short Haul." California: Fiber Network Engineering, Inc., n.d., 1-10.

"radio." *Encyclopeida Britannica.* <http://www.britannica.com/eb/article?eu=108703&tocid=query=radio>.

Rainal, Attilio J. "Laser Clipping Distortion in Analog and Digital Channels." *Journal of Lightwave Technology,* 15.10 (October 1997): 1805-1807.

---. "Limiting Distortion of CATV Lasers." *Journal of Lightwave Technology* 14.3 (March 1996): 474-479.

Ramos, Francisco, and Javier Marti. "Compensation for Fiber-Induced Composite Second-order Distortion in Externally Modulated Lightwave AM-SCM Systems Using Optical-phase Conjugation." *Journal of Lightwave Technology,* 16.8 (August 1998): 1387-1392.

RAND. *MR-960-A: Emerging Commercial Mobile Wireless Technology and Standards.* 1 July 2002 <http://www.rand.org/publications/MR/MR960>.

Rivera, Carlos, and Payman Arabshahi. *Vector Quantization*. 15 May 2002 <http://www.dsp.jpl.nasa.gov/members/payman/icee93.pdf>.

Rohde, Ulrish L., T.T.N. Bucher, and Jerry Whitaker. *Communications Receivers*. New York: McGraw-Hill, Inc.,1997.

Rosales, R., and M.K. Jackson. "Silicon Bipolar Wideband Frequency Modulator and Demodulator for Analog Fiber-Optic Transmission." Vancouver: University of British Columbia, n.d.

Ryan, Gerald P, ed. "Dense Wavelength Division Multiplexing." *Communications & Technology Guide Series*. Massachusetts: Applied Technologies Group, 1997.

Ryba, Marc, and Raul Matuszak. *Testing 256 QAM Transmission of Data over HFC*. 3 May 2002 <http://www.cedmagazine.com/ced/9612/9612d/html>.

Sabeus Photonics. *A Brief History of Optical Fiber Grating*. 17 June 2001 <http://www.sabeus.com/Gratings.cfm>.

Schatzkin, Paul. *The Farnsworth Chronicles*. 25 January 2002 <http://www.farnovision.com>.

Slater, J.N. *Cable Television Technology*. Sussex, England: Ellis Horwood Limited, 1988.

Society of Motion Picture and Television Engineers (SMPTE). *Standard 259M-1997: Serial Digital Interface for 10-bit 4:2:2 Component and 4 fsc NTSC Composite Digital Signals*, 1997.

Sony Corporation. "The Arrival of Betacam." 28 August 2002 <http://www.sony.co.jp/en/Fun/SH/1-16/h2.html>.

"Sony Pulls Plug on Betamax VCRs." *AP Online*. 27 August 2002. 27 August 2002 <http://www.excite.com/article/20020827/D7LLRAI00.html>.

Strachan, David. "An Introduction to Digital Television." *SMPTE Journal* (March 1995): 118+.

---. "Video Compression." *SMPTE Journal* (February 1996): 68-73.

Strachan, David, and Randy Conrod. "Digital Signal Conversion." *SMPTE Journal* (June 1995): 356-358.

Sumitomo Electric Industries, Ltd. *Non-Zero Dispersion Shifted Single-Mode Fiber for Metro WDM System*. 2 July 2002 <http://www.sei.co.jp/fbr-opt-eng/premium/premium.html>.

Tektronix, Inc. *NTSC Video Measurements: The Basics*. Oregon: Tektronix, Inc., 1997.

"telegraph." *Encyclopedia Britannica*. <http://www.britannica.com/eb/article?query=wilhelm+gintl&eu=11900&tocid=76405>.

Thomas, Jeffrey L. *Digital Basics for Cable Television Systems*. New Jersey: Prentice-Hall PTR, 1999.

Thompson, Brad. *Calculating and Measure Noise Values*. 3 May 2002 <http://www.tmworld.com/articles/2002/05_noise.htm>.

Tiernan Radyne ComStream, Inc. *Video Performance Measurements in DTV Transmission Systems*. San Diego: Tiernan Radyne ComStream, Inc., 2001: 1-10.

Tucker, Rodney S., and Douglas M. Baney. "Optical Noise Figure: Theory and Measurement." Optical Fiber Communications Conference Anahiem, CA. 17-22 March 2001: 1-18.

U.S. Congress. *Telecommunications Act of 1996*. Pub. LA. No. 104-104, 110 Stat. 56 (1996).

Video Technology Pages. *Video Signal Standards and Conversion Page*. 12 June 2002 <http://www.epanorama.net/links/videosignal.html>.

Walker, Marc S. "Serial Digital Video Distribution from the Present to the Future." *BTS Technical Reports*, 2 (n.d.): 115-132.

Weiss, S. Merrill. *Issues in Advanced Television Technology*. Massachusetts: Focal Press, 1996.

Whitaker, Jerry C. *Standard Handbook of Video and Television Engineering*. 3rd ed. Ed. Blair Benson. New York: McGraw-Hill, Inc., 2000.

"World TV Standards." 11 Sept. 2002 <http://www.tvresource.com/resources/standards.htm>.

Appendix C

Fiber Optic Symbols

Military Symbols

These symbols, included in military standard MIL-STD-1864A, are used wherever symbols for fiber optic parts are required.

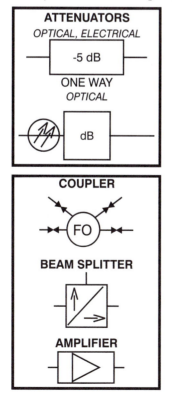

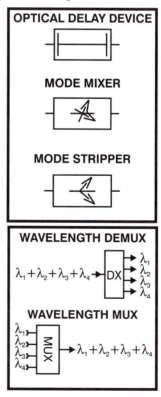

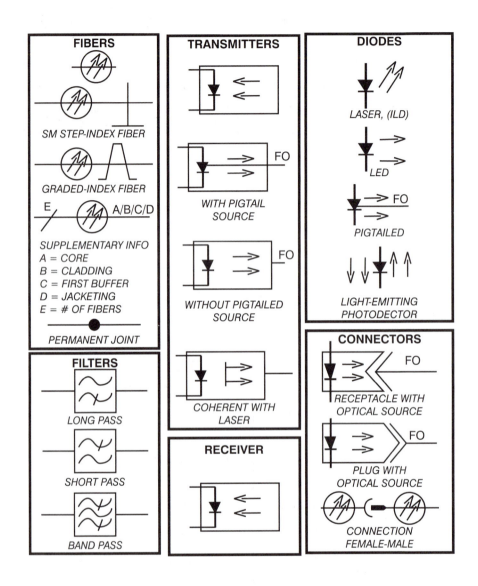

FIBERS
SM STEP-INDEX FIBER

GRADED-INDEX FIBER

E   A/B/C/D

SUPPLEMENTARY INFO
A = CORE
B = CLADDING
C = FIRST BUFFER
D = JACKETING
E = # OF FIBERS

PERMANENT JOINT

FILTERS
LONG PASS

SHORT PASS

BAND PASS

TRANSMITTERS
WITH PIGTAIL
SOURCE

FO

WITHOUT PIGTAILED
SOURCE

FO

COHERENT WITH
LASER

RECEIVER

DIODES
LASER, (ILD)

LED

FO

PIGTAILED

LIGHT-EMITTING
PHOTODECTOR

CONNECTORS
RECEPTACLE WITH
OPTICAL SOURCE

FO

PLUG WITH
OPTICAL SOURCE

FO

CONNECTION
FEMALE-MALE

Common Cable Television Symbols

These symbols were made part of the National Cable Television Association's (NCTA) "Recommended Practice for Measurements on Cable Television Systems."

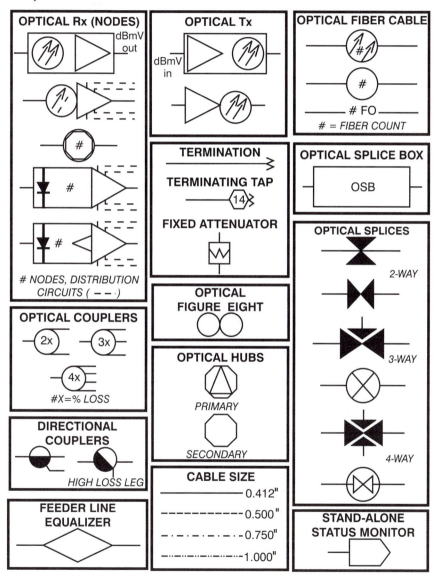

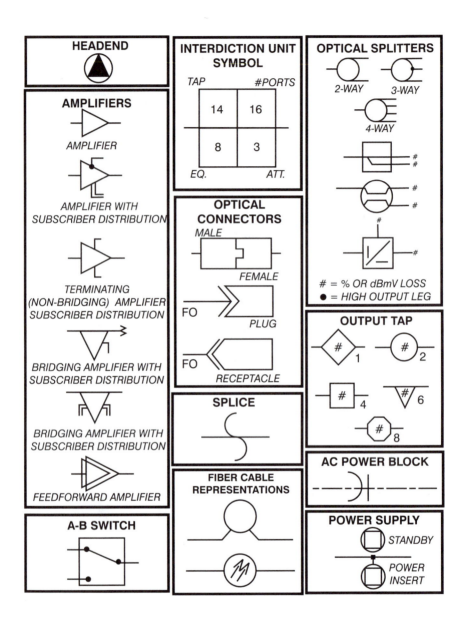

Appendix D

Television Standards

A number of standards exist to describe video transmission, fiber optic or otherwise. These standards break down into numerous categories for a variety of applications. This appendix does not claim to be exhaustive, although every effort was made for accuracy and completeness. For simplicity, this appendix will cover only standards currently in force and not list the myriad of developing standards.

Broadcast Standards: NTSC, PAL, SECAM

Broadcast standards combine technical and legal definitions for television broadcasting. They include NTSC, PAL, and SECAM standards.

NTSC

NTSC broadcast standards include the recommended standards (RS) published by the EIA. This format is basically synonymous with composite video when referring to a video signal.

RS-250C

RS-250C is used to evaluate a received television picture. This requires some knowledge about the transmission path as requirements differ for RS-250C short-haul, RS-250 medium-haul, and RS-250 long-haul. Each of these paths is defined by the number of intermediate processing devices and the type of path. RS-250C determines coax feeds with D/As, microwave, fiber optic, and satellite transmissions as well as mixes of all of the above. Each of the three paths have their own level of performance standards which assure picture quality rather than sync and timing.

RS-250C also specifies that certain video signals must be used to make picture quality evaluations and recommends certain test signals to complete the measurements. A performance standard similar to RS-250C, called NTC-7, defines only one delivered condition and is quite specific about which test signals to use.

RS-330

EIA recommended standard for signals generated by closed-circuit TV cameras scanned at 525/60 and interlaced at 2:1. This standard resembles RS-170, but it omits horizontal sync pulses during the vertical sync pulse. Also used for color television studio electrical signals.

PAL/SECAM

PAL and SECAM video standards have six basic color categories. The color categories are as follows:

PAL

Standard used in the United Kingdom and much of Europe. Similar to the NTSC standard. This standard bears a line/frame rate of 625/25 per second. This breaks down to 576 separate horizontal lines of raster arrayed vertically (625 lines including the vertical interval), with 50 fields per second (25 interlaced frames per second). This standard is black and white compatible with PAL-N, SECAM-V, and SECAM-H.

PAL-M

PAL-M more closely resembles NTSC than standard PAL. The line/frame rate is 525/30 per second containing 486 separate horizontal lines of raster arrayed vertically (525 including the vertical interval), with 60 fields per second (30 interlaced frames per second). PAL-M is not compatible with PAL, but the black and white signals are compatible with NTSC. Brazil is the only country that uses this format.

PAL-N

Possesses the same standards as PAL, but a lower, 3.58 MHz subcarrier allows the transmission of a narrow channel band.

SECAM

Possesses the same line/frame rate as PAL.

SECAM-V

Essentially the same as PAL and PAL-N.

SECAM-H

Essentially the same as PAL, PAL-N, and SECAM-V. Also known as MSECAM.

In addition to these variations, PAL and SECAM also maintain different system specifications. For example, a country can use the SECAM color system and the M transmission system. The table below outlines the system specifications for PAL B, G, D, I, and N, and SECAM D, M, K, K1, E, L, and H. These specifications originated from the International Radio Consultant Committee (CCIR), the predecessor of the ITU-R, the radio communications sector of the International Telecommunications Union.

Table D.1 – ITU-R System Specifications for PAL and SECAM

	PAL B	PAL G	PAL/ SECAM D	PAL I	PAL/ SECAM M	PAL N	SECAM K	SECAM K1	SECAM E/L	SECAM H
Scanning Lines	625	625	625	625	525	625	625	625	625	625
Vertical Frequency	50 Hz	50 Hz	50 Hz	50 Hz	60 Hz	60 Hz	50 Hz	50 Hz	50 Hz	50 Hz
Horizontal Frequency	15.625 kHz	15.625 kHz	15.625 kHz	15.625 kHz	15.750 kHz	15.650 kHz	15.625 kHz	15.625 kHz	15.625 kHz	15.625 kHz
Interleaving	2/1	2/1	2/1	2/1	2/1	2/1	2/1	2/1	2/1	2/1
Frames	25	25	25	25	25	25	25	25	25	25
Video Bandwidth	5 MHz	5 MHz	6 MHz	5.5 MHz	4.2 MHz	4.2 MHz	6 MHz	6 MHz	6 MHz	5 MHz
Channel Bandwidth	7 MHz	8 MHz	8 MHz	8 MHz	6 MHz	6 MHz	8 MHz	8 MHz	8 MHz	8 MHz
Audio Carrier	+5.5 MHz	+5.5 MHz	+6.55 MHz	+6.0 MHz	+4.5 MHz	+4.5 MHz	+6.5 MHz	+6.5 MHz	+6.5 MHz	+5.5 MHz
Next Channel Edge Relative to fp	-1.25 MHz	-1.25 MHz	-1.25 MHz	-1.25 MHz	-1.25 MHz	-1.25 MHz	-1.25 MHz	-1.25 MHz	-1.25 MHz	±2.38 MHz
Upper Sideband	5 MHz	5 MHz	6 MHz	-5.5 MHz	4.2 MHz	4.2 MHz	6 MHz	6 MHz	6 MHz	5 MHz
Lower Sideband	0.75 MHz	0.75 MHz	0.75 MHz	1.25 MHz	0.75 MHz	0.75 MHz	0.75 MHz	1.25 MHz	1.25 MHz	1.25 MHz
Audio Modulation & Polarity	AM/ Neg.	AM/ Neg.	AM/ Neg.	AM/ Neg.	AM/ Neg.	AM/ Neg.	AM/ Neg.	AM/ Neg.	AM/Pos.	AM/ Neg.
Audio Modulation	FM ±50 kHz	FM ±50 kHz	FM ±50 kHz	FM ±50 kHz	FM ±25 kHz	FM ±25 kHz	FM ±50 kHz	FM ±50 kHz	AM	FM ±50 kHz
Audio Deemphasis	50 mS	50 mS	50 mS	50 mS	75 mS	75 mS	50 mS	50 mS	None	50 mS

Component Analog Video (CAV)

Betacam

Betacam is the name for both a video recording format and the equipment used to record and play the format, developed by Sony Corporation. As a format, Betacam offers a high-quality images based on the component video standard of three signals, one for luminance (Y) and two for chrominance (U and V). This standard records all three signals independently using compressed time-division multiplexing. The U and V signals are recorded on one video track while the Y signal is recorded on a second video track, eliminating cross-color and cross-luminance effects inherent in composite video. As equipment, the format records on a ½" tape running at 105 mm/s and has several variants. The most common Betacam format, Betacam SP, uses a high grade metal oxide tape for recording. Digital Betacam is a full 4:2:2: digital variation of the Betacam, and the most recent variant, Betacam SX, offers MPEG-based digital compression to extend the running time compared to digital Betacam.

Betacam represented a second generation format after Sony's Betamax. Betamax first hit the market in 1975 and sold as many as 18 million units worldwide over time, but the company refused to share its technology at the time. Sony's competitor, JVC, displayed a willingness to share the technology behind their VHS (video home system) format, allowing VHS to eventually dominate the home video market, even as it does today (although DVD players are quickly gaining popularity). In addition to Betacam VTRs and VCRs, all Betacam tapes can use Betamax technology. However, Sony discontinued the production of all Betamax equipment in the year 2002. Betacam, on the other hand, continues to find use in today's high-quality video applications.

RGB/GRB

RGB transmission offers the highest quality audio/video signals in both the broadcast and computer video industries. It uses one wire for each color and usually incorporates RF shielding on each wire to reduce interference between the three color signals. GRB is the matrix decoded version of NTSC with sync added to all three channels. Reversal of the non complex RGB to GRB format is consistent with the green signal corresponding to the Y or luminance signal in the other color difference (B–Y and R–Y) formats.

MII

MII is similar to Betacam, developed by Matsushita. As with Betacam, MII format comes in a 3-wire or 2–wire version and involve the component time-division multiplexed (CTDM or CTCM) nomenclature in the latter case. This video format complies with SMPT/EBU N10. The three signals in this scheme are luminance, scaled B-Y, and scaled R-Y.

SMPTE/EBU N10

The Society for Motion Picture and Television Engineers (SMPTE) and the European Broadcasting Union (EBU) have adopted their own color difference formats to remove brand name association of BetaCam or MII. These formats operate in a similar fashion.

S-Video

Abbreviation for super-video, this technology transmits video signals over a cable by dividing the video information into two separate signals: one for chrominance, and the other for luminance. When sent to a television, which is designed to display separate luminance and chrominance signals, S-video produces sharper images than composite video, which transmits video as a single signal over one wire.

CCTV Video Standards

RS-170

RS-170 is the U.S. standard video format for black and white (monochrome) television signals. It requires a 15.75 kHz horizontal interlaced scan frequency and a 60 Hz vertical interlaced scan frequency. The signal encodes light intensity as a function of position, which is represented by time. The light intensity value are represented by voltage. An RS-170 signal contains both image and timing information. This standard may also be called monochrome NTSC.

RS-343/RS-343A

EIA recommended standard for non broadcast high resolution monochrome video. Used by computer systems and high resolution video cameras. RS-343A is a very high resolution monochrome CCTV standard based on RS-343.

ITU-R and ITU-T Recommendations

Analog Signals

- J.61: Transmission Performance of Television Circuits Designed for use in International Connections
- J.62: Single Value of the Signal-to-Noise Ratio for all Television Systems
- J.86: Mixed Analog and Digital Transmission of Analog Composite Television Signals Over Long Distances

Digital Signals

- J.62: Single Value of the Signal-to-Noise Ratio for all Television Systems
- J.80: Transmission of Component-coded Digital Television Signals for Contribution-quality Applications at Bit Rates near 140 Mb/s
- J.85: Digital Television Transmission Over Long Distances, General Principles

- J.86: Mixed Analog and Digital Transmission of Analog Composite Television Signals Over Long Distances
- J.88: Transmission of Enhanced-definition Television Signals Over Digital Links
- J.89: Transport Mechanism for Component-coded Digital Television Signals Using MPEG-2 4:2:2 Including all Service Elements for Contribution and Primary Distribution
- J.112 Annex A: Digital Video Broadcasting (DVB) Interaction Channel for Cable TV Distribution Systems (prepublished version)
- J.184: Digital Broadband Delivery System: Out-of-band Transport

SMPTE Standards

Analog Signals

- SMPTE 15M-1998: Television Analog Recording, 1 inch Type B Helical Scan, Basic System Parameters
- SMPTE 19M-1996: Television Analog Recording, 1 inch Type C, Basic System and Transport Geometry Parameters
- SMPTE 253M-1998: Television, Three Channel RGB Analog Video Interface

Digital Signals

- SMPTE 240-M-1995: Television, Signal Parameters, 1125 Line High-definition Production Systems
- SMPTE 244M-1995: Television, System M/NTSC Composite Video Signals, Bit-parallel Digital Interface
- SMPTE 259M-1997: Television, 10-bit 4:2:2 Component and $4f_{sc}$ Composite Digital Signals, Serial Digital Interface
- SMPTE 260M-1999: Television, 1125/60 High-definition Production System, Digital Representation and Bit-parallel Interface
- SMPTE 292M-1998: Television, Bit-serial Digital Interface for High-definition Television Systems
- SMPTE 305.2M-2000: Television, Serial Data Transport Interface (SDTI)
- SMPTE 310M-1998: Television, Synchronous Serial Interface for MPEG-2 Digital Transport Streams
- SMPTE 344M-2000: Television, 540 Mb/s Serial Digital Interface
- SMPTE 348M-2000: Television, High Data Rate Serial Data Transport Interface

Appendix E

Societies, Conference Sponsors, and Trade Journals

Societies and Conference Sponsors

Advanced Television Systems Committee (ATSC)

1750 K Street NW, Suite 1200
Washington, D.C. 20036
TEL: (202) 828-3120
http://www.atsc.org

Building Industry Consulting Service International, Inc. (BICSI)

8610 Hidden River Parkway
Tampa, FL 33637-1000
TEL: (813) 979-1991
USA: (800) 242-7405
http://www.bicsi.org

The Consumer Electronics Association (CE)

2500 Wilson Boulevard
Arlington, VA 22201-3834
TEL: (703) 907-7600
http://www.ce.org

DV Expo East and DV Expo West

CMP Media, LLC
600 Harrison Street
San Francisco, CA 94107
TEL: (415) 947-6000
http://www.dvexpo.com

Electronic Industries Association (EIA)

2500 Wilson Boulevard
Arlington, VA 22201-3834
TEL: (703) 907-7500
http://www.eia.org

European Conference on Optical Communication (ECOC)

Nexus Media Limited
Nexus House, Swanley, Kent, BR8 8HU, UK
TEL: (44) 1322-66-00-70
http://www.ecoc-exhibition.com

European Optical Society (EOS)

Klaus-Dieter Nowitzki
Holleritallee 8
30419 Hannover, Germany
TEL: (49) 0-511-2788-115
http://www.EuropeanOpticalSociety.org

Fiber Optic Association, Inc.

2 Florence Street, 3rd Floor
Malden, MA 02148
Tel: (781) 367-2400
http://www.theFOA.org

Institute of Electrical and Electronics Engineers (IEEE)

445 Hoes Lane
Piscataway, NJ 08855-1311
TEL: (732) 981-0060
http://www.ieee.org

Institute of Electrical Engineers (IEE)

Savory Place
London, WC2R CBL-UK
TEL: (44) 0-20-7240-1871
http://www.iee.org

International Society for Optical Engineering (SPIE)

PO Box 10
Bellingham, WA 98227-0010
TEL: (360) 676-3290
http://www.spie.org

International Telecommunication Union (ITU)

Places Des Nations, CH-1211
Geneva, 20, SWITZERLAND
TEL: (44) 22-730-6141
http://www.itu.int

Lasers and Electro-Optics Society (LEOS)

445 Hoes Lane
PO Box 1331
Piscataway, NJ 08855-1331
TEL: (201) 562-3892
http://www.i-LEOS.org

National Association of Broadcasters (NAB)

1771 N Street, NW
Washington, D.C. 20036
TEL: (202) 429-5300
http://www.nab.org

National Cable Television Association (NCTA)

1724 Massachusetts Avenue N.W.
Washington, D.C. 20036
TEL: (202) 775-3550
http://www.ncta.com

National Electrical Contractors Assoc. (NECA)

3 Bethesda Metro Center, Suite 1100
Bethesda, MD 20814
TEL: (301) 657-3110
http://www.necanet.org

National Electrical Manufacturers Association (NEMA)

1300 North 17th Street, Suite 1847
Rosslyn, VA 22209
TEL: (703) 841-3200
http://www.nema.org

National Systems Contractors Association (NSCA)

625 First Street SE, Suite 420
Cedar Rapids, IA 52401
TEL: (319) 366-6722
http://www.nsca.org

North American Broadcasters Association (NABA)

PO Box 500 Station A
Toronto, ON M5WIE6
TEL: (416) 598-9877
http://www.nabanet.com

Optical Society of America (OSA)

2010 Massachusetts Avenue N.W.
Washington, D.C. 20036
TEL: (202) 223-8130
http://www.osa.org

Society of Broadcast Engineers (SBE)

9247 N. Meridian Street, Suite 305
Indianapolis, IN 46260
TEL: (317) 846-9000
http://www.sbe.org

Society of Cable Television Engineers (SCTE)

140 Philips Road
Exton, PA 19341
USA: (800) 542-5040
TEL: (610) 363-6888
http://www.scte.org

Society of Motion Picture and Television Engineers (SMPTE)

595 West Hartsdale Avenue
White Plains, NY 10607
TEL: (914) 761-1100
http://www.smpte.org

Telecommunications Industry Association (TIA)

2500 Wilson Boulevard, Suite 300
Arlington, VA 22201
TEL: (703) 907-7700
http://www.tiaonline.org

Underwriters Laboratories (UL)

333 Pfingsten Road
Northbrook, IL 60062-2096
TEL: (847) 272-8800
http://www.ul.com

Fiber Optic Trade Journals

Cabling Installation & Maintenance

Ten Tara Boulevard
Fifth Floor
Nashua, NH 03062
http://www.broadband-guide.com/cim

CCTV Applications & Technology

Burke Publishing Company
15825 Shady Grove Road, Suite 130
Rockville, MD 20850

Communications Convergence

CMP Media, Inc.
600 Community Drive
Manhasset, NY 11030
TEL: (516) 562-5000
http://www.cconvergence.com

Communications Technology

PBI Media, LLC Corporate Office
1201 Seven Locks Road, Suite 300
Potomac, MD 20854
TEL: (301) 354-2000
http://www.pbimedia.com

Electronic Design

Penton Media, Inc.
1100 Superior Avenue
Cleveland, OH 44114-2543
http://www.elecdesign.com

Fiberoptic Product News

Cahners
301 Gibraltar Drive, Box 650
Morris Plains, NJ 07950
TEL: (973) 292-5100
http://www.fpnmag.com

Laser Focus World

Pennwell
1421 S. Sheridan
Tulsa, OK 74112
USA: (800) 331-4463
http://www.pennwell.com

Lightwave

Pennwell
1421 S. Sheridan
Tulsa, OK 74112
USA: (800) 331-4463
http://www.pennwell.com

Optics & Photonics News

Optical Society of America
2010 Massachusetts Avenue, NW
Washington, D.C. 20036
TEL: (202) 223-8130
http://www.osa.org

Photonics Spectra

Laurin Publishing Co.
Editorial Offices
Berkshire Common
PO Box 4949
Pittsfield, MA 01202-4949
TEL: (413) 499-0514
http://www.photonicsspectra.com

Spectrum Magazine — IEEE

Editorial Board
New York, NY 10001
TEL: (212) 419-7555
http://www.spectrum.ieee.org

WDM Solutions

Pennwell
1421 S. Sheridan
Tulsa, OK 74112
USA: (800) 331-4463
http://www.pennwell.com

Video Trade Journals

AV Video Multimedia Producer
PO Box 3034
Northbrook, IL 60065-3034
TEL: (847) 559-7314
http://www.avvideo.com

Broadband Networking News
PBI Media, LLC Corporate Office
1201 Seven Locks Road, Suite 300
Potomac, MD 20854
TEL: (301) 354-2000
http://www.pbimedia.com

Broadcasting & Cable
PO Box 15157
North Hollywood, CA 91615-5157
USA: (800) 554-5729
http://www.broadcastingcable.com

Broadcast Engineering
Primedia Business Magazines & Media
PO Box 12914
Overland Park, KS 66282-2914
http://www.industryclick.com

Satellite Business News
1990 M Street, NW, Suite 510
Washington, D.C. 20036
TEL: (202) 785-0505
http://www.satbiznews.com

Sound & Video Contractor
Primedia Business Magazines & Media
PO Box 12914
Overland Park, KS 66282-2914
http://www.industryclick.com

Via Satellite
PBI Media, LLC Corporate Office
1201 Seven Locks Road, Suite 300
Potomac, MD 20854
TEL: (301) 354-2000
http://www.pbimedia.com

Video Age
216 East 75th Street
New, NY 10012
TEL: (212) 288-3933
http://www.videoageinternational.com

Video Systems
Primedia Business Magazines & Media
PO Box 12914
Overland Park, KS 66282-2914
http://www.industryclick.com

Vision Systems Design
Pennwell
1421 S. Sheridan
Tulsa, OK 74112
USA: (800) 331-4463
http://www.pennwell.com

Appendix F

General Reference Material

Concerning Numbers

Système Internationale or SI Units, known as the metric system, use the following prefixes to express large and small numbers.

Table F.1 – Names and Symbols for Metric Prefixes

Prefix	Symbol	Multiplier	Scientific	U.S. Word
exa	E	1,000,000,000,000,000,000	10^{18}	quintillions
peta	P	1,000,000,000,000,000	10^{15}	quadrillions
tera	T	1,000,000,000,000	10^{12}	trillions
giga	G	1,000,000,000	10^{9}	billions
mega	M	1,000,000	10^{6}	millions
kilo	k	1,000	10^{3}	thousands
hecto	h	100	10^{2}	hundreds
deka	da	10	10^{1}	tens
deci	d	0.1	10^{-1}	tenths
centi	c	0.01	10^{-2}	hundredths
milli	m	0.001	10^{-3}	thousandths
micro	μ	0.000 001	10^{-6}	millionths
nano	n	0.000 000 001	10^{-9}	billionths
pico	p	0.000 000 000 001	10^{-12}	trillionths
femto	f	0.000 000 000 000 001	10^{-15}	quadrillionths

Table F.1 – Names and Symbols for Metric Prefixes (Continued)

Prefix	Symbol	Multiplier	Scientific	U.S. Word
atto	a	0.000 000 000 000 000 001	10^{-18}	quintillionths
Mil	N/A	1/1000 of an inch	1 mil = 25.4 microns	
Micron	N/A	1/1,000,000 of a meter	1 micron = 1 micrometer (μm)	

Constants

The following is a partial list of constants that are pertinent to the use of fiber optics and electronics:

1. **Speed of Light in a Vacuum**
   C = 299,792.5 km/s = 29.98 cm/ns = 299.8 mm/ps = 11.8in/ns = 0.983 ft./ns.

2. **Speed of Light in Fiber (Refractive index = 1.45)**
   C = 206,753.4 km/s = 20.68 cm/ns = 206.8 μs/ps = 8.140 in/ns = 0.6779 ft./ns

3. **Electronic Charge**
   q=1.602 x 10^{-19} Coulombs

4. **Planck's Constant**
   h = 6.625 x 10^{-34} J•s = 4.135 x 10^{-15} eV•s = 6.625 x 10^{-27} erg•s

5. **Boltzmann's Constant**
   k = 1.3804 x 10^{-23} J/°K = 8.616 x 10^{-5} eV/°K = 1.3804 x 10^{-16} erg/°K

6. **Energy-Wavelength Conversion Factor**
   hc/e = 1239.8 eV nm = 1.2398 eV•μm

7. **Wien's Displacement Law Constant**
   λmax•T = 2.9878 x 10^{6} nm•°K = 2897.8 μm•°K

8. **k•T at +300°K**
   0.0259

9. **Characteristic Impedance of Vacuum**
   Z_0 = 376.7 Ω

10. **Pi (π)**
    3.1415926535

Conversion Factors

The following is a list of common conversions that pertain to fiber optics and electronics:

Table F.2 – Conversion Factors

To Convert from:	To:	Multiply by:
μm (micrometers)	mils	0.03937
	inches	0.00003937
	Angstroms	10,000
	nanometers	1,000
mm (millimeters)	inches	0.03937
	feet	0.003281
cm (centimeters)	inches	0.39370
	feet	0.03281
m (meters)	feet	3.281
	inches	39.37
	cm	100
	mm	1,000
feet (ft.)	inch	12
	cm	30.48
	meter	0.3048
inch (in.)	feet	0.08333
	cm	2.54
	meter	0.0254
electron Volt (eV)	erg	1.602×10^{-12}
	Joules	1.602×10^{-19}
	kilowatt-hour (kW-hr)	4.45×10^{-26}
	Watt-hour (W-hr)	4.45×10^{-23}
	milliwatt-hour (mW-hr)	4.45×10^{-20}
	Watt-second (W-sec)	1.602×10^{-19}
	milliwatt-second (mW-sec)	1.602×10^{-16}
	Photon Frequency	2.41768×10^{14}
Photon Frequency	eV	4.136×10^{-15}

Table F.2 – Conversion Factors (Continued)

To Convert from:	To:	Multiply by:
erg	Joules	10^{-7}
	eV	6.242×10^{11}
Watt (W)	milliwatt (mW)	1,000
	microwatt (μW)	1,000,000
km (kilometers)	miles	0.62137
	feet	3,280.8
	mm	1,000,000
kg (kilograms)	pounds	2.2046
g (grams)	oz. (ounces)	0.03527
	pounds	0.0022045
°C (Centigrade)	°F (Fahrenheit)	1.8 then add 32
°F	°C	subtract 32 then divide by 1.8
°K (Kelvin)	°C	= °C + 273.16
N (Newton)	pounds	0.2247
kg/km	pounds/mile	3.5480
kPa	PSI	0.14511

Appendix G

Optical and RF Conversions

Table G.1 – Optical dBm to Optical mW Conversion

Optical Power		Optical Power		Optical Power		Optical Power	
(dBm)	(mW)	(dBm)	(µW)	(dBm)	(nW)	(dBm)	(pW)
30	1000.00	0	1000.00	-30	1000.00	-60	1000.00
29	794.33	-1	794.33	-31	794.33	-61	794.33
28	630.96	-2	630.96	-32	630.96	-62	630.96
27	501.19	-3	501.19	-33	501.19	-63	501.19
26	398.11	-4	398.11	-34	398.11	-64	398.11
25	316.23	-5	316.23	-35	316.23	-65	316.23
24	251.19	-6	251.19	-36	251.19	-66	251.19
23	199.53	-7	199.53	-37	199.53	-67	199.53
22	158.49	-8	158.49	-38	158.49	-68	158.49
21	125.89	-9	125.89	-39	125.89	-69	125.89
20	100.00	-10	100.00	-40	100.00	-70	100.00
19	79.43	-11	79.43	-41	79.43	-71	79.43
18	63.10	-12	63.10	-42	63.10	-72	63.10
17	50.12	-13	50.12	-43	50.12	-73	50.12
16	39.81	-14	39.81	-44	39.81	-74	39.81
15	31.62	-15	31.62	-45	31.62	-75	31.62
14	25.12	-16	25.12	-46	25.12	-76	25.12
13	19.95	-17	19.95	-47	19.95	-77	19.95
12	15.85	-18	15.85	-48	15.85	-78	15.85
11	12.59	-19	12.59	-49	12.59	-79	12.59
10	10.00	-20	10.00	-50	10.00	-80	10.00
9	7.943	-21	7.943	-51	7.943	-81	7.94

Table G.1 – Optical dBm to Optical mW Conversion (Continued)

Optical Power		Optical Power		Optical Power		Optical Power	
(dBm)	(mW)	(dBm)	(µW)	(dBm)	(nW)	(dBm)	(pW)
8	6.310	-22	6.310	-52	6.310	-82	6.31
7	5.012	-23	5.012	-53	5.012	-83	5.01
6	3.981	-24	3.981	-54	3.981	-84	3.98
5	3.162	-25	3.162	-55	3.162	-85	3.16
4	2.512	-26	2.512	-56	2.512	-86	2.51
3	1.995	-27	1.995	-57	1.995	-87	2.00
2	1.585	-28	1.585	-58	1.585	-88	1.58
1	1.259	-29	1.259	-59	1.259	-89	1.26
0	1.000	-30	1.000	-60	1.000	-90	1.00

Table G.2 – Optical mW to Optical dBm Conversion

Optical Power		Optical Power		Optical Power		Optical Power	
(mW)	(dBm)	(µW)	(dBm)	(nW)	(dBm)	(pW)	(dBm)
1000.00	30.00	1000.00	0.00	1000.00	-30.00	1000.00	-60.00
900.00	29.54	900.00	-0.46	900.00	-30.46	900.00	-60.46
800.00	29.03	800.00	-0.97	800.00	-30.97	800.00	-60.97
700.00	28.45	700.00	-1.55	700.00	-31.55	700.00	-61.55
600.00	27.78	600.00	-2.22	600.00	-32.22	600.00	-62.22
500.00	26.99	500.00	-3.01	500.00	-33.01	500.00	-63.01
400.00	26.02	400.00	-3.98	400.00	-33.98	400.00	-63.98
300.00	24.77	300.00	-5.23	300.00	-35.23	300.00	-65.23
250.00	23.98	250.00	-6.02	250.00	-36.02	250.00	-66.02
200.00	23.01	200.00	-6.99	200.00	-36.99	200.00	-66.99
150.00	21.76	150.00	-8.24	150.00	-38.24	150.00	-68.24
125.00	20.97	125.00	-9.03	125.00	-39.03	125.00	-69.03
100.00	20.00	100.00	-10.00	100.00	-40.00	100.00	-70.00
90.00	19.54	90.00	-10.46	90.00	-40.46	90.00	-70.46
80.00	19.03	80.00	-10.97	80.00	-40.97	80.00	-70.97
70.00	18.45	70.00	-11.55	70.00	-41.55	70.00	-71.55
60.00	17.78	60.00	-12.22	60.00	-42.22	60.00	-72.22
50.00	16.99	50.00	-13.01	50.00	-43.01	50.00	-73.01
40.00	16.02	40.00	-13.98	40.00	-43.98	40.00	-73.98
30.00	14.77	30.00	-15.23	30.00	-45.23	30.00	-75.23
25.00	13.98	25.00	-16.02	25.00	-46.02	25.00	-76.02
20.00	13.01	20.00	-16.99	20.00	-46.99	20.00	-76.99
15.00	11.76	15.00	-18.24	15.00	-48.24	15.00	-78.24
12.50	10.97	12.50	-19.03	12.50	-49.03	12.50	-79.03
10.00	10.00	10.00	-20.00	10.00	-50.00	10.00	-80.00
9.00	9.54	9.00	-20.46	9.00	-50.46	9.00	-80.46
8.00	9.03	8.00	-20.97	8.00	-50.97	8.00	-80.97

Table G.2 – Optical mW to Optical dBm Conversion (Continued)

Optical Power		Optical Power		Optical Power		Optical Power	
(mW)	(dBm)	(µW)	(dBm)	(nW)	(dBm)	(pW)	(dBm)
7.00	8.45	7.00	-21.55	7.00	-51.55	7.00	-81.55
6.00	7.78	6.00	-22.22	6.00	-52.22	6.00	-82.22
5.00	6.99	5.00	-23.01	5.00	-53.01	5.00	-83.01
4.00	6.02	4.00	-23.98	4.00	-53.98	4.00	-83.98
3.00	4.77	3.00	-25.23	3.00	-55.23	3.00	-85.23
2.50	3.98	2.50	-26.02	2.50	-56.02	2.50	-86.02
2.00	3.01	2.00	-26.99	2.00	-56.99	2.00	-86.99
1.50	1.76	1.50	-28.24	1.50	-58.24	1.50	-88.24
1.25	0.97	1.25	-29.03	1.25	-59.03	1.25	-89.03
1.00	0.00	1.00	-30.00	1.00	-60.00	1.00	-90.00

Table G.3 – Optical dB to % Change

dB	% Change
1	25.89%
0.5	12.20%
0.2	4.71%
0.1	2.33%
0.05	1.16%
0.02	0.46%
0.01	0.23%
0.005	0.12%
0.002	0.046%
0.001	0.023%

The Decibel

The decibel (dB) provides a means of representing large power ratios as manageable, small numbers. This allows overall gains and losses to be calculated by addition and subtraction, rather than by multiplication and division. A ratio of power P_1 to power P_2 in dB is described as:

$$dB = 10 \cdot Log_{10}\left(\frac{P_1}{P_2}\right)$$

Ratio of two voltage measurements, V_1 to voltage V_2:

$$dB = 20 \cdot Log_{10}\left(\frac{V_1}{V_2}\right)$$

Power Conversions

While dBmV and dBµV expressions of power contain an upper case V for voltage, these values do not convey voltage. They are expressions of power. Several conversions exist to translate between these power references.

- dBmV: A power measurement of "x dBmV" indicates that a particular signal is x dB greater than 1 millivolt in 75 Ohms. Conversely, a negative dBmV value indicates that the signal is x dB less than 1 millivolt in 75 Ohms. The equation to convert x millivolts to x dBmV is:

$$dBmV = 20 \cdot Log_{10} \, (x \text{ millivolts})$$

- dBμV: A power measurement of "x dBμV" indicates that a particular signal is x dB greater than 1 microvolt in 75 Ohms. Conversely, a negative dBμV value indicates that the signal is x dB less than 1 microvolt in 75 Ohms. The equation to convert x microvolts to x dBmV is:

$$dB\mu V = 20 \cdot Log_{10} \, (x \text{ microvolts})$$

To convert dBmV to dBμV, add 60 to the dBmV reading:

$$x \, dB\mu V = x \, dBmV + 60$$

- dBm: A measurement of "x dBm" indicates that a particular signal is x dB greater than 1 milliwatt. A negative dBm value indicates that the signal is x dB less than 1 milliwatt. To convert x milliwatts to dBm:

$$dBm = 10 \cdot Log_{10} \, (x \text{ milliwatts})$$

A power level, in dBmV, can be converted directly to power in dBm, if the impedance, Z, is known, so to convert x dBmV directly to dBm:

$$dBmV = 10 \cdot Log_{10} \left[\frac{10^{\left(\frac{X}{10}\right)}}{Z \cdot 1000} \right]$$

The inverse operation is also possible if impedance is known, so to convert dBm directly to dBmV:

$$dBmV = 10 \cdot Log_{10} \left[Z \cdot 1000 \cdot 10^{\left(\frac{X}{10}\right)} \right]$$

Impedance Mismatch

Frequently, the input impedance of a measuring device does not match the impedance of the system under test, requiring a correction of the value. The equation for this correction is:

$$\text{Correction (in dB)} = 10 \cdot Log_{10} \left(\frac{Z_I}{Z_S} \right)$$

Where Z_I is the impedance of the instrument, and Z_s is the impedance of the system under test.

Conversion Formulae

The following tables provide conversion formulae for all common units of a video signal level measurement. Find the current units (left of table), and use the corresponding formula under the "To Units" column.

Table G.4 – Units to dBmV and dBµV

	To dBmV	To dBµV
Volts (V)	$20 \cdot Log_{10}\left(\dfrac{V}{10^3}\right)$	$20 \cdot Log_{10}\left(\dfrac{V}{10^6}\right)$
Watts (P)	$20 \cdot Log_{10}\left[\dfrac{\sqrt{Z \cdot P}}{10^3}\right]$	$20 \cdot Log_{10}\left[\dfrac{\sqrt{Z \cdot P}}{10^6}\right]$
dBm	dBm + 30 + 10·Log$_{10}$(Z)	dBm + 60 + 10·Log$_{10}$(Z)
dBmV	dBmV	dBmV + 60
dBµV	dBµV - 60	dBµV
Where Z = impedance of the system.		

Table G.5 – Units to V, P, and dBm

	To Volts (V)	To Watts (P)	To dBm
Volts (V)	V	$\dfrac{V^2}{Z}$	$10 \cdot Log_{10}\left(\dfrac{V^2}{10^3 \cdot Z}\right)$
Watts (P)	$\sqrt{P \cdot Z}$	P	$10 \cdot Log_{10}\left(\dfrac{P}{10^3}\right)$
dBm	$\sqrt{10^{\left(\frac{dBmV}{10}\right)} \cdot Z \cdot 10^3}$	$10^3 \cdot 10^{\left(\frac{dBmV}{10}\right)}$	dBm
dBmV	$10^{\left(\frac{dBmV}{20} - 3\right)}$	$\dfrac{1}{Z} \cdot 10^{\left(\frac{dBmV}{10} - 6\right)}$	dBmV + 30 - 10·Log$_{10}$(Z)
dBµV	$10^{\left(\frac{dBmV}{20} - 6\right)}$	$\dfrac{1}{Z} \cdot 10^{\left(\frac{dBmV}{10} - 12\right)}$	dBµV + 30 - 10·Log$_{10}$(Z)
Where Z = impedance of the system.			

Table G.6 – Units to dBmV for Impedance

		50 Ω	75 Ω	300 Ω	600 Ω	Z_2
From dBmV at Impe-dance Z_1	50 Ω	0	+1.76 dB	+7.78 dB	+10.79 dB	$+10 \cdot \text{Log}_{10}\!\left(\frac{Z_2}{50}\right)$
	75 Ω	-1.76 dB	0	+6.02 dB	+9.03 dB	$+10 \cdot \text{Log}_{10}\!\left(\frac{Z_2}{75}\right)$
	300 Ω	-7.78 dB	-6.02 dB	0	+3.01 dB	$+10 \cdot \text{Log}_{10}\!\left(\frac{Z_2}{300}\right)$
	600 Ω	-10.79 dB	-9.03 dB	-3.01 dB	0	$+10 \cdot \text{Log}_{10}\!\left(\frac{Z_2}{600}\right)$
	Z_1	$+10 \cdot \text{Log}_{10}\!\left(\frac{50}{Z_1}\right)$	$+10 \cdot \text{Log}_{10}\!\left(\frac{75}{Z_1}\right)$	$+10 \cdot \text{Log}_{10}\!\left(\frac{300}{Z_1}\right)$	$+10 \cdot \text{Log}_{10}\!\left(\frac{600}{Z_1}\right)$	$+10 \cdot \text{Log}_{10}\!\left(\frac{Z_2}{Z_1}\right)$

Where Z = impedance of the system.

Common Conversion Factors
1 mW (10^{-3} Watts) in 75 Ω = 0 dBm = 48.75 dBmV
0 dBm = +107 dBμV in 50 Ω
0 dBmV = +60 dBμV
0 dBmV (50 Ω) = +1.76 dBmV (75 Ω)

Index

Numerics

1 dB Compression Point (P_{1dB}) 183
4:1:1, see Video Signals, DTV
4:2:0, see Video Signals, DTV
4:2:2, see Video Signals, DTV
4B5B Encoding 205, 279
4*fsc*, see Digital Modulation
8B10B Encoding 279

A

Absorption, see Attenuation
Acceptance Angle, see Total Internal Reflection
Add-Drop Multiplexer (ADM) 280
    Optical ADM 313
ADM, see Add-Drop Multiplexer
Aliasing, see Compression
Alignment Sleeve, see Connectors, Parts of, Coupling Device
AM, see Amplitude Modulation
Amplified Spontaneous Emission (ASE) 280
Amplifier 183, 281
    Amplifier Noise Calculation 183–186
    Linear Amplifier 183, 321
    Optical Amplifier 252, 253, 313
    RF Amplifier 215, 228
Amplitude Modulation (AM) 3, 27, 34, 36–37, 139, 181–190, 280
    Baseband 194
    RF Carrier 35, 36, 194, 195

Vestigial-sideband AM 35, 40, 42, 194, 195, 210, 211, 228, 327
Amplitude Noise, see Noise
Amplitude, see Digital Modulation, Pulse
Analog 2, 43, 148, 281
Analog-to-digital Conversion, see Digital Modulation
Analog Video, see Video Signals
Angle of Incidence, see Total Internal Reflection
ANSI 281, 310, 323
APC, see Connectors, Types of, Angle Polished Connectors
APD, see Detectors, Avalanche Photodiode
APL, see Video Signals
Arrayed Waveguide Grating (AWG) 282
Asymmetrical Distortion, see Distortion
Asynchronous Transfer Mode (ATM), see Data Networks
AT&T 11
ATM, see Data Networks
ATSC 4, 18, 281, 349
Attenuation 24, 58, 148, 281
    Absorption 25, 280
    Rayleigh Scattering 25, 65, 135, 319
Audion Tube 10, 13
Automatic Gain Control (AGC) 181, 182, 280

Fiber Optic Video Transmission